Leave While the Party's Good

Leave While the Party's Good

The Life and Legacy of Baseball Executive **Harry Dalton**

LEE C. KLUCK

University of Nebraska Press
LINCOLN

A portion of chapter 8 previously appeared, in different form, in "This Is the Way: The Baltimore Orioles, the Oriole Way, and the Influence of Harry Dalton from 1969 to 1971," *NINE: A Journal of Baseball History and Culture* 29, nos. 1–2 (Fall–Spring 2020–21). Used by permission of the University of Nebraska Press. Copyright 2021 by the University of Nebraska Press. A portion of chapter 16 previously appeared in "October 3, 1982: Harvey's Wallbangers Clinch Division in Season Finale," in *Harvey's Wallbangers: The 1982 Milwaukee Brewers*, ed. Gregory H. Wolf (Phoenix: Society for American Baseball Research, 2020).

The University of Nebraska Press is part of a land-grant institution with campuses and programs on the past, present, and future homelands of the Pawnee, Ponca, Otoe-Missouria, Omaha, Dakota, Lakota, Kaw, Cheyenne, and Arapaho Peoples, as well as those of the relocated Ho-Chunk, Sac and Fox, and Iowa Peoples.

Library of Congress Cataloging-in-Publication Data
Names: Kluck, Lee C., author.
Title: Leave while the party's good: the life and legacy of baseball executive Harry Dalton / Lee C. Kluck.
Description: Lincoln: University of Nebraska Press, [2024] | Includes bibliographical references and index.
Identifiers: LCCN 2023040937
ISBN 9781496222893 (hardback)
ISBN 9781496240002 (epub)
ISBN 9781496240019 (pdf)
Subjects: LCSH: Dalton, Harry, 1928–2005. | Baltimore Orioles (Baseball team)—History. | Milwaukee Brewers (Baseball team)—History. | Baseball managers—United States—Biography. | Baseball executives. | BISAC: SPORTS & RECREATION / Baseball / General | HISTORY / United States / 20th Century
Classification: LCC GV865.D265 K58 2024 | DDC 796.357092 [B]—dc23/eng/20231026
LC record available at https://lccn.loc.gov/2023040937

Designed and set in Adobe Text by A. Shahan.

This work is dedicated to a host of people who did not live long enough for me to cross the finish line but were always there for me.

To Pete Friedrich of Washington Elementary, who always treated me like a big deal even though he himself was larger than life. I miss you, my friend.

To John Kekar of the Rosholt High class of '95, who saw a redeemable quality in an awkward high school kid and treated him like one of the cool kids when very few did.

To Jack Brooks of the Rosholt High baseball program, who let me hang around his baseball team even though, like Harry Dalton, I was better off the field than on.

To Burt and Loyce Kluck of the Town of Sharon, who nurtured my love of baseball during countless afternoons on Hwy J and taught me the importance of the midgame nap in the recliner.

To Barbara Brostowitz Bugar of Loyal, Wisconsin, whose story reminded me that no ordeal was insurmountable and that a higher education was possible no matter what the odds.

To Sally Kent of the University of Wisconsin–Stevens Point, who was the first historian who thought I could "do the work" of a professional. I finally figured out how to get paid, Sally. Thanks for believing in me.

To Harry Dalton of West Springfield, Massachusetts, thanks for teaching the people around you that hard work should be rewarded sometimes. Everyone has taken good care of me, Harry, and I have you to thank for that because they saw in me what you fostered in them. I hope you like my attempt to make sense of it all.

Contents

Preface

It was just like old times in Milwaukee. The weather was warm, the Brewers were hot, and the "Dalton Gang" was the guest of honor. It could have been 1978, 1982, or 1987. But it was 2018, and Harry Dalton was there only in spirit. Still, on a night that featured a team that Dalton would have been proud of (an abundance of pitching and enough power for two teams) and appearances by his wife and family that would have made him smile, you could not help but think of the man who built the first winner in the franchise's history.

That night, before the game, in the hours he once dedicated to work, while the smell of grilling wafted in from the parking lot ritual that is tailgating in Milwaukee, they installed a picture of him at Miller Park for everything he had done at County Stadium. The plaque and its location are unassuming, much like the man whom it honors.

No matter where it is or how big the footprint, that plaque is well deserved. Harry Dalton was special, and he made the places he went special. Milwaukee is a wonderful example. That city is only part of the story, however. To tell the story of Harry Dalton, one must trek the globe, from Massachusetts to South Korea. From Baltimore to California. From Orange County to Cream City and finally to the sun-drenched lands of Arizona.

Harry Dalton loved all these places, and they all informed his life. However, much like the plaque in Milwaukee and another in Baltimore that celebrate his greatest professional accomplishments, he never tried to overwhelm his surroundings. He just wanted to be one with the world. Because of that, Harry Dalton often slipped into the background of a time or place. Still, if you look hard enough, you can find the man behind the plaque.

What follows is a story that will give you a map.

Acknowledgments

In the twenty-first century, it is often said that successfully completing a massive undertaking requires a village. If that is the case, my village is a sell-out crowd at County Stadium. That may seem counterintuitive given that writing is a solitary endeavor. Still, if I have learned anything from Harry Dalton, it has been that the best products come when you accept the input of others.

First and foremost, thank you to the Dalton family for the support you gave me. I especially want to thank Pat Dalton for sharing the love of her life with me and allowing me to tell his story to the world. As for Harry and Pat's daughters, Kim, Cindy, and Debbie carry the best of both of their parents, and that inherited inquisitiveness and drive have made this a better book by 1,000 percent.

I would also like to thank the countless friends, family, and coworkers of Harry Dalton and those who played for him; they have all made my work a living, breathing thing. Of particular note, thank you to Nolan Ryan, Robin Yount, the late Brooks Robinson, Ted Simmons, and the late Andy Etchebarren. I would be remiss if I did not mention that Pete Vuckovich came up big for me just like he did Harry Dalton. Pete, I could not have captured a true sense of who Harry was without your help.

As was the case with the Dalton Gang, I found that my decisions were also improved by the help of extremely qualified executives. Thank you to Commissioner Emeritus Bud Selig and his daughter Wendy Selig-Prieb for their time spent describing what it was like to have Harry Dalton lead their team. I would also like to thank Dan Duquette, the late Sky Skibosh, Bruce Manno, Mario Ziino, Michael Hamacher, and the best traveling secretary in the game, Jimmy Bank, for sharing what it was like to work for and sometimes even laugh with Harry and the cast of characters he assembled in Milwaukee.

Finally, a team is only as good as those covering it. The old sportswriter in Harry Dalton would appreciate that I got such fine help from fourth estate members Peter Gammons, Tracy Ringolsby, Tim Kurkjian, Ross Newhan, Ron Rapoport, Susan Shemanske, Gregg Hoffman, and the incomparable Tom Haudricourt.

On the academic side, a historian is only as good as the archivists who lead the way to source material. In Cassidy Lent and team at the Giamatti Research Center at the National Baseball Hall of Fame and Museum, I got to work with the best in the business. Thank you.

Any work that I do is colored by my affiliation with some of the best baseball scholars in the world through *NINE: A Journal of Baseball History and Culture* and the NINE Spring Training Conference. Like any rookie, when I first walked into the "clubhouse" that was our cozy little ballroom/workshop in Tempe I was awestruck and wondered how I had achieved the right to be there. As I settled in, though, people like John Thorn, Larry Gerlach, Dan Ardell and his late wife Jean, David Pegram, Steve Treder, Andy McCue, Lisa Alexander, Rob Bellamy, Jim Walker, Judith Hiltner, Willie Steele, Roberta Newman, Stephanie Liscio, Steve Geitschier, and my dear friend Paul Hensler nurtured my work and showed me that I belonged in that room just as much as they did. I am a lucky man to call them and countless others my friends.

In terms of friends, I am one of the luckiest people in the world because I have a support system that includes so many wonderful folks. First, to all my friends who have helped me through countless anxiety attacks, I cannot thank you enough. Mental health is as important as physical well-being, and I would not be here if it were not for all of you who helped me when my brain told me I wasn't good enough.

As it is with a lot of people, in the friend department I am truly blessed to have a few who may as well be family. Gwen Goetting, Katherine Schoofs, Mike Lynch, Randy Jones, and Nora Puetz all fit that description and then some. THANK YOU!

I would also like to specially thank Amy Boldt, Colleen McFarland-Radamacher, and Abbie Betinis for their continued friendship through so many stages of my life. Words cannot express what a privilege it is to call you all my friends.

Finally, I would like to thank my family for all their support. My parents, Chris and Barb Kluck, have been with me through every stage of this journey and have never shied away from helping me. Thank you for teaching me what I need to have every day to make it through life.

To my siblings Joe and Lacey, I know it's a shock that your brother is long-winded enough to write a book. Thanks for reading this far. Love you.

To the Outlaws that are the Lorenz clan, thanks for taking in the black sheep of the family. Love you all.

To Jack, Aaron, Jane, Coleson, William, Shelby, Roar, Obie, and T, this is my opportunity to remind you that anything is possible if you just keep moving in life. Uncle Lee is proud of you all.

Lastly, to Carla. This ride is wild and there are times when I would not have blamed you for getting off. Still, you look at our life with a passion and a sense of adventure and you just hang in there. I really never believed that I would find someone who could put up with me and my challenges and yet here you are. I love you more than all the tea in England. You are a wonderful friend and a great sounding board, and I could not imagine a better person to share my life with. Thank you for everything, always.

Introduction

We are at a point in baseball history when the men who built baseball teams are appreciated as much as the men who play the game on the field. This phenomenon is not new, to some degree; men like Branch Rickey, George Weiss, and Larry MacPhail earned fame while building winning teams. However, with the proliferation of social media and the twenty-four-hour news cycle, Major League Baseball executives' lives and actions are scrutinized as never before.

This period could rightfully be called the era of the celebrity executive. Because of this increased popular interest, there has been an influx of books about how various executives built winning teams. Some of these books are a rehash of the stories of executives who built teams at different points in the game's history, written by authors of both academic and popular histories. One executive baseball writers have grossly overlooked is Harry Dalton.

Mentions of Dalton in works on MLB team building do not extend much past his successes in that effort, and even those references are few and far between. Historians and fans alike are unaware that Dalton often learned more when his teams did not win a pennant, and they do not see how he and his group dealt with adversity or the game's changing nature so as to stay relevant in a sport that swallowed up people who became complacent. Dalton, who worked for three teams for over forty years, was a game-changing executive whom others emulated for many reasons.

That emulation does not make Dalton unique. He was successful, and success breeds copycats in most lines of work, especially in professional baseball. What makes Dalton different from Branch Rickey, Frank Cashen (the man who followed Dalton as the primary team builder in Baltimore), Pat Gillick, John Schuerholz, Billy Beane, or Theo Epstein?

All those men won at different points; how they won became how other people tried to win.

The significant difference between them and Harry Dalton is versatility. Harry Dalton won with both big payrolls and small ones. He won before and after free agency. He built winning teams from nothing. To do this, Dalton had to be versatile and creative; he was not a one-trick pony. He was a firm believer in building from within but also willing to leverage the players he had to acquire a player who would improve his team. He would change managers if he thought doing so would help. He even knew when not to force winning. This willingness to change made him better than his peers, and it shows.

During a career with teams in Baltimore, California, and Milwaukee, Dalton defined baseball executive excellence in terms of his team-building skills. His teams in Baltimore were the best in baseball during the late 1960s and early 1970s and some of the best teams in history. He left the California Angels with all the necessary pieces in place to secure their first period of prolonged winning in the late 1970s, albeit those winning seasons came after Dalton had left. Finally, he built some of the most consistently competitive teams in baseball during the 1980s and early 1990s in Milwaukee despite dealing with a changing financial climate that threatened to swallow up his small-market team. An in-depth study of Dalton's career would allow scholars and fans alike to track the innovative team-building methods of a master during one of the most chaotic periods in baseball history.

Baseball aficionados would find that Dalton's methods were different from those of his predecessors. His front offices combined features of a major corporation, a college seminar, a barroom, and the family dinner table.

Dalton changed how baseball teams handled decision-making in the team-building process. He wanted the opinions of everyone who worked for him. He did not do this so that he could lay blame if a decision went wrong. He did it so that he would have the best information available. Harry Dalton was an information junkie. He knew that his odds of making a better decision grew exponentially if he had good information. Therefore, Dalton took his ego out of the equation when he decided what to do. He did not care if the person sharing information was a trusted advisor or the office's lowest assistant. He just wanted helpful information, whether anecdotal or statistical. Sometimes gathering that information came with a fair amount of healthy, heated debate.

There were times when the Dalton Gang members and their associates would almost come to blows over who had better information. In the end, though, because Harry Dalton believed in them, much as a father or an uncle would, they understood that no matter how they came to a decision, they would stand by each other and him. The top organizations in baseball do this routinely in the twenty-first century; the fate of teams is collective, and this phenomenon of solidarity started with the Dalton Gang. Dalton's legacy is much more than team building, however.

Harry Dalton should be considered the first modern baseball executive. As Frank Cashen, one of his contemporaries, pointed out, when Dalton became the chief team builder for the Baltimore Orioles in the winter of 1965, he was not an actual general manager because he did not concentrate on ancillary things such as promotions, vending, media contracts, and upkeep of the stadium like his predecessors had. Cashen meant this as a slight to Dalton, to make himself look better for the historical record. However, when readers consider all of baseball history, Harry Dalton's hiring by the Orioles to oversee baseball operations alone was a turning point in the game, not an admission of weakness.

Beginning with Dalton, no one did everything the way scholars of team-building history have shown; baseball's business became more complicated due to the advent of television, expansion, and the changing nature of the sport's finances vis-à-vis the players, and thus the game left generalists like Branch Rickey behind. Instead, offices were structured so that staff members became content experts, and those who oversaw them were middle managers who had a grasp of the larger picture but did not focus on everything. Harry Dalton was the first of a new breed of executive, and he created a mold for others to follow.

Dalton's innovation extended to how he dealt with people. There was no denying that Dalton was in charge and the final arbiter of all decisions. He was the boss. What made him different was that he looked to empower people no matter their job. This idiosyncrasy meant taking a less militant view of free agency informed by a Curt Flood–like battle over the ability of players to shape their careers. Dalton was the first player's GM, and baseball would be better for it.

Dalton's career is also meaningful because he was a continuation of the game's deep thinkers. His name should be uttered in the same breath as Branch Rickey, Larry MacPhail, and Billy Beane. Dalton worked during one of the most transformative periods in baseball history. He had opinions on all the hot-button issues of his time. Moreover, people wanted to hear his opinions. Owners, his fellow midlevel executives, up-and-coming front office personnel, reporters, and fans all wanted to know what Harry Dalton thought about things like scheduling, the changing nature of the relationship between players and management, free agency, rising salaries, or how the game was played on the field. It is time for historians to follow in the footsteps of Dalton's contemporaries. Dalton had a great mind, and exploration of it will allow for a better understanding of baseball between 1953 and 1994.

Finally, Harry Dalton's career is meaningful because he was an educator to many top executives in baseball history. The Dalton front office tree has branches that still touch the game during the twenty-first century. Frank Cashen, Lou Gorman, John Schuerholz, Bruce Manno, and Dan Duquette learned professional baseball from Harry Dalton. Finally, others, like Pat Gillick and Ted Simmons, were exposed to the "Dalton Way" as players before they began front office careers. Because of this reach, Dalton's methods need to be studied so that future generations can appreciate his influence on others.

This book will also go beyond baseball and show that Harry Dalton was much more than his job. As one of his daughters explained, "Baseball was all-consuming" for him. However, each of his daughters and his wife are quick to point out that he was a loving father who never let his job get totally in the way of him being there for his family. The people who worked for Dalton reiterated the presence of this humanistic side. He was loyal and could laugh at himself and make others laugh with him. He seemed egoless and to see himself as just another rank-and-file employee of the owners. In many players' minds, this mentality meant that Dalton had more in common with them than with ownership. To fully understand Harry Dalton is to realize that this part of him existed right alongside the cerebral executive who was out to win.

Finally, the last goal of this book is to give Harry Dalton a voice. Since his death in 2005, Dalton's employers and a fair number of employees have taken his absence as an opportunity to shape the narrative of what it was like working with and for him. They have also taken credit for some things he did but for which he never felt the need to receive credit. This proclivity makes the offending parties look better in the eyes of historians while marginalizing Dalton. A full biography will correct this distortion.

The mechanics of accomplishing these goals are somewhat simplistic, given the complexity of the subject. In the different portions of Dalton's life, I wanted to highlight different moments that encapsulate Dalton's team-building approach, his more in-depth thoughts on baseball, his role in off-the-field issues, and his demeanor and interactions with people in his life. My approach was "big picture" in nature with events on the field but more concentrated on Dalton and his approach with players and team management. The book focuses on how Harry Dalton built his teams and kept them competitive and how he shaped the world around him both professionally and personally. However, I do offer a closer look at game play when Dalton's teams were involved in the postseason or went through a period of prolonged excellence. Those seasons receive extra on-field attention because even though this book is about more than Dalton's most successful teams, winning was still a massive part of his legacy.

First, I outline Dalton's life before baseball. This part of my narrative will show that from an early age, he developed traits that would shape the rest of his life.

Then I cover his career in Baltimore and establish how his early days with the team organization there would inform his later years in higher management and the rest of his baseball career. This portion of the book also shows how Dalton came to national prominence and how he functioned as the first modern baseball executive in the way he set up his offices and dealt with people.

Dalton's move to California follows, with material covering the challenges he and his gang faced in building the California Angels into a winner, how free agency caused Dalton to improve his team-building approach, how other staff members' jealousy of Dalton hastened his departure from California, and how his budding family experienced life in California.

The next phase of Dalton's baseball career came as he moved to Milwaukee. The narrative covers him turning the team into a winner in the late 1970s and building one last pennant winner in the early 1980s while he worked toward labor-management harmony.

The text also provides a look at how Dalton kept the Brewers relevant despite the changing economic structure of the game and how he managed to stay relevant as a father with a maturing family in the late 1980s and early 1990s. A discussion of Dalton's time in Milwaukee concludes with the anticlimactic end to his career, which was still filled with moments of brilliance.

The last section covers Harry Dalton's life as a private citizen, including his untimely death. The book then discusses why he still matters to those who work in, follow, and study baseball and argue for his induction into the Baseball Hall of Fame.

A mix of sources informed my writing of Dalton's story. On the one hand, this work relies heavily on interviews conducted with people who played for, worked for, and were personal friends of Dalton. Also, Dalton's family contributes much to the text to present what it was like living with Harry Dalton. Family interviews include multiple conversations with all three of his daughters and his wife, Pat. Dalton's daughters have given invaluable information on what it was like being a "Dalton Girl," and Pat provided critical insight into not only her career as a baseball executive's wife but her husband's demeanor at and away from the ballpark.

On the baseball side, erstwhile front office staff, such as Dalton's former secretary in Milwaukee, some of his former protégés, and former players, contributed to this work. The players include Hall of Famers, everyday players, and the proverbial last man on the roster. This way, a complete picture is captured.

Finally, various friends from all walks of life have shared memories to give the reader a well-rounded picture of Harry Dalton.

Beyond interviews, the author has mined countless period media sources that outline Dalton's professional life and put his moves in context. Finally, where possible, the author has used oral histories and autobiographies of Dalton's contemporaries, along with his archived papers, to enrich the details of the events described and lend opinions on Harry Dalton.

Leave While the Party's Good

1

An All-American Son of the Commonwealth

1928–54

The early days of Harry Dalton's life would greatly inform his later life on two counts. First, his life before baseball shows that family profoundly influences the story of Harry Dalton. Throughout his life, whether it was augmenting his parents' income, taking time off during spring training to meet his wife's sister, or leaving the office early to watch one of his daughters participate in an activity, Harry Dalton always had time for family. His early life also establishes that Dalton showed a high degree of intelligence that would forever shape his interactions with others.

Dalton's familial connections span the U.S.-Canadian border and present a story that is very characteristic of English-speaking Canadian immigrants.

According to Bruno Ramirez, a historian of immigration and ethnic history, one of the most overlooked stories vis-à-vis immigration to the United States is that of the Anglo-Canadians.[1] They have remained largely invisible even as scholars have learned more and more about German, Irish, Polish, and French-Canadian immigrants to the United States. This absence from the immigration story has occurred, writes Ramirez, even though "for every French-Canadian who immigrated to the United States [between 1880 and 1930], two Anglo-Canadians did likewise."[2] This migration pattern is present on both sides of Harry Dalton's extended family.

On the Dalton side, Harry's fraternal grandfather, James Dalton, was born in 1844 in Nova Scotia. By the age of thirty-seven, the bookkeeper was married with three kids, and he also identified himself as a member of the Church of England. This household actually had an Irish German heritage, and the middle child was Harry H. Dalton. Harry was born on April 1, 1871, in Halifax.[3] By 1901 the thirty-year-old middle child had begun a career in sales in the hardware industry. He had also married and fathered three children. The youngest of these was Jack Ingles Dalton.[4]

The other side of Harry Dalton's family tree was also rooted in Canada. His maternal grandfather was a baker by the name of Thomas O'Malley. Thomas was born in 1868, and Thomas's wife was the former Harriet "Hattie" Boutilier. Hattie was the third of eight children born to William and Mary Boutilier. She was nineteen in 1891 and lived with her widowed father, her maternal grandfather, and her brothers and sisters, who ranged in age from six to twenty-one. A year later, she married O'Malley.[5]

The couple continued to live in Halifax during the early part of their marriage. Thomas and Hattie's first child, a girl named Florence, was born there in 1893. Then, in 1894 the family immigrated to Lowell, Massachusetts. A year after they moved, Hattie gave birth to a second daughter, named Mary.[6] The couple's next forays into expanding their family met with mixed results. In 1899 Hattie was pregnant with twins. She gave birth to them in the middle of February. Catherine was born first, and her brother, Roy, followed. Unfortunately, tragedy struck. Catherine died one day after her birth. Eleven days later, Roy succumbed to the same illness.[7] The couple recorded no more births until 1902, when Hattie gave birth to Edna Frances O'Malley on January 16.[8]

Despite being born in Massachusetts, Edna O'Malley attended school back in Halifax. According to family lore, it was most likely at this time that she met Jack Dalton. There are very few details of their courtship, and what is known is that Jack Dalton attended both high school and technical college in Nova Scotia and followed his family when they immigrated to the United States in 1925.[9]

The family came to the United States via Boston on the SS *Northland* from Yarmouth, Canada. How long they stayed in Boston is unknown. However, the family left Massachusetts at some point and migrated to Florida. When the Daltons reached the Sunshine State, the family's men took up the one occupation they knew best—sales. During that first year, Harry, Jack, and Jack's older brother Arthur, a World War I veteran, all resided at 35 North Hill Street in Orlando with Harry's wife, Ada, and worked for the Joseph Bumby Hardware Company.[10]

In 1926 the family dynamic went through significant changes. In a somewhat odd coincidence, both Dalton brothers were married within a day of each other in August 1926. The first ceremony occurred on August 24 in an Orange County, Florida, courtroom. That day, Jack married Edna O'Malley. The date Edna had immigrated back to the United States is unknown. However, it is safe to assume that she was back in the country either in late 1925 or early 1926 because she listed her address as 35 North Hill Street on her marriage license. On August 25 Arthur married Hazel Harvey, formerly of Halifax, who also listed her address as 35 North Hill Street. North Hill Street remained the family home until 1928.[11]

In 1928 the Daltons (Harry, Ada, Arthur, Hazel, Jack, and Edna) moved to 602 Stetson Avenue in Orlando. Harry and Arthur still worked for the Joseph Bumby Hardware Company during this period. However, at some point Jack took a job as a Sunoco gas station manager in Orlando.[12] This situation did not last long, however. Sometime in 1927, Edna became pregnant. Instead of trying to make a go of it in Florida, the Dalton brothers and their brides moved back to Massachusetts. Arthur and Hazel settled in Winthrop.

Meanwhile, Jack and Edna made West Springfield their home base. It was here that the life of Harry Dalton began. West Springfield, Massachusetts, located on the banks of the Connecticut River, was first incorporated in 1774 after having been a portion of the Springfield land grant of 1636. It had acquired its modern boundaries by 1855, when Holyoke separated from West Springfield. By 1915 the town had evolved from an agriculturally reliant area centered on commercial farming to a hub for the Boston and Albany Railroad.[13] Fifteen years later, the town had a population of 16,684.[14] Four members of that population resided in the Dalton household at 408 Belmont Avenue.

The 1930 federal census listed Jack as a hardware salesman, and the same census classified Edna as a homemaker. Also in the house were two Daltons named Harry. The first was Jack's father, who had moved in with Jack and Edna following Ada's death sometime in 1929 while the couple was still living in Florida. The second, Harry Ingles Dalton, was born in Springfield on August 23, 1928.[15] He would be the only child of Jack and Edna Dalton and, from an early age, demonstrated talents and interests in several subjects.

Harry showed high intelligence in his earliest youth. In 1941, while in the seventh grade at West Springfield Junior High, he was routinely cited for his academic excellence. His academic prowess continued through his time at West Springfield High School, culminating with his graduation in 1946, when he was named a high honor winner in the senior class.[16]

Beyond his high marks in class, Dalton was active in the school's clubs. He received recognition in his junior year for his excellent play on a lackluster soccer team. Dalton's senior year of 1946 was the high-water mark. That year the skinny senior with a pompadour was the assistant editor of the yearbook and a Pro Merito Society member, thanks to his 4.0 GPA.[17]

As a teenager, Harry became a connoisseur of the arts and evolved into a civic-minded citizen. Like many teens of his generation, he loved the music that would become known as "big band" sound. Music was such a big part of his life that Harry would often sit by a radio listening to concerts from New York and Chicago and chart the playlists for future reference.[18] Beyond writing out the music played by others, Harry also took the time to create his own literary work. These writings showed a dichotomy that would be present for his entire life. On one hand, Dalton was capable of deft humor. For instance, during his senior year, Dalton penned a poem titled "Excursion" that appeared in the yearbook; it was about a perilous trip to the city junkyard. As for what Dalton used as a muse, "Excursion" probably has more than a grain of truth, considering that the poem conveniently featured two classmates as the protagonists:

Over the hill in a cloud of dust
Sails Robert's Fine Food truck, "Junkyard or Bust"
The fenders are shaking; the running boards off,
And all through the journey the motor doth cough.
The dashboard says fifty but that can't be true.
For Donald doth never exceed twenty-two.
He spots a cute redhead up on the right,

Ah Ha! Watch it Donald! You just missed a light
The junkyard comes closer; will he reach it in time?
The danger is great, but his joy is sublime
He pictures his glory when the job is well done,
And glory he gets because they pay him no mon—
All of a sudden, comes a voice through the door,
It's McBride in back, stretched out on the floor,
He has an announcement; it is one of great need,
But Donald is anxious; he increases his speed.
The end of the journey is nearing quite fast;
The junkyard approaches; he'll make it at last
And as we depart from this lad of great spunk,
He stands there disgusted. He's left home the junk![19]

Not content with just penning this tongue-in-cheek ditty, Dalton, a former American Legion Boys State representative, used his writings to show that he was cognizant of the larger world around him and that that world was changing. The class of 1946 had lived through a world war. They had seen friends go off to fight and the advent of the atomic age, with all the terrifying and promising effects of that new technology. With all this in mind, Harry Dalton used his assistant editor's platform on the yearbook to remind his classmates that diplomats had failed to maintain peace twice in the twentieth century, that atomic weapons did not guarantee human survival of a third world war, and that "people now known as teen-agers are the ones slated to shoulder the burden" of any future conflicts. Because of this, Dalton cautioned that his generation of Americans would serve themselves and the world best by practicing the values of "religious tolerance, racial tolerance, and political tolerance," which the Germans and Japanese had abandoned before World War II. In doing this, Dalton felt that when it was time for his cohort to lead America, they could "courageously take our place in the world as citizens of a democratic nation with the preservation of world peace upmost [*sic*] in our minds."[20]

With such an understanding of the larger world so clearly laid out in front of the reader, it is easy to forget that Harry Dalton was also one of those "teen-agers" upon whom the world would place the burden of the future. He had a job as a playground supervisor; he was the captain and scorekeeper for a sandlot baseball team, although his skill level meant that he did not play much. He also liked girls. According to his senior yearbook, "Flash" Dalton "talked continuously" and often asked his classmates, "What's comin['] off here?" He also had a penchant for knowing "all the girls." These girls included a "blonde top" in Montreal who had caught Harry's eye. Due to this ability with the opposite sex, Dalton's classmates deemed him the "Playboy" of the graduating class, whose theme song "Is You Is or Is You Ain't (My Baby)" was a popular hit by Louis Jordan and fit Dalton to a tee.[21]

With all these interests, it is hard to imagine that Harry Dalton had time for anything else. However, he spent summers traveling with his parents. Family vacations included a car trip to Maine that would remain a cherished memory. He also routinely rode into Boston with Jack and Edna and went to Fenway Park to watch the Red Sox in the era of Ted Williams, Johnny Pesky, and Dominic DiMaggio.[22]

The well-rounded nature of his teenage years is the epitome of what colleges look for when high school students apply for admission, as was the case even in the 1940s. Therefore, it is no surprise that Harry's days in West Springfield were, for the most part, numbered. The fall after his high school graduation, Harry set out to a place he would always be proud of: Amherst College.

In 1946 Amherst College was in the middle of a two-pronged transition. On the one hand, the college was transitioning into a new curriculum that would take effect in 1947.[23] On the other hand, like the rest of America, Amherst was emerging from four years of war.

Amherst College was founded in 1821 as the Amherst Collegiate Institution. In 1825 it received its charter from the Massachusetts legislature to operate as Amherst College and graduated its first class—twenty-five male students. The institution featured progressive thinking from the faculty and student body right from the beginning. In 1828 the student body formed a governmental unit known as the House of Students to "ensure more order on campus." It initiated reforms that included drafting laws protecting the school buildings and ensuring students observed mandatory study hours. The school was also progressive on the athletic fields. In 1859, in a game that took three and a half hours and twenty-six innings, Amherst defeated rival Williams College in the first intercollegiate baseball game in history. Finally, as the Civil War was poised to begin, Amherst became the first college in the United States to offer hygiene and physical education instruction to promote student health. With this history, a curriculum change does not seem as daunting as it would be for an institution with a less progressive pedigree.[24]

Amherst also had a history of aiding in the war efforts of the United States. In 1917 the federal government began operating the college and did so for the duration of the American involvement in World War I. During that time, the students formed an Army Reserve Officer Training Corps detachment and a Student Army Training Corps unit.[25] The college's close ties with the military continued after the outbreak of World War II. In March 1941 Amherst became one of the colleges affiliated with the U.S. Navy Preflight V-5 program, which took college students from all over and made them naval aviators. Then, in July 1942, the college rolled out an accelerated course designed to allow students to graduate in three years. Following this move, other military training commands began operating schools at Amherst. Running two obstacle courses became mandatory for the student body and all military trainees.[26] With the war's end, the entire campus was looking forward to a return to a peacetime footing. Harry Dalton and the class of 1950 entered this changing environment.

Harry Dalton began his time at Amherst as an English major. Dalton's selection of English is not shocking, given two overriding factors. First, Dalton's earlier writings show an excellent grasp of the written word. In addition, the English Department was the crown jewel of Amherst's academic program, thanks to the strength of a faculty that included Robert Frost and Theodore Baird.[27]

The college expected Dalton and his fellow English majors to complete 120 credit hours to meet graduation requirements. For those credit hours students had to complete four electives, including classes in language, literature and the arts, social studies, philosophy, mathematics, and natural sciences. Dalton would have also had to show proficiency in a foreign language and achieve required standards in physical education and public speaking.[28]

Dalton also maintained a full extracurricular life. During his senior year, he was the sports editor of the *Amherst Student* newspaper, worked in the college news service disseminating Amherst news to the outside world, and was a member of Theta Delta Chi fraternity.[29] He also made lifelong friends. Bill Nesbitt was Dalton's roommate at the Theta Delta Chi house. Harry and the bespectacled Nesbitt became fast friends, and Harry also quickly became friends with the future Mrs. Nesbitt, who would visit often. Dayle Jones remembered that the college-aged Harry, despite looking taciturn in his Delta Chi picture, was "easy to be around" and that he kept "everyone in stitches" with a "killer sense of humor."[30] Humor was a lifelong trait. One of the people with whom Dalton had his share of laughs was classmate Danny Galbreath. Danny's father, John, had made a fortune in the real estate market during his thirties and forties. This windfall allowed him to start a successful thoroughbred stable, which he purchased in 1935, and to buy a controlling interest in the Pittsburgh Pirates in 1946.[31]

Despite these connections, Harry Dalton did not ask for special treatment when looking for a job following graduation. He did not have to. Thanks to his work with the student newspaper and the college's news bureau, Dalton was recognized at graduation with two different awards. The first, awarded to him by the Sphinx, an undergraduate honor society at Amherst, was for Dalton's contributions to the athletic department through his reporting. The second award named him the school's journalist of the year. Graduation was a star-studded affair featuring speeches laced with Cold War rhetoric (that Harry Dalton accepted as truth) by Smith College president Benjamin F. Wright and future secretary of state John Foster Dulles, both of whom received honorary degrees.[32] As for Harry Dalton, with his diploma in his back pocket, he moved back to West Springfield. Once there, he would become the first Dalton male not to go into sales. He was going to work in the newspaper business.

Fresh out of Amherst, Dalton took a job on the sports desk at the *Springfield Sunday Republican*. His first byline appeared on July 9, 1950, when he covered the third round of the Springfield Republican City Golf Tournament.[33] From there, armed with a clear, concise writing style, Dalton became a jack-of-all-trades for the *Sunday Republican*. The following week, after an interview with the head coach of the Cornell "Big Red" squad, Dalton used Cold War terminology to describe the school's college football dominance. Specifically, Dalton informed readers that "a red menace" in the form of the Cornell University football team was ready to dominate the Ivy League that fall as the "Cornell grid machine battles its way in search of its third straight Ivy League title."[34]

Dalton's budding sports journalism career continued in the fall of that year. In August he returned to his alma mater to give a less than nuanced but not quite biased appraisal of the Amherst football team's upcoming prospects under their new head coach, John J. McLaughry.[35] Then, in September, Dalton turned his sights back to the local sports scene. The budding journalist wrote his longest story to date on the third annual "Midget Derby" soapbox race in mid-September.[36] It was shaping up to be an exciting fall for Harry Dalton as he brought the sights and sounds of local sports to readers of the Springfield newspaper. Unbeknown to them, however, events on the Korean Peninsula and in Baltimore would guarantee that Harry Dalton would never write another news story in Springfield.

In June 1950, as Harry Dalton, Danny Galbreath, and the rest of the Amherst class of 1950 prepared to graduate, they, along with the rest of America, were reminded that the United States was by then a global power locked in an ideological struggle that had battlefields the world over. The catalyst of that reminder was the invasion of South Korea by its northern neighbor in an attempt by the north's communist leadership to reunify the country. The communist north's desire for reunification arose from a deal that had been made as Harry Dalton was finishing his junior year at West Springfield High.

Following World War II's end, the United States and its Soviet allies administered the Japanese military's surrender in Korea and oversaw the running of that country. The arrangements agreed upon during the surrender were set to expire in 1949, when the United Nations would schedule free elections that would decide the fate of Korea vis-à-vis the country's form of government. In the meantime, the Soviet Union and the United States exerted their influence over various newborn governments. Because of this, Korea was caught in the middle when relations between the two superpowers began to turn. The result was a landmass split into two different populations with two different benefactors. Above the Thirty-Eighth Parallel, North Korea was a communist government backed by the Soviet Union and led by Kim Il Sung. Below that line, Syngman Rhee led South Korea and received aid, including military assistance, from the United States. U.S. support for South Korea was unacceptable to the North Korean government, which actively sought Soviet approval to fight a war of reunification. They were finally permitted to begin this war in June 1950.

The attack launched by the North Korean People's Army against the U.S. and Republic of Korea military positions was a complete shock to the vastly unprepared American army, which had grown complacent after years of occupation duty. As a result, by the fall of 1950 the U.S. Army, along with follow-on troops provided by the U.S. Marine Corps as part of a United Nations force mobilized to stop the North Koreans, were in danger of being pushed off the southern half of the Korean Peninsula.[37] At this moment, Harry Dalton, no doubt driven by a love of his country and an understanding of his generation's role in the larger world, quit his job and enlisted in the fledgling U.S. Air Force.

The U.S. Air Force, born out of the Army Air Force of World War II, began life in 1947. From that time, thanks to a firm belief that it had almost single-handedly ended World War II and an even more assertive public relations machine reinforcing this notion with the American citizenry, the U.S. Air Force was seen as the perfect fighting force for a world where aviation, tied with the threat of the atomic bomb, was the ultimate equalizer. American pilots were proving this in Korea. The first generation of jet aircraft was pairing with propeller-driven holdovers from the American victory in World War II to secure a toehold on the Korean Peninsula.[38]

It would take Harry Dalton a while to contribute to the air force record in Korea. He attended enlisted men's basic training at Lackland Air Force Base in San Antonio, Texas. He was stationed at Standiford Field in Louisville, Kentucky, which opened in 1941 and doubled as the city's commercial airport.[39] He then attended specialized training at Carlisle Barracks, an army post in Pennsylvania, in the spring of 1952.[40] While at Carlisle, Dalton was enrolled in a multiservice six-week course in public information. The course had 108 graduates from every military branch and was commanded by Rear Admiral Thomas Binford. At the end of the course, Private Dalton was the top graduate.[41] This performance marked Dalton for even bigger things.

After a short period back at Standiford, Dalton was assigned to Officer Candidate School (OCS) back at Lackland. OCS was designed to turn civilians and select enlisted personnel like Dalton into leaders. While there, Dalton learned the tenets of command expected of a new lieutenant in the service. OCS was six months long, and afterward Lieutenant Dalton used some of his leave in the summer of 1952 to serve as best man for Don Nesbitt (who was in the U.S. Army Signal Corps at Fort Lee, Virginia) when he married Dayle Fort in South Orange, New Jersey.[42] After his leave, Dalton went to his first duty post as an officer.

Harry Dalton spent the next portion of his career as a project officer attached to the Ground Observer Corps (GOC) stationed at Ent Air Force Base in Colorado Springs, Colorado. The air force modeled the Ground Observer Corps on the British method of using civilians to identify aircraft types and numbers during air raids against England during the Battle of Britain. The United States implemented the system during the earliest days of the Cold War out of fear of Soviet attacks on the United States.[43] As a project officer with the program, Dalton was tasked with welcoming the aviation press corps and explaining the GOC program. This job included welcoming a writer from his former civilian employer in July 1952. Through this visiting reporter, Harry quickly told the folks at home two significant pieces of information. First, he told readers that "although his folks now live in Baltimore, Springfield will always be his home." Second, Lieutenant Dalton was heading to Korea.[44]

The air force command prosecuting the war in Korea was known as the Far East Air Forces (abbreviated as FEAF and pronounced to rhyme with "thief"). During the war, FEAF maintained bases in both Japan and South Korea, and Lieutenant Dalton would spend time in both places as he served as a combat correspondent. Today combat correspondents are known as embedded reporters, and they are stationed with combat units and report on the goings-on in those units for their readers. In Dalton's case, this meant going on combat missions up and down the Korean Peninsula. It is unknown whom Dalton's readership included. What is certain is that along with his Korean Service Medal, National Defense Service Medal, and United Nations Service Medal, Dalton's personal correspondence also shows that Dalton won a Bronze Star for merit, which was awarded in conjunction with these missions.[45]

With this track record, there is no doubt that Harry Dalton could have extended his air force career beyond the thirty-seven months that he served. However, he was discharged from the air force, and the first stop he made was to see his parents in Baltimore. This trip would change the trajectory of his life.

2

Present at the Creation for Forty-Five Dollars a Week

1954

True to his word, Harry Dalton moved to Baltimore to be with his parents. As for what had brought Jack and Edna to Baltimore, it was once again the nomadic life of a salesman that had influenced the Dalton family's relocation. In the fall of 1950, Jack had taken a sales position with Bacharach's Sporting Goods, which billed itself as "Maryland's Largest Sporting Goods Store." Thanks to a degree of subterfuge by Bacharach's, the mustachioed Jack Dalton was in turn billed as a firearms expert who had "forgotten more about fine guns than the average man learns in a lifetime." The subterfuge occurred because Bacharach's made it seem that Jack Dalton had worked in conjunction with the Springfield Armory while the family lived in Massachusetts. This was not the case; Jack never worked for the armory. However, the assertion looked good in print.[1]

Now discharged from the service, Harry Dalton was without a job for the first time since he left for Amherst. According to Dalton, he had decided that he would try and hook on with a Major League ball club to work in public relations.[2] Ever since his days on West Springfield's sandlots, Dalton had understood the game better than he played it. Even at a young age, this tended to mean that his friends placed him in various administrative roles instead of putting him in the lineup. This leadership ability allowed Dalton to foster hope that he would get to work in a baseball team's front office one day. Thanks to machinations occurring in the boardrooms of Major League Baseball, Harry Dalton would get his chance.

To put it kindly, by 1953 the St. Louis Browns were seen as the laughingstock of the American League and had been for some time. The Browns' former general manager and partial owner Bill DeWitt summed up the situation best. "Most of the other clubs had players in the minors that were better than the players we had on the Browns," he said. Meanwhile, off the field, "the Browns had a hell of a time because the [St. Louis] Cardinals were so popular and the Browns couldn't do a damn thing. . . . We didn't have any attendance money to build up the ball club with."[3] Any ownership group could see that moving the Browns from St. Louis was the only alternative.

The Browns' owners first tried to do so in 1941, with Los Angeles in their sights. This western move would have been a game changer for a sport that was an East Coast monopoly up to that point. Most important, a move of that kind would have opened a new fan base for Major League Baseball. However, the American League owners had misgivings about letting the Browns relocate to the Golden State. First, having the Browns as the sole Major League entry on the West Coast would create travel and scheduling issues for the league. Furthermore, the other owners feared that the native sons and daughters of Los Angeles would not back an also-ran.[4] Fortunately for them, the world changed as the Browns made their pitch.

The 1941 winter meetings began on December 9, 1941. Two days earlier, the Empire of Japan had attacked U.S. military forces throughout the Pacific. These attacks reached a crescendo with the Japanese sneak attack on Pearl Harbor, Hawaii, which left U.S. forces in the region crippled. Consequently, on December 8, President Franklin D. Roosevelt asked Congress to declare war on Japan. Congress approved, and America was now at war. Because of this, baseball was thrown into limbo for a time. Moreover, moving a team to California seemed ludicrous, so the Browns would stay put.

The war years were somewhat successful for the perennial losers. In 1944 the Browns even captured the pennant in a depleted American League. Still, despite a change in ownership and the pennant win in 1944, the team returned to the basement following the war. This poor performance precipitated another ownership change. This time, the sometimes abrasive, always entertaining Bill Veeck Jr. purchased a controlling interest in the team.[5]

Veeck was already well known in baseball circles. His father, William Veeck Sr., had worked for the Chicago Cubs, and Bill had owned the Minor League Milwaukee Brewers of the American Association, where he perfected the art of promoting his team and himself. He then purchased a controlling interest in the Cleveland Indians following service in World War II. Veeck brought the city on Lake Erie a World Series title in 1948 with a roster that included stars Larry Doby, Satchel Paige, Bob Feller, Bob Lemmon, and Lou Boudreau.

Following Cleveland's success, Veeck looked for new worlds to conquer and settled on the St. Louis Browns. In June 1951, Veeck purchased the Browns from Bill and Charley DeWitt. His team played out the 1951 season in St. Louis as well as the 1952 campaign. He then tried to figure out how to move the team. In a perfect world, Veeck wanted to bring Major League Baseball to Milwaukee. The people in Wisconsin were baseball crazy; they loved Veeck and his antics and were building a new municipally funded ballpark. Conditions were perfect for Veeck and the Browns. There was only one snag. The right to put a Major League team in Milwaukee belonged to someone else.

Lou Perini, a construction magnate from Boston, owned the Boston Braves and had his Triple-A affiliate in Milwaukee. Veeck would have to buy the rights to Milwaukee to put the Browns there. Unfortunately for him, Perini was in the same predicament as Veeck. Perini's solution, a closely guarded secret, unlike Veeck's proposed move, was to relocate the Braves to Milwaukee for the 1953 season.[6] This left one city as a viable option for Veeck: Baltimore, Maryland.

Like Milwaukee, the city of Baltimore had particular strengths that made it attractive as a prospective site for Major League Baseball. On the one hand, even though the local team was no longer in the Majors, the city had supported winning baseball in many guises. The great Baltimore teams of the 1880s and 1890s had helped transform the way baseball was played league-wide. The city had also experienced success at the Minor League level in the 1910s and 1920s, when the Minor League Orioles dominated the International League. Then, during the war years and in the immediate aftermath, the Baltimore Elite Giants of the Negro National League became the next in a long line of successful teams from Baltimore when they won pennants in 1942 and then again in 1948, marking a competitive streak that lasted the whole decade. Besides being a baseball town, Baltimore also had a publicly funded stadium on the way. Finally, the local team had an owner who wanted out of direct ownership. For decades, the Dunn family, which had been involved in Baltimore baseball since the earliest days of the game in the city, could not underwrite a team by itself anymore. Conditions were ripe for Veeck to move the Browns to Baltimore in time for the 1953 season, except for one significant problem. The other owners in the American League, by and large, could not stand Veeck.

The nature of their dislike for Veeck was twofold. First, most of them felt he made a mockery of the game on the field. During his time in St. Louis, Veeck had already sent 3-foot-7-inch Eddie Gaedel into a game to bat and had let fans attending home games manage the team using placards to dictate strategy to the Browns' manager. Finally, perhaps, more important, he looked to change the game off the field. Veeck believed that players should have more freedom to choose their employer and that owners should split profits gained through the new medium of television.[7] Willingness to upset the status quo led to a negative vote of 6–2 when Veeck asked permission to move. Veeck tried again after the 1953 season, and this time he failed to get permission by a vote of 4–4 during the owners' meetings in September, just before the World Series. Moreover, it looked like the American League was shifting away from moving to Baltimore, with California now targeted as a landing spot.

At that point, the movement to get Baltimore back in Major League Baseball needed something to shake it up to secure the bid. The answer was complete local control. With Mayor Thomas D'Alesandro Jr. as the loudest supporter of the move and a voice promising the city government's full support, it fell to Baltimore's elite to secure a team. Luckily, a group of men had planned for this eventuality. Aristocratic lawyer Clarence Miles was the front man and a minority stockholder, while most of the money came from a mix of Baltimore's upper crust, including the president of the National Brewing Company, Jerold Hoffberger. This group had enough clout to buy out Veeck's 80 percent of the Browns, as well as enough money left over to satiate Clark Griffin, the owner of the Washington Senators, whose team would be impacted the most by another team moving into his territory of control. Another vote followed this move. The result? Big league baseball was back in Baltimore.[8]

The team officially moved operations in November 1953. At that point, the organization began lining up the men who would make the baseball decisions on behalf of the ownership group. Ultimately, Art Ehlers would become the first general manager, Dick Armstrong was the head of public relations, and Jim McLaughlin, the only holdover from the team's days in St. Louis, was the new farm director. This was the environment that newly discharged Harry Dalton hoped to join.

Legend has it that Harry Dalton walked into the Baltimore Orioles' offices fresh off the street. While this would make for a move that sounds straight out of central casting, the reality is more in line with current practices. He sent the Orioles his résumé.

In a letter dated October 27, 1953, Dalton outlined his intention to seek employment in the public relations department with the club. His qualifications earned Dalton an interview with Dick Armstrong, the head of PR for the Orioles. At the end of that interview, Armstrong told Dalton that he should speak to the Orioles' farm director, Jim McLaughlin, who was also looking for an assistant. It was during this second meeting that Dalton struck pay dirt. Dalton was officially hired two days before Christmas in 1954 as the assistant farm director. His salary? Forty-five dollars a week.

It was a job that came with some unique challenges. The offices at the time were not at Memorial Stadium, so many of Dalton's early days with the team were spent running messages from his boss McLaughlin at the offices in Baltimore out to GM Art Ehlers at the stadium on Thirty-Third Street. According to Dalton, it was not the easiest way to earn his keep in a new job, but he would not have traded it for anything. "We had to run back and forth for meetings . . . but for a guy who wanted to get into baseball, hell, I'd have gone fifty miles," Dalton told an interviewer.[9] Just because he was now in the big leagues did not secure glamour for

Harry Dalton. In fact, during his early days with the team, Dalton was working two jobs.

"I was young. I was driving a cab at night to pay off college loans and everything else. I didn't even have a car. I'd take the trolley to work, get a trolley back [to his parents' house], and go out to College Cabs in Towson, right by the fire station on York Road. I'd moonlight at night for four or five hours trying to get myself out from under."[10]

While he was "trying to get out from under," Dalton was exposed to events and people that would shape his later life. One of them was Joe Hamper. Hamper was an infantryman in Europe during World War II, and the Germans captured him during the Battle of the Bulge in late 1944. After he returned stateside, he attended Johns Hopkins University and became a CPA. In the winter of 1954, he noticed a newspaper ad for an accountant with the Orioles organization. Hamper applied and got the job. "Harry was one of the first guys I met," he told an interviewer. "Somebody introduced him to me. People were just working there. Nobody had any titles. . . . I was just in the accounting department."[11] Hamper and Dalton became fast friends who bonded over their time in the military. While performing his duties for the Orioles and driving a cab, Dalton also learned baseball at the foot of Jim McLaughlin. He would quickly become Dalton's mentor.

Although he would later claim not to be a "Baseball Man," Jim McLaughlin was a lifer in the game. His career began when he worked for Bill DeWitt with the St. Louis Browns. Along the way, while the Browns were mired in their losing ways, McLaughlin developed scouting methods that would alienate him from his peers yet revolutionize the scouting industry.

McLaughlin's scientific method was basically to look beyond a player's physical tools to what he would eventually call the "skills that cannot be seen with the eye."[12] He taught Dalton (and the scouts under his charge) to look at these attributes in players:

Attitude: desire, drive, willingness, hunger, attention
Mental: intelligence, baseball sense, teachability, knowledge of the game

Winner: stomach, heart, competitor, pride, confidence
Personality: improvement, consistency, maturity, adjustment, stability, temperament, disposition
Background: family, habits

Armed with information about what intangibles and incidentals made a great ballplayer, Dalton took the next step in his baseball education by watching enough talent to know what physical tools would help the fledgling Orioles climb out of the American League cellar. During that first season, and throughout the rest of the 1950s and into the early 1960s, the best place for Dalton to learn would be at the Orioles' Minor League spring training complex in Thomasville, Georgia.

A Minor League spring training complex in multiple cities seems archaic to the modern fan. These days, parent teams train and evaluate all their players, no matter what level they occupy in a team's system, in a centrally located venue, either Arizona or Florida. This way, clubs can monitor their investment in players on a daily basis. In the 1950s this was not the case. Teams often had training facilities in two places, and the Orioles were no different. Thanks to a deal made by Bill Veeck with local authorities in Yuma, Arizona, the Major League Orioles headed west for their inaugural spring campaign. Meanwhile, Jim McLaughlin, Harry Dalton, and the team of Orioles scouts set up a Minor League training camp in Thomasville.

The name Thomasville, Georgia, evokes an image of a slow-paced southern town with an idyllic city center. It is much like that today and mirrors what Harry Dalton first saw in the winter of 1954. Little did he know that the spartan conditions in the town hard on the Georgia-Florida state line, a town best known for growing roses, would provide players and the Orioles' young assistant farm director with the ideal environment in which to learn the game of professional baseball. Why? Because there was very little to do other than eat, sleep, and watch baseball.

The Browns first came to Thomasville in 1952. They set up shop on a former Veterans Administration property that was built, naturally, like a military base. As such, there were very few amenities. The players slept in barracks on cots. Those in charge even used reveille to wake the masses. Physicals were given en masse. On the field, the conditions for the hundreds of Minor Leaguers in the camp were not much better from the players' standpoint. Future Hall of Famer Jim Palmer remembered that Thomasville's complex was short on practice fields and creature comforts: "They really only had one real park . . . two Ping Pong tables. . . . If you lost, you waited two hours."[13] Despite the place's flaws, Thomasville did have its charms.

According to Harry Dalton, it was the best place to learn the game as a player and an evaluator of talent. "It was a huge complex, actually just south of Thomasville," he recalled. "We had our own administrative building with two offices and a big meeting room. A kitchen and a dining room. Barracks-style serving. Then about eight typical military barracks buildings where you put up thirty cots. It was perfect, really perfect. Pines, beautiful grounds. There was a ballpark with a small grandstand, the main field. Then they built an adjacent field next to the ballpark, just off the grounds on city property, and then on the grounds, they built two more diamonds for us, so we had four to work with."[14]

The preparation for this work would start long before Dalton got to Thomasville. January would be filled with Dalton getting player contracts in the mail and setting dates for the players to report to the following year's Thomasville camp. Then, in February, Dalton and McLaughlin would ink the Minor League managers and Dalton would go to Thomasville to help prepare the facility. Once the camp opened, Dalton spent most of his time in his office shuffling paper with help from a secretary recruited from the local population. He would keep track of contracts and how many Minor League options a player had left before he either had to be promoted to the Majors or the Orioles would risk losing him. When he was not in the office, Dalton was on the field in a technologically enriched environment learning to evaluate players. In the early years, Bill Enos ran the Orioles' Minor League spring camp.

Enos was from Massachusetts, and during his first camp he reinforced the scientific feel of the Orioles organization. He introduced things like walkie-talkies for communication. This innovation made Dalton's office the communications base for the camp, complete with a Teletype machine. Other innovations occurred in the field. For instance, "Iron Mike" pitching machines allowed hitters to take as many swings in a batting cage as was necessary, which meant that training camp wouldn't burn out the pitchers.[15]

These innovations, combined with Jim McLaughlin's work, helped reinforce the Orioles' belief that the organization had moved into "modern times" and had to use "modern methods to train ballplayers."[16] This mantra would be the foundation of Harry Dalton's long career.

According to Dalton, the learning did not stop when the sun set on Thomasville. "We had long days, then you'd go have a beer in the Bird's Nest," he recalled. The Bird's Nest was a spare room in the staff barracks that became the Baltimore team brain trust's de facto after-hours club. According to Dalton, this was where the scouts and the other brass did the gritty work of building a roster. "We'd have cold cuts, cheese, beer, and soft drinks, and people would start to unwind. Then you'd go to dinner at six-thirty and we'd have a meeting at seven, and those meetings would usually go to ten o'clock because we kept talking about players," he remembered. After that, it was back to the Bird's Nest, where talks would go until the early hours of the morning. This, Dalton would say years later, "created a tremendous sense of organization" among the staff.[17]

As one can imagine, there was not much time for a social life in Thomasville. Orioles recruits had long days on the field, and men like Harry Dalton had long nights discussing the team's future. When they were not in meetings or too tired from playing, the staff and the players could find a few distractions in town. For the players, there was a drive-in diner where they could try their luck with the southern belles of Thomasville. Meanwhile, the staff headed to the Elks Lodge. There they could get a drink and socialize (over bingo) with the town fathers. This ritual activity usually led to the dating life of Harry Dalton becoming a topic of discussion between the Orioles brass and their counterparts. When that occurred, the main objective was to get Dalton a date with one of the daughters of Thomasville's elite. Orioles insiders even had him linked to Claire Varnedoe, the college-age daughter of the mayor of Thomasville, who was home from the University of Georgia.[18]

With a full schedule, the days in Thomasville passed quickly for the skinny, crew-cut-wearing Dalton. Soon it was time to break camp and head north, where he would begin his first regular season in baseball.

Once the 1954 season began, the Major League Orioles struggled. Being assigned to the farm department, Harry Dalton did not see much of their troubles. Jim McLaughlin was, first and foremost, a facilitator, and he left Baltimore only when he had to. McLaughlin's preference not to leave Baltimore meant that Harry Dalton saw many of America's Minor League hotspots.

In Dalton's first season, the Orioles' Minor League system stretched five levels, from Class D at the low end to Class Double-A at the top. Geographically, the Orioles had teams from Quebec up in Canada (Class C Thetford Mines), into South Dakota (Class C Aberdeen) and through the American West (Class A Lewiston, Idaho), down through Texas (Double-A San Antonio), Oklahoma (Class D Ada), and Kansas (Class A Wichita), then into the Southeast with teams in Arkansas (Class C Pine Bluff), North Carolina (Class D Marion), South Carolina (Class B Anderson), and Georgia (Class D Cordele), and finally up through Virginia (Class D Wytheville) and ending in Pennsylvania (Class B York). Having so many destinations on his itinerary allowed Harry Dalton to see a large portion of small-town America and a ton of baseball. More important, this allowed him to quickly become a good judge of talent on the diamond and in his surroundings while acting as an advance man for the Orioles' farm department. For example, in September 1954 Dalton wrote home to his parents from a prospect camp held in Burlington, Iowa. He noted that "Burlington is an old city and not a particularly beautiful city." However, it suited the purposes of the Orioles contingent because "it's not too big, and the prices aren't too high." Dalton was also quick to point out that from a group of thirty-five players, only one or two looked like potential pro players, but that was enough to make the camp worth the Orioles' time. From Burlington, Dalton went on to Columbus, Ohio, before stopping in Baltimore and finishing the month setting up another camp, this one in York.[19]

While Dalton was on his way to Burlington, events in Baltimore had the potential to end his baseball career before it began. Although the city was happy to be back in the Majors, losing began to grate on the fan base. As a result, even before the end of the 1954 season, the ownership group looked for their top officials for 1955. By late August they had settled on their top target.

In 1954 the Chicago White Sox's manager was a rail-thin Texan considered one of the big leagues' most profound thinkers. His name was Paul Richards. Born in Waxahachie, a town south of Dallas, Richards had made his Major League debut for the Brooklyn Dodgers in 1932. He would play eight seasons as a catcher and win one World Series with the 1945 Detroit Tigers, for which he also doubled as pitching coach.

Richards would play his last game in 1946 and then became a manager for the second time (he had managed in the Minors in the late 1930s) for the 1947 season. Richards then spent the next three seasons managing in the Minors in Buffalo and Seattle. Then, in 1950, after another losing campaign, Richards was hired by the White Sox.

At the helm of the White Sox from 1951 to 1954, Richards helped return the team (which had fallen on hard times since their dominance in the 1910s) to the top of the American League. His teams won eighty-one games in 1951 and 1952. The Sox followed that up with eighty-nine wins in 1953 and ninety-four in 1954. Near the end of that season, Richards, who had helped transform the team by developing some of its best talent and had become known as the "Wizard of Waxahachie," made it known that he wanted a three-year extension if he was to stay in Chicago.

General Manager Frank "Trader" Lane was all for the move. Unfortunately for Lane, the Comiskey family, who still owned the White Sox but were living up to their penny-pinching reputation, would only agree to a two-year deal for the explosive Texan. Richards fielded offers from other clubs. Chief among these was the Baltimore Orioles. They were unsure if they wanted Richards to be the GM or the field manager. They knew they did want him. It was perhaps the worst-kept secret in Baltimore.

On September 9 Orioles manager Jimmy Dykes told the *Baltimore Sun* that Art Ehlers had informed him that the club planned to fire the two of them at the end of the season, with Paul Richards filling one of the vacated roles. The firing came to fruition less than a week later. Baltimore hired Richards on September 15; he even ended up with both jobs. The duality of Richards's role seemed to jeopardize the jobs of rest of the baseball staff, especially when Richards reported that "he would have to tear into the club from top to bottom."[20] What ultimately saved Harry Dalton was the honesty of his boss.

Jim McLaughlin was not known for pulling punches. During his first meeting with Richards, which was supposed to be his "last meal," he told the incoming GM that Baltimore's farm system was "horseshit." He then proceeded to outline how it could be improved. This summation and subsequent plan jibed with what Richards already thought.[21] It ultimately saved McLaughlin's job as well as Harry Dalton's.

3

Competing Philosophies and Losing Baseball

1954–61

It did not take long for Paul Richards to make his mark as manager in Baltimore. First, in November 1954 he made the largest trade in baseball history. Baltimore sent pitchers Don Larsen and Bob Turley and infielder Billy Hunter to the Yankees, along with four players to be named later. In return, Richards got nine players, including Yankees stalwart Gene Woodling. This move was only the tip of the iceberg. Richards made two separate trades in December that overhauled the roster further. On December 6 he sent Jim Brideweser, Bob Chakales, and Clint Courtney to the Chicago White Sox, getting four players in return.[1] A week later Richards sent two Minor Leaguers and cash to the Brooklyn Dodgers for infielder Billy Cox and pitcher Preacher Roe. Trades were only part of Richards's arsenal, however.

By the admission of team accountant Joe Hamper, the Orioles' ownership group had not understood what it took to underwrite a winning baseball team financially.[2] Paul Richards was determined to show them by getting them to spend. His favorite method? Doling out loads of money to unproven talent. In 1955 alone, he signed six "bonus babies" for a grand total of $226,000. The math worked out to an average of $38,000 per player. This put the Orioles in a roster bind due to a unique rule.

In 1947, to curb spending on young talent, Major League Baseball instituted a bonus rule, which meant that if a player received more than $4,000 as a bonus, he would have to stay on the Major League roster for two seasons and not be assignable to the Minor Leagues. This rule hamstrung the Orioles, and five of the spots on the team's active roster had to go to rookies signed by Richards. This is where the second problem arose. Every one of Richards's bonus babies was overmatched at the Major League level. The final problem with the Richards overhaul using bonus babies was that he quickly alienated any friends among the ownership group or people in the player development department.

As Harry Dalton would later say, Richards "just came in and bamboozled the owners." That played well with Dalton because, as he later said, "he [Richards] shocked ownership into realizing that if you wanted to be competitive, this is what you had to do." The owners, however, quickly wondered where their money was going. And then there was the opinion of the player development staff. Richards often circumnavigated Jim McLaughlin and his scouts when signing bonus babies. According to Dalton, "He would just get a call from Dutch Dietrich or one of his other cronies saying 'this kid[,] you've got to sign him.' He would give him fifty thousand, seventy thousand, whatever it took." That created a rift between Richards and McLaughlin and their respective charges.[3]

One person who did not necessarily get caught up in the test of wills going on in Baltimore was Harry Dalton. He was beyond loyal to McLaughlin but managed to get along well with Richards. The way he achieved this was to continue to work hard. Dalton's player evaluation skills showed particular improvement. By the winter of 1955, Dalton had become the go-to spokesperson for the farm department when media outlets were looking for opinions on players. In February of that year, Dalton provided readers of the *Baltimore Sun* with a glimpse into the plans for eight different players. In a series of articles that ran in the newspaper, Dalton told readers that a four-year pro from Canada, pitcher Bill Diemer, had a great shot of making the Orioles' roster if he could curb his penchant for food. While just 5 feet 10 inches tall, Diemer weighed in at 205 pounds. According to Dalton, this made Diemer a liability for the Orioles: "He [Diemer] has a tremendous appetite . . . in fact, that appetite worries us more than his arm."[4]

Once the season started, Dalton was still on the road scouting prospects. His road trips began in the early spring, with the first stop in Thomasville to set up the spring camp with McLaughlin. From there, it was up and down the Minor League chain from York, Pennsylvania, to San Antonio, Texas. As these trips continued into the 1955 season, one thing became apparent to Dalton and the others who saw the "Baby Birds." They were improving at the Minor League level. By the end of the 1955 season, the Orioles placed six of their ten affiliates in the playoffs. This was an increase from having just two teams in the playoffs in 1954. Despite working against each other, thanks to the mutual animosity between their bosses, the scouts who worked for Jim McLaughlin and the informal scouts tasked by Paul Richards began to find players who could win. The winning—and losing—at the Minor League level was running parallel with that of the Major League club: despite the continued outlay of large bonuses and flipping of the roster, the Orioles continued to lose in 1955.

Paul Richards's first season in charge of the team began with six straight losses. The Orioles were 23-55 at the All-Star break, and at 115 games in, they were 36-77. They ultimately won 57 for the year and finished 39 games back of the New York Yankees.[5] Doubt began to creep in among some in the ownership group that Richards could make the Orioles a winner; it was his fiscal irresponsibility that fed such doubts rather than his team's performance on the field. However, despite what he called his "infirmities," Richards still found favor with the team president. In October, before Richards and the other front office staff members left for the World Series in New York, Clarence Miles reiterated that Richards was in for the long haul. The team president went as far as to say that "as long as I have anything to do with this club, Paul Richards will continue to guide the destiny of the Orioles."[6] There was only one problem. Clarence Miles was on the way out.

Miles had alienated most of his fellow board members by allowing Richards to be fiscally irresponsible during his first two years. Thus, in November the board voted Miles out as club president. In his place, "a new coalition leadership took charge," with active roles for real estate mogul and part-owner James Keelty and fellow owner and investment banker Joseph Iglehart.[7] For Richards, McLaughlin, and Dalton, the active role played by Iglehart had the most significant impact. Simply put, the days of Richards spending blindly were over. From that moment forward, McLaughlin and Dalton had the power to build a winner from within, if not necessarily with the general manager's support.[8]

The Orioles' Minor League office had much work to do to build a winning team. It took Dalton and McLaughlin years to find the right mix of players and to rid the team of dead weight. Part of finding a winning mix was deciding how large of a Minor League system the team could sustain.

In 1954 the Orioles, thanks to the St. Louis Browns' administrative work, inherited the most extensive farm system in baseball, with twelve teams.[9] McLaughlin quickly pointed out to Richards that an extensive system was counterproductive from a baseball standpoint. He reiterated this in the winter of 1954, when he and Richards announced that the Orioles would be reducing the number of its farm teams to eight clubs and that this would mean the release of one hundred players. When pressed on the reasoning behind such a move, McLaughlin explained it succinctly. The team was not "curtailing the flow of minor league talent into Baltimore." They were moving to "weed out" the players in the system who would never contribute at the Major League level. This culling would make room for players who would. McLaughlin described the system as an accordion, and it contracted and grew with the goal of "developing prospects for the major club."[10]

Once McLaughlin and Dalton had the appropriately sized system for what they wanted to accomplish, the next job was to find players who would be able to help the Orioles at the Major League level. McLaughlin and Dalton planned to develop a system of amateur scouts to help fill the rosters of the fledgling team's affiliates. By 1956 that system had been developed, with two levels of oversight. At one level, the Orioles had three general assignment scouts, and below that was a set of area scouts spanning the country; by 1956 that second set of scouts numbered twenty-three men. Each of these local "bird dogs" had his finger on the pulse of a given local baseball scene. From the Northeast (Joe Cusick of Cranston, Rhode Island) to California (Mike Catron of Compton, California), their job was to suggest players for McLaughlin. The Orioles even had an international scouting department, which consisted of one person.

This beat was an extension of a plan McLaughlin hatched before the 1955 season. That year he sent Fred Hoffman to scout the European Command, with varying results.[11] In 1956 Rex Greaves, who listed his address as 9 Ernst Schwendler Strasse, Frankfurt am Mein, was tasked with finding hidden gems among the soldiers and airmen stationed in Europe to help defend West Germany. He did not expect to find two natural German citizens who had learned their baseball from members of the Army of Occupation after World War II. Claus and Hanjorg Helmig were discovered by Greaves in the winter of 1956, just in time for a tryout at spring training.[12]

No matter where the scouts were based, Harry Dalton was their conduit to Jim McLaughlin. In what would become a trademark trait, Dalton developed a good rapport with the scouts in the field. Of course, all this work did not help the Orioles immediately. Throughout his career, Harry Dalton would tell owners that productive Minor League systems did not crop up overnight; they had to be built over time. This delay guaranteed that the Orioles would continue to struggle at the Major League level for the foreseeable future.

In 1956 Baltimore finished sixth place in the AL with a record of 69-85. However, in 1957 the club finished at .500 for the first time. McLaughlin, Dalton, and their charges continued to work through it all. Dalton's work ethic did not go unnoticed. In 1956 he was considered a possible replacement for the general manager of the franchise's top Minor League club, in San Antonio. He further made a name for himself after the 1957 season. In November of that year, Dalton received a note from the team's lawyer, Herb O'Connor. O'Connor noted, "The very thorough report of the 1957 activities which you prepared brought some very complimentary remarks at each of the stockholders' meetings." He then suggested that Dalton's report become a yearly occurrence so that it could be used by James Keelty when he met with the board.[13] Dalton's work ethic was noteworthy in the Minor League department and did not go unnoticed.

Joe Hamper was still impressed with the Minor League office's work ethic fifty years after seeing it. "We had a hard-driving, hard-working, minor league department," he recalled. "Those people worked harder than anybody I ever saw. Jim had a definite program and plan for what he wanted to do. And Harry was an exceptionally bright, hard-working guy."[14] McLaughlin did have a plan, and Dalton firmly believed in it. The program even had a name that quickly became a mantra. If you asked McLaughlin or Dalton, the Orioles would be "Homegrown by 1960."

McLaughlin and Dalton truly believed it could happen. In 1958 the Major League Orioles finished four games below .500. However, the farm system was again productive when McLaughlin and Dalton evaluated it at the end of the Minor League season. Of note was the play of center fielder Willie Tasby. Tasby, who signed his first contract in 1950 out of high school in Shreveport, Louisiana, was one of the first Black players signed by the St. Louis Browns. By 1958 it seemed that Tasby would be ready for a shot at the Majors when Dalton mentioned him in a mid-August media briefing.[15] Of course, even this notion received pushback from Paul Richards when he noted that in his mind, the chance that the farm system would produce Major League talent in time for 1959 was "slight."[16]

With Richards holding an opinion like that, the mission of McLaughlin and Dalton seemed insurmountable. However, their luck was about to change. The Orioles' ownership was fed up with Paul Richards's attempts to build a winner and manage the team simultaneously. It was time to bring in a separate general manager, and the owners even had a candidate in mind.

Leland Stanford "Lee" MacPhail Jr. grew up in baseball. His father, Leland Stanford "Larry" MacPhail, had turned the Cincinnati Reds and the Brooklyn Dodgers into winners during the 1930s and 1940s and was part owner of the Yankees during the postwar period. He was best known for having a cavalier managerial style, fueled by baseball acumen, showmanship, and alcohol. With his father's career as his background, Lee MacPhail began working for the Brooklyn Dodgers in their massive Minor League system in the days before World War II. After a stint in the navy during the war, Lee MacPhail worked for the New York Yankees, first as GM of the Yankees' Triple-A club in Kansas City, then as farm director. By 1958 MacPhail was the assistant GM of the best club in baseball.

At that time, the Orioles began making overtures to get MacPhail to visit Baltimore. The first attempt to entice him occurred in an unlikely place. Late in the year, as the Yankees looked to be on their way to another pennant, Paul Richards met with MacPhail in the visiting clubhouse at Yankee Stadium to discuss his possibly moving to Baltimore. Then, after the season, Joe Iglehart met with MacPhail again. MacPhail admitted that neither he nor his wife wanted to leave the Yankees or the comfort of their life in New York. Throughout the fall, deciding what he wanted to do would be a struggle.

While Lee MacPhail was considering a move from New York, Harry Dalton had an equally life-changing experience during the 1958 season. As should be evident, the charming, funny, good-looking Dalton never had a problem finding a date. However, no one could hold his attention for longer than a few dates. That all changed when Ann Haines, a mutual acquaintance through an Amherst friend, set Dalton up on a blind date with a girl Haines knew from their Goucher College days.

Patricia "Pat" Booker was the oldest daughter of Archy and Evalyn Booker of Bronxville, New York. She was a student at Goucher College in Baltimore, and thanks to a change in schedules, she needed a date to her senior formal. In stepped Haines with Harry Dalton. The match turned out to be one made in heaven.

Pat Booker was born in 1936 and split her time growing up between Bronxville, trips to Manhattan, and summers at a camp upstate with her sister "Winki." In the fall of 1958, Pat Booker was on the way to concluding a career at Goucher College, where she had made quite the name for herself. She was a member of the Political Science Club, was listed in *Who's Who in American Colleges and Universities*, and found time to chair the Campus Activities Committee of the Student Organization governing body.[17] Moreover, she had a quick wit and wrapped all that up in a diminutive, raven-haired frame with equal parts grace, elegance, and youthful exuberance colored by a childhood in the upper-middle class.

On the first date Dalton impressed Booker with both his sense of humor and grace under adversity. Dalton's dry wit came out early. Pat remembered that Harry was supposed to pick her up at 7:00 p.m. As sometimes happened, Dalton was running late. He made a point to call Pat to let her know. As for his excuse for his tardiness, Dalton let Pat know that he was running late because his "wife and kids" had arrived in Baltimore. Although she was unsure if he was joking or not, Pat remembered that if he was joking, Dalton had a great sense of humor.

Dalton's grace was shown much later in the evening when at dinner, with three other couples, Dalton was charged for a more expensive entrée despite his date having ordered a different dish in order to appear that she was "trying not to gouge" her date. Instead of making a scene with either the restaurant staff or Booker, Dalton paid the first price and avoided confrontation.

That evening led to a second date, and the second ignited a budding romance. As the spring wore on, Dalton never had Booker too far from his mind. He even went as far as to mail clippings from the *Baltimore Sun* about the graduation at Goucher College (Pat graduated in absentia) to Pat while she was in Europe—no small feat considering he did not know what hostel she was staying in. His drive to track her down impressed Booker even more. Soon she was writing about her "Oriole Man" in a diary she kept. When she returned, the two set a night for a third date while Pat was job hunting in New York City.

It was this date that gave Pat Booker a glimpse into the life of someone who cared for someone in baseball. The date was in New York during the World Series of 1958. That day's game between the New York Yankees and the Milwaukee Braves ran long. Consequently, Pat was left unescorted in the Commodore Hotel's lobby on East Forty-Second Street, near Grand Central Station. At the time, the Commodore was still one of the more upscale hotels in New York City, before urban decay would set in late in the 1960s.

However, no matter the hotel's reputation, as Pat quickly pointed out, her date left her in a tough spot. "Women did not sit in the hotel lobby or the bar waiting for a man."[18] Because of these social conventions, the young coed spent time waiting for her date by going in and out of the lobby restroom. When he did arrive, Dalton showed another hallmark of his personality. He was totally engaged on his date and with Pat. They got so lost in each other's company that Pat even missed the last train back to Bronxville. This ability to focus on the person he was with in the moment would help to mitigate the reality that his career put so many constraints on his time. With his personal life on seemingly safe footing, Harry Dalton could again focus on work as he and the baseball staff in Baltimore got a new boss.

While Lee MacPhail loved working in New York, the reality of his employment with the Yankees finally changed MacPhail's mind. One day, as he was weighing a move to the Orioles, the Yankees' principal owner, Dan Topping, called MacPhail into his office and simply told him his chances of becoming the Yankees' GM any time soon were very slim, thanks to the success of George Weiss. With this in mind, MacPhail agreed in November 1958 to become the new general manager of the Orioles.[19]

This move had an immediate impact on the running of the Orioles. MacPhail's appointment was a game changer for McLaughlin and Dalton. MacPhail understood the importance of a healthy farm system. He grew up around his father, who had used the farm system to build the Reds and Dodgers into winners. Lee MacPhail then served as general manager of the Triple-A Kansas City Blues (an affiliate of the New York Yankees) before becoming the Yankees' farm director during their dynastic years in the early 1950s. MacPhail's move to the Orioles changed the outlook for McLaughlin and Dalton, who from that moment forward decided to implement their strategy to make the Orioles a winner from within.

MacPhail liked what he saw when he looked at his staff. "Jack Dunn, Harry Dalton, and Bob Brown were good young guys who worked hard," he recalled.[20] Moreover, although MacPhail would be in the office more than Richards in the winter, the new boss allowed his young charges to have fun.

Two individuals who took advantage of this were Dalton and Brown, who had a lot in common. First and foremost, they had both graduated from Amherst College. While Dalton wrote about sports in his college years, Brown was the starting left fielder on a team that routinely took on clubs like Army and Princeton before he graduated in 1953. They also had the military in common. In Brown's case, he spent "30 Months in Japan with the Army intelligence corps chasing down Soviet spies and their signals." Brown also spent time in the newspaper business. At twenty-five, he was the head copy boy for the *Washington Post* while moonlighting with the CIA.[21]

Bob Brown came to work for the Orioles in the fall of 1957, thanks partly to another Amherst College alumnus. The head traveling secretary and PR man with the Orioles was John S. Lancaster, who ran into Brown at an Amherst homecoming social and announced he was looking for an assistant. By the time MacPhail became GM, Brown was doing most of the public relations work while Jack Dunn was the titular head of the two-person department. When Brown was not working, he played practical jokes on Dalton and Joe Hamper, and the three men became inseparable. Around that same time, their team began to show signs of life on the field.

By the spring of 1959, the Minor League system's talent was almost ready for the Majors. Meanwhile, the Orioles' roster mainly consisted of older players who seemed past their prime. But the 1959 Orioles shocked the baseball world by playing over .500 ball before the All-Star break, and they then flirted with the lead in the American League. They stumbled but still finished the season six games under .500, at 74-80.

For Harry Dalton, the 1959 season was a reiteration of the previous five seasons. He spent most of his time on the road and talking to the press, and he was the top spokesperson when *The Sporting News* came looking for a comment on the struggles and apparent rebirth of demoted bonus baby Dave Nicholson.

Nicholson, a high schooler out of St. Louis and the top prospect in the country in January 1958, was signed for an estimated $110,000. His signing with Baltimore was so significant that it made headlines in the January 28 *Baltimore Sun*. Nicholson's signing was on the sports section's front page, and the front section carried a headline about bombings in Ankara, Turkey, where the U.S. embassy was one of the targets.

During his rookie season, Nicholson struggled with the bat at three different stops in the Orioles system, and his troubles persisted in Amarillo as 1959 got underway. Nicholson's struggles prompted the Orioles to demote him to the Class C club in Aberdeen, South Dakota, for the rest of the season. In Aberdeen, Nicholson began to flourish. Dalton pointed out, "Certainly Dave was disappointed, but he realized it was best for him." Dalton then paid Nicholson the ultimate compliment when he said that he "had never seen anyone who received so much money show so much ambition and desire."[22]

Finally, the 1959 season saw Dalton get a temporary promotion. In July of that year, Jim McLaughlin suffered a minor heart attack that would sideline him for much of the season. It fell to Dalton and Richards's crony

Eddie Robinson to pick up the slack. So Dalton ran the organizational Minor League meetings and was the top attendee for the club when they went to Columbus for the Minor League meetings in August. Dalton then wrapped up his 1959 season with a trip to Los Angeles for the first all–West Coast World Series in baseball history.[23]

Dalton's promotion was temporary because McLaughlin was back for the 1960 season. It looked, on paper, to be a promising one for the Orioles. Lee MacPhail had convinced ownership and Paul Richards that the best way forward for the club would be a sustained youth movement. The 1959 Triple-A club in Vancouver was loaded with talent and had finished in second place in the Pacific Coast League. Nicknamed the "Kiddie Corps," the 1959 Vancouver Mounties provided numerous players to join existing talent like Brooks Robinson and form the 1960 Orioles.

The club did not disappoint. The Orioles were 26-15 on June 1. Even after a five-game losing streak, they were 45-38 at the All-Star break and only four games out of first place. Things were going so well in Baltimore that Harry Dalton felt he had enough security to get married.

He and Pat had dated for almost two years, and they both felt they had found the love of their lives. All that was left was to make it official. Their wedding was a significant social event given Pat's upper-middle-class upbringing, and their engagement made both the *Baltimore Sun* and the *New York Times*. The couple was married Saturday, July 9, entering the season's second All-Star break. They had the ceremony at Christ Protestant Episcopal Church in Bronxville with two officiants, and the witnesses were Pat's sister Winki and a friend, Leni Schwartz, who had attended Goucher with Pat and was also her roommate in New York.

Meanwhile, Joe Hamper was Dalton's best man, and Don Nesbitt was the other groomsman. By all accounts, it was a great day, one that concluded with a reception for 120 at the Booker home in Bronxville. It prefigured the gatherings that would become a Dalton family staple in the future. After the ceremony there was a four-day honeymoon in the Poconos and then it was back to a one-bedroom apartment in the Rodgers Forge section of Towson, Maryland. The second half of the baseball season meant it was time to get back to work.[24]

With the All-Star breaks behind them, the Orioles settled in for the long march to the end of the season. Baltimore was 54-45 after a 2–1 win over the Chicago White Sox on August 1. August would be their best month, and the Orioles fueled speculation about winning a pennant as they remained stubbornly in contention. Early on, most fans took a wait-and-see attitude. However, thanks in large part to the offensive punch of Brooks Robinson and rookie Ron Hansen and the pitching of Steve Barber, whom Dalton had a hand in bringing into the Orioles fold, Baltimore was one game back of the New York Yankees as the calendar turned to September and the two teams met for a three-game series in Baltimore.

On the first night, Milt Pappas threw a complete-game three-hitter and got offensive support from Walt Dropo as the Orioles blanked the Yankees 5–0, putting the Orioles in a tie for first place. The next night, Brooks Robinson hit a two-run homer, and Jackie Fisher scattered seven hits as the Orioles won 2–0, to go up by a game. Finally, in front of over thirty-four thousand people on Sunday, Chuck Estrada notched his sixteenth game of the year as the Orioles won 6–2. The sweep gave them their seventh straight win and a two-game advantage.

The sweep of New York was the high-water mark of the season for the Orioles. While they did not play horribly the rest of the way, they could not hold onto their tenuous lead. Ultimately they would fall back in the standings and finish eight games back in second place. Still, there was plenty to like for the team's fans or a front office member as the team looked to 1961. There was only one problem as far as Lee MacPhail and others were concerned, and it was that Jim McLaughlin and Paul Richards did not get along and could not coexist. According to MacPhail, their relationship grew so toxic that even players became labeled as either "a McLaughlin Player or a Richards Player," depending on which group had signed them.[25]

This schism led MacPhail to let McLaughlin go in January 1961. The Orioles explained that McLaughlin was leaving for personal reasons.[26] However, most people knew the real story, or at least they thought they did: they knew he did not get along with Paul Richards.[27] The real issue was more specific than that.

In the summer of 1960, the Orioles were in the running to sign standout high school pitcher Dave McNally out of Billings, Montana. McNally, a diminutive lefty (5 feet 10 inches, 185 pounds), was a multisport star and virtually in another cosmos on the pitching mound. His talent placed him head and shoulders above his competition and often his own teammates as well. One night in July, facing an outmatched opponent during his final American Legion baseball season, McNally fanned twenty-seven batters. This tour de force included four strikeouts in one inning and five in another when McNally's catcher could not handle his offerings.[28] Performances such as these guaranteed that scouts hounded McNally, and one of those hounds was Jim Wilson of the Orioles. Wilson covered the West Coast for Baltimore and saw plenty of McNally, thanks to an American Legion program that took him throughout the region. After two visits with McNally and his mother, brother, and a lawyer who was a family friend (his father had died on Okinawa during World War II), Wilson, with the blessing of Jim McLaughlin, offered McNally an $80,000 signing bonus in September 1960. After some soul searching, McNally accepted.[29] There was only one problem: McLaughlin had not told Paul Richards that he had given Wilson permission to offer that much. At that moment, Paul Richards decided to become fiscally responsible. That was too big an outlay on unproven talent. McLaughlin was out.

As for who would replace McLaughlin, there was no debate; Harry Dalton was the clear choice to continue McLaughlin's work. Years later, Dalton would be pragmatic when describing his feelings about the promotion. "I was thrilled, but I was upset about Jim, because without Jim I'd be back at the *Springfield Daily News* writing sports."[30]

Whatever his feelings were, his bosses felt Dalton was ready to take the next step in his baseball career. His experience had everything to do with it. He had learned for seven years from Jim McLaughlin and helped bring in talent that had done a lot to turn the situation around in Baltimore.[31]

Equally as important, given the rift that had developed in the club's talent department, Dalton had achieved all this with a significant degree of humility. Even at a young age, he felt that success in baseball was a team effort on the field and in the scouting office. This belief would be one of his underlying working principles for the next thirty years and would endear him to those who worked for him. Never was this more evident than in Dalton's working relationship with the men who would play such a prominent role in his maturation and success over the coming years. They would become known as the Dalton Gang.

4

The World of Harry Dalton

1960–65

As Harry Dalton made his way through his career, the game of baseball and the business that surrounded it would change in significant ways. Through all these changes, Dalton's best asset was his ability to surround himself with knowledgeable people, create an environment where they felt valued, and empower them to do their job. Dalton's earliest days as the Orioles' farm director manifested this trait when he helped repair the rift between the scouts and the front office that had developed during Jim McLaughlin's and Paul Richards's dual reigns. His ability to mend fences in that regard would create a loyal core of individuals who would continue to help stock a farm system that was the envy of baseball.

To understand how Dalton got this opportunity, one must first understand the structure of baseball front offices in the earliest days of his career. As historians of the sport have shown, front offices evolved over time. Mainly, they became more specialized. In the late 1950s and early 1960s, this specialization had not yet taken hold everywhere. Thus, when Harry Dalton became the Orioles' farm director, he was also the de facto head of scouting. In this role, he maintained constant contact with the men whom Richards had largely ignored.

His first job was to reassure those scouts that they had an essential role in the organization. The first way he did this was to let them know that the scouting department was not broken. In one of the first interviews he gave after becoming the new farm director, Dalton said that he did not see "any need for radical changes in the farm policies we [the Orioles] have worked together for the last seven years [to develop]. . . . I think those policies have proven sound. I hope we can continue to get our share of the outstanding [amateur] free-agent prospects and a little more."[1]

In Dalton's mind, the need to find "a little more" was wholly predicated on the Orioles needing to stay competitive when competing for younger players, who were the backbone of their roster.[2] He also did not care what position those players occupied or if the Major League club already had three outstanding players at one position. He wanted the best player available. He articulated this philosophy early in his tenure.

In March 1961, as he was about to set off to Thomasville for spring training, the thirty-two-year-old Dalton was asked if, now that the Orioles had a solid infield, including Brooks Robinson at third, Rookie of the Year shortstop Ron Hansen, and Orioles farmhand Marv Breeding at shortstop, his scouts would now focus on building a core group of outfield prospects. Dalton thought about the question for a second and then replied that the reporter's theory "sounded good" but that, in his mind, a structured plan left a team open to complacency. "You think you're set in a certain position, concentrate on something else, and one injury throws the whole thing out of balance," he commented. Dalton felt a better solution to combat this was to "ferret out [whomever] you thought were the best prospects and try to sign them."[3] The Orioles would need to rely on the men Paul Richards had shunted to the background: scouts.

By spring training of 1961, Dalton was overseeing six regional scouts who helped manage thirty lower-level regional assignment scouts.[4] Most of these individuals were holdovers from the McLaughlin/Richards days. That did not mean Dalton felt that he had to thoroughly clean house to find scouts loyal to him. Dalton took stock of his charges and concluded that few teams in baseball could compete with the Orioles' scouts in evaluating talent and signing players out of the colleges and sandlots of America.[5] Because of this, Dalton made very few changes during his first off-season in charge.

All the area supervisors stayed in place and continued cross-checking the reports of their assignment scouts who had received tips from associate "bird dog" scouts. Former Minor Leaguer Don McShane worked in Northern California, while former Major Leaguer Fred "Bootnose" Hoffman worked in the southern part of the Golden State. In the Upper Midwest, Orioles scouts were overseen by former Major League pitcher

Hal Newhouser, while Jimmy Russo would cover the Lower Midwest and Texas from his home in Missouri. Finally, Art Ehlers was the cross-checker for the Southeast, while another former Major Leaguer, Fred "Beauty" McGowan, handled the Northeast.

Below them, the area assignment scouting staff was full of men who would soon make names for themselves. Two would help Dalton shape baseball for the next thirty years.

The first was already a local legend in Baltimore. Walter Youse, a man with a booming voice and a body that was the epitome of barrel-chested, began coaching amateur teams in Baltimore before World War II. After being discharged from the navy, Youse worked as a Minor League manager. However, after two losing campaigns in the low Minors in 1946–47, Youse returned to Maryland. For a time, he ran a bar in his hometown while becoming a high school and amateur coach. During this time, he came to the attention of Paul Richards.

Richards was looking for inroads in the local baseball scene and gave Youse a job as a part-time scout beginning in 1956. In 1957 Youse helped acquire lefty pitcher Steve Barber, who would become a member of the Kiddie Corps. Youse then became a full-time scout in 1959. In that capacity, he would evaluate and sign fellow Baltimorean Tom Phoebus in 1960. With that track record, Youse was the type of scout with whom Harry Dalton wanted to fill the organization.

Another scout who fit the Dalton mold and would become a trusted advisor was former Major League pitcher Ray Scarborough. From Mount Gilead, North Carolina, he began his career during World War II. After two years in the navy, he returned to baseball and finally retired in 1953 with a record of 80-85. After his retirement, Scarborough ran his own business, and then in 1960 he joined the Orioles as a scout.

Many of these men made a lasting impression on their bosses in the coming years. "Youse was terrific," Dalton recalled. "So was Jim Russo. McShane was a hell of a scout. Fred Hoffman didn't sign a lot of people, but when Freddie talked about liking a ballplayer, you listened."[6]

Harry Dalton also made a quick first impression on them. Simply put, he was the type of man for whom a scout wanted to work. Walter Youse called Dalton "a smart boy who knew the strong points and the weak points of the people who work for him." Perhaps most importantly, even at an early point in his career, Dalton listened to others. He understood that he did not have all the answers.[7] Moreover, the scouts who worked for Dalton loved that he knew about players in the same way they did. "When Harry was farm director he knew every player in that minor league system," Youse said. In Dalton's earliest days with the club, Jim McLaughlin readily admitted that "the new kid, Harry Dalton," knew more about the players in the lowest levels of the system than he did.[8] This encyclopedic knowledge endeared him to the scouts who worked for Dalton when he was the farm director. Finally, Dalton earned the respect of the scouts who worked for him because he worked as hard as they did and led the same life. Unlike Jim McLaughlin, Dalton did not spend all his time in his office in Baltimore.

Dalton's travel schedule was as full as the one maintained by the scouts he oversaw. In June 1961 Bob Maisel of the *Sun* reported that Dalton was often only in Baltimore long enough to "clean up a few details at his office, pick up some clean clothes and his wife, and hit the road again." At that time, he had logged trips to Miami, Florida, and Thomasville (for Major and Minor League spring training), as well as "California, Virginia, Boston, Pennsylvania, and Omaha, just to name a few," he said. When he was home, Harry Dalton could be found in Memorial Stadium's caverns, even when the Major League club was on the field.[9]

Jerry Sachs, who would go on to a long career in public relations and management inside and outside of sports, was a junior PR staffer for the Orioles when Dalton took over as the farm director. He recalled that the front office members would try and sneak away to catch the game on the field as much as possible, except for Harry Dalton. "Harry was buried in his office," Sachs said.[10]

Dalton's dedication to his job did not mean that his charges did not take issue with some of his stances from time to time. Money was a big issue. Walter Youse remembered that he had to fight tooth and nail with Dalton to get a raise once he became a full-time scout.[11] Others felt that Dalton was not as good a judge of talent as he thought.

The primary example of this divergence of opinion occurred in 1965, the inaugural year of the MLB amateur player draft. That year, Johnny

Bench, from Binger, Oklahoma, was one of the top high school players in the country. Orioles scout Jimmy Russo had seen Bench play numerous times and had recommended to Dalton that the Orioles take him with the team's No. 1 pick (fifteenth overall). They passed on him in the first two rounds. Instead, they drafted a catcher from Dartmouth whom Dalton had seen personally, Dick Horton; he spent three years in the Minors and never made it out of Class A ball. Bench went on to a seventeen-year Major League career that ended with enshrinement in the Baseball Hall of Fame.[12] Still, Harry Dalton would always be a person for whom scouts liked to work.

With a solid scouting base, Dalton could transition the rest of the scouting department. In retirement, Dalton would remember that he "got things winnowed down to the point that the scouts who didn't fit what we wanted were gone."[13] This winnowing occurred over the next few seasons, with the first set of changes occurring during the winter of 1961.

Dalton faced a mini-crisis, his first on the job, in September of that year. The catalyst for this event was none other than Paul Richards.

Richards, named the American League Manager of the Year in 1960, left the Orioles in early September to become the general manager of the Houston Colt .45s expansion team after the departure of their first GM, Gabe Paul. Many in the press felt that Richards's departure from the Orioles would have a disastrous trickle-down effect within the scouting department if and when his cronies left Baltimore to follow their benefactor. In fact, the mass exodus did not occur. However, Dalton did replace Eddie Robinson, the Baltimore field director, and Hal Newhouser, the Midwest regional supervisor.[14]

The Orioles expected Robinson's departure. He had served as Richards's eyes and ears in the farm department, and Lee MacPhail, Dalton, and Richards had already discussed letting Robinson out of his contract when Richards left. The Orioles also thought that Newhouser would leave to follow Richards.[15] Instead, he took a scouting job with the Cleveland Indians.

To fill these vacancies in the immediate aftermath of the departures, Dalton did some shuffling. First, he hired former Major Leaguer George Selkirk to fill the role of the departing Robinson. Selkirk, who was from

Canada and had spent nine years with the Yankees as a player, took over as a special assignment scout. He scouted players for the Minors and Majors and evaluated both levels for "future trading material."[16]

Dalton also noted that the team would hire a scout to fill the vacancy left by Newhouser. However, Dalton quickly pointed out that the new individual, whoever he was, would not automatically become a supervisor, which Newhouser had been. In keeping with the trend of rewarding those with Orioles employment longevity, Dalton noted that "we [the Orioles] prefer to promote from within our own system and among the scouts we have."[17] This loyalty further cemented Dalton as an excellent man for whom to work, and he had the bonus of keeping the scouts who had helped build the Orioles' farm system, which was quickly becoming the envy of baseball.

What the Orioles had done with their Minor League system in the seven years before Harry Dalton became the farm director was just short of miraculous. When the Browns left St. Louis, the farm system was emptied of prospects. Now the Birds had stockpiled enough talent that they were often winners at the Minor League level. The reason for this winning was not just because of talent, however. The Orioles were developing a culture that nurtured talent, making rookies into proven players, and Harry Dalton was at the forefront of this development.

Under Dalton, when Minor League prospects entered the system, they were taught how Baltimore wanted them to play baseball. Eventually, this would become known nationally as the "Oriole Way," and it was seen as a sort of unique formula, especially as the team got more successful. According to Dalton, however, the instruction was much more informal initially. Dalton allowed experts on specific topics to pass their knowledge to the younger players. "It wasn't like we sat back and said, 'OK, let's establish the Oriole Way . . .' Ray Scarborough on pitching, Billy Hunter on-field play and baserunning, and various others contributing because of their position or experience," he recalled.[18] The core instruction began when a player got to Thomasville, and it would continue once he joined his Minor League team.

By the time Dalton took over for McLaughlin, the contraction of Minor League teams was well underway and nearing the end. As noted earlier, the Orioles ran twelve teams at the high point, and in 1961 that number was nine teams. From 1962 to 1965 the Orioles operated six teams except for one year when they had a partial working agreement with a team in Aberdeen, South Dakota.

Much like today, each of these Minor League teams had its vibe and presented particular challenges to players assigned there. The challenges started the minute the "Baby Birds" arrived in Thomasville. Tim Sommer, who would pitch eight seasons in the Minors for the Orioles and had his first interaction with Harry Dalton via a telegram telling him to gain weight, remembered that his first spring in Thomasville put him face to face with vestiges of the Civil War.

"There was one particular bar a few of us always gravitated towards during our afternoon visits to town," he recalled. Within this bar, Sommer would often meet "grandsons of men who actually fought in the Civil war" who would spend their time replaying old battles and trying to figure out how their grandfathers could have been victorious instead of defeated. This phenomenon led Sommer to believe that while certain parts of Thomasville could accept the Orioles' presence because the players had "some hint of fame," they were primarily seen as Yankees who "were intruders and non-believers as to their cause."[19]

Thomasville was not just different for the white players. It was a strange new world for Minor Leaguers from other countries who were generically categorized as Black by the local population. One of these was José "Rene" Paredes. Paredes was from Nicaragua and would be Tim Sommer's roommate during much of his early career. One day a group of Orioles hands decided to go to the local Dairy Queen in Thomasville to break the boredom of table tennis and baseball. Some white players told Paredes to order by telling the clerk at the window that he wanted to fornicate with her. Paredes had no grasp of English, and the players in question seemingly had no idea about race relations in Georgia. The result was that Paredes was on the verge of being detained by the Thomasville Police Department. Luckily for him, before that occurred his teammates showed that he was the butt of a horrible joke. Still, he was cautioned not to return to town.[20]

The culture shock continued as the club assigned players to various teams in the system, and the regional culture manifested itself in diverse ways. In one case, Don Baylor, a Black player who had grown up poor in Texas, was shocked by the poverty he found in the coal company town of Bluefield, West Virginia, where he was assigned to play Class A ball in 1967: "I thought I grew up poor. . . . I thought growing up in Clarksville was tough, but they had it a lot tougher."[21]

Regardless of the shock at seeing how people lived in the towns where the young Orioles played, these Minor Leaguers would be managed by a group of men who continued their education and melded them into winning ball clubs. One of these men was Earl Weaver, and he and Harry Dalton would forge a working relationship in the coming years that would be one of the most productive in baseball history.

Weaver was born and raised in St. Louis, and he was exposed to professional baseball at a young age, thanks to his father. "My father owned a cleaning plant, and he did the uniforms for both the St. Louis Browns and the St. Louis Cardinals," he recalled.[22] Weaver would be signed as a second baseman by the Cardinals, and he played in the Minors until 1956. At that point, Harry Dalton saw something in Weaver that would connect their lives for years.

On a trip to Knoxville, Tennessee, Dalton worked on securing the city's unaffiliated club as an Orioles farm team. While there, he could not help but notice Weaver, the Smokies' player-manager, and thought he would be an excellent fit for the Orioles. Dalton's observation led to a discussion with Jim McLaughlin, and ultimately Weaver got a contract managing the Orioles' Class D Fitzgerald, Georgia, club in 1957.

While in Fitzgerald as a player-manager, Weaver quickly established that he would fight for his team in any situation. Sometimes this was even done literally. One night he grounded out and jumped into the opposing dugout to brawl with the other team.[23] He was pummeled, but that fight would be an excellent metaphor for Weaver and the Orioles' Minor League system during Harry Dalton's reign. They did not quit.

The Orioles' farm system would produce eight pennant winners from 1961 to 1965, including three league titles in 1964: the Northern and Midwest League titles in Class A and the Eastern League title in Class Double-A. Moreover, the Orioles' Minor League system had an overall winning percentage of .527 while Dalton was the farm director.[24] Win or lose, Dalton was always around to offer a kind word or a pointed word of correction to both players and managers.

Tim Sommer recalled that in 1964, while he was having his best year in pro baseball, at 13-2 for the Fox Cities Foxes of the Class A Midwest League, Dalton was in the stands after a particularly dominating start. After the game, Sommer expected Dalton to congratulate him on his performance. He did not expect Dalton to stop and tell the catcher from that night that he was impressed with how the backstop had shepherded Sommer through the game.[25]

The cerebral Dalton took in everything. Moreover, he rarely raised his voice above a conversational tone when he spoke, which would become a trademark at home and work. This included tense occasions, such as the time he had to rein in the fiery Earl Weaver.

As Dalton and his scouts continued to build a winner, Weaver steadily moved up through the system along with his players. The diminutive, volatile Weaver left behind a trail of broken umpires and flabbergasted league presidents along the way. Finally, Dalton had to intercede.

"I had to fly into Springfield, Massachusetts, once, when [Weaver] had the Elmira [New York] club in the Eastern League," Dalton recalled. "He got real out of line one night—threw a bunch of bats on the field . . . just went in the dugout and took all the bats and threw 'em on the field. And he had a mishap like that a couple of weeks before, and I was worried that he was going to get [suspended], so I just flew up, did not tell him I was coming, just walked in the ballpark and took him out after the game. I laid down the law. . . . This is it or else."[26]

Weaver was not the only bump in the road that Dalton faced as farm director. Another prime example involved the Major League Orioles' trip to Aberdeen, South Dakota, in June 1964. By twenty-first-century standards, it seems strange that a Major League club would play one of its Minor League affiliates during the middle of the season. However, at that time such games were commonplace because of the publicity they would garner for both the Major League club and the affiliate.

As a part of this trip, Dalton felt that it would be good for himself, Lee MacPhail, and Orioles manager Hank Bauer to take in a regular-season game between their Aberdeen affiliate and the Chicago Cubs' affiliate in St. Cloud, Minnesota, given the fact that the airport in Minneapolis was only seventy miles from St. Cloud. There was only one problem. After driving that distance, Dalton arrived at an empty park. Dalton found out he had read the schedule wrong. The game was in Aberdeen. Once the trio arrived back in Minneapolis to catch a flight to Aberdeen, Dalton's trip did not improve.

The Orioles prepared to take a Douglas DC-6 to Aberdeen. The aircraft was the epitome of luxury at the time. But there was another problem. The runway at the airport in Aberdeen could not have a DC-6 land safely under normal circumstances. The oversight made Dalton remark in his trademark dry sense of humor that "they've sold 4,000 tickets for the game and 6,000 to watch us land."[27]

Despite his failure as ad hoc travel agent, there was no denying that Harry Dalton had built a farm system that was the envy of baseball. The best evidence is that the Orioles lost eighteen players during the December 1962 Rule 5 draft.[28] Nevertheless, by the end of the 1965 season, the Orioles' scouting/farm system had produced twenty players out of the twenty-four on the Major League roster of a team that won ninety-four games. The Orioles had transitioned to contender status, and the only question that remained was when the Major League club would win the American League pennant. People in Baltimore, including Dalton himself, did not realize that the wheels were in motion to make the Orioles and their farm director the most recognizable names in baseball.

5

Changes

WINTER 1965

Although the Orioles were now contenders, the end of the 1965 season was a time of significant change for the team. The catalysts of the changes were both internal and external and would help to set the stage for the rise of the Orioles as a power within baseball and the emergence of Harry Dalton as one of the game's best team builders, one of baseball's profound thinkers, and the first modern executive in the history of the game.

The first spark igniting the post–1965 season shifts in Baltimore occurred in New York. This phenomenon had of course had happened before, when Lee MacPhail was enticed from New York to join the Orioles in Baltimore. It turned out that a change in New York would also lead to MacPhail's departure from the Orioles. However, this time it was not the needs of one team that would return MacPhail to the Big Apple but rather Major League Baseball's needs.

Baseball commissioner Ford Frick, who had served in that role since 1951, overseen considerable growth in the game, and ushered in what many people felt was the game's second golden period, announced his retirement in 1964. As a part of that announcement, Frick rolled out a new structure in the commissioner's office: various new department heads would help the commissioner oversee the promotion and growth of the game. In addition, Frick pushed for the creation of a chief of staff who would report to the commissioner.[1] This chief of staff position became vital when the owners selected a baseball neophyte to oversee the game. That outsider, picked from a list of 150 candidates in the fall of 1965, was William C. Eckert, a retired air force general. Eckert, who had seen combat in World War II, was the ideal candidate for commissioner if the only criteria were that the selected individual should know nothing of the game.[2] It then became necessary to find someone to shepherd Eckert through his early days in office. To many in baseball, that person could only be one man—Lee MacPhail.

MacPhail had considered leaving Baltimore previously. In 1964 he almost returned to New York when he was offered a position with the Mets as heir apparent to club president George Weiss, his old boss when the two were with the Yankees organization. Ultimately, MacPhail did not leave Baltimore that year, because he waited too long to decide. Now, with the job offer to be chief of staff to the new commissioner, he was on the fence again with his decision-making, but this time there were two significant differences. First, MacPhail viewed taking the job as Eckert's deputy to be a "mandate," thanks mainly to his family's long history in the game.[3] Perhaps more important was that the Orioles had a new principal owner: Jerold "Jerry" Hoffberger.

Hoffberger had been a minority owner since the Orioles came to town. His family was deeply entwined in the fabric of Baltimore and had business interests throughout the city. In Jerry's case, he was the president of National Brewing Company, a major sponsor of the Orioles over and above his ownership stake. However, other events in New York pushed this lifelong Baltimorean to the Orioles ownership group's forefront.

In 1964, as their dominance atop the American League was waning thanks to an aging team, Dan Topping and Del Webb, the Yankees' principal owners since 1945, began to look for a buyer for their club. Simultaneously, the Columbia Broadcasting System (CBS) sought to diversify its corporate holdings. Thus, it came to be that Topping and Webb would sell 80 percent of the club to CBS (which would also have an option to buy the remaining 20 percent) for $11.2 million, in time for the 1965 season.[4]

The sale of the Yankees opened the door for Hoffberger to buy the Orioles because Joe Iglehart, with whom Hoffberger had had a falling out over his unwillingness to put him on the Orioles board of directors, also had stock in CBS, and this dual ownership created a conflict of interest. Iglehart would have to divest himself of his stake in the Orioles or CBS, and he chose to sell his Orioles shares to Hoffberger. In turn, this move triggered a clause whereby the other principal owner of the Orioles, Zanvyl Krieger, would also be forced to divest most of his shares. National Brewing Company (that is, Hoffberger) thus became the principal owner of the Orioles.[5]

What Hoffberger's ownership meant was very clear in MacPhail's mind. There was no real guarantee that Hoffberger would want to keep MacPhail with the Orioles. "I always felt he hadn't had anything to do with hiring me, and I wasn't really his person," MacPhail said.[6] On the contrary, Hoffberger did not make any drastic moves with the operation other than appointing a trusted staff member to evaluate the team. This man was Frank Cashen, a former reporter and longtime National Brewing Company executive.

As for what Cashen's duties would be with the Orioles, it is apparent that Jerry Hoffberger knew that one of the first things on the agenda would be to make the Birds relevant in the minds of Baltimoreans. Cashen, a former newspaper reporter and a public relations wizard, could do that. The other thing that Hoffberger felt he had to do was to make the Orioles a more streamlined business. Deciding how best to do those things successfully would fall to Cashen. Hoffberger also clearly saw this position with the Orioles as a temporary stop for Cashen. "Whenever I see something in one of my businesses that needs bolstering, I send Frank in. He's done it for me before in other businesses. I think in about two years, we'll have things running smoothly with the Orioles, and Frank can come back to the brewery," Hoffberger commented.[7] As for why Cashen needed to be away from the brewery, Hoffberger felt he had a two-pronged problem.

First, Hoffberger, who believed that MacPhail had neglected day-to-day operations while in charge of the team, wanted to streamline the front office. Hoffberger's goal was to have Cashen design and oversee a new office hierarchy to fix that problem.[8] Cashen's second and perhaps most important job was to put the Orioles on par with the Baltimore Colts of the NFL in terms of public image. This was necessary because the Orioles were not on many hometown sports fans' minds. Some alarming anecdotal evidence backs this up.

Even those who worked for the Orioles were rabid Colts fans. Joe Hamper would remember that he was a "fanatic Colt fan" and that the Orioles were "second-class citizens" in the eyes of the people of Baltimore.[9] This feeling of having second-class status even existed inside Harry Dalton's home. Pat Dalton would remember the lean years of the Orioles, a time when she felt she had to hide the fact that Harry worked for the team. "In those days, the fledgling O's were always like a bridesmaid," she said. "Johnny Unitas [the Colts' star quarterback and one of the faces of the NFL] was big-time, and all that mattered. I remember attending [a] Christmas party. The hostess asked me what Harry did. I sort of whispered the Orioles."[10]

Fixing the public's perception of the team would likely take some prolonged winning, an influx of money, and the right people to lead the effort.

As for the right person willing to spend money on marketing to make the team more visible, the Orioles could not have found a better pair than Jerry Hoffberger and Frank Cashen. Joe Hamper remembered that "Jerry brought new vigor to the team's marketing. He had a high visibility in the community and was very outgoing. . . . Hoffberger's family had deep roots in Baltimore, and it was as if he was really running the club for the benefit of the city. . . . He changed the image of the ballclub."[11] Furthermore, in Cashen he had found someone who went out of his way to ensure that his employer was always out front in the community.

What Cashen did not have was experience with the business of baseball. Even he understood that. Two facts reinforce this. When he joined the club, Cashen declined Hoffberger's offer to become the GM of the Orioles. This decision put Cashen outside the baseball operations team.

Moreover, Lee MacPhail noted that both Hoffberger and Cashen had urged him not to take the job as chief of staff to the baseball commissioner. Still and all, Lee MacPhail announced that he would leave the Orioles. On that same day, the speculation over who would replace MacPhail began. It quickly became a two-horse race, and each candidate had an upside.

The first candidate was Jack Dunn III. Dunn was, as noted earlier, part of Baltimore baseball royalty. However, despite his having "baseball knowledge aplenty," Frank Cashen decided Dunn was not a "head guy."[12] That left Harry Dalton.

The upsides of promoting Dalton were numerous. He was young, and he was intelligent. He also had the respect of the scouts and the Minor League managers, and the players were familiar with him. In many ways, he was the ideal candidate. The only question that Frank Cashen had was whether Dalton could handle all that went with being the head of a front office. The answer, as Cashen saw it, was yes. With a small amount of help.

That proviso was because Cashen did not think Dalton, whose official title would be vice president in charge of baseball operations, could handle being a general manager in the traditional sense. "GMs in those days were the Chief Operating Officers of the clubs, and in charge of everything: radio and television, the stadium, the playing field, the Minor Leagues, ticket sales, public relations, club publications, spring training, and of course, the Major League club," Cashen stated.[13] Because of all these ancillary duties, Cashen felt that Dalton was not ready to be named the GM and "that a lot of those duties" would need to be done by himself, thus making Dalton Cashen's "number one assistant in many ways."[14]

There is one problem with this assertion when considering Harry Dalton's career. Whatever Cashen believed later, Harry Dalton was *not* Frank Cashen's assistant. In a modern sense, Cashen was a business manager and Dalton was the general manager, as baseball fans understand the job today. Cashen saying Dalton was not the GM is more a matter of semantics and a possible attempt to soften the blow that someone else would be receiving the lion's share of the credit regarding baseball decisions. When looking at the realities of the situation, it becomes apparent that Harry Dalton was ushering in a new era of executive management in baseball. The era of generalists like Branch Rickey, George Weiss, and Buzzie Bavasi was effectively over.

Gone were the days when the front office bosses would expect a GM to shoulder the whole load of running a team. Teams were big business, and as team operations grew in complexity through the 1960s, baseball faced challenges posed by the increasing popularity of professional and college football. To offset this, baseball clubs increasingly needed experts in the correct positions off the field to ensure they were enacting intelligent business practices that would maximize profits in an environment where baseball was not the only form of sports entertainment. Jerry

Hoffberger had this environment in mind when he made Frank Cashen the point man for turning around Baltimore's public perception of the Orioles. Cashen was a business expert. Hoffberger had also used him as a fixer at his racetrack and brewery before sending him to the Orioles. The type of business did not matter. Frank Cashen could make a business successful with the parameters mapped out, and Jerry Hoffberger expected this to happen again, as the fact that Hoffberger saw Cashen's position with the club as temporary suggests. Cashen's role was not to build a winner on the field. That fell to Harry Dalton.

As such, regardless of title, Dalton was the GM of the Orioles, and that was how people in Baltimore saw him. It was how reporters who covered the team saw him. From this point forward, that is how history will remember him, and that is the way this book will refer to him, no matter which of his team employments is under discussion. Not doing so would be both archaic and a disservice to Dalton and every modern GM that followed. Harry Dalton was the first in a new breed of GMs that every other team emulated in structure and hoped to emulate in substance.

Of course, just because Dalton was the GM of the Orioles did not mean that he was free to make decisions willy-nilly. As Cashen put it in his introductory press conference, Dalton did have to "brief" him before making a trade.[15] As such, Dalton made sure that he and Cashen got along. However, the respect Dalton gave Cashen was that of a man who saw his counterpart as an expert in his chosen field. Pat Dalton would go on to say that Harry believed Cashen to be "simply the gate keeper [*sic*] for J[erry] Hoffberger. A good PR guy but not a baseball man." As such, Dalton "accepted that and tolerated Frank."[16]

Dalton also had to answer to Jerry Hoffberger. As Dalton pointed out in an interview with author James Edward Miller, this was more straightforward than one might have thought, especially since Dalton was new at his job. "When Jerry gave me the job . . . he said: 'I've only got one piece of advice for you: as long as you make more right decisions than wrong ones, you'll never have any trouble.' . . . He was a hands-off operator," Dalton related.[17] The new general manager's first decision would help make him an overnight sensation, and the groundwork was laid by his former boss, Lee MacPhail.

According to Lee MacPhail's recounting, to not throw his replacement into the pool's deep end, Hoffberger asked MacPhail to "please stay through the Winter Meetings."[18] MacPhail acquiesced to that request and represented the club at the gathering in Miami. As for what he was looking for on his trip to the Magic City, on the day that *The Sporting News* announced MacPhail's departure, Orioles correspondent Doug Brown reported that MacPhail was in the market for a starting outfielder and a relief pitcher to help put his old club over the top.[19] MacPhail's agreeing to stay begs the question: why would a person taking a new job work so hard to improve a team that no longer employed him? Simply put, MacPhail was a professional and understood that the Orioles faced a unique situation in 1966.

As 1966 dawned, the American League was in a transitional phase. The New York Yankees had been the crème de la crème of the American League almost continuously since the 1920s. However, although the team had performed well in the early 1960s, the wheels quickly fell off following an appearance in the 1964 World Series. In 1965 the Yankees had finished 77-85 in the ten-team American League. That total left them in sixth place, a distant ten games behind the fifth-place Cleveland Indians. Now, with a change in ownership, what would become of the Yankees was unknown. This situation opened the door for other teams to move up.

In 1965 that team was the Minnesota Twins. The budding contenders from the Midwest had won 105 games, and it took the Los Angeles Dodgers 7 games to dispatch them in the World Series. Despite this dominance, the Twins were not the only team having an outstanding season in 1965. The Chicago White Sox won 95 games, while the Baltimore Orioles had 94 victories. Despite this finish, Lee MacPhail and the Orioles' front office felt they lacked one or two pieces of the winning puzzle. Specifically, "what the team needed was one more good hitter with power—preferably a right-handed hitter."[20] To find this piece, MacPhail was willing to part with a lot if the return ultimately benefited the Orioles. This type of trade was possible because of the strength of Harry Dalton's Minor League system.

On the one hand, the Orioles had a preponderance of infield depth thanks to Davey Johnson's play. Johnson had shown great promise throughout the last three seasons with the club in Rochester, New York, and had earned a call-up at the end of the 1965 season. According to speculation in the press, Johnson's performance made veteran Luis Aparicio available, as well as second baseman Jerry Adair. Moreover, the Orioles had a surplus of pitching, and this depth made twenty-year-old Wally Bunker, John Miller, or even staff ace Milt Pappas available. Finally, thanks to the emergence of John "Boog" Powell as a candidate to play either a corner outfield spot or first base, MacPhail floated veteran Norm Siebern's name as trade bait.[21]

As for what MacPhail wanted in return, it was apparent from the beginning that he wanted the missing bat to play the outfield: "We figure Curt Blefary [a rookie who had hit twenty-two home runs and won the Rookie of the Year in the American League in 1965] is established in the left field. However, in Center and Right, Paul Blair [an up-and-coming outfielder in the Orioles system] and Sam Bowens [an established big leaguer who had played in the Orioles' outfield on and off since 1963] could have problems. We need a player who can jump right in there."[22] Luckily for MacPhail, he got plenty of offers and quickly consummated some deals for lower-impact players.

On December 2 MacPhail traded Norm Siebern to the California Angels for twenty-one-year-old outfielder Dick Simpson. Then, in a more significant move, MacPhail sent veteran outfielder Jackie Brandt and prized pitching prospect Darold Knowles to the Philadelphia Phillies for reliever Jack Baldschun. This deal gave the Orioles something they were looking for: help in the bullpen. Of course, at the time, Baltimore fans most likely felt it was a steep price to pay. As late as the winter of 1965, Knowles was one of the Orioles organization's top pitching prospects. In January that year, Harry Dalton went so far as to say that Knowles was one of two pitchers in the farm system who could win consistently. Dalton believed that Knowles was a winner because, despite his below-average velocity on his two-seam fastball, Knowles "has a fine curve and good control."[23] Unbeknown to the Orioles fan base, however, the acquisition of Baldschun had given the team the chip it needed to fulfill its goal of getting an impact hitter who could play the outfield. The

Cincinnati Reds made this possible by being ready to cut ties with the one outfielder in the league who could reshape any lineup.

The 1965 Reds had won eighty-nine games and finished a distant fourth in the National League but only eight games behind the pennant-winning Los Angeles Dodgers. However, like the Orioles, the Reds felt that they were only one or two pieces away from climbing to the top. In their case, Reds GM Bill DeWitt felt the team needed pitching to go with the best offense in the league.[24] With this in mind, he was ready to make a bold move by acquiring Frank Robinson.

Born in Beaumont, Texas, in 1935, Robinson grew up on the West Coast in a racially diverse neighborhood in Oakland, California. While attending McClymonds High School, he had his life changed by his baseball coach, George Powles. He saw potential in Robinson and cultivated his talent, and Frank dedicated his young life to using baseball as a way out of Oakland. The Cincinnati Reds helped him reach his goal in 1953 during the second wave of Major League integration.

After being signed for $3,500 in 1953, Robinson began his march through the Reds' Minor League system despite facing the peril of racial segregation while playing in places like Ogden, Utah, and Columbia, South Carolina. Then, in 1956, at the age of twenty, Robinson was promoted to the Major League Reds and quickly became a standout member of the team and a formidable slugger. Robinson capped his rise in 1961 when he won the National League Most Valuable Player Award after earning a .323 batting average, belting 37 home runs, and driving in 124 while the Reds won the National League pennant.[25] It seemed like the sky was the limit for the young slugger. However, because of what many see as an underlying institutional racism that permeated the Reds organization, it did not work out that way.

Robinson pointed out that as the team's makeup changed (coinciding with improved play on the field), he became a team leader with the club. He was more likely to voice his opinion instead of staying quiet, as he had early in his career. Because of this, he began to run afoul of management and was branded a troublemaker. Robinson's stock continued to drop when he ran afoul of Bill DeWitt during his first meeting with the new GM. During that meeting, prior to which DeWitt kept Robinson waiting in the lobby way past their appointed meeting time, DeWitt voiced the opinion of some in the organization, including himself, whom Robinson had never met, that Robinson did not always hustle.[26] However, Robinson's place on the team was secure despite these issues. Then he got into legal trouble.

In February 1961 Cincinnati police arrested Robinson after several incidents at a diner. The evening started poorly when Robinson, accompanied by friends, got into a minor altercation with teenage patrons in the diner. Although this incident did not lead to formal charges, police exacerbated the situation when two officers called to mediate the dispute referred to Robinson and his friends as "boys." A short time later, Robinson and his friends returned to the diner to finish the meal they had left behind. They were then the targets of throat-slashing gestures from the cook. This gesture provoked Robinson to draw a .25-caliber pistol he carried. Once again, the cook called the police. This time, the officers who had responded to the earlier call asked Robinson to produce his gun. At that time, Robinson lied and said he did not have one. When police discovered that he did, Robinson was arrested and jailed on a $1,000 bond that the club refused to help him pay.[27]

This unsavory episode, combined with a perceived belief that Robinson was actually older than his age of record (he was thirty), led DeWitt to feel that he could trade Robinson without any negative consequences, especially if he could trade for the pitching help he believed would get his Reds over the top. This line of reasoning opened the door for the Orioles to acquire the outfielder they desired, and all it would take was trading Milt Pappas, the newly acquired Jack Baldschun, and Dick Simpson.

This news was broken to Harry Dalton the morning of his introductory press conference. Dalton was announced as the GM of the Orioles on December 8, 1965, in a series of moves meant to streamline the Orioles' front office. Before this announcement, Dalton discovered he could make a huge splash on his first day. "Lee [MacPhail] came in and said, 'Here's your first decision,' and handed me a slip of paper with three names on one side and Frank on the other," Dalton said.[28] At that point, MacPhail left the ultimate choice up to Dalton as to whether executing the trade was a good idea or not.

Dalton is on the record as being all for the trade, despite the perceived baggage of getting Robinson. He made his decision, as usual, after checking with the members of the Dalton Gang. The blockbuster trade was going to happen. In a move that would become a Harry Dalton trademark, he asked DeWitt for another player because, as baseball fans would see over the next thirty years, Dalton was always looking to get more talent, especially pitching. In this case, Dalton remembered that the Reds had a left-handed prospect in the Florida State League whom the Dalton Gang had liked. So, as Dalton recalled, he asked DeWitt for this FSL pitcher because he felt that DeWitt was fleecing him in the three-for-one deal and that another player would make the Orioles look good in the public eye. DeWitt rebuffed Dalton and ultimately offered Roger Craig, whom Dalton "didn't want any part of." This tiff jeopardized the whole trade package, and later MacPhail cautioned Dalton not to "blow this deal."[29]

Aside from MacPhail's opinion, Dalton also had to weigh Hank Bauer and Frank Cashen's input. There are conflicting reports on how Bauer felt about the deal. On the one hand, Dalton, who was with Bauer when Lee MacPhail brought the trade to him, said the former U.S. Marine was all for the deal. Conversely, Cashen remembered that Bauer "didn't want to make the deal."[30] Bauer's reasoning was twofold and largely dovetailed with Cashen's ideas on the deal, as Cashen reported them in 2001: "Number one, no one wants to give up their best pitcher. That was Pappas. And second, Frank Robinson had a terrible reputation."[31] Cashen went on to elaborate that, in his mind, "if you've got a bad apple in the barrel, get him the hell out before the rest of the barrel goes bad."[32] Armed with all this information, Dalton went home after a party for the departing MacPhail, and, in another move that would become a Dalton staple, he "slept" on the trade. He awoke on December 9, 1965, and agreed to the deal.

As could be imagined, there was fallout. Robinson feared moving to highly segregated Baltimore, where he had had troubles earlier. Meanwhile, Pappas, who had recently bought a home in Florida based on information that he would remain in Baltimore and partake in spring training at the Orioles' camp in nearby Miami, felt betrayed by the club.[33] Frank Cashen announced to the Baltimore media that he hoped the acquisition of Robinson would help the club change its image and help the team "gain more friends in the negro community."[34] How did Harry Dalton feel about the consummation of the trade?

His initial reaction was to exclaim that the Orioles now had "cannons at the four corners!" with Robinson and Curt Blefary in the outfield and Boog Powell and Brooks Robinson at first and third base.[35] Once he calmed down, his analysis was measured and calculated. "Robinson can go along with Brooks, who has been carrying our right-handed load, while Blefary and Powell balance the power beautifully from the left side," he stated.[36] Dalton, always the former Minor League director, was also quick to point out that the new Robinson was a defensive upgrade, ran the bases well, and had a "quick and accurate" throwing arm. Dalton also understood that while the offense and outfield got better, the pitching was, at least on paper, downgraded by the move. Dalton was not overly worried. Dalton quickly praised Pappas on the starting side but noted that the Orioles had "four solid starters . . . and seven youngsters who have the stuff to compete and win a job next year."[37] Meanwhile, Dalton pointed out that Rule 5 draftees Moe Drabowsky and Gene Brabender, Wisconsin sandlot star, would help the bullpen.[38] All that remained for the new GM was to put all the pieces together for 1966.

6

Can You Believe It?

1966

The Orioles' acquisition of Frank Robinson did not mean that Harry Dalton's work to prepare for the 1966 season was over. He also needed to find the right combination of players to put around Robinson. Furthermore, as he settled into his new role he had to hire a replacement for himself as head of scouting and the farm system. Ultimately, he decided that the best move would be to split those duties between two individuals.

For the position of farm director, he had a host of candidates. One of these was his assistant, Lou Gorman, who was a Massachusetts product and had worked for the Orioles since the winter of 1963. Since that time, he had learned a lot from Dalton, whom he found to be "thorough, capable, and intelligent. . . . He was approachable and a people person." Gorman would even say that when Dalton was "demanding and a stickler for details," it was a teaching moment that made Gorman develop a "great deal of respect for his overall ability as a baseball executive and for him personally."[1] However, when it came to Dalton's replacement, Gorman recalled that Dalton had reservations about Gorman's experience level. Still, since Dalton was a big believer in people who believed in themselves, when Gorman outlined his argument for why Dalton should hire him, it made enough of an impression that Dalton hired Gorman after a few days of deliberation.[2]

With Gorman hired for the farm system role, Dalton set out to find someone who could oversee the scouting department. He ultimately hired a man who would help shape Dalton's career until Dalton left the game.

By 1966 Walter Shannon had devoted much of his time to baseball. He began his career in St. Louis with the Browns and became one of Branch Rickey's young Cardinals scouts in a department that would help redefine baseball and make the Cardinals a powerhouse through the late 1960s. From there, Shannon moved to Cleveland in 1962, and it was from there that Dalton hired him to head the Orioles' scouting effort. As for why Dalton went with Shannon, the root of the decision was that, as Lou Gorman would reiterate, "Dalton was always impressed with Shannon's ability."[3]

This ability was twofold. On the one hand, Shannon was a great judge of talent. His signings for the Cardinals included Tim McCarver and Bob Gibson. The other reason Dalton wanted to bring in Shannon was that the longtime scout brought to the organization a wealth of knowledge that aligned with Dalton's proclivities. Dalton would always look for ways to increase knowledge that would help him and his staff. Moreover, he was always looking to increase the number of people willing to speak their mind. Dalton's offices were very collegial environments. Dalton wanted others to challenge him and stand behind their arguments even if Dalton, the final arbiter, felt differently about an issue. From his earliest days in Baltimore, Dalton taught others the game, exposed them to people like Shannon, and gave them a voice so that they could have ownership in decisions and learn how to weigh the pros and cons of the choices they made. This mentality would make him and his teams better. It would also influence a future generation of baseball executives.

With behind-the-scenes work completed before the team went to Miami and Thomasville, Dalton sought the right blend of players to position around Frank Robinson. His decisions were more straightforward due to his own work as a farm director. By the time the Orioles went to camp in Miami in the spring of 1966, they had several standout players at various positions.

Third baseman Brooks Robinson anchored the infield. By the 1966 season, the one-time bonus baby known as "Brooksie" or "Brooks Robbie" had blossomed into one of the Majors' best third basemen. Brooksie, by his tenth year in the league, had won seven straight Gold Gloves, had led the league in games played by a third baseman five times, led the league in fielding percentage six times, and was routinely in the top ten when using current metrics like range factor or total runs saved.[4] Beyond his defense, Robinson had blossomed offensively. He was named the American League MVP in 1960 when he hit .328, clubbed 28 home runs, and drove in 118 runs.

In the middle infield, the Birds were a combination of experience and youth. At shortstop, the Orioles had placed their faith in veteran glove-man Luis Aparicio. Aparicio had made his name in the Majors with the Chicago White Sox as a slick-fielding, base-stealing contact hitter. He came over to Baltimore in the winter of 1962 for former Rookie of the Year Ron Hansen; bonus baby Dave Nicholson; Pete Ward, who was coming off a lackluster Major League debut in 1962; and future Hall of Famer Hoyt Wilhelm (who was nearing the end of his career). At second base Dalton placed Texas A&M product Davey Johnson, whom the Orioles signed in June 1962. He had made his Major League debut in the spring of 1965 and looked to have the starting job in 1966.

The other cannon on the infield was at first base. The Orioles had signed John "Boog" Powell out of Key West, Florida, in 1959. From that moment, he had worked his way up the Orioles pipeline despite a fluctuating waistline. He made his Major League debut in 1961 and showed moments of being a big-time contributor. The best example was in 1964, when Powell, who then played in the outfield corners, hit .290 with 39 home runs and 99 RBIs. Despite lower numbers in 1965, Powell figured to start most of the Orioles games at first base in 1966.

Dick Brown did the bulk of the catching in 1965 and was the front-runner to start. Beyond Brown, the Orioles had veteran Charlie Lau and rookie Andy Etchebarren as possible backups.

In the outfield, the Orioles looked set, thanks to Frank Robinson, now in right field. In the other two spots, the Orioles featured former Minor League Rule 5 selections Curt Blefary in left field and Paul Blair in center. There was also veteran Russ Snyder, who could play all three outfield positions.

Who would pitch for the Orioles was the big question that Harry Dalton had to answer that spring, since the Orioles had traded Milt Pappas in December. The team still had Steve Barber from the Kiddie Corps of 1960. The staff looked like a mix of young arms, including Wally Bunker, Dave McNally, and Tom Phoebus. Two prospects for the 1966 staff were relative unknowns at the Major League level, and a third was a journeyman.

At 6 feet 5 inches, Gene Brabender (pronounced BRAH-bender) was the most intriguing of the unknowns. Brabender was signed in 1961 by the Los Angeles Dodgers and spent the next two seasons working through their system. In 1963 he was drafted into the army, went through basic training, and then found himself stationed outside Baltimore and serving in the military police. Thus, he was the best pitcher for the Aberdeen Proving Ground Bombers until he was discharged from the army in the fall of 1965. At that time, the Dodgers had left the gigantic, bespectacled pitcher unprotected in the Minor League Rule 5 draft. This allowed other pro scouts, who had missed him the first time, to get a look. One of these was Walter Youse, who saw Brabender pitch in the army, liked what he saw, and recommended that the Orioles draft him.

The other unknown came with more of a history. Jim Palmer was one of the most sought-after pitchers in the country in 1963, after playing for his hometown Arizona State Sun Devils. At that time, the Orioles got the inside track on Palmer thanks to his college coach, Bobby Winkles. In the summer of 1963, Winkles supplied an amateur team in South Dakota (subsidized by the Orioles) with players, and now, in 1966, he suggested that Palmer join the Baltimore roster. The result was that the Orioles found a transformative arm. Harry Dalton recalled that after he had seen about fifteen pitches from Palmer, he told scouts Jim Russo and Jim Wilson to try and sign him.[5]

Once he signed with the Orioles, Palmer was not in the Minors long. He pitched for Aberdeen as an eighteen-year-old rookie and went 11-3 with a 2.51 ERA in nineteen starts. He then won four more starts for the Orioles' instructional league team in Florida in the winter of 1964. These performances gave Palmer the inside track to the Majors; he broke camp with the Orioles and made his debut on April 17, 1965, pitching two innings against the Boston Red Sox in relief. A little less than a month later, Palmer would make his first start. This time, he pitched seven innings and gained a no-decision. This performance would lead to five more starts during his twenty-seven-appearance campaign, ending with Palmer earning a 5-4 record.

Sandwiched between the prospect Palmer and the suspect Brabender was right-hander Moe Drabowsky. Drabowsky had been in the Majors since 1956 and had pitched for three other teams (Chicago Cubs, Cincinnati Reds, and Kansas City Athletics) as both a starter and a reliever. He got to Baltimore the way Brabender had; the Orioles selected Drabowsky in the 1965 Minor League Rule 5 draft, and manager Hank Bauer quickly slotted Drabowsky into the bullpen.

With this core group in place, the media quickly proclaimed Baltimore the AL front-runner. However, not everyone was convinced. On the eve of the exhibition season, Bob Maisel of the *Baltimore Sun* pointed out that the Orioles seemed weak up the middle of the field, especially at catcher and in center field. In Maisel's mind, the vital issue at those spots was whether Paul Blair at center and Charlie Lau or Andy Etchebarren at catcher would hit well enough. The Orioles brass quickly dismissed these worries, especially when discussing the possible lack of production behind the plate. Coach Billy Hunter quickly defended Etchebarren: "All the scouts tell me that Etchebarren was one of the best defensive catchers in the minors last year. . . . And like Hank [Bauer] says, if our big guys don't hit, we are wasting our time worrying about the rest of it anyway."[6]

One person who bought into that philosophy was Harry Dalton, especially when it came to carrying the light-hitting Etchebarren. Dalton had seen him catch for years in the Minor League system, and he knew that the strong defensive catcher could help lead the Orioles pitching staff. Ultimately, this led to Dalton convincing Bauer and Frank Cashen that Etchebarren should handle the bulk of the catching despite his offensive deficiencies. Etchebarren said Dalton made this quite clear to him one day in the spring of 1966: "Harry looked at me and said, I don't care if you hit .200. You are going to catch every day."[7]

There was speculation among the players as to whether the Orioles could gel as a team with the catching situation settled. According to Boog Powell, as Frank Robinson took his first swing in Baltimore's batting cage, he quickly assuaged the worry that they would not come together. In a story that names several players watching Frank Robinson pound a home run over a set of palm trees, the Orioles knew they had "just won the fucking pennant."[8] This excitement, however, was tempered by some ugliness Robinson's wife experienced back in Baltimore.

By 1966 Baltimore and the surrounding area had a deep history of racial disharmony. Nowhere was this more evident than in the housing practices of the city. Although the federal courts had outlawed agreements known as "covenants," used to bar ethnic families from living in white neighborhoods in 1948, de facto segregation existed in many areas.[9] This unwritten rule of segregation extended to every Black citizen, including members of the Colts and Orioles teams. Thus, when Frank Robinson first moved to town in January, he had more than the usual share of difficulty finding a place to live with his wife and family. This situation came to a head in February while Robinson was in Florida for spring training.

One day his wife phoned him to say that realtors told her that there was no housing available. Furthermore, in one alarming case, she was denied a chance to look at a house after the realtor realized that the "Mrs. Robinson, whose husband played for the Orioles," was not the white Mrs. Brooks Robinson but the Black Mrs. Frank Robinson. All this caused Frank to call Jerry Hoffberger and let him know that he would need to leave Florida to resolve the situation and that he might have to leave the team permanently. Ultimately, the team owner stepped in and applied pressure of his own. The Robinsons finally found a home in the integrated neighborhood of Ashburton, just in time for the start of the season. The first crisis of the season was averted.[10]

On the field, the Orioles made believers of the naysayers early. The players came out of the gate blazing in April. The season began with two wins over the Boston Red Sox on April 12 and 13. The Orioles suffered their first defeat two days later when they dropped the home opener to the New York Yankees 3–2. They did not lose for the rest of the month. They swept series from the Yankees, Washington, California Angels, and Detroit during that time.[11]

Frank Robinson quickly showed Baltimore fans that he was not too old. In twelve games he hit 5 home runs, drove in 5 runs, hit .463, and had an OPS of 1.561. He was on a roll that included home runs in his first three games. Thanks to an old baseball tradition, Frank also helped bond his new team off the field.

The so-called Kangaroo Court has a rich history in baseball. It is an informal proceeding whereby team members are fined various token amounts for doing things incorrectly during a ball game. In most cases, the court is a good way for a team to bond and playfully rehash things after winning a game. In 1966, at the urging of Billy Hunter, Frank Robinson installed himself as the judge, jury, and executioner of the Orioles' court. Robinson presided in the clubhouse; he sat at the front of the room and wore a string mop on his head. According to his teammates, no one individual or incident was off limits. This included Harry Dalton. One day Dalton walked into the Orioles' clubhouse after a victory. Robinson then informed Dalton that he was fining him for not shining his shoes. At that time, the room went silent because the assembled group wondered if Robinson had finally overstepped. Dalton slowly took his wallet out and paid the fine. From that moment on, most players felt that Dalton was willing to let them have their fun when it came time to unwind, and he participated if the players "picked their spots."[12]

Unfortunately, there were not many reasons to celebrate in May. The Orioles returned to earth with a record of 14-16 and finished the month three games back of first place. Still, there were bright spots. The bullpen looked to have stabilized thanks to the pitching of rookie Eddie Watt. The right-hander from Iowa made twelve appearances in May and won four of those games, including a couple of one-run decisions. Watt also notched a save and soaked up some valuable innings. Nowhere was this more evident than on the last day of May, when, after being staked to a 6–0 lead, Dave McNally gave up four runs while securing only one out in his half of the first. Watt then entered the game and surrendered only one more run in eight and two-thirds innings in what turned out to be a 14–5 Baltimore win.

Still, as the calendar turned to June, Baltimore was three games back, and there was speculation that Harry Dalton would be looking to make a trade to better his team before the June trade deadline. That speculation turned out to be correct. With his team back on the winning track at the start of June, Dalton moved veteran second baseman Jerry Adair to the Chicago White Sox for veteran reliever Eddie Fisher. This move coincided with a six-game winning streak.

Two losses and five more wins followed, and during that time the Orioles continued to jockey for the top spot in the American League. A large part of this success was thanks to Frank Robinson. By the middle of the month, following a 6–4 Orioles win, Robinson was leading the American League with a .350 batting average, he was tied for the league lead in home runs with 16, and he led the league with 50 RBIs. At that time, the Orioles were one game ahead in first place, and they would never relinquish that spot.

The continued Orioles dominance did not mean that Dalton took the summer off. However, there is evidence that he had time to concentrate on other baseball issues. This duality would become commonplace for Dalton. His legacy goes far beyond his skill as a team builder. As Commissioner Emeritus Bud Selig noted in 2019, MLB officials first consulted Harry when baseball owners were considering or confronting a change in the game.[13] He was one of the most cerebral executives in the game's history. In the summer of 1966, he argued that Major League Baseball would best serve its customers and players by shortening the season.

Harry Dalton was not the first to suggest that baseball rethink its schedule. Before expanding the schedule to 162 games in 1961, various owners had suggested shortening the number of games in 1963; Dodgers owner Walter O'Malley called the schedule "ridiculous." The following year, Calvin Griffith of the Minnesota Twins recommended shortening the schedule to 153 games.[14] Meanwhile, fans watched the NFL's alluring made-for-TV product and its 14-game schedule in ever-growing numbers.[15]

Dalton proposed a rational solution: shorten the season to 144 games with "128 single contests and eight doubleheaders." This shift would ultimately cut the off days on the schedule, but it would provide a league-wide off day every two weeks. According to Dalton, it also had the potential to extend the careers of the game's biggest stars while keeping fans interested. He understood that his plan was not perfect in many respects. However, he felt "someone has to jump in with a concrete proposal." Ultimately, the "Dalton Plan" was shouted down by his fellow executives.[16]

Gabe Paul, the GM of the Cleveland Indians, noted that baseball was a "game of continuity," with the "high spots building up the low spots" in the season schedule. In Paul's opinion, shortening the schedule to the proposed 144 games would throw off that balance. Others, like GM Jim Campbell of the Detroit Tigers and Kansas City Athletics owner Charlie Finley, believed that a 153-game schedule should be adopted.[17]

Beyond issues with the proposed length of the schedule, others took issue with Dalton's assertion that players were "tired" under the current season structure. However, on the day that *The Sporting News* ran the Dalton proposal and rebuttals, it also ran two articles on the same page that quoted both Willie Mays and Brooks Robinson saying that there needed to be a revamp of the schedule. These two stars felt that day-night doubleheaders and night games on getaway day were causing the players to tire unnecessarily, and so they believed there needed to be a change.[18]

Ultimately, the Dalton Plan did not get off the ground. However, this series of events illustrates that Harry Dalton could see when and where the game needed to change, and he was not afraid to offer possible fixes where his contemporaries offered empty talk. He again illustrated this in July 1966, when he called out the hypocrisy of his college baseball counterparts as it pertained to the perceived exploitation of players.

Dalton's comments did not come out of the blue. In three separate issues of *The Sporting News*, the editors of the self-proclaimed "bible of baseball" laid out the various viewpoints of those on both sides of the exploitation issue. On July 30, a week after the last article ran, Dalton wrote to *The Sporting News* and weighed in. As expected, he defended pro baseball, saying that in his mind "there is no question that the college people are much more vocal about this problem than we [professional baseball] are." According to Dalton, this situation caused the overriding narrative that professional baseball was not acting in the college players' best interests. Dalton moved quickly to assuage this belief. In his mind, he and others believed that "there are many sincere and dedicated college coaches who art [*sic*] truly interested in their players and their [the players'] welfare." There were yet others whose "hypocrisy is indicated by their desire to improve their own position at the expense of any athlete available to them." In Dalton's mind, these coaches "are the men who are complicating the efforts being made by professional baseball men and responsible college people to bring about a satisfactory relationship [between professional and college baseball]."[19]

While the media, owners, fans, and Dalton's fellow GMs discussed the merits of his scheduling plan, Dalton defended organized baseball from naysayers in college baseball, and his team kept winning. The Orioles were 58-29 at the All-Star break, which was good enough for an eight-game lead in the American League over the Detroit Tigers. As for the reasons for the Orioles' success, they outscored their opponents, just as predicted. Even after being shut out in a 4–0 loss to California on July 10, the Orioles' runs scored versus runs against heavily slanted in the club's favor. The Orioles had outscored the competition 443–300. A large part of that success was the play of the Robinsons. However, the Orioles were also getting great performances from Luis Aparicio (second in the AL in runs and third in hits) and Boog Powell (second in RBIs and third in home runs). Beyond the play of the team's stars, the Orioles were also getting positive performances from less well known players going into the season.

One such performer living up to Dalton and Hank Bauer's faith was Andy Etchebarren. The pug-faced catcher from Whittier, California, was impressing both pundits and his teammates. One who was incredibly impressed was Aparicio, who told *The Sporting News* that, in his opinion, Etchebarren was the Orioles' MVP of the first half: "I'm not taking anything away from Frank and Brooksie. They've been great. But the thing is, you expect them to be great. We didn't expect Andy to be this good—at least, I didn't. . . . What would we have done without him?"[20]

The Orioles were also getting timely performances. Dalton would recall years later that one of the hallmarks of that '66 club was winning no matter the situation. "We won a lot of dramatic situations. . . . Teams have years like that, when everything goes right," he said. "It's almost an intangible."[21] Finally, the Orioles were successful in the first half of the season, and some felt it was because they came together off the field. This bonding took many forms. Whether it was parties featuring barbecue smoked by Boog Powell and washed down by National Bohemian beer provided by Jerry Hoffberger or locker room pranks perpetrated by Moe Drabowsky, the Orioles stayed loose and liked each other. This quality showed on the field in the second half of the season.

The Orioles were 19-10 in July, ending the month in first place by thirteen games. With that big a lead, many fans and writers believed it was not a matter of *if* the Orioles would win the pennant but *when*. Veteran sportswriter Sam Lacy shared this sentiment.

Lacy first came to prominence in the 1940s as a champion of integration in baseball while on the *Chicago Defender* staff. From there, he took his talents to the *Baltimore Afro American*. While at the *Afro*, Lacy would write his influential "A to Z" column. On July 26 Lacy dedicated the column to teaching Black Baltimore about Harry Dalton. Like many others, Lacy did not discount the play of stars like Frank Robinson and Brooks Robinson. However, in Lacy's mind, Dalton deserved the credit for the Orioles' success because he took risks while other front-office executives in the American League "played their hand close to the vest." The risks Dalton took included trading away Jerry Adair, placing his faith in Davey Johnson, and starting Andy Etchebarren. If any of those risks had failed, Lacy surmised, it would have been the death knell for the rookie executive. Because they worked and because of Dalton's ability to gamble in instances like that, Lacy believed the Orioles' manager was the person Baltimore should recognize for "putting the wings on the bird."[22]

The Orioles continued to march to the pennant in August despite a .500 record for the month, which they finished at 14-14. Still, as the calendar turned to September, Baltimore had an eleven-game lead, and they had outlasted potential tragedy thanks to a team party gone wrong.

Eerily, the party had been held at the house of a local undertaker. This time, thanks to the presence of a pool and, one can only assume, a fair amount of National Brewing Company product, the Orioles were blowing off steam on land and water. This party had almost disastrous effects on the season. First, in an attempt to throw reliever Moe Drabowsky in the pool, Boog Powell slipped and suffered a cut above his eye. "I fell back and hit my eye on the corner of a doorjamb. I just laid it wide open. It was ugly," he recalled. Ultimately, Powell would require a trip to the local emergency room, where he attempted a small amount of subterfuge with hospital staff before returning to the party. "[Outfielder]

Curt Blefary and I grabbed someone else's hospital card and went to the emergency room. . . . Everybody was sniggering because they knew it was me," he said.[23] If that was the worst thing that happened that night, the memory would probably be lost to history. Except that Powell's night was topped when Frank Robinson tried to swim. One can imagine that Robinson took to the water in the spirit of camaraderie. Besides, the world-class athlete had some of the best hand-eye coordination on the planet. Wading in a pool should not have been a problem, but Robinson could not swim and quickly sank to the bottom of the pool. Luckily, Andy Etchebarren was paying attention, and he was able to rescue Robinson before the slugger suffered irreparable harm.[24]

With that event behind them, the Orioles continued to play .500 baseball in September. Along the way, Frank Robinson would take over the top spot in every major offensive category in the American League. By mid-September Robinson was hitting .316 with 49 home runs and 120 RBIs. He also had scored 120 runs and was slugging .644. Provided that his batting average held out, he had a shot at winning the Triple Crown by leading the league in home runs, batting average, and RBIs—not bad for an outfielder his previous team had traded because he was deemed too old.

Finally, the day that Harry Dalton and the Orioles had worked toward since 1954 arrived on September 22. In front of a smattering of 5,250 fans at Kansas City's Municipal Stadium, the Orioles won their first American League pennant. As for the game itself, it was never really in doubt. Jim Palmer threw a complete game while scattering five hits, surrendering one run, and striking out eight. Meanwhile, the Orioles offense carried the day, scoring two runs each in the third, fifth, and sixth to provide a cushion for Palmer. Then, on a hard-hit liner into the gap in left-center field, left fielder Russ Snyder sprinted to his right and made a diving catch to end the game and secure the pennant.

The win set off a party for the ages. Players doused each other with condiments from the postgame buffet and threw Hank Bauer in the whirlpool. The Orioles virtually destroyed the visiting clubhouse. As for Harry Dalton, he kept a low profile that day. The one thing he did was to phone his friend Lee MacPhail and thank him for his help in making the day a reality. His quiet approach was an oft-repeated behavior. No matter his success, he would never forget those around him who helped him succeed.[25]

With the pennant sewn up, Harry Dalton's professional life became one of fielding questions. In the immediate aftermath, reporters wanted to know if pitcher Steve Barber, who had won ten games and posted a 2.30 ERA on the way to his second All-Star game appearance, would be available in the World Series. Barber had developed tendinitis following his last start of the season in California, and his arm was still hurting. Ultimately, Dalton would not rule Barber out, but he also said it would take a few days to see if the swelling would go down enough for him to pitch. Beyond Barber's health, reporters also wanted to know what Dalton thought about keeping the team together for 1967. Dalton knew the players would be asking for raises in the coming year.

In terms of his players, as the World Series neared Dalton was quick to point out that the Orioles were willing to face the vaunted Los Angeles Dodgers with the team that had won them the pennant. The Orioles considered their chances at defeating the Dodgers in the Series; Jim Russo and Al Kubski reported that Baltimore "can beat this club" in their report to the team before the Series. The reason, according to Russo and Kubski, was that although the Dodgers had "good [starting] pitching and a great bullpen," the Orioles knew that the Dodgers "don't score with power or the big inning." Instead, LA tried to "make a few runs hold up."[26] This insight was backed by the fact that despite having the most wins in the National League, the Dodgers finished eighth in runs scored per game. Of course, this meant that the Dodgers' pitching staff went a long way to making the team a winner.

At the heart of the Dodgers' pitching staff was perhaps the best left-right tandem in baseball during the late 1950s and early 1960s. From the right side, Don Drysdale was an intimidating strikeout pitcher who had gone 85-54 with 930 strikeouts from 1962 to 1965. Meanwhile, the Dodgers offered up arguably the best pitcher in baseball from the left side. Like Drysdale, Sandy Koufax had begun his career with the Dodgers in Brooklyn. Koufax was a wild-throwing, gangly teen who seemed destined for mediocrity on the mound. Once the team moved to LA, however, Koufax would quickly come to dominate. From 1962 to 1965 he was 84-25 with an ERA of 2.02 and 1,127 strikeouts. During that time, the man who would become known as "The Left Arm of God" won three Cy Young Awards as the best pitcher in the Majors and one MVP while finishing second twice.

What the combined records of Drysdale and Koufax did not show, however, was that time was creeping up on both men. In 1966 Drysdale went only 13-16 in forty starts. Moreover, his strikeouts were down, and his hits allowed per nine innings were up. Kubski and Russo also noted that the power-pitching Drysdale had "two bad knees" and "one leg is completely taped," making it difficult for him to push off or pivot.[27] Statistically, Koufax could not have looked better, as his 1966 season was another banner year. He led the league in wins, shutouts, complete games, innings pitched, ERA, and strikeouts. There was only one problem. He was in tremendous pain, and getting to the mound for his start took a massive effort.[28]

Against this backdrop, Harry Dalton and the Orioles took a DC-8 to LA for the Series' first two games. The first game occurred on a sunny afternoon on October 5, with Dave McNally taking on Don Drysdale, who was making his fifth career start in the World Series. As it turned out, both teams played to their scouting reports. On the one hand, the Orioles played for the big inning. In the first, after a Russ Snyder walk, Frank Robinson put a home run into the left-field bleachers that avoided Tommy Davis's glove. Then, with the Dodgers still reeling, Brooks Robinson bombed another homer to left, giving the Orioles a 3–0 lead after half an inning.

Staked to that lead, some pitchers go on to cruise to victory. Not so for McNally. For most of his start, he was wild and inconsistent. The Dodgers took advantage of this by running and chipping away, as was their style. In the first inning, McNally walked shortstop Maury Wills, who promptly stole second before being stranded. Staked to a 4–0 lead in the second following a Russ Snyder RBI single, McNally surrendered a home run to Dodgers second baseman Jim Lefebvre to start the Dodgers' second. Then McNally promptly gave up a ground-rule double to

Wes Parker (which most likely would have been a triple if not for fan interference) and a walk to the next hitter, Jim Gilliam. He then got John Roseboro to line out to Snyder and retired pinch hitter Dick Stuart on a fly ball to center for the second out before striking out Maury Wills.

McNally was in trouble again in the third. The inning started well enough, with McNally inducing a pop-out to short by Willie Davis. He then walked the next three hitters. McNally's day was officially over with one out and the bases loaded. In his place, Bauer brought in clubhouse clown Moe Drabowsky. Drabowsky was 6-0 during the regular season, but he was also famous among his teammates for clubhouse pranks. He would quickly become a World Series hero, but he had to get out of his inherited jam first.

He quickly got a third of the way out when he fanned Parker for the second out. He then gave up a run and charged to Dave McNally when he walked Jim Gilliam, which scored Lou Johnson to make it 4–1. From there, however, Drabowsky, known for a three-pitch mix of a fastball, curveball, and slider, induced a pop-out from John Roseboro for the final out. From that moment on, Drabowsky cruised.

In the fourth, he struck out the side swinging while up 5–2. He did the same in the fifth. This time he got Lou Johnson, Tommy Davis, and Jim Lefebvre all swinging. He got his eighth strikeout in the bottom of the seventh when he fanned former Brave Wes Covington to start the inning. He got Wes Parker swinging in the eighth inning as the Dodgers went down 1-2-3. Finally, Drabowsky notched his tenth and eleventh strikeouts of the day when he fanned John Roseboro and pinch hitter Ron Fairly in a 1-2-3 ninth to secure the win for Baltimore.

After the game, all the talk centered on Drabowsky. Dalton deflected any possible role in finding the piece of coal that turned into an October diamond when asked why he felt that Drabowsky the journeyman pitcher was worth the $25,000 fee in the previous Rule 5 draft. "Charley Lau kept telling us about him for a year or so. . . . Hank [Bauer] liked the way he threw for him in Kansas City," Dalton said, adding that "one of our scouts by the name of Charley Wallgren followed Moe when he was with Vancouver and turned in a real favorable report on him."[29] Dalton then concluded his remarks by heaping more praise on Hank Bauer.

"I've said all year that Hank did a tremendous job handling our pitching," Dalton stated. "This is just another example. Everybody said Drabowsky was a loser, and his record [48-81 to that point] seemed to prove it. Hank figured he had the stuff to come out of the bullpen, do a job and look at the results. Moe was 6-0, had some big saves, and now he does this."[30]

Of course, any good feelings about what happened in Game One were short-lived, with Game Two scheduled for the next day. Game Two featured a ceremonial first pitch by Hank Bauer's old Yankees manager, Casey Stengel. Then, Jim Palmer and Sandy Koufax took the mound.

After the game and before the official baseball party of both teams, the commissioner's office and the parties of both league presidents took six aircraft back to Baltimore for Game Three.[31] Like the game before, Harry Dalton had to answer questions about where he had found a particular pitcher. With Palmer, he was once again quick to lay the credit at someone else's feet, and this time it was Paul Richards. However, the general manager did point out that he thought that every day "this kid had everything to be a great pitcher. . . . He had a great arm, a great fastball, and a great body." After the game, the media asked Dalton about his role in finding the man of the hour. With Blair, Dalton once again put the credit for success on the shoulders of his scouting department. "Jim Russo and Dee Phillips turned in very favorable reports on Blair off his play in Class C [with the New York Mets in 1962]," he said.[32] The Orioles selected Blair in the 1963 Minor League Rule 5 draft and signed him to a $12,500 contract. Once again, Dalton's decision came up roses, no matter who began the search. The Orioles sat on the verge of winning the World Series, vindicating the work of himself and the men who worked for him.

Whether Dalton and the Birds would get vindication came down to the right arm of Dave McNally. In a reiteration of Game One, McNally took on Don Drysdale. This time, befitting the stakes, both pitchers were on their game. A crowd of 54,458 fans saw both men dominate the lineup early on, with very little traffic on the bases for either team. Then, in the fourth, as he had done so many times in 1966, Frank Robinson provided a shot to the offense just when the Orioles needed it.

This time, the Triple Crown winner and eventual MVP came up in the Baltimore fourth with one out and nobody on. Drysdale missed with a fastball middle-in, and Robinson deposited the ball on a line into the left-field stands. The homer was estimated at 410 feet, and the Orioles led 1–0.

With that lead, McNally was masterful. He would induce back-to-back double plays in the fifth and sixth innings to keep the Dodgers at bay following hits. McNally, who gave up four hits total, worked clean innings in the seventh and eighth. Finally, in the ninth inning, one of Harry Dalton and Jim McLaughlin's first finds made the Orioles the best team in baseball. It was not smooth sailing, however.

McNally opened the inning by striking out Dick Stuart on a fastball down the middle for the first out. The Dodgers then sent their second straight pinch hitter to the plate. Al Ferrara, who was hitting for Drysdale, punched the first pitch from McNally up the middle for a single. At that point, McNally appeared to be rattled. This nervousness facilitated a conference between McNally and shortstop Luis Aparicio while the Dodgers brought in Nate Oliver to pinch run. With Oliver on first representing the tying run, McNally walked speedster Maury Wills to put the tying run at second and the go-ahead run at first with one out. At this point, McNally toughened. He got Willie Davis to fly out lazily to Frank Robinson, and the runners could not advance. Then, after a visit from pitching coach Harry "The Cat" Brecheen, McNally jumped ahead of Dodgers RBI leader Lou Johnson 0–2. Down to his last strike, Johnson swung and lifted an easy fly to center, where Paul Blair, who had entered the game as a defensive replacement, waited. The Orioles were champions of the baseball world.

On the field, separate parties broke out in the outfield and infield. Etchebarren and Brooks Robinson quickly smothered McNally. Meanwhile, the outfield of Snyder, Blair, and Robinson mingled with fans who had managed to exit the stands onto the field.

When the dust finally settled, the Orioles, whom the country doubted had enough pitching, had blanked the Dodgers for thirty-three consecutive innings while securing the first American League sweep in the series since 1950. As he would throughout his career, Harry Dalton credited someone else when talking about the baseball operations staff's role in the win.

This time, as players and front office staff alike basked in the win, Dalton went out of his way to recognize all the hard work put in by the scouting staff. "The scouting report of Jim Russo and Al Kubski is a typical example of the dedication of all the people connected with the organization that helped bring this ball club to the point that it has reached today," he said. "There are so many men in the field—the scouts, and managers—who worked so hard to put this ball club together that it is impossible and certainly unfair to single out any single one."[33]

Now that he had congratulated his team and his staff, there was only one thing left to do before he started thinking about the 1967 season: party. Dalton was never one to let his emotions get the best of him. Even in the best of times. However, on the night of his first World Series victory, Harry Dalton danced with his wife and smiled. He also was loose with the team checkbook. At one point during the team party out on York Road, Andy Etchebarren, also dancing with his wife, asked Dalton when he could expect his offer for the 1967 season. Dalton's reply? "How about right now?" At that point, Etchebarren tried to put off Dalton, stating that they were both having a good time and that it was not the right time. Then Dalton sweetened the deal. If Etchebarren signed right that minute, he could sign for $13,000. The raise was a 100 percent increase for the catcher. Etchebarren would have to negotiate with Dalton if he did not sign that night. Etchebarren, who would become a lifelong Daltonite at that moment, signed the deal.[34] In some ways, it was the cap to a Hollywoodesque season. The longtime employee helps his team reach the sport's pinnacle, gets the girl, and stays likable. However, the credits did not roll with Harry Dalton on the dance floor in his wife's arms, smiling at the camera. Soon enough, it was time to try and stay on top for 1967. Little did Dalton know that he and the country would face two tumultuous years in which neither would fare very well.

7

A Different Reality

1967–68

In the twenty-first century, a sports season feels endless for the fan. Thanks to the internet and the proliferation of content, the coverage is total, and there is very little dead time. In the 1960s, the only person for whom this was true was the general manager of a fan's favorite team. Harry Dalton's work for 1967 started shortly after 1966 ended.

On paper, there was very little for Dalton to accomplish. In the days before free agency, as long Dalton sent out a contract to a player, and the player, who had no real alternatives, signed it, the Orioles would have the same team that ran to the pennant in 1966. Any changes would be of Dalton's design, and he had confidence in the players he had on the Major League roster and in the Minors. That did not mean that he did not have opportunities to make deals. At one point the Cubs were willing to part with former Rookie of the Year, perennial All-Star, and eventual Hall of Famer Billy Williams. The problem was that it would cost Dalton one or both of the Orioles' top prospects. In hindsight, some of his scouts felt that it would have been a move worth making, and for years they wondered about why Dalton passed on an outfield with Frank Robinson and Billy Williams in the corners.[1] However, Dalton would always be able to judge when it was worth trading a player to upgrade his team and when it was prudent not to make a move. In his mind, this was one of those times. "Of course, we could use Williams, but our crying need is not for offense. We could be greedy and sacrifice our future by giving up young talent," Dalton stated.[2] In 1967 that future talent was two-pronged, and Dalton felt both men could lead the Orioles to further glory.

First baseman Mike Epstein and shortstop Mark Belanger could not have been any more different in physical makeup or their strengths on the field. Epstein was a hulking, college-educated former football player with prodigious power. Though from New York, he had gone to the University of California, Berkeley, and played for the U.S. Olympic team in 1964 before being signed by the Orioles.

The Orioles quickly marked Epstein for potential stardom when he joined their system. Harry Dalton, then serving as the farm director, went as far as to say that he felt that, given time, Epstein could "hit 50 homers" in a season.[3] Epstein backed up Dalton's faith by posting stellar stats in his first two seasons in the Minors. After brief stops in rookie ball in Florida, Epstein posted 30 home runs and 100 RBIs in 1965 at Class A Stockton and won the Player of the Year in the California League.[4]

Epstein was *The Sporting News* Minor League Player of the Year in 1966, when he posted a .309 average with 29 home runs and 102 RBIs at Triple-A Rochester. Mark Belanger was the antithesis of Epstein. Belanger came from a hardscrabble background in western Massachusetts. He was a high school star and the definition of an all-field, no-hit shortstop, which was more common in the 1960s than now. That did not stop Harry Dalton from showering praise on him. In February 1967 Harry Dalton said he would "never trade Belanger."[5]

With Dalton heaping praise on his untouchable twosome, it is possible to think as Dalton did: the Orioles had no visible problems coming off their victory in 1966. A closer look does show cracks, however.

On the one hand, the pitching, which had been superlative in the World Series, was still thin, given Wally Bunker's and Steve Barber's injuries. On the other hand, certain players, including Russ Snyder and Andy Etchebarren, had their peak years in 1966. Luis Aparicio and Frank Robinson had aged another year, and there were questions as to whether they could continue to perform at the same level.[6] Dalton was not worried publicly. However, he did not assume they'd keep the pennant just because they had won it the year before: "We're the No. 1 club now and will see the best pitchers and the best efforts from everyone." He then pointed to the Twins, Indians, and White Sox as teams ready to challenge the Orioles.[7] It turned out that Dalton and those covering the Orioles were right to see threats from other teams, thanks to many factors.

The Orioles' problems began in spring training when Jim Palmer developed arm trouble. According to Palmer, his shoulder pain started in 1966 and had not improved over the winter.[8] Then there was the case of Mike Epstein.

With the production he had during those first seasons in the Minors, Epstein felt that he was a lock for a job with the Orioles in 1967. There was only one problem. The Orioles had Boog Powell at first base, and Epstein did not adjust well to the outfield in spring training that year. Largely due to those two factors, when the final roster reduction for Opening Day was made, the Orioles sent Epstein back to Rochester. His response would be a harbinger of Harry Dalton's relations with players as baseball continued to evolve into a sport in which the players had more leverage. Epstein refused to report to Rochester and called Dalton a liar for walking back a supposed promise to trade him if he did not make the big club out of spring training.[9]

Throughout his career, Dalton always tolerated people casting aspersions on his team-building skills. People's opinions on how a GM did something were part of the game, and managers had to have thick skin to survive. One thing Dalton would not allow, however, was someone taking shots at his character. He was thus quick to defend himself against Epstein's attacks. "I'd have been a fool to make a promise like that," he stated. "Mike and I discussed his situation last winter, of course, but what I said was that I wouldn't stymie his career."[10] Ultimately, Dalton agreed to trade Epstein after the 1967 season if he had not been called up to Baltimore. However, this did not placate Epstein, and he did not report to Rochester as the season began.

Finally, as the Orioles got ready to break camp in Miami, Frank Robinson's right knee was balking. Robinson was "confused" when he contemplated why the knee, operated on in the winter of 1966, was giving him trouble. No matter the reason, it put his status in doubt as the season began.[11]

Things did not improve for Harry Dalton and the Orioles as they got to Baltimore. Unlike in 1966, when the team started fast, the defending champs sputtered in April, with an 8-8 record in the first month. May was not much better. Even though Frank Robinson was on pace to win another Triple Crown, the team could not maintain a winning streak. They went .500 in May and lost Jim Palmer for almost a month when he finally gave up battling through the pain in his shoulder following a drubbing in Boston, where he barely made it out of the first inning before being asked to be removed.[12] By mid-May the Orioles were in last place. Harry Dalton tried to arrest the slide by continuing to look for pitching to help his beleaguered club. His efforts to find arms began in early April and would continue all year. He even gave Mike Epstein his wish by trading him in May for Senators lefty Pete Richert.[13]

Ultimately, Dalton was in a no-win situation. When he did not make a move, fans wondered if he was "living off the [Frank] Robinson deal." When he did make deals, fans and writers questioned why he made them.[14] Luckily for the Orioles and their fans, Dalton did not care if the press roasted him. What fans did not realize at the time, and what became apparent throughout his career, was that Harry Dalton could discern when a significant move would help a team in the hunt and when it was best to make smaller moves that would make the team better in the long term. He held by that in 1967, even if it meant taking flak from the uninitiated.

One thing that helped Dalton avoid getting bogged down in the negativity that season was his devotion to his growing family. By the summer of 1967, Harry and Pat had three young daughters. Five-year-old Kim was the oldest. Cindy followed, in September 1965. Finally, Debbie arrived during spring training in 1967. The girls would quickly become the center of his private life. Along the way, Dalton, whom his oldest daughter Kim remembered as being "the perfect father for girls," liked to "trout fish and work in the yard."[15] By his own admission, however, his job did not allow him to do either frequently. Routinely, Dalton's workday stretched from "9 A.M. until midnight when the Orioles are home," and he did not see the girls till breakfast the following day.[16] When he did slide up to the table, the once rail-thin Dalton, who steadily gained weight as he lived on press box buffets and wonderful meals prepared by his wife, flaunted breakfast convention. He liked hamburgers or Italian food for breakfast—whatever Pat had cooked for dinner the night before. It drove Evalyn, his much more conventional mother-in-law, crazy.

Regardless of Evalyn Booker's opinion about his eating habits, she could not deny that her son-in-law loved his family and had reached a point where his work supported them and gave them perks that few got to experience. Harry and Pat both remembered that Harry's job allowed their family to travel. For example, Pat and the girls accompanied Harry to Miami for spring training every year. During one of these trips, Dalton and his family made two unlikely friends they were in a unique position to help, thanks to Harry's celebrity in baseball. These women would quickly become like second mothers to the girls.

When in Miami, the Orioles stayed at the McAllister Hotel. The McAllister, built in the early 1920s, was Miami's first skyscraper, and by the 1950s the three-columned building with boutique shops on the lower floor had become the preferred hotel of the business traveler who wanted to be downtown in Miami.[17] By the 1960s the McAllister, like many hotels in the city, employed many people from the community of Cubans who had flocked to South Florida after Fidel Castro's rise to power. Among those expatriates was Miriam Diaz and her younger sister, Celia.

The story of the Diaz sisters is unique to their time and place. In 1960 Father Bryan O. Walsh of the Catholic Welfare Bureau began a secret operation codenamed Operation Pedro Pan. At its core, Pedro Pan was an agreement of cooperation between the U.S. State Department and Catholic Charities of Miami. After Castro came to power, the operation initially sought to evacuate from the island children whose parents were fighting against him. The effort soon expanded to all Cuban families who wanted to flee out of fear for their future under the new regime. More than fourteen thousand unaccompanied Cuban children between the ages of six and eighteen were sent from the beleaguered island to Miami. The operation began in 1960 and continued until flights between Cuba and the United States ended just before the Cuban Missile Crisis.[18] On board some of the last of the flights, in September 1962, were eighteen-year-old Miriam and eight-year-old Celia.

Less than a year later, Miriam, hired as an elevator operator at the McAllister Hotel, had a chance meeting with Harry Dalton. Dalton and Miriam had numerous conversations, and eventually Miriam, during her breaks, would spend time with Kim Dalton. Ultimately, this relationship would lead to Harry Dalton having a role in reuniting Miriam and Celia with their parents.

In 1965, following the opening of Cuban immigration to the United States by President Lyndon Johnson, the United States began "Freedom Flights," operated with the Cuban government's begrudging blessing. These flights brought Operation Pedro Pan parents from exile in Mexico to Miami to reunite them with their children. As a part of that process, early in 1965 Harry Dalton sent letters on behalf of the Diaz family that showed that Miriam was gainfully employed in the United States and that it was in the best interest of the U.S. government, through the Cuban Refugee Assistance Program, to allow Miriam and Celia to reunite with their parents. This move cemented the Dalton and the Diaz families' relationship when the girls' parents came to the United States in 1965. That led to many cherished, mutual memories. These included Mr. Diaz providing Mrs. Dalton with milk for Cindy and Debbie that came from the supply for the McAllister when Mr. Diaz worked the freight elevator at the hotel beginning in 1966. The Dalton girls began learning Spanish from Miriam and Celia, and Harry Dalton taught Celia how to score a baseball game. All these events helped Harry keep things in perspective as his 1967 season got more difficult by the end of June.[19]

Near the end of that month, Frank Robinson suffered a significant injury that would impair his performance for the rest of the season. Robinson tried to take out Al Weis, the second baseman of the Chicago White Sox, in retaliation for a hard slide on Orioles catcher Andy Etchebarren the night before. Unfortunately for the Orioles, the hard-nosed Robinson missed Weis. Instead, Weis's knee hit Robinson in the eye and knocked him unconscious. Robinson would suffer a concussion, some swelling of the brain, and nerve damage.[20] Most of these aftereffects would dissipate after a few days, but double vision would plague Robinson for the rest of the season. He would be in and out of the lineup for a month and a half.[21] At that point, Harry Dalton would continue trying to help his struggling team. He made a series of smaller trades and called pitching up from the Minor Leagues. Neither helped the Orioles get back into the tightest AL race in recent memory. By the start of August, the Orioles had risen from last place, but their pennant chances were slim as they sat thirteen and a half games behind the Chicago White Sox.

While his team was struggling on the field, Dalton shifted his focus to the future during the team's annual fall meetings, held in mid-September. As in years past, the attendees were the scouting department, the Minor League managers, and the front office staff, and the main goal was to discuss how they could do their jobs better to help the team win. Usually, this meant reshuffling the scouting staff or making a coaching change at the Minor League level. In 1967, however, Dalton felt the best changes were a matter of addition and subtraction. To begin the rebuilding effort, Jim McLaughlin returned to Baltimore after two years away from the game and a successful stint in Cincinnati, where he had helped draft Johnny Bench.

It seemed like an odd move for a team to make after the debacle that ended with McLaughlin's dismissal. But Dalton was now in charge, and above all else he was extremely loyal to those loyal to him. No one fit that bill more than McLaughlin. As noted earlier, Dalton truly felt that he would not have been in baseball if McLaughlin had not taken a chance on him. Therefore, when McLaughlin became available, Dalton jumped at the chance to bring his mentor back into the fold. It is a scenario that Harry Dalton would repeat numerous times over the next thirty years.

As for what Dalton felt McLaughlin could bring to the table, he was hired officially as an assistant to Walter Shannon, who was the scouting director. Specifically, Dalton noted that McLaughlin's duties would be to coordinate the "scouting and negotiations of unsigned baseball free agents—college, high school, and amateur prospects."[22] This specialization of roles was necessary because Dalton understood that the game was changing, and he had to change with it. As he had when he took over for Lee MacPhail, Dalton understood that one man could not run the whole scouting department. In this case, as Dalton pointed out at the time, he rehired McLaughlin because "free-agent scouting is more complex today than ever as the competition for talent increases."[23]

McLaughlin's rehiring occurred on the first night of the organizational meetings and was the team's most extensive development move that year. However, Dalton used the meetings that year to set in motion something that would reshape his team for years to come.

All season the Orioles had struggled to hit their stride, and by September the team was floundering. While injuries and down years accounted for this, Dalton was not convinced that there was not an underlying issue centered in his dugout. Dalton dispatched Jimmy Russo to assess the Orioles. Russo's final appraisal was that the coaching staff was a large part of the problem. The result was that on September 28 Dalton, with the blessing of Hoffberger and Cashen, fired three of four coaches on Hank Bauer's staff.

Let go were pitching coach Harry Brecheen, bullpen coach Sherm Lollar, and first base/hitting coach Gene Woodling. As for why Dalton decided to fire most of the coaching staff even though he did not hold the coaches "responsible for the Orioles' current plight," he felt that he could "help the performance of the ball club by making these changes."[24] In their places were three of Dalton's trusted lieutenants. Earl Weaver took over at first base after guiding Rochester to the top of the International League despite Dalton calling up a large part of his pitching staff. Like Weaver, the new pitching coach, George Bamberger, had strong ties to the Orioles and had served as the team's Minor League pitching instructor the previous four seasons. He had also pitched for the team when the Orioles first came to Baltimore. Finally, Earl Hoscheit, who had served as a scout for Dalton in the Midwest after numerous seasons as a field manager and coach in the Minors for various teams, took over as the bullpen coach after the season ended in October.

The one change that Dalton did not make was firing Hank Bauer. Being retained as manager did not mean that Bauer felt safe in his position. With Earl Weaver seemingly waiting in the wings to manage at the Major League level, Bauer understood the pressure was on for him to perform better. To that end, the former marine, who had seen combat in places like the New Georgia Islands and Okinawa and had twice been awarded the Purple Heart after suffering injuries in combat, vowed to be more rigid in 1968.[25]

The team that Bauer would shower his toughness upon continued to evolve thanks to Harry Dalton and his gang's work. That year, baseball held winter meetings in Mexico City, and the Orioles were the major players. Dalton made his big, tough move on November 29, when he traded Luis Aparicio back to the Chicago White Sox, along with Russ Snyder and Minor League fixture John Matias, for starting pitcher Bruce Howard and utility player Don Buford. Dalton later commented that the Orioles' goals at the meeting had been to upgrade the pitching staff and the bullpen and to obtain a utility player.

This move immediately strengthened the Orioles for 1968 by accomplishing two things. First, it opened a spot for shortstop Mark Belanger. Utility player Buford was a two-sport star at USC, playing for the legendary Rod Dedeaux in baseball and starting as a two-way star on the football field on some less-than-stellar Trojans teams.[26] The White Sox had signed Buford in 1960, and he rewarded their faith by showing surprising power as he played his first full season in the Majors in 1964. Still, by the winter of 1968, Buford had struggled enough at the plate and in the field that he was available to Baltimore. While the media saw him as a throw-in, Dalton quickly sized him up as a possibly essential member of the team because he would be able to "add pinch-hitting strength from both sides and be able to give [Davey] Johnson and [Brooks] Robinson rest periods as well as play in the outfield."[27]

A month after the MLB winter meetings and just before Christmas, Dalton and his wife went to Puerto Rico. This time, he was off to watch a contingent of Orioles, managed by Earl Weaver, play for Santurce in the Puerto Rican Winter League. The Santurce connection for the Orioles had begun in the winter of 1966. At that time, Weaver managed the Santurce Crabbers, and Harry Dalton took the opportunity to develop a working agreement with the perennial title contender. The Santurce GM, Hiram Cuevas, would remember Harry Dalton fondly and see the deal as mutually beneficial to both teams. "We [Cuevas and Dalton] had good chemistry and developed a good friendship," he said. "Every player under Dalton had first refusal to play in Puerto Rico, and my friendship with Harry never interfered with the business aspects [of running Santurce]."[28] What Dalton got for the Orioles was a way to judge how far along his players were in their development against some of the top talent in baseball and determine if they could help the Orioles. This relationship was highly beneficial in the lead-up to 1968, when Dalton got a look at Elrod "Ellie" Hendricks.

By 1968 Hendricks, born on St. Thomas in the U.S. Virgin Islands, was a journeyman player. He had initially signed a contract with the Milwaukee Braves in 1959 at age eighteen. After playing two years for the Braves in their Minor League system, Hendricks was released in December 1960 and spent 1961 out of organized baseball. He was still playing winter ball in Puerto Rico, however. At this time, playing for Santurce, he caught the eye of scouts for the St. Louis Cardinals. This time, Hendricks would play parts of two seasons before being let go by the Cardinals. Once again, he took comfort in playing for Santurce as he tried to figure out his next step.

That step would lead to Mexico, where Hendricks would play the best part of Jalisco's 1965–67 seasons and put up substantial power numbers. At that time, the California Angels, who had come into Major League Baseball in 1961, had a working agreement with Jalisco and would end up shuffling Hendricks between Jalisco and their stateside Double-A and Triple-A teams. Once again, Hendricks could not make a go of it north of the border; he appeared in only thirty-one games over those two seasons in the Double-A Texas League and Triple-A Pacific Coast League. Despite this inability to stick, Hendricks would return to Santurce every winter. There, he caught the attention of Earl Weaver, who used Hendricks as a hard-hitting backup catcher as Santurce won the pennant in the winter of 1966–67. Weaver was so impressed by Hendricks, now in his midtwenties, that he forwarded a recommendation to Harry Dalton. Frank Lane, Dalton's special assistant, agreed that the Orioles should pick up Hendricks in the Rule 5 draft at the winter meetings in Mexico City.[29]

The move to get another catcher might seem odd, given that Dalton was still a fan of Andy Etchebarren and would remain so for the whole of Etchebarren's career. However, Harry Dalton never let personal relationships get in the way of building a better team. Because of Hendricks's perceived ability to hit, and hit for power, Dalton and his brain trust were more than willing to give him a look in spring training ahead of the 1968 season.

Before Dalton fully turned his mind to building his team, however, he was asked to lend his intellect again to the larger baseball community. This time, the league drafted Dalton to help define how expansion teams in Seattle and Kansas City, set to start playing in 1969, would stock their teams during the expansion draft scheduled for mid-October 1968. This work was necessary because the American League clubs wanted to "give the new expansion clubs better representative teams at the start than was the case in 1961 when the new Washington and California clubs were stocked with players."[30]

To meet their goal, Dalton, Lee MacPhail, Minnesota Twins owner Calvin Griffith, and GM Jim Campbell of the Detroit Tigers devised a plan in which teams were allowed to protect fifteen players from their forty-man roster. Fifteen players was a reduction from the twenty-five allowed in 1961. As Dalton noted, he and his cohorts understood that under this plan "the clubs will lose players they won't want to lose," but to Dalton, the reason for using fifteen as the maximum number of protected players was a simple matter of mathematics: "Under the old plan, the expansion clubs theoretically got the twenty-sixth best, twenty-seventh, twenty-eighth, twenty-ninth, thirtieth, and thirty-first."[31] By Dalton's calculations, this time Seattle and Kansas City would be able to get the sixteenth, twentieth, twenty-fourth, twenty-eighth, thirty-second, and thirty-sixth best players. Each club would also get five picks in the Minor League portion of the Rule 5 draft and two picks in the amateur draft.

Dalton quickly pointed out that while this might seem like a lot for the existing teams to give up, the drafting teams would monetarily compensate the league teams to help offset talent loss. Specifically, each Major League pick would cost $175,000, and each player selected in the Minor League Rule 5 draft would cost $25,000. Dalton hoped this stipulation would allow the existing teams to restock their numbers to improve the whole league. Reinforcing the existing teams was important because as Dalton, who always understood the larger picture of his work, noted, "A league is only as strong as its weakest club."[32]

With the expansion draft finished in February, Dalton could turn his attention back to his squad. It was perfect timing. Spring training was right around the corner, and Dalton had a few significant issues to consider before his team went to Miami.

The first was which nonroster players from their system the team would invite to Major League camp. As the roster took shape, the Dalton Gang was willing to look seriously at five other rookies besides Hendricks. This group included outfielders Curt Motton, Merv Rettenmund, Dave May, Cuban-born utility infielder Chico Fernandez, and pitcher Roger Nelson (who was traded to Baltimore for Aparicio with Don Buford). Dalton and his gang believed that looking at that many rookies was a gamble worth taking because many of the big pieces to the Orioles puzzle were still in place—if Dalton could get these veterans signed.

As the winter wore on, of crucial concern was shortstop Davey Johnson's status, the "cannons" of Frank Robinson and Boog Powell, and outfielder Curt Blefary. In Boog Powell's case, the critical question was whether Dalton would push for a pay cut following Powell's lackluster 1967. At the heart of Dalton's thought process was Powell's inability to control his weight.

According to Powell, his weight had been a point of contention between him and Dalton for most of his time in the Majors and an especially sore spot during spring training of 1965; Powell tipped the scales at over 260 pounds at one point. Powell remembered that this led the club to make him start a weight loss program. Ultimately, he missed his target by a half pound. This perceived failure caused Dalton to levy a fine on the big Floridian. Powell's response was to throw five dollars at Dalton's feet to protest the fine before walking away in silence.[33]

In the winter of 1968, Powell's weight was again a concern for the Orioles, and Dalton told him to report to camp at 240.[34] Along the way, Dalton reminded the slugger how much his weight influenced his performance and affected his pocketbook. Dalton forced Powell to sign a contract for 1968 for a marginal pay cut—around $5,000 less than the $42,000 he made the year before.[35]

With Powell's experience fresh in the reader's mind, this is an excellent time to discuss Harry Dalton's negotiating style. With the reserve clause in place in the 1960s and early 1970s, it would be easy to assume that Harry Dalton negotiated with players at that time much as his contemporaries did. This would mean that he tried to keep salaries down and accomplished this goal by inflating players' failures and downplaying their successes. However, the fact that Dalton wanted a pay cut for Powell should not indicate that Dalton was looking to hold down player salaries as a rule. Dalton did not feel that his primary job was to argue that a player did not have a good year when he obviously did. Over the years, numerous players would point out that they always felt Harry Dalton was fair when negotiating with players, and a few thought he was downright generous compared to others with whom they had worked.[36] They all said that he treated them as more than a commodity. That did not mean that he was quick to part with the owner's money. One good example was the case of Brooks Robinson.

When asked in 2018 about his relationship with Dalton, Brooks Robinson would remember that he considered Dalton a "terrific guy"; however, he and Dalton "always had a little bit of an adversarial relationship. He was trying to keep the budget down, and I was always trying to get paid more. . . . We did not see eye to eye on everything. One year I held out for an extra $500. I was in Florida, and I went a whole week without signing. He told me to stop by to see him after batting practice in Miami. I said, 'Harry, I want $500 more.' He said he was going to leave the office for about 10 minutes and I should contemplate [*sic*] about it. When he came back, I told him, 'Harry, it's plain and simple. I want $500 more.' He said that he'd give me that $500, but I better remember how I took advantage of him for $500 next year when it can time to negotiate."[37]

In the spring of 1968, Frank Robinson, Davey Johnson, and Curt Blefary used the same tactic with Dalton, though the amounts they demanded were drastically different. As camp opened, Blefary wanted a "considerable boost" over the estimated $20,000 he earned in 1967. Meanwhile, Johnson wanted a "token $2,000 raise" on an estimated salary of $14,000.[38] Both men succeeded to some degree; Blefary received a "fair and decent raise" of $5,000 on his estimated salary of $20,000, and Johnson got twice what he asked for when Dalton raised his salary to $18,000.[39] Then there was Frank Robinson.

In Robinson's case, both Dalton and Robinson told the media they were willing to come to an agreement. It was just a matter of finding the number that both men could live with. Dalton tried to placate Robinson with another year at $100,000. He felt that maintaining that salary level was reasonable since the slugger had missed so much time the year before.[40] Robinson quickly rejected this status quo offer, stating that if the Orioles were going to be "ridiculous," so could he. Robinson then asked for $150,000 for 1968.[41] This stalemate persisted for most of the winter. Eventually, as spring training opened in Miami, Robinson came down to $120,000, and Harry Dalton came up to $110,000. It looked like both sides were at an impasse. Robinson even hinted that he might return to California.[42] Finally, on March 7, Dalton and Robinson agreed on a $115,000 deal that, in Dalton's words, made Robinson one of the highest-paid players in baseball history at that time.[43]

With Frank Robinson signed, attention turned to the action on the training fields and dugouts in Miami. Early in camp, Earl Weaver regularly led a team of second teamers over the starters. Weaver's performance fueled speculation by fans as to if or when he would replace Hank Bauer. However, as longtime sportswriter Bob Maisel pointed out in the *Baltimore Sun* late in spring training, Weaver had been a model citizen who had worked as hard as anyone to reinforce Bauer's message, and there was no friction between the two men.[44] This single-mindedness led to a productive camp, leaving Harry Dalton hopeful for a strong finish.

The day before the Orioles left Miami, Dalton told *Sun* staff that the Orioles could not be counted out despite any perceived shortcomings. Dalton, who would always value pitching depth, felt that despite not having a twenty-game-winner on the pitching staff in 1967 and injuries to Dave McNally and Jim Palmer in the lead-up to 1968, the Orioles had enough arms to compete. "Last year, [Tom] Phoebus had a 14-9 record on a sixth-place club," a local sportswriter noted.[45] Bauer led his birds north at the beginning of April with a brief stop in Atlanta for an exhibition series with the Braves. It would quickly replace any good feeling for the Orioles, and the country soon plunged into one of the most tumultuous periods in its history.

The Orioles arrived in Atlanta during the late afternoon of April 4. The plan was to play Friday night (April 5), Saturday night (April 6), and Sunday afternoon (April 7), before returning home for Opening Day on April 9.[46] That plan was thrown into chaos shortly after the Orioles arrived with the Dalton family in tow.

Four hundred miles away in Memphis, Tennessee, the Reverend Martin Luther King Jr. was preparing to attend a dinner in his honor at a local minister's home. He was in Memphis to participate in a peaceful protest in solidarity with striking Black sanitation workers. At 5:55 p.m. local time, King stepped onto the balcony in front of his room at the Lorraine Motel to take in the heat of the escaping day. Six minutes later, a gunshot rang out, and King was severely wounded. One hour later, King was pronounced dead. The news quickly spread throughout the country.[47]

In Atlanta, King's hometown, officials began to prepare for the city's reaction. Meanwhile, the Orioles brass and the hotel quickly put the team and their guests on what Pat Dalton would describe fifty years later as "lockdown." With three small children to entertain, Pat Dalton made her way to the hotel lobby with the kids. There, Harry Belafonte, who was also staying in the hotel, helped Pat with six-year-old Kim, three-year-old Cindy, and one-year-old Debbie.

The next few days passed fitfully. Officials canceled the game on the night of the fifth due to bad weather and fear of civil unrest.[48] The next night, the Orioles would win 4–3 on a Mark Belanger home run. However, sports quickly became eclipsed by crisis. By the morning of the sixth, riots had erupted in cities throughout America. The Orioles and Braves canceled their game for that day. Also, Pete Richert was lost to the team when the Department of Defense federalized his Maryland National Guard unit before deploying it to Washington DC. Officials hoped that the Sunday game could be played. That turned out to be wishful thinking. As riots continued in cities all over the country, the situation became more tenuous and the priority of sports was lost. Not without controversy, however. As baseball historian Paul Hensler notes, the commissioner's office response to King's death was rudimentary and "awkward."[49] Ultimately, it was up to the teams to decide if they would postpone the start of the season. This lack of institutional direction made a challenging situation even more chaotic, and pundits throughout the country wondered if Commissioner Eckert was the right man to lead baseball.[50]

Baltimore faced more significant issues as things worsened on April 6. Riots began a little after five that evening when white merchants, fearing for their businesses, opened fire on Robert Bradby, who was leaving a bar on North Gay Street on the east side of the city. At first, Bradby had nothing to do with a growing crowd up the street from the bar. However, in response to the gunfire, Bradby, who was Black, threw a Molotov cocktail through a house window. He then migrated with the growing crowd farther down Gay Street, where the rioters burned down two furniture stores three blocks from the initial incident. The riots quickly spread, and a state of emergency was declared in Baltimore by 8:00 p.m.[51]

The riots would continue all through the next day. The Orioles' departure from Atlanta was in serious jeopardy. Once again, Pat Dalton faced safeguarding her children in a highly complicated and fluid situation. The Orioles were finally escorted to the airport in Atlanta at midnight on April 8. The Orioles took off without incident shortly after that. Once in the air, they were confronted by a very surreal situation.

Don Buford remembered the mood among players, especially the Black contingent of the Orioles, being very somber. The team was already unified in terms of race relations and was the antithesis of the city of Baltimore, where racial tensions had flared for decades.[52] With the Orioles, the color of someone's skin did not matter. Everyone, white or Black, wanted to win. Buford said that this extended to Harry Dalton, who viewed players only in terms of ability. Because of that, players of both races respected Dalton. Thus, because they could play together, they could also mourn together and stay unified despite the more significant issues at play in their city.[53]

Meanwhile, Pat Dalton tried to keep the girls entertained and on their best behavior as the Orioles headed toward an unknown situation back home. Fifty years later, she remembered that she had two things in her favor. First, the girls adored Brooks Robinson, and he would help her with the kids—especially Debbie, who was a year old—during the flight. Once Pat had the girls settled, she began to take stock of the situation. She could see fires on the ground from other riots all the way back to Baltimore. That visual proof of widespread unrest led to a certain degree of uncertainty and trepidation. One of the biggest fears was making it home from Memorial Stadium without coming in contact with the riots. Ultimately, there was only one way around that. The team would be bused home with a police escort, and they would pick up their cars the following day. Finally, at 4:00 a.m. on April 9, once Harry had seen that all the players were home safe, the Daltons were the last ones off the bus at their home. Spring training had officially ended.[54]

The city the Daltons returned to was in turmoil. On April 7 Governor Spiro Agnew went as far as to tell President Lyndon Johnson that Baltimore was the site of an "insurrection." In response, the president authorized the XVIII Airborne Corps (the parent organization of the Eighty-Second Airborne Division) to deploy elements to the city, resulting in 1,900 paratroopers patrolling the city. The total grew to 3,400 on April 9.[55]

Meanwhile, the Orioles attempted to turn their minds to baseball. As of the morning of April 9, the scheduled home opener against Oakland, on tap for the next day, was still in doubt due to conditions in Baltimore.[56] Beyond that, Harry Dalton scrambled to fill holes in his roster that arose as a result of the riots and the war raging in Vietnam.

By the summer of 1968, the war (and the draft that was a part of it) was nothing new. The United States had had American troops in combat roles in Vietnam since 1965, and draft quotas grew with each passing day. Baseball was not immune to the impact of the war. Historian Paul Hensler skillfully points out that one of the biggest jobs of the GMs of the era was staying up to date on the draft status of every man in the Minors and Majors.[57] Dalton was no different in that regard. Like his counterparts in other cities, Dalton had to take a different approach to team building because of the war.

Dalton's best hope was to get his Major League players assigned to National Guard or Army Reserve units to serve their time without deploying to Southeast Asia. It is important to note that Dalton did not see what he was doing as circumnavigating the system. While his thoughts on Vietnam do not survive, anecdotal evidence shows that Harry Dalton firmly believed that if players and front office staff were drafted, they should serve their time in some fashion. However, he was not above working the system, as many of his cohorts did. A prime example of this is Hall of Fame executive John Schuerholz's case, which played out in the spring and summer of 1966.

Schuerholz was born and raised in the Baltimore area and went to the State Teachers College at Towson, where he starred on the baseball team. After graduating, he failed the Marine Corps Officer Candidate School physical and had a somewhat sobering tryout for the Orioles that ended with him helping Walter Youse track sixty-yard-dash times instead of playing. Schuerholz then took a job as a teacher in the Baltimore school system. The school system paid well, but he quickly realized he did not want to make teaching a career. In a move reminiscent of Harry Dalton's early effort, he sent a letter to the Orioles that eventually landed on Frank Cashen's desk. Cashen remembered Schuerholz as being from the "good stock" of a local family, and he forwarded the letter to Lou Gorman, the new farm director. Gorman met with Schuerholz and quickly hired him as his assistant in time for the 1966 season. To Schuerholz, it seemed like a dream fulfilled. There was only one problem. When he left his teaching job, which earned him a draft deferment, his former employer informed Schuerholz's draft board that he was now available for the draft. Soon a notice arrived in the mail stating that he should report for a pre-induction physical.

Schuerholz was not too worried. He had failed his Marine Corps physical because of significant hearing loss in one ear. At the time, that was enough to keep him out of the service. However, when he went before the army medical board, he got a rude awakening. The climate had changed. The army told Schuerholz that he would be classified 1A and should be prepared to be drafted. This looming eventuality led to a discussion with Lou Gorman about his options. Gorman then set up a meeting between Schuerholz and Dalton in the early part of the season in 1966. Dalton quickly told him that while he could not, nor would he, get Schuerholz out of the army completely, the Orioles saw promise in Schuerholz. As such, Dalton told Schuerholz that Dalton would contact the team's source within Army Reserve hierarchy and get Schuerholz assigned a stateside billet. Consequently, he spent his time in the summer of 1966 at Fort Knox, Kentucky, and then in Maryland instead of on active duty in Vietnam.[58]

In 1968 similar arrangements saw the Orioles lose pitcher Pete Richert and second baseman Mark Belanger when the government federalized their respective units for riot control duty in Washington.[59] Catcher Larry Haney and outfielder Paul Blair were also possibly slated for a call-up to federal service. When asked about this in the press, Harry Dalton quickly pointed out that federalization was a fact of life for teams. "Anytime a man is a member of such a unit, he is always subject to recall to active duty," he noted.[60] In the end, neither Blair nor Haney, who was out of the Opening Day lineup thanks to two broken fingers, was called up, and the season finally began on April 10.

When the season got underway, the Orioles showed early signs of life. They would go 10-6 in April and follow that up with a 16-13 record in May. They would even climb into first place for a short time at the beginning of the month. By June most of that early bloom had wilted. The team scuffled and suffered their first losing month. Meanwhile, Harry Dalton again showed his humanistic side to the world when Senator Robert F. Kennedy, a Democratic presidential candidate, was shot in the Ambassador Hotel's kitchen in Los Angeles following his win in the California presidential primary. He would die shortly after midnight on June 6, 1968. That night, while preparing for the amateur draft, Dalton talked with United Press International (UPI) syndicated columnist Milt Richman. The call was supposed to be about Dalton's plans for the upcoming draft, but it quickly evolved into a conversation that showed that Dalton thought more than baseball.

Dalton confided to Richman that, like many people affected by the tragedy, he could work during the day without too much interference. At night, however, his mind would turn to the larger world. Dalton summed his thoughts up this way: Kennedy's death, which worried his mind and put "fear in his features," was more than "terrible." Dalton wondered aloud if America had lost its collective sanity in 1968. "My God, please tell me what on earth is happening to us all?" he mused. "Has everyone lost his simple sense of common decency?" Dalton's thoughts then turned to his family and how the world events might affect it.[61]

"I'm telling you, when my wife and I got up this morning and heard what happened, both of us were sick. . . . I have a little girl who's going to be six in July. . . . She's my oldest, and I love her dearly, the same way I do my others. . . . But what's going to happen to them? Where if you don't necessarily agree with what someone says, you go out and get a gun and kill him?"

This sort of introspection was not uncommon for Dalton. He would always be known as a man who thought about more than his job. Baseball was but one of his passions. To be sure, it was his strongest passion outside of his own family, but it was only part of him. What shocked Richman and another friend of Dalton, who was part of the conversation, was that in this instance Dalton could not take even a small amount of solace in his job. When the friend mentioned that despite the day's events, Dalton's Orioles had won the night before (a 7–1 home win over the California Angels), a dejected Dalton replied, "Who cares?" This shocked the friend. "You mean you're not happy about winning the ball game?" Dalton replied quickly and in the authoritative way that was familiar to his daughters and those who knew him well: "Not really. Nobody won today. We all lost."

On the field, Dalton's team continued to be inconsistent. After winning the night Kennedy was shot, the Orioles would lose their next three games, including both ends of a doubleheader to Oakland on Friday, June 7. They would reel off three wins before dropping four more games, including both ends of another doubleheader to Oakland on June 16. Along the way, the Vietnam War forced Dalton to consider again how to shuffle his roster. While they had been fortunate enough to avoid active service in the April domestic unrest, Paul Blair and Larry Haney had been alerted that their units were going on active duty. Of the two, Blair, considered by some to be the best defensive center fielder in the American League, was the more significant loss.[62] This possibility forced Dalton and his gang to consider how best to fill the potential void.

Dalton thought Baltimore had three options: to seek a trade for a veteran center fielder, promote an outfielder from the Orioles' Minor

League system, or play rookie Dave May, who was already on the roster and could slot into center. Dalton was quick to point out that because of May's struggles (.141 average) and an unwillingness for other teams to give up what Dalton felt was a viable replacement, the best option was to promote Merv Rettenmund from Triple-A Rochester, where he was as a valuable lead-off hitter.[63]

In the end, the Orioles split the difference. On June 15 Dalton did make a trade for an outfielder when he sent underperforming pitcher Bruce Howard to Washington for outfielder Fred Valentine. They still planned to call up Merv Rettenmund if Blair went on active duty. Despite attempting to hedge his bets this way, Dalton had to defend himself and his trading philosophy. This time, fans balked that Dalton had traded away a pitcher for whom he had seemingly paid a premium (Luis Aparicio) for a less than ideal fill-in for Blair. Dalton was quick to say that he was not in the business of holding onto a player to save face.

"I told Hank [Bauer] in Spring Training, look, just because we gave up Luis to get this fellow, don't feel like you have to force him into the rotation. . . . If he doesn't do the job you want, we'll try something else," Dalton said. Furthermore, he argued, "why should I hold on to him [Howard] in hopes that he will eventually come around and make the deal look better?" He recognized that "any time you make deals, you're going to make some good ones and some bad ones. You just hope the good outnumber the bad." The key to any trade, Dalton said, was that "once you make a trade, you have to forget it and evaluate things as they are the next time a problem arises."[64] This was also the case when Dalton evaluated the effectiveness of his managers. He proved this in July.

As the All-Star break approached, the Orioles were above .500. However, despite being in a better place record-wise than in 1967, Dalton felt something was not quite right with his team. In his mind, the problems started with Hank Bauer. "Hank was sort of a laissez-faire manager," he said.[65] In Dalton's mind, this lackadaisical, hands-off approach was detrimental to the team's overall performance. Dalton thus resorted to the most drastic measure in his team-building tool kit. At the All-Star break, with the Orioles ten games back of first in the standings, Dalton fired Bauer.

As Bauer recalled, "When they made the change, I was at home in Kansas City, and Dalton called me from the airport. He asked me if I was going to be home because he was coming out. I hung up and told my wife I was getting fired." From there, Bauer recalled that the situation was even tenser. "He comes in a cab and tells the driver to keep the meter running. That is a bad sign. I offer him a beer; he takes a sip and tells me they are going to make a change."[66]

Dalton would remember that he loved Hank Bauer as a person, and he hated having to fire him.[67] Much like with players, however, Dalton was not sentimental when it came to managers. As noted before, Dalton wanted to win and would put the best person in the position to help his club do that. In this case, that person, to no one's surprise, was Earl Weaver.

As Weaver recalled many years later, there was a cloak-and-dagger element to his hiring. Right after Dalton called Bauer to tell him he was on his way, his next call was to Weaver. "The first day of the All-Star break," Weaver remembered being at the pool with his wife, Marianna, "enjoying ourselves, and from the front office of this complex, they came out and said you got to go home, you have a very important phone call."[68] Worried that it may be someone calling about the death of one of his parents, Weaver ran home, where he spoke on the phone with Dalton. He recalled that "Harry Dalton told me, tonight, you go check in to some hotel or motel, get out of your apartment, take Marianna with you, and register as Earl Sidney, because you're going to be my major league manager."[69]

From there, Dalton flew in to see Weaver, and the two set about discussing his deal's particulars. As Weaver recalled, even though Dalton wanted him, making a deal was not as easy as one would have anticipated. Weaver recalled that Dalton would only go up to a certain amount of salary, "which didn't seem fair to me." This became especially true when Dalton told Weaver that he would have to give up managing Santurce in the winter. This revelation drove Weaver to push for a raise: "I really supplemented my pay by managing in Puerto Rico. . . . He [Dalton] didn't want me to do that. So, I said, Harry, come on now, we got to have something here. . . . So Harry was fair finally, and we agreed."[70]

That agreement would change the course of baseball history. Before that occurred, however, Dalton had to introduce Weaver and deal with any potential fallout. For Dalton the father, this meant going as far as alerting the Baltimore police just in case angry fans took their allegiance to Bauer too far and came after Dalton's family.

Weaver's introduction occurred in Baltimore on July 11, 1968. At that time, Dalton reiterated that he was making the change because "at this time, a change was in order to pick up the performance of the ball club."[71] He would elaborate later, saying he did not fire Bauer due to one specific incident during his tenure. Instead, Dalton felt that Bauer's biggest drawback was that he allowed a general malaise to settle in.

"We felt that even though we are six games over .500 right now—we felt we could be, or should be, playing better," Dalton said. "The club just has seemed to us to be more of a sputtering ball club than a forward-driving ball club. We feel the talent is here for it to be an aggressive, winning ball club. Sitting down at the All-Star Break after a half-season, reviewing everything, I felt a change was in order."[72]

Dalton's belief that the Orioles could be more aggressive was one of the reasons for hiring the fiery Weaver. "I think Earl Weaver is a winner—he has been a winner wherever he has gone," Dalton said. "He is aggressive. . . . He is a battler for his team, a battler for his organization, and a battler for what he thinks is right in running a ball club."[73] Years later, Dalton would take his evaluation of Weaver a step further: "He has a quick mind. His organizational abilities and his knack for understanding statistics are outstanding. He is not afraid to make a decision and sticks with it. He has plenty of guts and can get the most out of any baseball team."[74] These things aligned Weaver with Harry Dalton and guaranteed that the two men could work together. As for how that relationship would look, Dalton quickly pointed out that while he and Weaver would discuss the makeup of the team's roster, how to manage it would fall to Weaver. The dividend of that working agreement was a winning record for the rest of 1968.

The Orioles would go 48-34 with Weaver at the helm, and he would work with Dalton to shake up the team by shuffling the roster. On a day-to-day basis, Don Buford and Elrod Hendricks would earn more playing time. Of course, this had ramifications. The player most affected was Curt Blefary. After his Rookie of the Year campaign in 1965, Blefary had two productive years from 1966 to 1967. However, in 1968 Blefary struggled as he served in a utility role that saw him play four different positions, including spots in the outfield and catcher. These struggles along with Blair's and Hendricks's difficulties on the field led Weaver to sit Blefary for long stretches during the second half of the season. Blefary finally voiced his displeasure in September.

Ultimately, Blefary blamed Weaver, stating that the new manager would not play him at a set position, preferably in the outfield. He then announced that the outfield was the only spot he would play in 1969.[75] Weaver responded at the end of the season by noting that Blefary would "have to earn" a spot in the outfield. This proclamation caused more tension between the two men. Blefary called out Weaver again and questioned how the organization was using him. This was the final straw in the strained relationship. The Orioles quickly branded Blefary a clubhouse cancer and sought to trade him.[76] Harry Dalton succeeded during the winter meetings of 1968. In exchange for Blefary, Dalton picked up Cuban-born, screwball-throwing Mike Cuellar from the Houston Astros.[77]

With that addition in December, the team's core was in place on and off the field. This allowed Harry Dalton to take a much-needed vacation with his family. While he was gone, events in New York ushered in the potential to change Harry Dalton's career, much as had been the case when Lee MacPhail left Baltimore.

By the time of the winter meetings in San Francisco, the Major League owners had had enough of Commissioner William Eckert. Although they had given the baseball neophyte two years and plenty of opportunities to learn his job, not to mention the help of people like Lee MacPhail, Eckert never grew into the role. Oftentimes he left the owners with egg on their faces after a public debacle. His ineffectual leadership after the assassinations of Martin Luther King and Robert F. Kennedy did not help his position, nor did his response to the increasing role organized labor was playing in the game. In early 1968 he took a lukewarm stance when the players successfully fought for collective bargaining through their burgeoning negotiating arm, the Major League Baseball Players Association (MLBPA). He then compounded the difficulties by ruling in favor of the players in various cases in which he acted as the arbitrator during negotiations between the players and management.[78] Many felt that Eckert then put the final nail in his coffin when he was again seen as a friend of labor after American League president Joe Cronin fired two umpires for attempting to start an umpires' union and when Eckert was sympathetic to the pleas of the on-field adjudicators.

The result was Eckert's dismissal immediately after the winter meetings, while the owners were still ensconced in San Francisco. In a bizarre press statement handled by Eckert himself, the owners officially announced that he had resigned. Evidence suggests this is a misrepresentation; the owners had fired Eckert. When the press asked why they let Eckert go, the owners quickly downplayed any issues they may have had with Eckert. Instead, they pointed out that baseball needed a younger face and someone raised in the game to lead it. The primary reason was that ownership felt that the changing nature of the country's demographics warranted such a move. While this is mostly an excuse and code for someone whom ownership could manipulate, there was some justification for it. Eckert proved during the unrest of 1968 that he was from a different era. He struggled to manage a game dealing with many off-field issues, including race and labor relations and a growing group of players who did not mind speaking up for what they felt was right for them and other Americans. The question became: Who was that face? Many believed it was Harry Dalton.

For starters, Dalton was young. He had just turned forty in the summer of 1968. Moreover, despite his relative youth, 1968 was already his fifteenth year in the game. Finally, he was more and more of a celebrity who spoke for the game and who understood the hot-button issues that fans, players, and, perhaps most importantly, ownership saw as those that could influence the game going forward.

As was noted earlier, Dalton had already taken on the length of the schedule in 1966. He was also a member of several committees that helped shape the game's future on the field. This included working on potential rule changes and specifications for the use of artificial turf, and Dalton was always a proponent of a robust Minor League system, as well as allowing fans to vote for All-Star teams. This work endeared him to fans and media members who felt that baseball needed to embrace its past and plan for the future.

Dalton also managed to gain admirers among the ownership and within the clubhouse. From an ownership perspective, he was an excellent voice for what the owners saw as important. As illustrated by his championing of stronger player selection criteria during expansion, he understood that a strong product, in which all the teams were competitive, benefited the whole league and could drive up profits. He tried to keep player salaries down when he could. He also believed that players should exercise a degree of personal decorum (for example, the discussion of short versus long hair). Most importantly, he was leery of the rising power of the MLBPA. On the other hand, players respected Dalton because, as illustrated, he understood that players had concerns outside of baseball. War was on their mind. So were race relations and financial freedom. To them, Dalton understood that managing these issues was just as important as teaching them the correct way to cover first base or bunt a runner over.

The ability to move seamlessly among these three symbiotic, yet differently motivated groups made Dalton special in many eyes. UPI columnist Milt Richman best summed up this argument two weeks after Eckert's "firing by resignation." In his nationally syndicated column, Richman compared Dalton to the NFL's young commissioner Pete Rozelle (who was two years older than Dalton); he was getting loads of positive press due to his youthful approach to managing the league, which was quickly threatening baseball as the perceived national pastime. Moreover, Richman argued that Dalton could accomplish the challenging goal of being accepted by American and National League owners, and to that end he commented that National League members saw Dalton as "not having a speck of bias."[79]

Whatever qualities made Dalton a possible replacement for Eckert, in the end there is no evidence to suggest that the owners followed up with Dalton. Moreover, Pat Dalton was quick to note that Dalton would not have sought the position because of his love for the day-to-day work of building a team and competing.[80] The owners ultimately selected a young lawyer who had done work for the National League. His name was Bowie Kuhn, and he served as the commissioner until 1984.

As for Dalton, he continued to drive to make the Orioles the best team in baseball, and that is what they would become in very short order. At the heart of that success was an approach known universally as the "Oriole Way." What the Oriole Way encompassed or who the architect was is a hotly debated topic. What should not be debated is that Harry Dalton was a large part of the Oriole Way and its success.

8

The Best Team in Baseball

1969–71

When Harry Dalton hired Earl Weaver, he hoped the fiery, cerebral manager would give his team a spark that Dalton felt Hank Bauer did not provide. The reality was that Weaver was the final piece that would transform the Orioles into the best team in baseball from 1969 to 1971 and one of the greatest in baseball history. What made them so good? That is a question that reporters and scholars have asked for over fifty years. Was the team's success thanks to the skill of men like Harry Dalton and his gang in acquiring raw amateurs and molding them into professional talent? Was it the internal fire and no-holds-barred mentality of Earl Weaver that would not allow his teams to lose? Was it great coaching from the likes of George Bamberger that provided the foundation? Everyone has theories. The answer lies at the intersection of all three.

At the heart of the Orioles' success was the group of players whom Dalton had helped acquire after he came on board with the team. Individually, they were the best players in the league, having some of their best seasons during the period of Dalton's leadership of the scouting team.

The two Robinsons and Boog Powell were at the heart of the offensive attack. From 1969 to 1971, Frank Robinson would average 28 homers and 92 RBIs and twice finish in the top three in the MVP voting. Meanwhile, Powell would average 31 home runs and over 100 RBIs during the same stretch and win the 1971 MVP.[1] As for Brooks Robinson, he was his usual steady self. During the Orioles' period of dominance, he would hit .261 with 20 homers and 90 RBIs.[2] Around this core, Don Buford, Paul Blair, and newcomers like Merv Rettenmund would contribute to giving the Orioles one of the most potent offenses in history.

Of course, offense was not the only area in which the Orioles excelled. Brooks Robinson anchored one of the best infield defenses in baseball. From 1969 to 1971, Elrod "Ellie" Hendricks at catcher and the offensively minded Powell at first were the only players on the infield not to win a Gold Glove. Brooks Robinson and Davey Johnson would win yearly, and Mark Belanger would win in 1969 and 1971. In addition, Paul Blair would win a Gold Glove for his play in left each of the three years from 1969 to 1971. The Orioles' dominance extends to current sabermetric defensive stats as well. During this three-year period, the Orioles finished no less than second in fielding runs across all MLB teams. The fielding runs statistic measures the number of runs saved by the defense. In 1969 the Orioles would finish first overall, and Ellie Hendricks, Brooks Robinson, and Paul Blair would finish first at their respective positions. The Orioles would have players well inside the top ten in every position category for the other two years of the period.[3]

The final leg of the Orioles' success on the field was outstanding pitching. Not only was their pitching the best in baseball during the time in question, but it is also some of the most dominant in baseball history. From 1969 to 1971, Orioles starters were a combined 241-113 with an ERA of 3.04, and the relievers were 77-51 with a 2.84 ERA.[4] During a period of extended greatness, 1971 was the topper. That season, the Orioles would become the second team in Major League history to have four twenty-game winners in their starting rotation. Mike Cuellar and Jim Palmer, who had finally gotten over his shoulder woes, were 20-9. Meanwhile, Dave McNally went 21-5 in thirty starts, while newcomer Pat Dobson, traded for three players in the winter of 1970, went 20-8.[5] As for the bullpen, veteran Eddie Watt, who had his big league debut with the club in 1966, went 3-1 and was 11 for 12 in save attempts as the Orioles captured another pennant.[6]

This mix of pitching, defense, and a potent offense resulted in great baseball. Outfielder Merv Rettenmund, whom many believed could have started for any other team in the league, believed the Orioles were so good in those years that they lulled the average fan into a sense of boredom: "They were so good fundamentally that it was boring to watch, but baseball people, players, managers, writers, appreciated how great the team was."[7]

The Orioles' greatness was also born of preparedness filtering down from the top. Thanks to Dalton's leadership, all Orioles staff members and players knew their role when they joined the team. Readers will recall that Dalton reintroduced this overarching approach, with the help of Earl Weaver, during his time as the farm director. In 1970 Dalton officially codified the lessons. Don Pries, whom Dalton had hired in 1968 as a scout, would write the first actual manual, at the behest of Dalton, in 1969. *The Oriole Way of Baseball* covered everything an Orioles player, manager, or coach would need to succeed in the organization, and it would become the gold standard for instruction in all of baseball.[8]

As one might expect, *The Oriole Way of Baseball* was loaded with on-field instruction. Within its pages, a player would learn the Baltimore way to slide, take a cutoff, execute the hit and run, and attempt to pick off a runner. However, the manual went beyond this basic instruction, and that is where the Orioles separated themselves from their competition. The manual also taught Orioles players, managers, and coaches how to be professional. This training extended to how they would prepare and carry themselves before, during, and after the season.

As Don Pries relayed in the introduction to the manual to both the managers and players in the Orioles system, "THIS MANUAL IS FOR YOU—USE IT."[9] Moreover, it is important to note that the Orioles' front office saw the manual as something that would make every manager and player "a better-qualified *person* in his chosen profession."[10] Orioles players and staff were to use the manual to "prepare themselves mentally and physically to **Do A Job**."[11]

Like all jobs, this one came with a set of conduct rules that were as important to the organization as the technical skills of doing that job. These skills extend to time spent at and away from the ballpark, and while players were the manual's target audience, it was clear that the manager's job was to be a leader for the player at all times and to set an example for the players.

Players were to "conduct themselves as gentlemen at all times," both on and off the field.[12] Off the field, they were not to swear in public, gamble, yell back at fans, conduct lewd conversations with girls, drink to excess, eat "junk," or lie around in bed at the hotel during the morning.[13]

On the field, players were not allowed to consume beer in the clubhouse at the Minor League level. Players, whether in the dugout, bullpen, or clubhouse, were to be focused at all times. There was to be no eating on the bench or with the general public during a game. The team expected players to be on time for meetings, games, and buses. Both players and managers were to take pride in their appearance on and off the field. This included wearing shoes and socks at all times, maintaining grooming standards, including keeping their hair cut short, and ensuring that the clubhouse was orderly.[14] Finally, players and managers were to remember to "cooperate to the utmost with the local club," including making public appearances and doing other things that would "assist in bringing fans to the ballpark."[15]

These standards extended to the front office staff, and Harry Dalton was quick to practice what he preached. Ernie Accorsi, who would go on to be the general manager of several NFL teams, was director of public relations of the Baltimore Colts during the early 1970s. He recalled that when seeing Harry Dalton and his "gang" in public or at Memorial Stadium, they set the standard for how officials of a sports team were supposed to carry themselves, and their boss was right out front. "Harry wasn't a big bar guy," Accorsi recalled. "You didn't see him out all the time." Accorsi would also remember that Dalton was professional at all times in public or around the stadium.[16] Dalton's professionalism was especially on display when it came time to interact with Orioles fans. He was always willing to go the extra mile to show that the team cared about the people who paid to watch. Consider the story of Orioles fan and future Maryland state trooper Jeff Hewett:

> In 1969 I was 10 years old, and we made it to a game. After the game we stayed in the stadium parking lot to catch a glimpse of some of the players and get some autographs. On this particular occasion, I bought some black and white pictures of all the players in the stadium,

> in hopes of getting some of them signed. I did in fact did get a couple signed by Brooks and a few others. I briefly set the signed pictures down, and when I turned around, they were gone. I was devastated and began crying. A few minutes later, a car pulled up beside me and my Mom and wound down the window, and the gentleman introduced himself as Harry Dalton, the Vice-President and Player Personnel Director of the Orioles, and presented his business card. He asked if there was a problem, and my Mom told him the story, and he tried his best to reassure me that everything was ok and he would try to make up for the misfortune. He wrote down our information and sure enough within the next few days I received a baseball autographed by all the Orioles as well as 8x10 autographed photos of all the players.[17]

Hewett's story illustrates the prototypical Dalton reaction, one he routinely repeated, not because that was his job but because he held himself and those he worked with to a high standard of personal conduct. He genuinely wanted people to have a good experience when they interacted with the team, and he would help them do that when he could. Lou Gorman would say of Dalton, "Harry was smart and demanding, but with no ego." It shows in these situations.[18] Dalton also extended this humanistic approach to players. Consider the situation that befell pitcher Pete Richert.

Richert joined the Orioles in 1967 and would stay with the team through 1971. He remembered that in 1968, when his National Guard unit was federalized in the wake of the riots after Reverend King's assassination, he was set to close on a new home. The closing was contingent on him receiving his first check of the season, and being on active duty put that check at risk. Richert went to Dalton to see what his options were. In the end, Dalton arranged that the Orioles would honor Richert's check even though he was not with the team, thereby allowing Richert's family to move in.[19] Stories like these solidified Dalton's reputation as a good person for team players to have as their team's manager.

Dalton let players and staff be themselves. He understood that players and managers would treat edicts in *The Oriole Way* manual as mere guideposts once they got to the Majors, and so some players drank to excess and cheated on their wives.[20] Earl Weaver had his problems on and off the field as well; he continued to get ejected from games after he became the Orioles' manager, and he also had a well-known affinity for drinking that would get him in hot water as time went on.[21] Dalton never turned a blind eye to these things, as he had a strong moral compass. However, he understood that players and managers alike were human, and they needed grace when he could allow it.

In this way, Dalton was the first modern general manager to see players as more than a commodity. He saw them as people first and foremost. As such, he understood the importance of valuing their opinions, that no two players were the same, and that their personal lives could affect their on-field performance. By considering this, Dalton built good relationships with each player, whether he was an All-Star or the twenty-sixth man on the Major League team roster. This ability to identify with everyone made Dalton "the best GM in baseball," according to many of the players who worked for him.[22]

The final aspect of Dalton's personality that helped make his late Baltimore teams some of the best in baseball history was his lack of need for the spotlight. He routinely let others take credit for the success that was partially his. That way, he could focus on keeping the Orioles moving in the right direction. If Frank Cashen wanted the press to see Frank Cashen as the most critical figure in the Orioles equation, Dalton let him. He would do this with Earl Weaver as well.

Writers, historians, and fans have had countless opportunities to outline how Earl Weaver changed the fortunes of the Orioles. Harry Dalton quickly agreed with them, saying that Weaver was a tremendous motivator and tactical manager.[23] He also acknowledged that for Weaver to be effective, Dalton had to allow him to be a firebrand.[24] Harry Dalton was secure enough with his talents to allow Weaver to flourish in this way. Weaver never forgot that. Of Dalton, he would say simply that Harry Dalton was a Hall of Famer: "The year I was inducted into the Hall of Fame [in 1996], Harry and Pat were there and all I could think of is why me and not him. If not for Harry, this could not have happened."[25]

What happened in Baltimore between 1969 and 1971 was a generational amount of winning. The Oriole Way conceptually covered how that got done on the field.

First and foremost, Earl Weaver was an inspired choice and one whose managerial style fit his team and his boss. He truly believed that "pitching, defense, and the three-run homer" could carry the day in any situation, and he was willing to be cerebral in his roster and lineup construction.

Weaver's teams did not play for one run. They did not give up outs by bunting. They did not steal many bases, because stolen bases could cost a team outs. His teams also worked the count while at the plate. In terms of defense, Weaver believed in a potent double-play combination specifically and a strong middle of the diamond as a general rule. With pitching, Weaver believed it was "easier to find four good starters than five."[26] All of these thoughts helped define the Orioles between 1969 and 1971.

Weaver was also a clear communicator with his team, a skill that helped his players prepare from one game to the next. Pete Richert remembered that players were often clued in days ahead of time. "One time, we are on the plane heading to Boston, and Earl comes up to me and says, 'At some point, Yastrzemski is going to come up in the sixth or seventh inning, and he's going to be yours,'" Richert recalled. "Sure enough, two nights later, Yastrzemski comes up and I knew that I was coming into the game. That stuff helps."[27]

Of course Dalton and Weaver were not the only ones to influence the Orioles during this time. Like the early days of the Oriole Way, the version the team used from 1969 to 1971 relied on the talents of multiple coaches who were as skilled at their jobs as Dalton and Weaver were at theirs. One such individual was George Bamberger.

When Bamberger joined the coaching staff in 1968, he quickly became known as someone who understood how to teach pitching mechanics and how to help pitchers navigate through tough stretches. At the heart of Bamberger's philosophy on pitching was a program that saw pitchers throw more, not less. In the off-season, this meant the following guidelines were in effect:

1. You should throw at least three times a week, more if possible. Throw outside where the weather permits, but if not possible, then be sure to find an indoor [venue] where you can throw regularly.
2. The third time you throw, start spinning curveballs and sliders. DO NOT THROW HARD. Concentrate on rotation only. Work on changeups. Practice holding men on when your arm is in fairly good shape. Use your catcher as a first baseman.
3. Run as much as possible to get your legs in shape. Physical conditioning can mean the greatest between a successful season and an unsuccessful season.[28]

Once the season began, Bamberger's ideas continued influencing pitchers throughout the system. Ultimately, a pitcher needed to make sure that he had "command of himself and command of his pitches" in order to be successful.[29] His "rules" for pitching were pretty simple: "The most important pitch is a strike. But the trick is to change speeds. Trying to pinpoint a pitch is crazy. Throw the ball down the middle, but don't throw the same pitch twice. Change the speed."[30]

When the raw talent of the Orioles players met the structured yet nurturing environment provided by Dalton and the teachings of Earl Weaver and his coaches, the Orioles became almost unstoppable.

The Orioles teams of the late 1960s and early 1970s were record-setters. They would average 105 wins during those years (109, 108, 101) and win three American League pennants by going 9-0 in the new league championship round of the playoffs. Finally, Baltimore would capture one more World Series title, in 1970. All this success was possible because the Orioles built the perfect environment for winning baseball when they combined great players with Dalton's structured yet nurturing environment and the teachings and mentality of Weaver and his coaches.

The average fan then asks: If the Orioles were so great between 1969 and 1971, why did they not win more than one World Series? The work of baseball writer Tyler Kepner provides the most coherent answer.

First, even though the fans and media place more importance on a World Series win or loss, the fact is that the games played in October are an extension of the game team members have been playing since spring training began. Within that context, a team's poor or excellent performance is the same one they experienced in March, June, or September. The same principle applies to individuals. As Kepner has shown, with a season's worth of equivalent appearances or at bats in the postseason, a player will play to his regular-season numbers.[31] In 1970 the Orioles would play to their norm and win a title. During the World Series in 1969 and 1971, the Orioles ran into teams and individuals who performed to their norm of equal excellence, so they lost close Series those years.

According to Kepner, the other factor overlooked when stating a team should have won more titles is the outstanding play of an outlier—someone who is an unlikely hero that has a run of superior play during October that offsets the outstanding play of the opposing team.[32] During their run between 1969 and 1971, the Orioles benefited from the play of such an individual, and they were also victimized by it.

In 1969 the Orioles' nemesis was the New York Mets' pitching staff. At the front of the rotation, the Mets had a future Hall of Famer, Tom Seaver, who had won twenty-five games in the regular season and would win the Cy Young Award at the end of the season. Behind Seaver, the Mets could rely on Jerry Koosman. Mets manager Gil Hodges and fans of the team saw the lefty as a solid starter whose role on the team was to serve as a catalyst; Koosman was often called upon to stop a possible losing streak before it started or to reinforce a positive start by Seaver. Finally, the Mets' third starter was Gary Gentry. Throughout 1969 and his career, Gentry was a middle-of-the-road starter. He was 13-12 for 1969, with ten no-decisions, and would finish three games under .500 for his career at 46-49 while having forty-five no-decisions. All three men would pitch to their norm in the World Series.

Seaver would lose Game One and then rebound to pitch a ten-inning victory in Game Four. In Game Two, Jerry Koosman did precisely what he did all year for the Mets by helping the team rebound from a loss in Game One by tossing a two-hitter in a 2–1 Mets victory in Game Two, which evened the Series. He would then back up Seaver's performance in Game

Four by throwing a complete game in the Game Five clincher. With three wins from their top two performers, the Mets needed one more win from Gentry. Gentry, who took a no-decision in his only start in the National League Championship Series, would win his only start (Game Four) in the World Series, with a small amount of help from an unlikely hero.[33]

In 1969 that hero for the Mets' pitching staff was Nolan Ryan. Ryan, who will enter our story to a much greater degree later, would pitch above expectations as he blanked the Orioles for two and a third innings to pick up a save for Gary Gentry in the Mets' 5–0 win in Game Four. In addition to Ryan, the Mets showed stellar play at essential times. Specifically, Tommie Agee and Ron Swoboda provided defensive gems in Games Three and Four that saved victories for the Mets.[34] These plays were enough to separate New York from a Baltimore team that went through an offensive slump during the Series.

In 1970 the Orioles were the ones who offered outstanding normative performances. In this case, Brooks Robinson provided highlight-reel defense and timely hitting on his way to winning the World Series MVP award. At the plate, Robinson would spur rallies in Games One and Two to secure for the Orioles a pair of one-run wins. On defense, Brooks Robinson, the man known as the "human vacuum cleaner," made some of the most iconic defensive plays in baseball history during the Series.[35] This play allowed the Orioles to take an edge into the third and fifth games, which they won in blowout fashion.

Finally, during the 1971 World Series against the Pittsburgh Pirates, the Orioles lost a seven-game affair that hinged on the normative play of Roberto Clemente and Steve Blass, as well as outstanding outlier performances from Nelson "Nellie" Briles and Bruce Kison.

Clemente was unbelievable in the field and at the plate. His twelve hits, including two doubles, a triple, and two home runs, would pace the Pirates' attack. In addition, he would make several throws, in keeping with his typical Gold Glove performance, that would thwart the Orioles' scoring chances.[36] Clemente's Series performance was in line with his play during his illustrious career, and the Orioles could not overcome the effort put forth in what many consider one of the most dominant performances in World Series history.

As for Blass, in keeping with his 15-9 record in 1971, he would win two starts in the Series. Most importantly for Pittsburgh, Blass threw a complete game four-hitter in a 2–1 Pirates win in Game Seven. Meanwhile, Briles would throw a two-hit shutout in Game Five as the Pirates won 4–0. The swing game was Bruce Kison's performance in Game Four.

Kison, a twenty-one-year-old rookie in 1971, entered Game Four after a short start by Luke Walker, who only got two outs in the first while giving up three hits and three runs. Kison would escape further damage and give the Pirates six scoreless innings. This performance, which included a single-game World Series record of three hit batters, allowed the Pirates to climb back into the game and eventually win it 4–3.[37]

All of these examples illustrate that winning titles is hard. Even if you have dominated the competition all year, things can and often do go differently in the World Series. Series losses should not detract from the overall evaluation of a team, however. This is especially true of the Orioles.

From 1969 to 1971, the organization was the bellwether of Major League Baseball on and off the field. To many, the Orioles had the best players, the best manager, and yes, the best GM. The biggest problem for Harry Dalton was that he had publicly undercut his value for the betterment of the team and the people he worked with for so long that even they started to believe that he was superfluous. They never repaid that loyalty privately with either a kind word or financial stability brought on by a multiple-year contract. The owners' failure to offer him such a deal fostered resentment and hurt in Dalton and sparked an idea that he might be better off with another team, on another coast. This notion not only launched a fight for his future in the game but also foreshadowed a coming battle between the players and management that would reshape the game on and off the field.

9

The Daltons Go West

FALL 1971

When Harry Dalton started to feel unhappy in Baltimore is unknown. What is a fact is that even as his team marched to the pennant in mid-August 1971, he quietly took a call from Gene Autry, the principal owner of the California Angels. Dalton would recall that Autry contacted him because "he didn't know what his club [the Angels] was going to do at the end of the season, but if they should make some changes, he wondered if I would be interested in something with the California club."[1] Always a man of principle, Dalton said that while he was happy in Baltimore, he would like to speak to Autry but that the Angels' major owner should first clear the conversation with Jerry Hoffberger.[2] Autry followed this call up with another a week later. This time "he [Autry] felt that they [California] would make a change, and they would like to talk to me."[3] Again Dalton reiterated, "I would only do that if they [California] talked to Baltimore first and [I] also stressed that anything that might take place could only happen after the playoffs and World Series."[4] Once again Autry agreed, and when he suggested that he would call Hoffberger after Labor Day, Dalton suggested that he call before that time so that everyone was aware as early as possible. This prompted Bob Reynolds, Autry's partner in the Angels and the manager of Autry's radio empire, to call Jerry Hoffberger. Once Reynolds contacted the team, Dalton had to tell Hoffberger and Frank Cashen why he would want to leave. Dalton's reasoning (and the way he stated it) is shocking on some level. He said he felt that the Orioles were telling him what was best for him in his career and that, by 1971, working in Baltimore under the constructs the Orioles had in place was "just like being owned."[5]

Dalton's thoughts are groundbreaking, especially when placed in the context of the history of labor relations in baseball. Wanting to test his value on the open market while not being made to feel like he was asking too much of his employer was not a new idea among players, nor was the idea of players as property. What is new is that in the past, historians and fans alike saw ownership and the players as two ends of a spectrum vis-à-vis labor relations, which is to say that players alone were property for the teams to control and that all team executives worked to maintain the status quo. Harry Dalton's situation shows that it is now time to reevaluate this generally accepted idea. This is especially true given that while Dalton was arguing that he should be free to decide where he wanted to work, a player was arguing the same thing in federal court.

Curt Flood broke into the Major Leagues at age eighteen, signing with the Cincinnati Reds in 1957. In 1959 he was traded to the St. Louis Cardinals and would quickly become one of the cogs in the Cardinals machine, which would win World Series titles in 1964 and 1967 and a National League pennant in 1968. In 1969 Flood would win his seventh straight Gold Glove in center field. That fall, in what could be considered a blockbuster deal, St. Louis traded Flood, journeyman outfielder Byron Browne, bullpen arm Joe Hoerner, and veteran starting catcher Tim McCarver to the Philadelphia Phillies for a package that included the often maligned but talented slugger Dick Allen. Under the employment system of the time, the trade should have gone through without a problem.

The National League introduced the reserve clause in 1880, and its legality was upheld by a host of court cases that granted baseball an antitrust exemption because the courts classified baseball as entertainment and not interstate commerce, thus allowing teams to maintain the rights to a player in perpetuity.[6] A team could tell a player how much they felt he was worth or give him a raise one year and an arbitrary pay cut the next. They could also tell him in which city he was going to play, and they could tell him when he was too old to work. In some cases, they could even tell a player how to conduct his life when aspects of his free time affected his job.

Moreover, if a player balked at any of these strictures, he could be told that he did not have the team's best interest in mind and that he was selfish. This paternalism, coupled with the legality of the reserve clause, left players facing the reality that the deck was stacked against them. With that fresh in their minds, most players, even those who tried to fight management, were left to complain mildly and then sign the contract they were offered. That all began to change with Curt Flood.

In a letter to Commissioner Bowie Kuhn written on Christmas Eve 1969, Flood stated, "After twelve years in the Major Leagues, I do not feel that I am a piece of property to be bought and sold irrespective of my wishes. I believe that any system that produces that result violates my basic rights as a citizen and is inconsistent with the laws of the United States." Flood then asked that Kuhn make it known to the baseball world that Flood was available for the upcoming 1970 season.[7]

As could be expected, Kuhn's response, penned on December 30, 1969, was grounded in the belief that while Flood was not a piece of property, his contract was standard for all Major League players. Therefore, "under the circumstances, and pending any further information from you [Flood], I do not see what action I [Kuhn] can take and cannot comply with the request [to become a free agent] contained in the second paragraph of your letter." This response set off a discussion between Flood and MLBPA chief Marvin Miller that ultimately led to a series of federal court cases (against the recommendation of Marvin Miller) that became known as *Flood v. Kuhn*. In these, Flood would argue that the reserve clause impeded his rights because the clause violated the Thirteenth Amendment to the Constitution that protected against indentured servitude. The first of these cases went to trial in 1970, and the Second U.S. Circuit Court heard the appeal in April 1971. Against this backdrop, Harry Dalton wrote a letter to Jerry Hoffberger arguing the same things that led Curt Flood to file suit against MLB.

Although the challenge Dalton penned to Hoffberger is undated, a timeline of events contained in Dalton's papers indicates that he wrote the letter in mid-September 1971. At that time, he quickly pointed out that his conversations with Hoffberger and Cashen regarding the possibility of talking to California about a job were "enlightening, helpful, and also disturbing."[8] As for why Dalton wanted to consider a new job with the Angels, the answer he gave was very much in keeping with the type of person he was at his core.

First and foremost, Dalton felt that a job with the Angels was worth exploring because he could "see the possibility of a more rewarding job for me and way of life for my family in California."

Dalton was, and always would be, a family-first individual. That was why he had worked at night driving a cab to help support his parents, and he thought a new job was the best fit for him at this point in his career. This was because the Orioles' owners apparently did not consider Dalton to be worth a long-term deal despite his success. In his mind, the necessity of working year to year opened his family and himself up to undue stress at that point. Moreover, after eighteen years and countless hours helping to build Baltimore into a winner, Dalton realized that even in his case, Hoffberger and Cashen would always look to do what they thought was best for the team before looking after their employees. As Dalton would confess, this left him "a little disappointed . . . perhaps hurt by the fact that after 18 years of satisfactory service, no one has said, 'Harry, what can we do to please you as well as ourselves.'" These circumstances motivated him to look out for himself and his family before defaulting to loyalty toward the club.

As for how his beliefs informed his decision to seek a position with California, Harry Dalton was a voracious reader who had consumed information at a prodigious rate from his earliest days; it remained one of the things that made him good at his job. To relax, he liked to read western fiction. The works of Wallace Stegner, a young Elmore Leonard, and Louis L'Amour were constant companions. These works helped shape Dalton's belief that there was something to the practical aspect of Manifest Destiny suggesting that dissatisfied persons should "go West," stake their claim, and seek betterment in their lives. That is not to say that Dalton did not appreciate his situation in Baltimore, but he was tired of the paternalism that the club used to try and thwart his efforts to improve his situation. This included a host of things that the owners attempted to do in the face of his possibly leaving for California. In Dalton's words, the Orioles had done the following:

1. Offer[ed] [the] job of Exec V.P. [in a position where he would not report to anyone but Hoffberger] by intimation only with no concrete offer or terms.
2. Appeal[ed] to my moral standards that Cal [California] violated [baseball's] system in approaching me as they did.
3. [Made] a veiled threat that I could be enjoined from joining the Cal [California] club by the action of Comish [Bowie Kuhn] if Balt[imore] presses complaint.
4. Appeal[ed] to my sense of duty and obligation that I would be leaving Balt[imore] in a lurch.
5. Pose[d] alternatives so that the only apparent way[s] for me to talk to Calif[ornia] are to resign or advise club [Baltimore] I want to leave and work elsewhere and ask JHC [Jerry Hoffberger] to help me get the job.

Situations like those described by Dalton were standard practice for ownership when dealing with an employee. This further illustrates that Dalton's experiences at the end of his tenure in Baltimore had much more in common with Curt Flood and the players that Dalton signed to contracts than they did with management. Frank Cashen did not see Harry Dalton as his equal despite the work Dalton did. This is evident in Cashen's thoughts on Dalton in his memoirs and is reinforced by anecdotal evidence from a host of people who knew both men.[9] Moreover, while Dalton always categorized his working relationship with Jerry Hoffberger as good, in this situation Hoffberger was equal parts paternalistic and insistent about taking care of the needs of his team before accommodating Dalton. The result is that Dalton felt "used to the hilt."[10] To clear the air, Dalton spent the back page of his letter to Hoffberger answering the accusations that Hoffberger and Cashen had leveled at him.

First, he pointed out that "while the opportunity for me to become Ex[ecutive] V.P. has always existed, it has never been pushed hard by the club and only now [that he was preparing to possibly leave] is it made to seem urgent that I move up to this post." Next, Dalton defended his conduct vis-à-vis the Orioles, Angels, and himself. As became evident during the Mike Epstein standoff, Dalton did not allow others to call his integrity into question. In this case, Dalton was quick to point out that in his dealings with California, he was "honorable and above board." This belief was rooted in the fact that Dalton had asked California to call Baltimore before speaking to him and that when Baltimore did not allow Dalton to speak to California, he had not called behind their back to get any details of a possible job. Dalton then let Cashen and Hoffberger know that if Baltimore still felt he and California had acted inappropriately, Dalton would go to the commissioner's office to determine if he was "in the wrong."[11]

If the commissioner's office did find that the Angels and Dalton were, in fact, duplicitous, Dalton felt that at that moment he would need to reconsider his career. In his mind, the Orioles had "benefited" from having Dalton with the club, and he believed there were very few employees with the Orioles who "have a greater concern for the welfare and success of the club" than he did. All these things led him to one conclusion: "if it is determined [by Major League Baseball] that an uncontracted employee in baseball is free to consider an opportunity to move to a job of higher authority and greater benefits only at the discretion of the employer, then, perhaps I am in the wrong business."[12]

The fact that his relationship with the Orioles had deteriorated to the point where he would consider quitting baseball altogether speaks volumes about the state of Dalton's psyche in the fall of 1971. This is historically relevant because it shows a side of the Orioles' success that has been mostly unknown until now. More importantly, the fact that Dalton cast his arguments in the language of proponents of free agency in baseball while they were arguing those very points in federal court is a revelation. This discovery has the power to change the narrative of baseball history at large and reinforces the importance of considering Dalton's career importance to be above and beyond that of a simple team builder.

To this point, there has never been evidence of an executive who acknowledged and identified with the players regarding their wanting freedom of movement in their jobs. Dalton's stance is groundbreaking, and when combined with his earlier comments on feeling like he was a piece of Orioles property, it leads to the conclusion that there is not much difference between Harry Dalton and Curt Flood when you take a broad view of their situations. This is true even though Dalton did not refuse to work until his situation was rectified. Yes, Flood sacrificed his career, making his case especially glaring. However, the fact that Harry Dalton would even put those things in writing is just as jarring.

Moreover, Dalton was not in a position to fall on his sword. His family depended on him as the primary breadwinner, and he could not choose martyrdom. That was why he ultimately backed away from his statement and told Hoffberger that he would abide by the Orioles' policies related to his employment. It still does not diminish the impact, however.

Dalton's belief in the free movement of talent in baseball would inform his career. He would never be considered a hard-line antilabor GM. This was because Harry Dalton understood what it felt like to be told you were not good at your job when you were. This would make him a favorite of players and occasionally put him at odds with the owners he worked for until the day he retired.

With his thoughts spelled out to Hoffberger and Cashen and the understanding that Dalton would not resign without another job in hand or rely on Baltimore to vouch for him with California or any other club, he set out to help his team finish the season strong. Ultimately, that work helped the Orioles reach a third straight World Series.

At the other end of the baseball world were the California Angels. They would finish the season ten games under .500. As foreshadowed by ownership, in October 1971 Dick Walsh, the team's GM, was fired. That ultimately opened the door for Harry Dalton, who began to negotiate with the Angels in earnest after the World Series. The Angels would hire him on October 27, 1971. The new situation was reminiscent of his early days in Baltimore, as the Angels were a relatively young franchise with an enthusiastic owner looking to prove himself. The result would not be a triumphant lap for Harry Dalton. However, that was in the future. In the present, the California Angels and their larger-than-life owner, country music icon Gene Autry, needed Harry Dalton as much as he needed the Angels.

Gene Autry was a baseball fan his whole life. He grew up playing American Legion baseball in his native Texas and played well enough that the

Cardinals offered him a Minor League contract. However, according to Autry, the railroad paid better, and he became a telegraph operator before going to Hollywood.[13]

Still, the game was always in the back of Autry's mind. He owned stock in the Los Angeles Angels of the Pacific Coast League for a time. Moreover, his radio station, KMPC, was the original broadcaster of the Los Angeles Dodgers when they moved west in 1958.

It was this final exposure that, in a way, brought Autry into baseball. In the winter of 1960, Autry's station negotiated with the Dodgers to keep their broadcasts on KMPC. According to Autry, he had been given assurances by Dodgers owner Walter O'Malley that the negotiations were a formality and that KMPC, which Autry had branded as a "sports station," would again be the Dodgers' radio flagship. Then, the vagaries of broadcast law, atmospheric science, and geography changed the course of events. Lake Arrowhead, California, lies roughly eighty miles northeast of LA in the middle of the San Bernardino National Forest. It was also where Walter O'Malley had a cabin that he retreated to when he wanted to escape the pressures of city life. There was only one problem. At night, when AM radio stations are required to "power down" (reduce their signal or turn off their transmitter completely) so as not to interfere with larger AM broadcasters, O'Malley could not get a clear signal to listen to the Dodgers. This led O'Malley to pull his KMPC offer. Quickly, Autry's station had no games, which led to drastic measures. He looked into buying a team to fill the airwaves.[14] This would be the first time, but certainly not the last, in which Walter O'Malley would shape the baseball decisions of the California Angels. For Gene Autry, O'Malley and his Dodgers were the gold standard. In some ways, it made sense. Without the Dodgers, there would be no Angels.

As was noted earlier when discussing the St. Louis Browns' potential move before the United States entered World War II, magnates had always considered California fertile ground for Major League Baseball. Baseball, and professional baseball in particular, had deep roots in California.[15] However, it was not until the early 1950s—oddly enough, during the peak power of Walter O'Malley's team in Brooklyn—that the Dodgers' owner began to think that relocating to California was his best hope for continued prosperity in the years to come.

According to biographer Andy McCue, O'Malley began giving serious thought to a franchise shift partly because of changing demographics in Brooklyn combined with a crumbling stadium infrastructure and partly because of the perception, thanks to the success of the Milwaukee Braves after their move from Boston with a beyond-sweet deal from civic leaders, that the grass was greener in a different locale.

Still, it was not until 1956, when the Dodgers began playing games in New Jersey in response to lackluster attendance at Ebbets Field and as a ploy to get the New York city fathers to begin thinking about what they were willing to do to keep the Dodgers in Brooklyn, that O'Malley also opened up back-channel negotiations with city officials in Los Angeles. There were initially a few hurdles to cross. O'Malley needed to find a second team to move west so that the National League could justify the travel to California for its six other members. He also had to navigate the unfamiliar politics of Los Angeles, which was a different world from the political climate of New York that he had mastered.

However, according to one historian, in the end "O'Malley was a man who complained he couldn't figure out who the boss was in Los Angeles and got everything he dreamed of."[16] Along the way, "the decision by O'Malley and [Horace] Stoneham (owner of the Giants who moved his team in tandem with the Dodgers) to move west was absolutely central to the making of modern Major League Baseball (MLB)."[17]

It would take the American League four years to respond to this historic move, and even then it was only when competition from a third league appeared on the horizon. In June 1959, in an attempt to change the face of baseball for a third time, relaunch his career, and ruffle more than a few feathers of the men who once employed him, Branch Rickey announced that he and various backers would be forming the Continental League in order to provide Major League–quality baseball to America's underrepresented—and growing—cities.

Initially, the Continental League aimed to begin to play in 1960. However, various issues with finding ownership groups in the league's two largest target markets, New York and Los Angeles, kept on delaying the proposed first year of play. Even with this delay, Major League owners were scared into action. To help maintain their fragile monopoly (and ever-growing profit margins), Major League owners announced in August 1960 that they had struck a deal with Continental League organizers to absorb four cities and add them to Major League Baseball. At the heart of this deal was a National League team for New York and an American League team in Los Angeles.

Much like the Continental League's attempt to join the baseball world, the American League's expansion into Los Angeles was not without problems. As baseball historian Andy McCue shows, the biggest stumbling block for American League expansion in Los Angeles was Walter O'Malley.

First, O'Malley would not sign off on Hank Greenberg and not-so-silent partner Bill Veeck as the new AL team's ownership group. Second, O'Malley wanted financial restitution from the new franchise for allowing it to enter Los Angeles and to offset costs that O'Malley had underwritten when moving the Dodgers to LA in 1958. The final stumbling block was that O'Malley wanted to guarantee that any American League team would play in Dodger Stadium while the new team's own facility was built.

Ultimately, Gene Autry and Bob Reynolds were the only potential ownership group willing to meet these demands. O'Malley and the rest of the American League ownership group quickly approved their selection. O'Malley's acquiescence would forever link Autry and O'Malley and set up unique conditions that would shape the Angels for decades.

On the field in the spring of 1961, after having had barely one hundred days to organize a front office, draft a team, and hold spring training, the Los Angeles Angels took the field. They would experience the many growing pains associated with an expansion franchise in any sport. That first year, the Angels lost. They would also suffer various indignities specific to being tied to the hip of the Los Angeles Dodgers and Walter O'Malley. This included paying for the maintenance of Dodger Stadium (famously, this included paying to have someone clean windows in club offices that were devoid of windows). Still, despite O'Malley's influence and having a diluted talent pool thanks to fellow owners who did not want to help build a rival into a winning club, the Angels would fight to maintain respectability on the field.

In the years leading up to Harry Dalton's arrival, the Angels fielded teams stocked with players who would have or had had productive careers—albeit before or after they left the Angels. The mid-1960s would see the emergence of Orioles farmhand Dean Chance and bonus baby Rick Reichardt, who were paired with a mix of aging stars and veterans. In 1966 the Angels finished 80-82 with Reichardt, Chance, infielder Jim Fregosi, and pitchers Marcelino López and Clyde Wright on a team with aging stars like Jimmy Piersall, Joe Adcock, Lew Burdette, and relief pitcher Jack Sanford.

This trend continued in the late 1960s and into the early 1970s. At various points, the Angels added players such as Jay Johnstone, Sandy Alomar, Aurelio Rodríguez, and Andy Messersmith to try and field a consistent winner. They would also sign Mickey Rivers from the Mets and Alex Johnson from the Reds and pair them with young pitchers like Dave LaRoche and Rudy May. Still, the team had two only two winning seasons for the first ten years of its existence, despite players who would be productive Major Leaguers. This is not horrible, considering the time it usually takes to build a consistent franchise.

The only problem was that Gene Autry believed that the Angels needed to be competitive with their in-city rivals, the Dodgers, from the moment of their conception. Considering the pedigree and longevity of the Dodgers, Autry did not do favors to those in his organization by comparing the two teams at that early point in time.

In contrast to the relatively new Angels, the Dodgers were a baseball blueblood. They had been among the best teams in the National League in the decade leading up to their move to California from New York. They won six National League pennants between 1947 and 1957, boasting rosters stacked with nationally familiar players like Gil Hodges, Pee Wee Reese, Jackie Robinson, and Don Newcombe.[18] Even though the roster turned over, the Dodgers were also the class of the league once they moved from Brooklyn. They won the World Series in 1959, 1963, and 1965 and another pennant in 1966 before they ran into the Harry Dalton–run Orioles in the World Series, won by Baltimore thanks to superior pitching and a retooled offense that relied on speed to help score runs.[19] Moreover, as the 1970s began, the Dodgers restocked their talent a third time with a core of young players, including infielders Steve Garvey, Ron Cey, and Davey Lopes, catcher Steve Yeager, and outfielders Bill Buckner and Bill Russell. This created a situation in which the Angels were playing second fiddle to the Dodgers among the fans and the media. As a result, the Angels would develop an institutional inferiority complex vis-à-vis the Dodgers that would color every team decision for the foreseeable future and was best summed up by Jim Fregosi: "We kept bringing in people from the Dodger organization into the Angels, and it never solved any problems."[20] This included bringing in Dodgers executive Dick Walsh as general manager late in the season in 1968 and Walsh's hiring of Harold "Lefty" Phillips as a manager in May 1969. Gene Autry hoped that the combination of Walsh and Phillips would bring stability and an element of the Dodgers' success to the Angels. Instead, the only thing the Walsh/Phillips dynamic created was distrust among the players.

In Walsh's case, players quickly began to see him as someone who spoke out of both sides of his mouth. Angels beat writer Ross Newhan felt this began and ended with how Walsh interjected himself into the players' private lives: "Players called him [Walsh] 'The Smiling Python.' He wrote letters to wives claiming that players were fooling around on them. Players hated him, and they were scared about what he might do. It was pretty grim."[21]

As for the issue with Phillips, it is apparent that the only person who felt Phillips was a capable manager was Dick Walsh. He had known and trusted "Lefty" Phillips from their days with the Dodgers. Phillips was a scout and the pitching coach for the Dodgers during the ascendancy of Drysdale and Koufax and had a successful six-week stint as interim manager of the Dodgers when a kidney ailment had sidelined manager Walter Alston in the summer of 1968. Phillips was initially a hard sell to Gene Autry; Autry wanted to promote Chuck Tanner, who had recently spent time in the Angels' farm system. Ultimately, Autry acquiesced, and Phillips took over the Angels. The club spent the next two and a half years underachieving while Phillips struggled with communication issues that, in conjunction with Walsh's tendencies, helped to cause an irreparable fissure in the Angels' clubhouse. The cataclysmic event? The treatment of Alex Johnson and the dysfunction it encapsulated.

One could argue that Johnson, a twenty-seven-year-old left fielder who had never spent more than two seasons with any club in his previous six seasons (with the Phillies, Cardinals, Reds, and now the Angels), had finally found his offensive stride coming into the 1971 season. In 1970, his first year with the Angels, he had led the American League in hitting at .329. Moreover, he had over 200 hits and led the Angels in every offensive category except home runs (finishing third with 14) and stolen bases (finishing second with 17), including the twenty-first-century metrics of on-base percentage (.370), on-base plus slugging or OPS (.830), and OPS+ (132).[22] Still, as the Angels went to Palm Springs for spring training in 1971, Johnson quickly went from being one of the Angels' best players to their biggest question mark thanks to a series of incidents throughout the spring and into the early part of the season in which Lefty Phillips accused him of not "hustling." In the spring, the Angels would fine Johnson repeatedly, and they would suspend him on June 28 for the remainder of the 1971 season.

Johnson's teammates were generally tight-lipped, with a few notable exceptions. De facto team leader Jim Fregosi presented the company line when he told the *Los Angeles Times*, "A man gets paid to play, and hustle is a part of the game. If you don't hustle, you shouldn't get paid. He [Johnson] was given every opportunity."[23] New Angel Tony Conigliaro agreed. Conigliaro was on the comeback trail after a beaning in 1967 had left the once-promising hitter with severe vision issues. Conigliaro acknowledged that you needed to play hard. However, he was one of the only people to point out that Alex Johnson had a mental illness that compounded the problems that every player felt over the course of the year.

Johnson's condition went unacknowledged by the Angels, and his varying moods put him at odds with teammates fed up with his inconsistent play and sometimes combative attitude. This led to a fight with Clyde Wright, in which Johnson brandished a stool at the pitcher, and to a situation involving infielder Chico Ruiz in which Ruiz pulled a gun from his locker and pointed it at Johnson. In the end, Johnson would take his case against the Angels to arbitration, ultimately winning a disability case against the club before finishing a thirteen-year career with a host of other teams.[24]

This is the world that Harry Dalton stepped into in the fall of 1971. The players were suspicious of management and scared of each other. The best offensive player from a year earlier was no longer on the team. Ownership was worried not about teams in their division but a team in another league. The Angels were a mess, and these factors would produce Dalton's first prolonged period of struggle as a GM. However, in the fall of 1971, that was all in the future. In the present, Dalton would set out to make the team a winner using the skills he had developed in Baltimore. He would attempt to overhaul the roster not once but twice and try to build a farm system from the ground up. The only question was, would he be given enough time to accomplish those goals?

1. ABOVE: Harry Dalton with his parents on a fishing trip to Maine in 1938. Dalton would always have a close relationship with his parents and a love of the outdoors. He counted the trip to Maine as one of his favorite memories. Dalton Family Collection.

2. Pictured in November 1945, "Flash" Dalton would develop an inquisitive mind, a great sense of patriotism, a life-long sense of humor, and a reputation as the class playboy during his years at West Springfield High School in Massachusetts. Dalton Family Collection.

3. ABOVE: Harry Dalton was always proud of his affiliation with Amherst College following his graduation in 1950. Here Dalton is pictured in his official Amherst photo from 1948. Dalton Family Collection.

4. OPPOSITE TOP: Following his time at Amherst College, Dalton would work as a reporter for the *Springfield (MA) Republican* before enlisting in the U.S. Air Force following the outbreak of the Korean War. Dalton, pictured being promoted to first lieutenant, would transition to the officer corps, serve stateside as a public affairs officer in Colorado, and then spend three years in Japan working for the Far East Air Forces and covering the fighting on the Korean Peninsula. Dalton Family Collection.

5. Following his discharge from the air force, Dalton would move to Baltimore to be near his parents. This relocation led to him applying for and getting a job with the Baltimore Orioles in the winter of 1953. Dalton's first job was as the assistant farm director. He is pictured here on the first day of the first Orioles Minor League camp in Thomasville, Georgia. Thomasville History Center.

US

6. ABOVE: Thomasville would be the professional incubator for Harry Dalton just like it was for Orioles players of the 1960s and 1970s. Pictured here as the farm director in 1964, Dalton looks on as various Minor Leaguers receive instruction from pitching instructor George Bamberger. Thomasville History Center.

7. OPPOSITE TOP: From 1969 to 1971, Dalton built the best team in baseball. The Orioles would win three American League pennants and a World Series under Dalton during that time. That type of dynastic winning led to "impromptu opportunities" for Dalton to use the clubhouse whirlpool. From the collection of Bob Brown, courtesy of Scotty Brown.

8. Dalton's success in baseball led to many special opportunities for the entire family. Here he is pictured in 1969 with Commissioner of Baseball Bowie Kuhn and President Richard Nixon in the East Room of the White House during the All-Star Gala celebrating one hundred years of professional baseball. Dalton Family Collection.

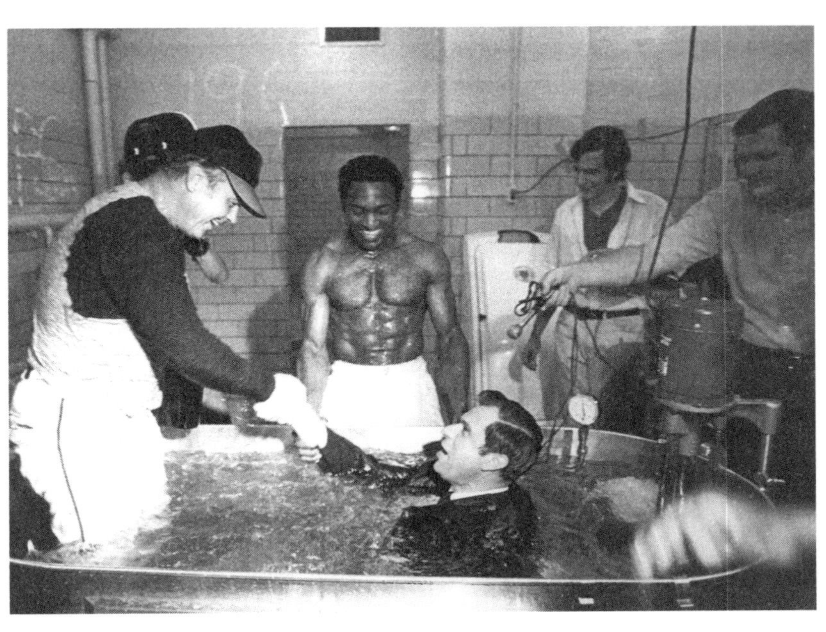

Chevron
STOP
ARTHRITIS
375

9. OPPOSITE: In a somewhat shocking move, Harry Dalton would leave the Orioles in the winter of 1971 for a chance to work for the California Angels. It would be the most difficult period of Dalton's career, though it would lead to opportunities to cement his relationships with his family. This included helping his wife, Pat, fundraise for various charities. Dalton Family Collection.

10. ABOVE: Despite his best efforts, Dalton would not have a winning season in California, though he would make the Angels a national talking point thanks to a trade for Nolan Ryan and the signing of Bobby Grich, Don Baylor, and Joe Rudi in the first year of free agency in baseball. No matter how his team was doing, whether it was the Orioles, the Angels, or the Brewers, Dalton never shied away from talking to the media to explain his thought process. Dalton Family Collection.

11. In the winter of 1977, Dalton would join his third and final team when he became general manager of the Milwaukee Brewers. Here Dalton is pictured with (*left*) Brewers owner and future baseball commissioner Bud Selig and (*center*) longtime GM and Dalton Gang member Frank "Trader" Lane at County Stadium in Milwaukee. Dalton Family Collection.

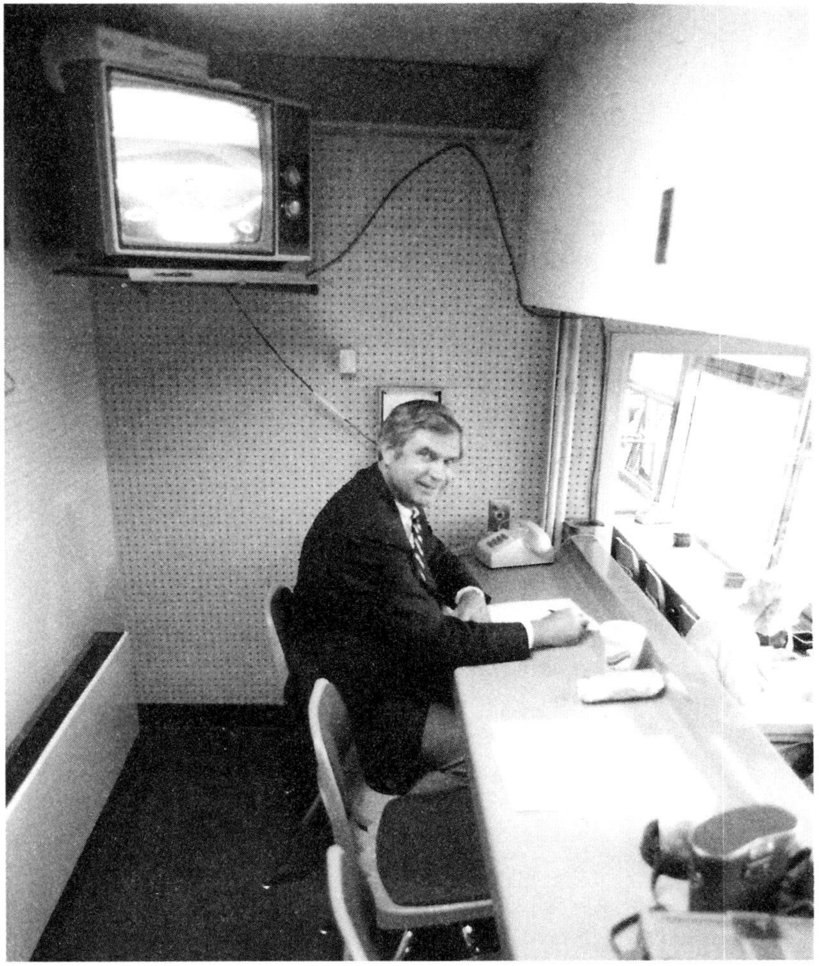

12. In contrast to his boss Bud Selig, Harry Dalton always presented a calm demeanor while watching a game in his box at Milwaukee County Stadium with a beverage and his ever-present scorebook. His most demonstrative outburst? Throwing his scoring pencil. Dalton Family Collection.

13. In the first five years that Dalton was in charge of the Milwaukee Brewers, the team would experience a meteoric rise to the top of the American League. It culminated with an American League pennant and World Series berth in 1982. That October would see Dalton and his team back on the national stage. This included interviews with Howard Cosell for ABC Sports and a reunion with Earl Weaver, who was working as an analyst for the network during the playoffs. Dalton Family Collection.

14. Although his team would fall short of a World Series title in 1982, losing to the St. Louis Cardinals in seven games, Harry Dalton would experience one more "victory" parade in the fall of 1982, when fans of the team saluted their heroes, including Harry and Pat Dalton, one final time that season. The day would be one of Dalton's favorite memories from working in Milwaukee. Dalton Family Collection.

15. Baseball insiders remember Harry Dalton as a tireless worker who never let himself get too far from a phone in case a deal needed to be made or an issue arose with his team. This meant that occasional stops were necessary during family outings so Dalton could "check in." Dalton Family Collection.

16. Throughout his career Dalton was an executive with whom players felt comfortable. This included times when he was around the batting cage or on the bench prior to games at Milwaukee County Stadium. Dalton Family Collection.

17. TOP: Thanks to his affable nature and his ability to be gracious even when things were not going well, Dalton would maintain positive relationships even with those with whom he might have had cause to be adversarial. A great example of that is his relationship with his former boss Gene Autry. Despite never having a winning season together, Dalton and Autry (shown circa the late 1980s) always maintained a good opinion of each other. Dalton Family Collection.

18. Dalton would not win another pennant in Milwaukee, but he would have plenty of great teams and plenty of great days at the ballpark in his later career. Here he is pictured in Palm Springs during spring training with Pat and his daughters circa 1990. Dalton Family Collection.

19. Retirement from baseball would bring continued adventures for Dalton, including spending time with Pat, celebrating the Hall of Fame induction of Earl Weaver in 1996, and reminiscing about his days in Baltimore as he was inducted into the Orioles Hall of Fame in 1997. Dalton Family Collection.

20. When he was not on the road in his later years, Dalton could be found at his home in Carefree, Arizona. His activities were wide ranging, from raising funds for the Desert Foothills Land Trust (which would name a trail after Dalton for his efforts) or entertaining in his home office (2002). Dalton Family Collection.

10

Getting His Hands in the Dirt

1971–72

With all that Harry Dalton had to accomplish with the Angels, his priority was to find a manager who could unify a divided dugout. Regarding candidates to replace Lefty Phillips, pundits were quick to speculate that Earl Weaver would be joining Dalton out West.

"I'd love to have him," Dalton said, "but he's under contract with Baltimore. I'm not going to raid that organization or try to. The Baltimore people know that, and Earl knows that." Dalton would say that he had several candidates in mind but would not rush his decision. "I'd rather take a little more time and get the right man than rush and pick the wrong one."[1]

Picking the "right man" took roughly a week. On December 6 the Angels announced that Del Rice, their Triple-A manager the year before, would lead the team. Rice was a former Major League player who had wanted to be a manager for as long as he could remember. By the time Dalton tabbed him, Rice was a longtime Minor League manager who had won a pennant with Salt Lake City and was named *The Sporting News* Minor League Manager of the Year in 1971.[2] Dalton was pleased with his choice. "I waited 40 days to make [my] choice," he said, "because I wanted to be sure to come up with the right man. Del fits the role completely as the man we need."[3]

As for how Rice categorized his managerial style, he quickly pointed out that he believed the Angels would "have fun" under him: "We're going to work hard, but we will have fun." Rice was also quick to distance himself from Anaheim during the Lefty Phillips era: "I don't know what went on here last summer. I wasn't here. I don't want to know. I want togetherness."[4] Those familiar with Rice thought he had an excellent chance to get it from his players. When asked about the new skipper, utility infielder Syd O'Brien pointed out that Rice "will make a good manager. He treats players like men."[5]

In terms of players, both Rice and Harry Dalton understood that they could not rely on the farm system to help the team in the short term. This paucity of players guaranteed that Dalton would look to make moves to bolster the roster ahead of spring training, and he had Gene Autry's blessing to do so. According to Dalton, he did not feel the Angels needed a total rebuild of the roster, but he did think his team needed a power hitter, a shortstop, and a catcher. Dalton made fast and furious moves to augment the team. At the end of November, the Angels selected four players in the Rule 5 draft and traded pitcher Dave LaRoche to the Minnesota Twins for veteran infielder Leo Cardenas. Then, at the winter meetings in Arizona, Dalton would be involved with a series of deals, both made and unmade, that would reverberate through the game.

Even before he named a manager, Dalton tried to reunite with Frank Robinson, whom the Orioles were shopping in the wake of his 28 home run, 99 RBI season. Eventually, though, the Orioles' asking price got too steep, leading Gene Autry to wonder if the Orioles did not want to trade with their former GM. Dalton also tried to swing a deal that would have made news on both coasts. On December 2 Dalton passed up a deal with the Dodgers that would have sent Bill Buckner, pitcher Claude Osteen, and Wes Parker to California for Angels ace Andy Messersmith. When asked why he did not pull the trigger, the usually cagey Dalton admitted that the sticking point had nothing to do with the Dodgers or the Angels. Instead, the deal stalled for Dalton when the Yankees would not send catcher Thurman Munson to the Angels for Jim Fregosi.[6]

It was shocking to Angels fans that Fregosi, the face of the franchise since its birth in 1961, would be on the trading block. By the winter of 1971, Jim Fregosi was the living embodiment of the California Angels. On the field, he was one of the best shortstops in the American League. This was especially true at the plate, where he hit enough to be a real threat for the early Angels' rivals. Off the field, he was the clubhouse leader, a favorite of Gene Autry, willing to back up management in the newspapers (e.g., the Alex Johnson affair), and still be considered one of the guys because he was comfortable enough partaking in the nightlife and extra female company afforded a young Major Leaguer in LA.[7] Thanks to a large contract and an aging body, he was also expendable by the winter of 1971.

On some level, even if Fregosi's body betrayed him, it was a stretch to many that the Angels would contemplate trading him. However, one condition of Dalton taking the job was that he would have the autonomy to change the roster however he saw fit. This became evident to the public when Dalton floated Fregosi's name in the press as possible trade material, and then Dalton traded for Cardenas. In the aftermath of that deal, Dalton pointed out that Fregosi could be traded but "only for the right price."[8] Ten days after acquiring Cardenas, Dalton got what he asked for.

On December 10, the last day of the interleague trading period, Dalton traded Fregosi to the New York Mets for a host of players, including catcher Frank Estrada, pitcher Don Rose, rookie right fielder Leroy Stanton, and a skinny right-handed pitcher from Texas whom everyone knew could throw a ball through a brick wall. However, not everyone was sure he had enough accuracy to hit the wall in the first place. His name was Nolan Ryan.

In hindsight, it seems like Dalton's trade for Ryan was on par with his acquisition of Frank Robinson for Milt Pappas, Jack Baldschun, and Wayne Simpson. History shows that Dalton would trade for a Hall of Fame talent and give up next to nothing to get it. At the time, however, the deal was not that cut and dried.

Contemporary reports of the deal make it clear that sportswriters of the time saw the deal for exactly what it was. One team (the Mets) was gaining a proven Major League talent in Fregosi, while the other (the Angels) was taking a flyer on a young pitcher who had not found his stride with the Mets despite much talent.

On the day of the deal, Mets manager Gil Hodges told the *New York Times* that, from the Mets' standpoint, "you always hate to give up on the arm like Ryan's," but he would not "hesitate to make a trade for somebody who might help us right now, and Fregosi is such a guy."

Mets GM Bob Scheffing took Hodges's comments one step further. In his mind, Ryan had run out of time to prove his worth. "I really can't say I quit on him," Scheffing said. "But we've had him three full years, and, although he's a hell of a prospect, he hasn't done it for us. How long can you wait? I can't rate him in the same category as Tom Seaver, Jerry Koosman, or Gary Gentry."[9]

Of course, in baseball, one team's sullied prospect is another team's future star. Harry Dalton did not know that was what he was getting with Ryan, but he was willing to part with Fregosi to find out. "We picked up one of baseball's best arms in Ryan," Dalton said. "We know of his control problems, but he had the best arm in the National League and, at 24, he is just coming into his own."[10] And Fregosi and Ryan? They both saw the deal as a welcome change.

Fregosi would tell Ross Newhan of the *Los Angeles Times* that while he felt he was a "better shortstop than [Leo] Cardenas," he was glad to be another ballplayer and not a mouthpiece and de facto captain, as he was in the Angels' clubhouse. As for what he thought of Dalton trading him, Fregosi could understand, even though he was miffed at the Angels generally. "The man [Dalton] wanted to express his authority," Fregosi said, "and I don't blame him. I don't think he has anything personal against me."[11]

Ryan expected the deal. He had asked the Mets to trade him that fall, and he had a feeling that the Mets would move him on the interleague trading deadline. As he recounted the story in March 2015, Ryan told his wife, Ruth, precisely that on the morning in question as he headed out to classes at Alvin Community College. Thinking back on it, Ryan thought that the Angels, after a dismal 1971, would be more open to giving a young player like him a chance.[12]

When the dust settled, Dalton realized that he had upset the natural order of things. However, like his attempt at moving Mike Epstein to the Orioles' outfield, Dalton was not worried about perception. "I believe Fregosi can still be productive," he said, "but I'm determined to put the 25 best players in uniform."[13] Fans of the Angels were not so sure. They lambasted Dalton in the press throughout California in the days immediately after the trade. One fan said that Dalton should "get the Most Valuable Dumbbell Award" for his dealing of Fregosi for Ryan and the signing of Cardenas "and a couple of minor leaguers."[14]

The aftermath of the Ryan-for-Fregosi trade is an excellent time to remind the reader that Harry Dalton did not care if fans or the media thought he had made a dumb move. However, this did not mean he did not care about the fan base of the team he was running. The old newspaper reporter in Dalton would never forget the fan who made the game what it was and allowed his team to make money. He always worked to give them the best available product (or the perception thereof). In California, this meant creating ties in the community. To help in this area, Dalton continued to specialize in his front office. This time, he hired Tom Seberg from the Dodgers to head the newly created position of community coordinator.

As Dalton saw it, "This [LA and Orange County] is a tremendous population area, but the Angels had not been staffed properly to take advantage of it. They weren't taking the club out into the community, and they weren't taking the players to the people. The fans love to get close to athletes and management, and I'm a great believer in the value of this type of program."[15] With this mandate, Dalton and Seberg took the Angels on the road to businesses throughout Orange County in February. Vada Pinson, Clyde Wright, and Rudy May went to a Laura Scudder's potato chip plant. Dalton, Del Rice, and others toured a mock-up of Skylab at McDonnell Douglas's space division in Huntington Beach. The whole goal was to improve relations between the Angels and their fans. This opened up some unique experiences for his family. One place where he went to foster a better relationship with fans was the Walt Disney Company. This led to the Daltons appearing in parades at the park for events like Opening Day. Kim Dalton, who was approaching her teen years in California, remembers this experience vividly: "I remember it so well. I thought we were the coolest people on the planet because of that parade."[16]

City hall also appreciated Dalton's efforts. Tom Liegler, who worked for the city of Anaheim, did not mince words when he reported that 1971 had soured the relationship between the city and the Angels. "Our relationship was definitely strained," he said, thanks mainly to Dick Walsh fostering a combative attitude with the city over the finer points of the lease at the Big A, as the Angels' stadium in Anaheim was known.[17] Liegler did not have those types of fights with Harry Dalton. "Harry and I both get to work before 8," Liegler reported, "and he'll call me just about every morning to see if there are any problems. The whole atmosphere is more relaxed."[18]

Ever the realist, Dalton understood that most fans just wanted a winning team. However, his efforts to improve relations with the fan base included giving them a better insight into how he planned to build the team. In short, winning would not happen overnight. "I don't believe in making a trade just to get a headline. This is going to have to be done in degrees," he said.[19]

The first step in attempting to build the winner that Dalton envisioned occurred in Holtville, California, a town located at the doorstep of the Marine Corps Air Station in El Centro, hard on the Mexican border. It was as hardscrabble a place to train a Major League baseball team as could be imagined. Nevertheless, for the first two weeks every spring, it was where the Angels went to get into shape at the outset of the spring training season. The living conditions were spartan; the players showered and changed in a barn known as "Autry's Corral." The weather was miserably hot during the day and unbelievably cold at night.[20] The Angels shared the grass beyond the walls of their four practice fields with grazing sheep.[21] An Angels beat reporter who had spent two weeks there in the late 1960s referred to it as "Stalag 17," after World War II's infamous German prisoner of war camp.[22] Like the Orioles facility in Thomasville, Georgia, Holtville became a proving ground for Minor League players and nonroster invitees to the Major League training camp. By the early 1970s, however, the whole team would spend time there, which quickly put Dalton at odds with his new addition, Nolan Ryan.

As Ryan would recall, the main point of contention between the two was that Holtville was closed to families. This required Ryan to do some creative thinking about housing his wife, Ruth, and young son, Reid, whom he was reluctant to leave alone in the new environs of Palm Springs.[23] Still, while Holtville was less than ideal regarding creature comforts, it quickly proved its worth by allowing players like Ryan to become acquainted with his new teammates and coaches without the added pressure of having fans around watching every move. This situation quickly paid dividends for Ryan, who built excellent working relationships with catcher Jeff Torborg and new pitching coach Tom Morgan—connections that would pay off later in 1972.

The early days at Holtville also seemed to put Harry Dalton at ease. As the calendar turned to March and his team prepared for exhibition games, Dalton felt that the Angels were improved from when he took over. "As far as I'm concerned, I've done what I wanted to do since I came here," he said. "We've tightened our defense, added speed and depth, and improved our power potential."[24] This did not mean that the team could not improve even further. "We certainly haven't added much power. In fact, we do not have what I would call an established power hitter," he commented. "I know we could use more socks behind the plate and in the outfield, but I'm more than happy defensively at those positions."[25]

Perhaps more important than the talent he had brought in was the change in attitude at the Angels' training camp. Simply put, the Angels seemed more at ease with Harry Dalton in charge of their collective fate. Numerous players and coaches quickly pointed out that Dalton was a "nice guy," and Nolan Ryan was among them. He would remember that Dalton was "pleasant and positive" and appreciated that Dalton gave him time to learn how to be a Major League pitcher, even though it took some patience in 1972, as Ryan continued to be wild during his spring starts.[26] Ryan was not the only one who thought Dalton was good for the Angels. Much like in Baltimore, even the "fringe" players at the Major League level appreciated how Dalton carried on relationships with them. In the spring of 1971, Jimmy Hutto was the epitome of a fringe big leaguer. The Philadelphia Phillies had drafted him in the seventh round of the inaugural amateur draft in 1965. He would make his Major League debut five years later and then be traded to Baltimore in the winter of 1970. After a productive year with the Rochester farm team for the Orioles in 1971, Hutto would find himself selected by the Angels in the Rule 5 draft in the winter of 1971. There, he would again come in contact with Harry Dalton, meeting him at spring training in Miami in 1971. He would quickly develop an affinity for the new GM. "Harry was a very straight-up kind of a guy and a much different type of general manager than I had been accustomed to in Philadelphia," Hutto said. "Harry told the truth no matter whether you liked it or not."[27] This was a trait Dalton exhibited throughout his entire career.

Dalton's ability to connect with players of all skill levels (and increasingly all socioeconomic levels as well) would serve him well throughout his career. However, as he continued to try and put a solid team on the field for California, issues off the field threatened to change the dynamics of how Harry Dalton and other GMs of the late twentieth century would relate and interact with players. Labor relations would soon become the No. 1 off-field issue in the game, and Dalton would soon find his personal beliefs on players' rights at odds with trying to help meet the agenda of bosses who looked to thwart the budding power of the MLBPA.

The idea of a players' union in baseball was not new in the 1970s. Various individuals had attempted to organize players throughout the history of the game. In 1885 star player John Montgomery Ward organized the Brotherhood of Professional Base Ball Players in response to National League magnates' attempt to cap salaries. The formation of this organization was met with applause by players, and by 1886 roughly 90 percent of the players in the National League (nine hundred players) had become members.[28] Ward followed up the creation of the Brotherhood by founding the Players League (PL) as direct competition for the National League in 1890. Despite attracting several high-profile players, the league would fold after one season, and the league's death would also spell the end of the Brotherhood.[29]

The next attempt to organize players occurred in 1912. This time, the forming of the Professional Baseball Players Fraternity was a response to what the players deemed unfair treatment in the aftermath of events of 1911 and 1912. The first event was the death of star player Addie Joss. Joss, a pitcher for Cleveland, died unexpectedly from meningitis in the spring of 1911, and league magnates enraged players when they refused to allow time off for the funeral. Then, in 1912 the Detroit Tigers staged a localized strike to protest the suspension of star center fielder Ty Cobb after he fought with a fan who had been heckling him. As word of the strike by the Tigers spread, players began to call for the formation of a union. Into that void stepped former player Dave Fultz, who helped to organize the Players' Fraternity in September 1912. This organization would push for, among other things, increased safety measures for the players. The high-water mark for the fraternity occurred in 1914, when American League chief Ban Johnson recognized it in response to the founding of the Federal League. The recognition of the fraternity was short-lived, however. Johnson disavowed the fraternity as the American and National Leagues began to make inroads against the Federal League. Then, when the union called for a strike prior to the 1917 season, the fraternity collapsed.[30]

The Players' Fraternity would be the last attempt to organize until after World War II, when a former National Labor Relations Board member, Robert Murphy, founded the American Baseball Guild to strike down the reserve clause. The guild was classified as a "prophetic failure." However, the short-lived union (1946 was the only year of operation) was thwarted when Major League Baseball agreed to create a players' pension fund in 1947.[31]

While the pension fund was seen as a win for the players because it led to the founding of the MLBPA, the whole arrangement was a house of cards. The players did not have a true union. As historian Charles Korr would illustrate, the MLBPA was a "house union" thanks to the inability of the players to elect its president.[32] This was the status quo until 1965, when the players felt it was time to elect a union chief who would be separate from the league and fight for the pension and other issues the players deemed important. This led to the creation of an MLBPA search and screen committee that consisted of player representatives Harvey Kuenn from the Pirates and Robin Roberts and Jim Bunning of the Phillies. This committee would spend most of the winter of 1965 looking for a suitable candidate and eventually settle on a man who would transform the MLBPA from a house union to one of the most powerful unions in the United States.[33]

By 1965 Marvin Miller was a seasoned labor negotiator. The diminutive New Yorker with a trademark pencil-thin mustache had spent the earliest days of his career with the War Production and War Labor Boards in Washington DC. Then, in 1950 Miller moved to the United Steel Workers Union (USW). He would spend the next fifteen years helping to make USW a powerhouse of organized labor.[34] When first approached about the MLBPA job, he was unsure that he wanted to run the inept organization. It was hardly a union at all. Eventually, though, Miller saw the merit of the move and took over as the head of the MLBPA in the spring of 1966 after he was voted in, 409–136, by the players and coaches (who had voting rights because they received pension benefits).[35]

From his earliest days, Miller would look to transform the union from a one-issue organization (the pension) to one that fought for an array of issues the players deemed essential. This would draw the wrath of the owners and GMs for the next eighteen years. Still, he would help the players win major concessions in 1968, outlined in the first collective bargaining agreement (CBA) in baseball history. It included an increase in the amount the owners would contribute to the pension fund and an increase in the minimum players' salary (to $10,000) and also called for the ability of players to ask for third-party arbitration of grievances. This series of victories would make Harry Dalton remark that Miller had the players "all stirred up."[36]

As the 1970s began, Dalton's opinion of Miller would be the opinion of many in baseball. This was especially the case as spring training continued in 1972. Still, as the circumstances of his leaving Baltimore indicated, Dalton's opinion of Miller and what he was trying to accomplish with the union ultimately softened. This led to an understanding of the players' stance on many issues. Still, the end of spring training in 1972 would test that newfound understanding as a labor showdown threatened to derail the start of the season.

Once again, pension contributions by ownership were at the heart of the argument between players and management. Specifically, ownership balked at increasing payment in line with the new television broadcast deal for 1971–72. Having the ownership contribution tied to the TV deal was not a new idea. Since the advent of the pension, the players and owners had made contributions following a 60/40 owners-players split of the proceeds of the sale of the World Series and as much as a 95/5 split of the All-Star Game television money. This changed in 1966 when Marvin Miller negotiated a flat contribution to counteract what he saw as ownership manipulating their contribution by hiding portions of the money received for the World Series and the All-Star Game with the revenue for the Game of the Week, which was not subject to a split.[37] In addition, a switch to a flat total guaranteed that the players would receive a portion of the growing income from televised games. As Rob Bellamy, a leading historian of baseball on television, notes, "the owners had made clear that they were not going to directly give the players a cut of the ever-increasing TV money."[38] A flat contribution guaranteed that the players would see part of the money. Finally, Miller used the flat contribution tactic to secure the long-term nature of the pension. Bellamy notes that after the advent of the pension, ownership saw it as a gift to the players that could go away if sufficient cash did not exist to fund it. What a flat contribution of the TV money guaranteed was that the union did not have to rely on ownership to decide if that money was available.[39]

Ownership made the first flat contribution in 1967: a $4.1 million lump sum. The next year's contribution was for the same amount. Problems began in 1969 when ownership negotiated a new three-year TV deal with NBC that netted the clubs $16.5 million. At that time, the players' union wanted to see an increase in the amounts paid to the pension fund over the deal's life. This was a nonstarter for ownership and led to a player boycott of spring training camps, though it was far from a blanket walkout; teams had some players report despite the union's stance. Ultimately, while the players did not see a graduated yearly increase in pension contributions, they pressured ownership into an increase to $5.45 million.[40] By 1971–72 the union was looking for a four-year CBA (to run concurrently with the new TV deal worth $71.5 million) and increases in pension contributions over the life of that contract that would help to offset inflation. The main areas in which this inflation was felt were in the cost of the health insurance plan covered by the union (the premium total had risen to $500,000) and the amount paid to players in the form of a pension check. The union sought a 17 percent increase in the owners' pension contribution to offset these areas, which equated to a $6.5 million contribution.

When the owners balked at that suggestion, the MLBPA offered to allow the owners to take the issue to arbitration. This, too, was turned down, and the players quickly began to plan for a strike. A group of owners that baseball writer Roger Angell would refer to as "Cro Magnon," including Gussie Busch of the Cardinals, Ewing Kauffman of the Kansas City Royals, and Dalton's former employer Jerry Hoffberger, were livid that players would consider a strike. They became dead set on using the issue to break the union.[41] Busch was the most vocal, going so far as to dare the players to strike: "We're not going to give another damn cent, and if they want to strike, let them strike." Gene Autry took another approach. Autry, who had spent years in Hollywood, where the influence of unions was prevalent, announced that he could always get out of baseball: "I say let them strike if they want to strike. . . . I can still back the horse out of the garage and make it that way." Others, like Bob Carpenter, the president and owner of the Philadelphia Phillies, were less antagonistic. "I'm sure that if we waited a few more days," he said, "we would have resolved the issue on our own, and the players would have come into camp on their own."[42]

While the owners expressed various degrees of rhetoric, the players' union was busy counting votes. According to Harry Dalton, the pension contribution issue was the most significant difference between the players' union and the ownership. In 1991 he would say that the most significant difference between the owners and the MLBPA was that with the latter, the sense of purpose and the message were clear because the structure of the union was "a pyramid with Miller at the top." Conversely, John Gaherin, the leader of the owners' Player Relations Committee (PRC), "was subject to twenty different viewpoints, twenty different vested interests, twenty different reasons for getting started [negotiating] or not wanting to get started."[43]

As for Dalton, his early comments mimicked the party line of ownership. On the very day that his team would vote 33–0 to strike if it came to that, Dalton told the *Los Angeles Times* that he understood the ownership position and that their financial situation was more fluid year to year than the average fan realized. "In bad years, you can take a real beating. Only the clubs in big markets have a cushion," he said. In true Dalton fashion, he then laid out a three-pronged plan to help the two sides bridge the ever-growing financial gap and mend fences in the current negotiations:

1. Legalize incentive contracts, under which a player's accomplishments would be weighted against a prearranged scale.
2. Establish a scale of base salaries, with a player paid so much for every year he is in the game. Raises would be on top of this, but owners would be allowed to cut more than the 20% now allowable [from one year to another].
3. Establish a scale of salary cuts. If a player, for example, makes $30,000, he could be cut 20%. If he makes $40,000, he would be cut 30%.[44]

Dalton's suggestions would fall on deaf ears. The players would vote 663–10 to strike, and the vote by his club of 33–0 would lead to a photo of Dalton with Marvin Miller that showed the GM's utter exasperation with the events occurring in baseball. However, from the commencement of the strike on April 1, Dalton's comments became more in line with his sense of humor as he tried to find levity in the work stoppage. For instance, in a weird turn of events, players and management still attended the Baseball Writers Association of America awards dinner in LA to celebrate the best players, managers, and executives for 1971. This event allowed Dalton to comment, tongue in cheek, that his new fireballing righty with control issues, Nolan Ryan, must be thrilled with the walkout because "this is the first strike he's been involved in all spring."[45]

Once the strike began, Dalton tried to stay busy. However, much of what he could take care of involved canceling flight reservations for early-season games. The strike would last thirteen days and show the owners that the MLBPA was much stronger than they had anticipated. In the end, eighty-six games were canceled and never made up, and every club felt some financial discomfort. According to Harry Dalton, the Angels were no different. "We've lost $200,000, and we only had two dates scheduled at home. The economic fallout is liable to go on for months, maybe several seasons," he said. Dalton also felt that the players would ultimately feel the financial hardship of the strike: "The average player is giving up $1,200 or $1,300 in salary now for some sort of small percentage gain in his pension 20 or 30 years from now."[46]

Financial ramifications aside, Dalton understood that once the season got going, the easiest way for his team not to feel the effects of the strike at the gate would be for the Angels (and the rest of the league) to put the best product on the field that they could. This was always a Dalton mantra. The former PR man knew that to get the most out of your audience, you had to give them something worthwhile to invest in, emotionally or financially. "I'm sure there are some fans discouraged, disturbed, and even angry," he said. "What we as a team and a league have to do is play in such a manner as to make them forget [the strike] in a hurry."[47] The Angels would make their fans forget. Unfortunately, however, the Angels did not replace memories of the strike with winning baseball early on. However, as the year went on, the Angels would show signs of vast improvement.

The Angels would go 5-8 in the truncated playing schedule for the month of April. From the start, this put pressure on Dalton, who in turn felt the need to address the Angels' dismal play with Del Rice. The two men met in a closed-door session that was reported in the press. When asked about his team's play and what he and Rice discussed in the meeting, Dalton quickly pointed out that the Angels had "four regulars not hitting," which did not leave much margin for error.[48] While Dalton was worried about the hitting, the Angels had pitching issues in April that quickly took over the narrative.

Andy Messersmith would win 1–0 on Opening Day and would not win the rest of the month, although he was occasionally a victim of poor run support.[49] Meanwhile, Clyde Wright was victimized by his defense in two of his starts. The defense was especially abhorrent on April 21, when two errors by the Angels led to three unearned runs for the Texas Rangers in a 7–6 Rangers win that saw California squander fourteen hits.[50] As for Nolan Ryan, he would be his inconsistent self in April 1972. He would strike out 15 hitters, walk 11 (including 5 each in two starts), and end the month with a 1-2 record.[51] To top it off, the bullpen was no help. In the April games, the Angels' bullpen would surrender 42 hits and 20 earned runs and have an ERA of 5.29 in thirty-four innings.[52] In short, this was not what Dalton expected when he sang the praises of his pitching staff during spring training.

The team would also struggle in May but less so. They would finish the month 13-15. The big, glaring problem was that the pitching staff, this time hindered by a rash of injuries, continued to underachieve. Ryan would suffer a pulled groin, shoulder problems sidelined Wright, and Messersmith would develop tendinitis in the middle finger on his pitching hand.[53] In the end, for the second straight month, the Angels would give up more runs than they scored, ending the month nine games out of first place with a record of 18-23.[54]

A second straight losing month led to the first postmortem of the season. Dalton believed that the Angels' issues came down to three factors: "One would be the injuries to our pitching. Two would be the fundamental mistakes that both veterans and rookies have made. Three would be a lack of scoring punch."[55] Pundits did not blame Dalton for these deficiencies directly. Injuries were a part of any season, and the Angels pitching staff just happened to run into a rash of them early in the season. Del Rice took the brunt of the blame for the lack of fundamentals, with his methods in spring training being called into question by the media. As for the lack of offensive power, sportswriter Ross Newhan quickly pointed out that from almost the first day Dalton was in charge in California, he was actively looking for a big bat to sit in the middle of the Angels lineup. He would even make a trade. The fact of the matter was that the landscape was bare in the American League that year, and Dalton, in his typical fashion, was not going to leverage the future for a better present if he didn't think it was worth it. This led him to pass on possible deals for sluggers like Frank Howard of the Texas Rangers and Willie Horton of the Detroit Tigers.

"I won't trade a Wright or Messersmith for the type of hitters available this year," Dalton said. He then called for Major League Baseball to reconsider allowing interleague trades in the season's first few months. Dalton also acknowledged that the dearth of available talent extended to the Angels' farm system, saying, "It's not the barren waste that it has been called, but there isn't a whole lot of immediate help."

It was not Dalton's fault that his team suddenly could not hit, pitch, or catch the baseball. Still, he understood that his fame preceded him, leaving him with a smaller window to learn the ropes in California. "I know the fans must be asking themselves, 'well, when is this super exec from the East going to do something,'" he said. Despite the struggles, Dalton still believed in his process, and he stood by it as he pulled back the curtain for the fans: "The point is, I can't tear up the nucleus of the future because of the past. I can't be pressured by the 11 years that came before I did." Dalton then concluded that he thought his plan for the Angels was progressing as he had planned: "When I took the job, I had three goals. One was to improve the team on the field. . . . Despite the injuries, we're only four games behind the pace of last year's team. . . . Two was to take the 1972 Angels out to the people of Orange County. Three was to beef up the farm system. The record may not show it, but I think we've made strides in all three areas."

No matter what he thought, Dalton understood that his team was not drawing at the gate. The Angels were roughly eighty thousand fans off their attendance figure from May 1971. However, according to Dalton, a lack of giveaways in the first few months of 1972 was the difference. Dalton wanted to lure fans to Anaheim by using the product on the field.

The product was much the same in the summer months as it was in May. The Angels would go 13-14 in June, 13-16 in July, and 13-14 in August. The starting pitching was much improved, thanks in large part to the improvement of Nolan Ryan. From April on, his innings increased while his walks, his ultimate nemesis, stabilized. Meanwhile, his strikeout totals skyrocketed. He would fan 43 in June, 83 in July, and 62 in August. At the same time, he would walk 27, 28, and 31. During that stretch, he would go 11-8. The catalyst for change was constant work with catcher Jeff Torborg and pitching coach Tom Morgan to smooth out Ryan's mechanics. The result, as 1972 progressed, was a repeatable delivery that started to bear positive results.[56] Ryan would go 19-16 and lead MLB in strikeouts (329) and shutouts (9). Of course he also led the league in walks (157) and wild pitches (18). True to form, Ryan had electric stuff. He was also inconsistent.

The Angels finally put a winning month together in September, going 17-11, including six one-run wins in a row to end the month. They would then finish the year by going 1-2 in October. In all, the second half of the season was an improvement record-wise; the Angels were 35-28. Still, the issues that had plagued the team in the opening months are what plagued them later in the season. They didn't hit with any consistency, and even though the starting pitching improved, the pitching staff surrendered more runs than the team scored. The team runs differential for the year was −79. This, combined with myriad other problems, made Harry Dalton feel the same about his team at the end of the year as he did at the end of April: his team was fundamentally deficient. "We missed cutoff men, threw to the wrong base, and ran poorly," Dalton said. This combination led him to conclude that he was "disappointed" by a team he thought should have finished at or above .500 for the year. As for who was to blame for the underperformance, Del Rice quickly became a target. He did try to defend himself and the methods he employed. However, in hindsight, he acknowledged that he did not get the best look at his team (veterans included) in spring training, which hurt in the long run.[57]

As for what Dalton thought he could do to help his team, he established that his main goal was to fortify the offense again. He also reiterated that he and his charges needed to improve the farm system. Finally, there was speculation that Dalton, who never shied away from changing managers if he felt it would help his club, would cut ties with Del Rice after one season. Over the next three seasons, Dalton would attempt to do all of those things and continue to increase the Angels' footprint in the greater Los Angeles area. It would be a struggle and take a lot out of Harry Dalton. Still, he would push to make the Angels the best team he could. Along the way, his most significant on-the-field risk would blossom into the best pitcher in baseball, and his family would continue to grow closer away from work even as Dalton's methods at work were called into question for the first time in his career.

11

Looking for the Right Combination

1973–76

From 1973 to 1976, Harry Dalton continued his attempts to fulfill his three goals for the Angels: making the farm system better, making the team on the field better, and making them relevant in Los Angeles. The results were mixed. On the field, the Angels would continue to struggle. However, Harry Dalton would not stop trying to find the best roster and management combinations to make the Angels a winner. He would also oversee an overhaul of the Angels' Minor League system and scouting department in an effort to produce more players in the wake of his predecessors' lack of attention to that issue. Finally, Dalton would continue trying to entice fans to Anaheim Stadium even as the specter of a successful Dodgers team haunted his efforts.

Along the way, he would keep working with his counterparts in collegiate baseball to bring the two sides closer together. He would also adapt successfully to the coming of free agency. All of this would help Dalton maintain his healthy relationship with countless members of the baseball community while his own teams struggled,

As he had done in Baltimore, Dalton started working in the fall of 1972 to make his team better for 1973. That September, Dalton held his first fall organizational meeting, bringing together a number of his scouts, the Minor League managers, and the Angels' front office staff. As usual, the agenda was jammed with meetings on topics ranging from scouting philosophy to player evaluation and playing techniques. All of these topics were designed to "put together an organization" and foster an environment where "hard work, loyalty, [and] pride" were second nature.[1]

The meetings also allowed Dalton to continue to shape baseball operations in a way that would leave his mark. To that end, an important addition was the standardization of terms used by the scouts to evaluate players. This became necessary because Dalton felt there was a degree of ambiguity in the terms used by the Angels to that point. For instance, prior to his tenure, "Tops," "Average," and "Not Desirable" were all terms that scouts used to describe prospects in the Angels system, and Dalton moved to eliminate them. Beginning in the fall of 1972, the Angels replaced those terms with a scale using "Excellent," "Good," "Fair," "Poor," and "Bad." Dalton also instituted a new numerical scale that rated prospects and their skills between 1 and 5, with 1 being excellent and 5 being bad.[2]

The fall meeting also allowed Dalton to fully evaluate the scouting staff. When Dalton took over in 1971, the Angels employed twenty-three full- or part-time scouts. Most of the team's scouting coverage focused on California, the only state with more than one scout. The most experienced of the scouts were Nick Kamzic and Dick Wiencek.[3]

Kamzic was from Chicago and had been a scout since 1948. He had worked for the Reds and the Milwaukee Braves before Roland Hemond hired him as a scout during the hurried creation of the California Angels. As for Wiencek, he began scouting in 1956 for the Washington Senators and continued to work for the team when it moved to Minnesota. He went to California in 1971. By 1973 both men had earned respect and made numerous successful signings, including Rick Reichardt for the Angels in 1964. Wiencek's early signings for the Senators/Twins included Hall of Famer Jim Kaat.[4]

With the exception of Wiencek and Kamzic, the Angels' scouting department was relatively inexperienced, and Tom Sommers, the farm/scouting director for the team since taking over for Roland Hemond, described numerous members of his department as inexperienced in both evaluation of talent and "being a good paper man."[5] This inexperience was not lost on Dalton, who, following the 1972 season, had various critiques on the scouts he had under contract. The most important of these was that the scouts needed to be forthcoming with information: "The front office runs on information—be sure we know what you know."[6]

As the '73 season approached, the inexperience of the scouting department continued to be an area of concern. In the team's budget document for the coming season, Dalton noted that the scouting budget for 1973 included hiring "two full-time scouts, three part-time scouts, and the new scouting director."[7] This increase came to fruition in January 1974, when Dalton, who was banned for one year from hiring any of his previous staff from Baltimore after the Angels were found guilty of tampering, hired Ray Scarborough and Al Kubski as full-time scouts in December 1973. He also hired Walter Shannon at that time to oversee the scouting department. From that point, there was a gradual phasing out of the Angels scouts who were on staff prior to Dalton being named the GM.

By 1975 the only members of the original farm/scouting department left were farm director Tom Sommers and Nick Kamzic. Sommers would recall that this led to hard feelings among the holdovers as time passed. "Harry had a tendency to only listen to the people he brought over from Baltimore, and it made things hard sometimes," Sommers recalled.[8] Of particular note, Sommers claimed that Dalton and Kamzic had a complicated relationship. However, this inability to listen to new voices should not be seen as one of the reasons why Dalton struggled in California. Instead, it is an example of the time-honored tradition in baseball of trusting the people you know. Bruce Manno, who would be trained by Dalton later in his career, explained the dynamic this way: "Usually, you can see the value of that person [one you have worked with longer] more than others since you have worked with them so long. . . . Their opinion still matters to you."[9]

Whatever the reasoning, Tom Sommers was quick to point out that as Dalton brought more and more people from Baltimore, the two groups worked well together daily. "Walter Shannon became one of my best friends and was a person I never met before he came with Harry," he reported. "All those guys were good baseball guys, and we worked well together."[10]

This ability to work together was necessary for the Angels as Dalton, Shannon, and Sommers tried to overcome years of neglect toward the farm system, which wasn't producing enough everyday Major Leaguers prior to Dalton's arrival.

To illustrate this, from 1968 to 1971, the Angels' scouting efforts produced two players who contributed to Dalton's early teams. In contrast, from 1972 to 1976, coinciding with Dalton's scouting overhaul, the Angels would produce seven Major League players. Under Dalton, the Angels would cast their nets wider thanks to the addition of scouts in areas like Florida, and they would operate tryout camps as well as back up their reports with information from the fledgling Major League Scouting Bureau.[11] Moreover, they would draft more college-age players, who were ostensibly closer to being ready to help the Angels at the Major League level.[12]

Most of these moves did have the desired effect. The percentage of players drafted by the Angels who would reach the Major Leagues would increase from 13 percent from 1968 to 1971 to 21.5 percent from 1972 to 1975.[13] There was only one problem. Many players whom the Dalton Gang drafted during that period would become viable Major Leaguers for other clubs thanks to trades put together after Dalton left in 1977. Still, by 1976 Dalton had righted the sinking ship that was Angels' Minor League system. This turnaround led *Sports Illustrated* to comment that "California could soon become a devil to beat."[14] Harry Dalton believed so too, but he knew that it would take longer than the average fan or journalist thought. When asked about his team in 1976, Dalton said he believed that the Angels could "move up" the standings by 1977 and that 1978 had the potential to be a "very, very, good year."[15] It turned out that Dalton was right. The Angels were a winner in 1978.

Nevertheless, as he predicted, it took every one of the intervening years to put a good team on the field. Still, Dalton would work tirelessly to ensure that the Angels continued to improve on the field. Moreover, in time, players and management would acknowledge that Dalton should be lauded for his work leading up to that moment, even though that improvement was not measured in winning seasons or pennants when Dalton was in charge.

From 1973 to 1976, the Angels would undergo a significant transformation at the Major League level in an attempt to turn the corner. The roster would see new faces every year. For example, by December 1974 Dalton had changed just over 75 percent of the Angels' roster since November 1972, and changes would continue.[16] The manager's office would also see numerous changes. Dalton would change managers so often, searching for the right fit, that the press dubbed him "Hangman Harry" for firing four managers in five years. None of these moves would see the Angels get over the hump in the AL West, though there were many factors (including the best team in baseball being in their division) contributing to the Angels' less than stellar status in the standings. That did not mean Dalton's teams were without promise. As longtime baseball writer Peter Gammons would put it in the spring of 2022, Harry Dalton would help make the Angels "something people wanted to watch."[17]

Dalton's first managerial change occurred shortly after his first season in charge; he fired Del Rice and hired Bobby Winkles as manager. As for what prompted the firing, Dalton felt that the Angels underperformed when it came to fundamentals, something he had mentioned in the spring and during his postmortem on the 1972 season. Dalton laid the blame at Rice's feet.[18]

Despite Rice wanting to keep the job, Dalton also felt that Rice did not maintain the enthusiasm necessary to help carry a team to a winning season. "I don't expect a constant rah-rah attitude," he said, "but when you are playing 162 games, there has to be an unbroken thread of determination."[19] Dalton felt that Winkles could provide that thread while also being in a better position to help the Angels reach the fundamental threshold Dalton felt was necessary. Much of that had to do with his background before coming to the Angels in 1972.

Born in Tuckerman, Arkansas, in 1930, Winkles spent seven years in the Minors as a middle infielder, including two stints in Triple-A ball sandwiched around service in the army coinciding with the Korean War. Winkles finally retired from play in 1958 and was hired in 1959 as the first varsity baseball coach at Arizona State University. Winkles would turn the Sun Devils into a national power over the next twelve years. He would win College World Series titles in 1965, 1967, and 1969, and his program would produce many high-profile Major Leaguers, including Rick Monday, Sal Bando, Reggie Jackson, Gary Gentry, and Larry Gura.[20]

Winkles joined the coaching staff of the Angels in 1971 at the urging of Del Rice, whom he had known for "10 or 12 years."[21] At that time, much like the hiring of Earl Weaver for Hank Bauer's staff in Baltimore, there was speculation that Winkles was the manager in waiting. As it turned out, the pundits were correct. Dalton announced Winkles's hiring at a press conference on October 12, 1972, and he became the first manager of a Major League club to have only college coaching experience.

As could be expected, given Dalton's reservations about the season just ended, his comments to the press about the hiring showed that he felt Winkles was an "aggressive leader and a man who could put together a system for teaching fundamentals." Dalton himself admitted that he was opening himself up to ridicule for hiring a manager with no previous pro experience. However, he believed that Winkles knew the game and that such knowledge transcended the level at which it was played.[22]

To help him along, Dalton swung a deal that he hoped would give Winkles the offensive punch the team needed. In late November 1972 Dalton traded the once untouchable Andy Messersmith, as well as veteran infielder Ken McMullen, to the Dodgers for utility man Billy Grabarkewitz, the once again too-old-to-play Frank Robinson, right-handed starter Bill Singer, first-year pitcher Mike Strahler, and a fleet-footed shortstop named Bobby Valentine.[23] This prototypical Dalton trade looked to fill multiple voids on the Angels.

The marquee player was thirty-seven-year-old Frank Robinson. There was speculation that Dalton, who would never shy away from signing someone he knew from a previous stop, reunited with Robinson as a long-term move to secure a future manager. Both men quickly dispelled this notion. Harry Dalton acquired Robinson to hit. In 1973 Robinson, who spent 127 of his 144 starts as a designated hitter, had plenty of power left in his bat to help the anemic Angels offense. He would rap out 30 home runs and drive in 97 RBIs in 1973 and follow that up with 20 homers and 63 RBIs in 1974—his last two productive Major League seasons.[24]

Meanwhile, Singer would provide valuable innings for the Angels in the wake of Messersmith's trade, and Grabarkewitz was a trade piece later in 1973 for veteran infielder Denny Doyle. As for Strahler, he would never reach the potential that the Dodgers or Angels saw in him, and he would be traded to Detroit later in 1973. He would spend much of the next two seasons in Triple-A before he retired. Then there was Valentine.

A certain type of player appealed to Harry Dalton, so it really is no surprise that he would be drawn to Bobby Valentine. Drafted in 1968 out of high school in Connecticut, the wiry (5 feet 10 inches tall, 189 pounds) Valentine had a meteoric rise through the Dodgers system and looked to be the heir apparent to Maury Wills after being converted to shortstop by his Minor League manager, Tommy Lasorda. However, after a leg injury, the still-effective Valentine was deemed expendable. Valentine immediately gave Dalton a sparkplug in the middle of the infield, and he quickly became a fan of Bobby Winkles and a fixture at short for California. As Valentine would describe it, "I played short almost every game when the season began, was batting third in Bobby Winkles['s] lineup, and was becoming the force that everyone expected me to be."[25] Then fate intervened.

Valentine was originally an outfielder when he came to the Dodgers, then shifted to short. With Valentine having that background, Winkles asked him to play in the outfield for a few games in mid-May. During the second of these appearances, on May 17, Valentine broke his leg after a collision with a tarp-covered outfield wall at Anaheim Stadium.[26] It would start a chain reaction that would see him unable to contribute for the rest of 1973 and turn him into a part-time outfielder for the Angels as he battled to stay in the lineup. Dalton would finally trade Valentine in 1975.

Despite the downside of missing Valentine for most of the season, there was a marked improvement in the 1973 Angels. Through the first half of the season, they were scoring more runs, thanks to Frank Robinson. Moreover, the pitching staff would provide the club with their first bona fide star since Jim Fregosi. In the spring and summer of 1973, Nolan Ryan took his first steps toward becoming the best pitcher of the 1970s and a future Hall of Famer. Ryan's pitching was still wild, however. He would lead the American League in walks in 1973, 1974, and 1976. In an era obsessed with wins and losses, Ryan would be a .500 pitcher, or close to it, for much of the next three years. Still, he was the drawing card that Harry Dalton needed to get people to care about the Angels.

No matter the individual accomplishments, Dalton understood that he had still not built a winner. Still, the team was getting closer to that level.

After playing solid baseball for the first two months of the 1973 season and even spending time in first place briefly in June, the Angels would go 10-19 in July before creeping back near .500 in August (12-14) and having a winning September (18-15). The Angels would finish 79-83 and fifteen games back in their division.[27] Under a different set of expectations, the 1973 season would have been a success in some aspects. The Angels played better than they had in 1972, and Dalton quickly acknowledged that. They set a team record for batting average at .253 and scored "175 more runs in '73 than they did in '72."[28] They had also found a viable No. 2 starter with the promotion of twenty-year-old Frank Tanana late in the season. He would go 49-38 with a 2.72 ERA over the next three years. He also felt that Robinson was the power hitter he had been searching for and that Nolan Ryan was great at the gate. "The exploits of Nolan Ryan alone probably made the season worthwhile," Dalton said.[29] This would be the case for the next three seasons and a multitude of seasons thereafter.

Ryan would strike out 383 batters in 1973, 367 in 1974, and 327 in 1976. These totals led the AL each of those years, and the 383 in 1973 is the modern baseball (1900–2022) record.[30] Moreover, Ryan became known as the type of pitcher who could no-hit the opposing team at any moment. He would throw two in 1973. His first no-no occurred during a May 15 game in Kansas City as the Angels battled to stay relevant, and the second happened exactly two months later when he no-hit the Detroit Tigers at Tiger Stadium. As it turned out, this season was the beginning of a baseball legend. Ryan would throw two more no-hitters for the Angels, one in 1974 and another in 1975.[31] He would also establish himself as the hardest-throwing pitcher in baseball history when he threw a fastball clocked at 100.8 miles per hour in a 1974 game at Anaheim Stadium.[32] Because of his effort, dedication to his family, and craft, Ryan became one of the favorite players of Dalton (and his family) during the latter's long career.[33]

Primarily because of Ryan, the Angels would never have a repeat of the dismal 1972 season, when they drew only 744,190 fans during their home schedule. In three of the following four seasons, the Angels would draw over a million fans. They would also just miss that mark in the one year during that stretch that they did not top a million (917,269 in 1974). It is safe to say that by 1976, much like he did with the farm system, Harry Dalton had created a better situation than the one he found when he got to Anaheim. Dalton would say at the end of the regular season in 1973, "We put a product on the field that the people responded to."[34] That would be the case for the rest of his time in Southern California.

Still, Dalton understood that no matter how well his team played, .500 was a necessary benchmark. That was a goal he set at the beginning of the year, and not achieving that goal meant he had not done his job successfully. The media had not yet turned on Dalton, however. In the fall of 1973, columnist Bud Tucker suggested that the Angels needed to hold a "Harry Dalton Sympathy Night," partly because of the many injuries that had plagued his club in 1973 and had delayed winning another year.[35] However, Dalton made no excuses and kept trying to find the right formula for a winning club.

Ahead of the 1974 season, Dalton made a ten-player trade with the Milwaukee Brewers that saw him send longtime Angel Clyde Wright, former "Kiddie Corps" member Steve Barber, veteran outfielder Ken Berry, and backup catcher Art Kusnyer for catcher Ellie Rodríguez, pitcher Skip Lockwood, part-time outfielder Joe Lahoud, and "Downtown" Ollie Brown. This was supposed to give the Angels the catcher Dalton thought the Angels needed. In the process, the Angels got younger and seemed, on paper, to have a core that could carry them to the future. This core included shortstop Dave Chalk (twenty-three years old); Bobby Valentine (twenty-four), who had moved to left field and whom Dalton felt could still help the team; and center fielder Mickey Rivers (twenty-five), who gave the team an added dimension with his speed and whom Dalton felt had "arrived" at the end of the 1973 season. There was only one problem. As time went on, Bobby Winkles became marginalized in his clubhouse thanks to a war between two factions of players.

On one side were players like Valentine who appreciated how Winkles approached the game. Bobby Winkles wanted his players to do things quickly. As Valentine would recall, Winkles "believed there was too much dead time. We weren't allowed to step out of the batters' box; relief pitchers were told to sprint in from the bullpen and sprint off the field."[36] This rigid approach, which worked with college players, was looked on with growing skepticism by veterans of the pro game. It eventually led to an open rebellion in the clubhouse. At the heart of the fight for the team was Frank Robinson.

Valentine would remember that every time Bobby Winkles would call a meeting, "as soon as Bobby walked out, Frank said something like 'well, that's bullshit.'" The infighting became common knowledge when Valentine made comments to a local group as he rehabbed his leg. This led to a fight between Robinson and Valentine in Dalton's office that set the tone for the 1974 season and ultimately spelled the end for Bobby Winkles.[37]

The Angels would start the year at 11-11 and score more runs than they gave up. The '74 season got progressively worse from there. May saw them finish 12-15. In mid-June Winkles had a meeting with Dalton in which he said it had become evident that he was to be fired: "Before the trading deadline, I [Dalton] very strongly suggested that we make some changes and that urging, or plea, or whatever you want to call it, fell on deaf ears."[38] On June 27, with the team mired in last place at 31-44, Winkles was fired. In his mind, two people were the cause of his failure: Frank Robinson and Harry Dalton.

Robinson felt that Winkles was not the manager of the Angels. Some went as far as to say that the person Robinson wanted to have to manage the team was Frank Robinson. Either way, Winkles admitted openly that he "couldn't handle him" and asked Dalton to trade Robinson.[39] That trade would have sent Robinson to the Yankees for Bill White. Robinson, however, had a no-trade clause in his contract and vetoed the deal when the Yankees refused to pay relocation costs for him and his family.[40] As for his beef with Dalton, Winkles argued that he was very seldom listened to. He and Dalton could "never get together on who should be on the ball club."[41] Whether Dalton ever listened to Winkles is open for debate. Tom Sommers said in hindsight that in his opinion Dalton did not give Winkles enough time to adjust to the pro game.[42] Still, Winkles would go only so far as to say that he was fired because "Harry thought I wasn't doing a good job."[43]

In retrospect, the Winkles hiring was a disaster. As for why it did not work or who was to blame, it is fair to say that the blame is, in some ways, a two-way street. As Tom Sommers noted, Dalton tended to value the opinion of only those he trusted. With that in mind, it is possible that Dalton overlooked Winkles's opinion regarding personnel.

Winkles had never evaluated a fully evolved pro player. Moreover, it can also be said that Winkles, in feeling that he should have "90 percent of the input" in the makeup of his roster, did not understand Harry Dalton's managerial style or the vagaries of pro baseball, in which teams are built by committee and not necessarily at the whims of the manager, as they are in college ball.[44]

Dalton would later privately admit that he felt Winkles was out of his depth in pro baseball.[45] This, of course, did not mean that he needed to fire Winkles after the dismal start in 1974. However, two specific factors probably contributed to the early release. First, even if Frank Robinson was not bitter about being passed over for the managerial position, he was in a unique position to report to Dalton on the running of the clubhouse. While players did not feel Dalton relied on "spies" to run his team better, Dalton was willing to listen to Robinson. Dalton felt that Robinson was a great leader and clubhouse presence and valued his opinion. Second, what cannot be overlooked is that by the summer of 1974, the pressure on Dalton was starting to mount. It would continue to build during the 1974 season. What made it worse was that for the first time in his life, Dalton would run into a manager who did not believe in his abilities as a team builder. That manager was Dick Williams, who would usher in the most contentious period Dalton ever experienced between himself and a manager in any of his forty years in baseball.

Bobby Winkles's lack of experience in the pro game makes one question why Harry Dalton would hire him. In a similar vein, it now seems like a no-brainer for Dick Williams to have been hired. His arrival seemed fortuitous in the summer of 1974. Williams had been a Major League manager for seven years by 1974 and had had three of his teams win the American League pennant. In 1967 his Boston Red Sox team came within one win of capping the "Impossible Dream" season with a World Series title. In 1971, after a season out of the game, Williams piloted the Oakland Athletics to 101 wins during the regular season before they fell to the Orioles in the American League Championship Series. In 1972 and 1973 Williams led the A's for the first two of their three straight World Series titles.

During this run, Williams would cultivate an environment that called for perfect execution at all times. Catcher Dave Duncan, who would go on to a long and successful career as a Major League pitching coach, would recall that Williams also hated losing, to the point of physical illness.[46] Despite his success, Williams, like many who would work for the mercurial A's owner Charles O. Finley, would grow weary of Finley's interference. This led to Williams quitting after the World Series win in 1973. He was still out of baseball when the Angels came calling.

The idea to hire Williams originated with Gene Autry. The Angels' owner would recall that his conversation with Harry Dalton was straightforward: "I think we need the best man we can find; I think we ought to go after Dick Williams."[47] With that mandate, Dalton pursued Williams and inked a deal with him that saw Williams make $100,000 over three years. On the surface, the Angels players and their boss were excited about Williams's arrival simply because he was different from Bobby Winkles. Nolan Ryan went on record saying, "I hope he is the disciplinarian I've been led to believe he is because that, right now, is where our greatest need is."[48] As for Dalton, he saw Williams as a winner who "is very much in tune with communicating with what is called today's ballplayer."[49]

Williams publicly indicated at the time that his most significant role was administering an attitude adjustment to the Angels. This included "getting 100 percent of what they [the players and coaches] have each day."[50] The Angels' record the rest of the year left the effectiveness of Williams in doubt. It also led others to speculate that Harry Dalton was to blame for the problems plaguing the Angels.

The first chink in Dalton's armor appeared in June 1974. At that time, Gene Autry received an anonymous letter from someone claiming to know intimately how others in baseball saw Dalton.[51] This person, who worked for a "major league club," was writing because he had respect for Autry and felt the owner wasn't getting all the relevant information about Dalton. That "information" contradicts everything ever heard about Dalton from those inside the game. The source, who claimed to have worked as a manager and scout during his time in baseball, told Autry that "Harry Dalton is not popular or well-liked with other baseball people or clubs. Over the years at Baltimore, he was a ruthless guy and tried to force trades down the throats of the other clubs." He then let Autry know that, for those in baseball, it was payback time, and Dalton's detractors were "glad to see him suffer," but they did not want to see Autry pay the price for Dalton's unwillingness to work with his contemporaries. This person believed that if Autry had not been sick with an eye ailment in the winter of 1971, he would have never hired Dalton because he would have been able to evaluate him accurately and would have seen his duplicitous nature. He then concluded the letter with a discussion of why he felt Autry would be better served by firing Dalton and rehiring Dick Walsh.

Dalton and Autry tried to discover the author of the note. Both men believed that it was someone who worked in the Angels organization. Two factors lend credence to this thought. The first is that the letter, dated June 22, arrived in Autry's office two days later with an Anaheim postmark. The second clue is that the author had intimate knowledge of the Angels' problems. This included the issues that Bobby Winkles had with members of the team, perceived deficiencies of coaches on Winkles's staff, and the rift that was growing thanks to Frank Robinson's issue with Winkles. The author also felt the solution was to rehire Dick Walsh.

There is no indication the letter moved Autry to reevaluate Dalton's position with the Angels. There is also no indication of a discussion about the accusations in the letter. Still, from the moment that letter arrived, the bloom was off the rose. Even Autry took measures to try and adjust how the team was run.

In the winter of 1974, Bob Reynolds left the Angels as president and part owner. In his place Autry hired Arthur "Red" Patterson, who had recently served as the Dodgers' public relations director. Initially, this did not look like it would cause many problems for Dalton. Autry hoped that Patterson would bring with him to Orange County some of what had made the Dodgers successful. He wanted Patterson to increase attendance at Anaheim Stadium through the use of inventive promotions and a robust speaking schedule while providing Dalton with more time to consider how to improve the on-the-field product.[52] In actuality, what Patterson's hiring did was make Harry Dalton's position tenuous. As Dalton would note, throughout 1975 Patterson would begin to weigh in publicly on baseball operations. This included pushing for the hiring of certain coaches (such as former Dodger Dixie Walker), "his [Patterson's] increasing involvement in the clubhouse and field areas," and "his recent public statements about trade possibilities with the Dodgers."[53] All of these things began to undermine Dalton, whether intentionally or not. Dalton also began to have problems with Dick Williams.

At the core of any problems between the two were differences in their demeanor. Dalton did not need to tell anyone that he knew his job, and Williams was willing to tell anyone that he knew best. This included Dalton. Williams had spent parts of five seasons with Baltimore. During that time, he claimed to have seen Dalton "rise meteorically to the top, seemingly through no fault of his own. In other words, Harry knew that I knew he didn't know shit."[54]

Moreover, Williams was not above calling out his team publicly. Famously, he even made a player cry one time. Dalton would have never felt the need to do either one. Williams also had issues with the makeup of the roster of his Angels teams. Gene Autry remembered that as Dick Williams got to see more of the club he inherited, he "lost his patience with a roster loaded with young players."[55] While Dalton saw this youthfulness as a benefit to the team, Williams saw it as a liability. To him, the team Dalton gave him was the "Peter Pans of baseball—nice, cute kids that would never grow up."[56] This cohort of "Peter Pans" included players whom Dalton felt were the backbone of any future success. The lost boys of Anaheim would compile a 36-48 record in the second half of 1974. Then the Angels would go 72-89 in 1975. They would not see .500

after April, and the team's run differential was an astronomically negative 628–723. The media laid most of the problems at the pitching staff's feet. The bullpen was substandard, and Nolan Ryan had a subpar year (14-12, 3.45 ERA), largely thanks to injuries he pitched around all year. More importantly, however, the 1975 Angels were offensively challenged. They hit only 55 home runs in 1975, and they struggled to score runs in other ways as well, thanks to a .246 average that would lead to the Angels scoring an average of only 3.90 runs per game. That was the second-worst total in the American League. The only upside to the offense was that Williams would get the team running. The Angels stole 220 bases, a figure that led the American League.[57] They still finished in last place.

Harry Dalton's strained relationships with Patterson and Williams, coupled with all the losses, meant that he did not find many things to smile about during his day. Still, even as his club struggled, he would find light in his day both in and away from the office. These things helped sustain him as the pressure mounted and helped to solidify his place as a person who loved the game of baseball while still loving his family.

As for baseball, much like in Baltimore, Dalton would find time to look at the game in a broad sense and try to use his experience to make it better. In California, this effort saw Dalton lead an exploratory committee to consider combining the umpiring staffs of the American League and National League into one entity, as well as work to continue improving relations between college baseball coaches and organized baseball development staff.

Dalton's work on the college committee is particularly interesting during this period. He would address the American Association of College Baseball Coaches at their national convention, and in an interview with *Collegiate Baseball Newspaper* he outlined his thoughts on how to improve the rocky relationship between colleges and professional baseball.

Dalton put the future player front and center in his comments. He felt both pro and college players would benefit from increased instruction and that this instruction be administered with college coaches and professional development departments working together. A "good future depends on the cooperation of all parties involved—school officials, NCAA, and Pro

People." This cooperation included colleges using "pro speakers" as part of "well-planned clinics." Dalton did not put the onus for improvement exclusively on the colleges. When asked if he had recommendations for pro teams looking to hire a college coach, Dalton wanted his cohorts to learn from his mistakes with Bobby Winkles by requiring an "apprenticeship in the minor leagues" and "closer cooperation between pro managers and coaches with college coaches discussing game strategy and handling personnel." Finally, Dalton felt that baseball, at no matter what level it was played, would be best served by a "national baseball Joe" program that saw the colleges and pro baseball look to subsidize at the local level coaches who would teach fundamentals without the pressure of "game conditions," which would "put more fun into practice."[58]

This last suggestion gets to the heart of something vital when understanding Harry Dalton. No matter what he was doing or where he would go, he loved the game of baseball and wanted to make the game as a whole better for everyone.

Dalton also loved his family and worked hard to be a relevant part of the lives of his wife and daughters. By 1975 Kim was thirteen, Cindy nine, and Debbie eight, and like most girls their age, they had busy social schedules, which included 4-H and youth softball for Cindy and Debbie. Beyond all these activities, Dalton tried to provide opportunities for family vacations, although baseball occasionally got in the way. For instance, in 1974 the Dalton family attempted to drive to Georgia to see Pat's sister Winki and her family at Christmas. They didn't count on the Oakland A's Catfish Hunter having his contract voided by the commissioner's office. This left one of the best arms in baseball up for grabs. As Pat Dalton would tell *Money* magazine, "The five of us traveled around the country with Catfish" as her husband tried to woo the pitcher from a pay phone.[59]

Despite these interruptions, family meant everything to Dalton, as another story from the time illustrates. During one season in California, Harry and Pat entertained Pat's sister Winki and her daughters for a few weeks in the middle of the season. During this time, Dalton was under tremendous pressure and was feeling the strain of his professional life.

Still, when he would get home, he was more than willing to spend time with his daughters and their cousins. One cousin, Winki's daughter Paige, took a particular liking to Dalton. "She [Paige] would spend the day going 'where is he . . . where is he . . .' then, when he would get home and even if he had a long day at the ballpark, she would follow Harry around, and Harry would just smile."[60]

Dalton also made time for Pat in his busy schedule. In one example, Dalton would help Pat raise funds for arthritis research. He would also support her as she raised money for Ronald Reagan during his 1976 presidential election campaign. Finally, they would entertain friends at their home in Tustin.[61]

Pat Dalton remembered that the camaraderie and close-knit community feeling of Baltimore was missing in California. Pat also recalled avoiding confrontation by crossing the street if she saw people approaching.

Things did not improve for Dalton in 1976, even though in the winter of 1975 he had traded for another power hitter. In a move Dick Williams applauded, Dalton traded pitcher Ed Figueroa and Mickey Rivers to the Yankees for Bobby Bonds.[62] On the surface, it seemed that Dalton had traded for an all-around star at the height of his powers. Bonds broke in with San Francisco in 1968, and from 1970 to 1975 he would hit 177 home runs, steal 232 bases, and have an OPS of .851.[63] Unfortunately, as would become a trend with Dalton, his key acquisition would not live up to his previous performance. Bonds would suffer a broken hand that would limit him to just ninety-nine games, while the Angels would hit only 63 home runs, their batting average would drop to .235, and they would average 3.39 runs per game.[64] The Angels went 5-12 in April, and according to Dick Williams, his veterans, except for Nolan Ryan, quit on him, and "the kids got scared."[65]

Williams's interpretation is suspect, however. By his own admission, he was to drive the younger players on the roster. This approach, for which Williams showed no remorse, fractured his team. The final blow for Williams would come on July 23, 1976, when Williams got into a screaming match after another loss. This time, Bill Melton was the target. As Williams would recall, the two men would get into a shouting match on the bus from LAX back to Anaheim following another loss.[66] The next day, after meeting with Williams and deliberating for most of the afternoon, Dalton fired him.[67]

For his replacement, Harry Dalton again tapped someone who understood the Angels' Minor League system. Norm Sherry was a former Dodger who had worked for the Angels since Dick Walsh hired him in 1969. Sherry was one of the few survivors when Dalton cleaned house in the farm system, and he would go on to manage Double-A ball in the Texas League for El Paso and Shreveport. He then worked from 1974 to 1975 at Triple-A Salt Lake City, guiding the club to the playoffs in 1975. Sherry was then put on the Angels' coaching staff in 1976.[68] When Dalton tabbed him as his interim manager, most of the younger players on the Angels were glad of the change.

The change in attitude in the Angels' clubhouse immediately impacted performance on the field. Under Sherry, the Angels would go 37-29 and finish in fourth place for the year. The improved play also had an impact on Harry Dalton's future. In September, Autry, in a move that he hoped would quell rumors that his front office was on the hot seat, extended Dalton's contract through 1979 and formalized the team's relationship with Red Patterson.[69] With this added job insurance, Dalton moved quickly to extend Norm Sherry.[70] At the press conference announcing the move, Dalton quickly pointed out that "if you were to project the Angels['] winning percentage under Sherry throughout the season, it would have been good enough to win the AL West title."[71] Beyond that information, Dalton felt confident that his team would enjoy a good season in 1977 with a healthy Bobby Bonds.[72]

Dalton also hinted at a new plan for the Angels in 1977, made possible by the first substantive change in the relationship between players and management since baseball became a game for professionals. For the first time, players on an expiring contract could seek a new deal with a different club than the one that signed them. This change would usher in a new era in baseball, help make the Angels a winner within a few years, and ultimately spell the end of the line for Harry Dalton in California.

12

New World, New Dalton, Same Results

WINTER 1976–FALL 1977

The catalyst for what was known as free agency occurred in 1975. At that time, independent arbitrator Peter Seitz ruled that players were not bound to a single team in perpetuity despite how ownership had interpreted the reserve clause to that point. Instead, players whose contract lapsed would be free to negotiate a new contract with their existing team and every other team in the league. This new ruling, formally known as the Messersmith-McNally decision, would change baseball's financial and competitive landscape forever. Teams could now remake themselves overnight. This new ability would also open up general managers to a new form of ridicule. GMs could be applauded for making a shrewd free agent signing or lambasted for wasting their team's money if a move did not work out.[1]

In the first year of free agency, Harry Dalton would experience both phenomena. He made the Angels into one of the first big-time "buyers" in free agency but then saw the Angels become one of the first teams to be snake-bit by a high-priced, underperforming addition. Ultimately, these things, combined with Gene Autry's obsession with the Dodgers, would lead to Harry Dalton's departure from California at the end of the 1977 season. How he got to that point is a fascinating tale about the changing nature of baseball.

Harry Dalton hinted at the Angels' plans to partake in free agency during the earliest days of the off-season in 1976. In his season wrap-up message, Dalton commented that the Angels were primed to be "financially aggressive" in pursuing players during the first winter under the new rules.[2] That year twenty-six players qualified to be "drafted" by potential suitors, including their current team. The maximum number of teams that could negotiate with any one free agent was twelve, each team was limited to signing two players, and each team could qualify for one additional signee for each player they had to enter the draft.[3] This rule would favor the Angels and bring about the first controversy of the free agency era. Initially, the Angels had four players in the draft pool, including Tim Nordbrook, who had been in the Baltimore system prior to coming to California in 1976; outfielder Paul Dade; infielder Billy Smith; and third baseman Mike Miley. Mike Miley would re-sign with the Angels prior to the draft. The other three would enter free agency, which would allow Dalton to sign a third free agent in a year with a talented class of players.

The initial list included several big names, including Reggie Jackson (who was finishing a one-year deal after being traded by Charlie Finley's A's to Baltimore). In addition, Baltimore stood to lose former Dalton Gang signee Bobby Grich. Finally, Finley stood to lose the last of the holdovers from his dynasty, including third baseman Sal Bando, outfielder Joe Rudi, catcher Gene Tenace, and bullpen ace Rollie Fingers. In addition, former Oriole Don Baylor was a free agent after spending one year in Oakland.

Any of these players would have made the Angels a serious dark horse in the AL West, and two would have made them a threat in a division devoid of a favorite. Harry Dalton would do better than that, and he would land three players who instantly made the Angels a serious contender and the first media darlings in the age of free agency.

Dalton's moves were fast and furious. On November 16 Dalton signed outfielder Don Baylor. Baylor was twenty-eight years old and coming into his prime as a player. Dalton would call him "one of the best young offensive players in the league."[4] Baylor would sign a six-year deal worth $1.6 million but quickly pointed out that Harry Dalton was the biggest reason he signed with California over the other eleven teams that sought his services. "The Angels are a class organization," he said. "I have dealt with Dalton, and Walter Shannon, their chief scout, before, and they haven't lost any of their class."[5]

Relationships also helped Dalton sign his second player of the offseason. One day after inking Baylor, the Angels signed Joe Rudi. While Rudi did not have a direct relationship with Dalton, the latter's ability to sell himself and his team to an agent helped seal the deal.

In this case, Jeremy Kapstein was the agent of both Baylor and Rudi. This allowed Dalton to foster a great relationship with one of the first so-called super agents. At the time of Rudi's signing, Kapstein let the world know that he was duly impressed with Dalton (and, by extension, the Angels organization). "We're talking about a quality organization with an environment to match," Kapstein said. "We not only talked about money but philosophy, housing, fans, and a number of other subjects as well. Harry Dalton spared no effort in being here, in staying in communication."[6]

This effort got Dalton and the Angels one of the most highly regarded outfielders in the Major League. Rudi was a great performer in big games, hitting .300 in his three World Series appearances, and earned three Gold Gloves.[7]

With Rudi and Baylor in the fold, Autry and Dalton gave differing opinions on whether they would attempt to sign a third player. When Rudi signed his $2 million deal for five years, Autry was quoted as saying that he had "hocked the horse" to pay for the spending spree, which led one to believe that the Angels were done buying. Dalton was noncommittal. "I'm neither optimistic nor pessimistic about signing a third player," he said. "I'm flying home . . . but will continue to pursue some conversations with Kapstein."[8]

Ultimately, Dalton would spend three hours in the air and return to Delaware, where Kapstein was headquartered. In a move that seemed unlikely at the start of the day, the Angels were now in a bidding war with the Yankees for Orioles second baseman Bobby Grich. Grich had graduated from high school in California, and Al Kubski quickly signed him for Baltimore. Grich then worked his way through the Orioles system and was on the team for their World Series title in 1970, though he did not play. Grich would finally break into the everyday lineup in 1972, making three All-Star games and winning four Gold Gloves from 1972 to

1976. Beyond the accolades, Grich also felt that Harry Dalton was "the best G.M. in baseball."[9] This opinion stemmed from Grich's experience with Dalton in Baltimore, where he saw the Orioles' general manager put players at ease. "When most G.M.s would come into the clubhouse," Grich recalled, "players would tense up because the boss was around. When Harry would come in, he was always bantering with guys, always smiling. He related to players, and everyone was equal."[10] When coupled with the Angels signing Baylor and Rudi, Grich began to change his mind about the Angels as a possible landing spot. When Grich and Kapstein relayed that to George Steinbrenner, the Yankees owner began to attack Dalton and his conduct in the initial days of free agency. Specifically, Steinbrenner took umbrage at the Nordbrook incident and threatened to have Grich's contract, if he signed with California, voided by the league. The signing of Grich would take a backseat to this drama, but ultimately MLB commissioner Bowie Kuhn saw no wrongdoing, and Dalton was cleared to negotiate with Grich.[11]

Dalton signed Grich the day before Thanksgiving in 1976. The deal was for $1.3 million over five years, and Dalton hoped Grich's ability to get on base would be the final piece of the offensive puzzle for the new-look Angels. When the dust settled, Dalton quickly thanked Gene Autry for "his heavy backing," saying that the owner had given the organization a "tremendous ball club."[12] Autry gave a tempered response: "I still don't believe all of this is good for baseball, so I'm not very happy about it. But this is how it is now, and there are certain facts of life we'll have to live with."[13] Dalton was much more pragmatic than the resigned Autry. On the day Dalton introduced Grich, Baylor, and Rudi to the public, he announced that he saw the coming of free agency as a fundamental shift in how he and his fellow GMs did their jobs.

"We're sort of at a crossroads," Dalton stated. "I think the unknown is probably always a little frightening to people. Certainly, this is an unknown situation as to what the net effect on baseball will be. I think we have reached a crossroads in the player development and player procurement fields in baseball. . . . We had the choice as the California ball club to continue the same highway, looking at your farm system, staying somewhat conservative, not going into the free agent market for multi-year contracts, or going down the new road. . . . By and large, we think this is the new direction of baseball, and we want to be there."[14]

Regardless of these signings' repercussions in the pro baseball world, the immediate result for the Angels was that they quickly became the darlings of both their fans and the national media. Immediately after the signings, the Angels had record ticket sales. In March 1977, Angels president Red Patterson told *The Sporting News* that the club had done booming business in every respect: "Group sales are up, advance sales, every phase of sales, priority parking, Stadium Club membership, everything is up because of the signings."[15] He added, "We are glibly talking about selling out our opening night for the first time in a park that has barely drawn 30,000 for an opener."[16] Of course, once the signings were made, the Angels still had to win games on the field. The ability of the Angels to do that took a severe hit almost as spring training opened. It was a foreshadowing for the whole season, and Harry Dalton gave a written record of the whole episode.

In the lead-up to the season, Harry Dalton kept a diary of the events surrounding his team. Much like the winter, the spring entries started out positive in tone. Players were quick to report, and even the desert weather in Holtville was pleasant as workouts began. Then Bobby Grich reported that he had a sore back due to "picking up an air conditioner."[17] This put Dalton on edge as the days went on. Then Grich's back became a full-fledged issue. On February 24 Dalton reported that "rain came up in mid-morning and cut the workout short about a half hour. Grich complained of his back and was sent in early to get heat." By the next day, Grich was in to see the team orthopedic specialist, Dr. Rasinski. He would categorize Grich's injuries as back spasms, and Grich would be on day-to-day status for the rest of camp.[18]

Aside from Grich's injuries, Dalton was happy with what he saw as February turned to March. On February 28 Dalton felt that the 1977 Angels were the "hardest working camp in baseball." He chalked up the work ethic to a change in demeanor from the lack of "pressure, ill feeling, or dictatorial attitudes" of the Dick Williams years. This even trickled down to the newly acquired stars. "Joe Rudi and Del Crandall [coach] run a mile and a half together at 7:30 A.M.," Dalton wrote. Don Baylor was one of a handful of players who went to a local health club to work on keeping his weight down.[19]

As March continued, Dalton was still impressed with his team. He was hopeful about the Angels' chances of winning the American League West even though Grich finally had to go back to Anaheim and spend a week in the hospital for his back. According to Dalton, much of his optimism stemmed from perceived deficiencies with the rest of the division, including Texas "having pitching problems" and Minnesota beginning to have financial woes.[20] The oddsmakers agreed and made the Angels the favorite to win the AL West at 7–5.

Anyone who has experienced spring training will say that it drags on after a certain point and is just another part of a grinding season. For Dalton, however, the middle of March brought more diverse work. At various points, there were trade offers to consider. He tried to swing deals for Sparky Lyle. He tried to bring Bucky Dent over from the Yankees, just in case Grich could not be ready for the start of the season. In the case of Dent, however, Dalton privately noted that he wouldn't mind acquiring him just to offer him to the Yankees to help the Angels fill a few more holes.[21] There were also discussions between Frank Lane, who had come over as a special assistant to Dalton, and Charlie Finley about Vida Blue. However, as the regular season approached, Dalton's mind turned to his team, and he made some difficult cuts. In the end, the Angels decided to "go with ten pitchers, including [Mike] Cuellar," whom the Angels had invited to camp, hoping he would pitch well.[22]

The Angels finally broke camp the last week in March. At that point, all that was left in the prelude to the regular season was the "Freeway Series" with the Dodgers. It was then that the sky began to fall in on the Angels. On April 1 the Angels lost to the Dodgers 5–0, and Nolan Ryan was injured throwing batting practice. During the game, Bobby Bonds reaggravated an ankle injury that had bothered him all spring. Finally, the next night, the Angels had to place backup shortstop Mario Guerrero on the fifteen-day disabled list. For the second season in a row, injuries seemed likely to derail the best-laid plans of Harry Dalton and the Angels. The result was a team that was inconsistent early in the season.[23]

The 1977 Angels did better at scoring runs in the season's opening months. However, this did not equate to wins. The team scuffled to a 9-13 record in April, and there were problems at every level. At the end of April and into May, the Angels suffered "seven losses in the last nine games" of the month. During this stretch, the Angels suffered from poor pitching and underachieving free agents. In his last Major League appearance, Mike Cuellar was roughed up on the mound in two appearances, including a blown save and a three-inning start. Overall, by May 15 the bullpen was 2-8 for the season with a 3.45 ERA. Offensively, the problems boiled down to one thing: Rudi, Baylor, and Grich were not living up to expectations. During an awful nine-game road trip, the three free agents combined to go "15-102." At the time, Dalton was clinging to the hope he had had during spring training. Still, he knew he had to make moves. Mike Cuellar was released, and outfielder Gil Flores, one of the last cuts in the spring, was recalled. Finally, Dalton would swing a trade for Dave LaRoche to strengthen the bullpen.

Regardless of what he did, however, Harry Dalton was seen as the main problem with the Angels, and fans let that be known in a series of letters to the editor of newspapers that covered the Angels. The consensus was that "Dalton is living on past reputation" and that "as long as Dalton is general manager, the Angels do not have a prayer."[24] Luckily for Dalton, the beat writers of the period did not come for him or stoke the fires fan acrimony. Harry Dalton was respected by the beat reporters. "Because he was a reporter," said *Los Angeles Times* beat reporter Ron Rapoport, referencing some of Dalton's pre-baseball work history, "Harry never really got too upset if you asked him a question that he knew you had to ask." Knowing the news business, "Harry would give you things," Rapoport added.[25] Tracy Ringolsby, who covered the Angels for the *Long Beach Independent* before moving on to an award-winning career at the *Rocky Mountain News*, remembered that Dalton was also willing to admit to reporters when he was in the wrong. The most vivid example occurred in the hours leading up to the trading deadline in 1977. "We [the Angels] were in Minnesota," Ringolsby recalled. "It was the night before the deadline, and the reporters were hanging out in the bar to see if the Angels would make a move before the deadline. Harry came in and looked at us, and told us to go to bed. That they weren't going to make a move. Well, the writers went to bed, and then Harry made a last-minute move. The next day at the ballpark, Harry came into the press box and apologized to everyone. He didn't want us to think that he was trying to fool us. He was good that way."[26]

The moves in question were for pitchers Gary Nolan of Cincinnati and Ken Brett of the Chicago White Sox. These moves were necessary because the Angels struggled to gel as June progressed. The month saw the Angels go 12-12, which was still underachieving, given the hype surrounding the team.

The most significant blow occurred when Bobby Grich played his last game of the season on June 8, when his injured back became too much of a problem. Still, Dalton felt that he "changed the entire complexion" of the Angels' pitching staff and had given his team what they needed to distance themselves from the competition in the AL West with his deadline moves.[27]

Two managers in Dalton's division agreed with that analysis. Manager Gene Mauch of the first-place Minnesota Twins felt that "nobody" could compete with the Angels' pitching now that they could pitch Ryan, Tanana, Brett, and Nolan in a four-game series.[28] Whitey Herzog, who was formerly a coach with the Angels and an interim manager for Dalton after the firing of Bobby Winkles, was now managing in Kansas City. Herzog was on record saying that Gene Autry was "trying to get him fired" by adding Brett and Nolan.[29]

Like every other thing Dalton tried to get the Angels on the winning track, the acquisition of Brett and Nolan did not help make the team a winner. Brett would go 7-10 over the rest of the year, and Nolan would only make three appearances before he was sidelined by arm troubles that had gone untreated in Cincinnati and would ultimately end his career. This, combined with the Grich injury and an underperforming Don Baylor, led to a horrible summer for Dalton and the Angels.

In July the Angels were fighting to stay above .500 once again, and Dalton, as he had previously, decided to change managers in hopes of giving his team an added boost. On July 11 Dalton fired Norm Sherry and replaced him with Dave Garcia, who had been serving as a coach.

As for why he made a move, with his team nine and a half games out of first place, Dalton suggested once again that the Angels' underperformance had much to do with the manager's style. He also understood that fans of the Angels had heard that before. Most people probably saw it as another case of what Dalton referred to as "the manager always gets it first because that's the thing to do." Dalton truly believed that he was making the right move, however, and was not "going to back away from that fact" just because of what had happened previously. Like his other managers, Dalton thought that Garcia had what it took to turn the Angels around, and he also felt that the new hitting coach, Frank Robinson, would make a difference.[30] In the end, Dalton was wrong. The Angels would finish 35-46 under Garcia, twenty-eight games back, and in fifth place in the West. They would spend their last day at .500 in early August; the only time they had been in first place was during the first three days of the season.[31]

The fallout for the 1977 season was almost instantaneous, and it had immediate repercussions for Harry Dalton. First, Gene Autry would be taking a more hands-on approach to running the Angels. Following what he called his "most disappointing season," Autry announced that he wanted to be involved in signings and trades and would also be assuming the title of president. As for who would be his second in command, Autry let it be known in mid-October that he wanted to bring on former Dodgers GM Buzzie Bavasi, who had been in the same position with the San Diego Padres.[32] This wish became reality after the move was finalized on October 21. As for his duties, Bavasi was named executive vice president and would be Autry's "right-hand man."[33] Autry quickly pointed out that Dalton would remain the GM, but he would report to Bavasi.

To say that you could not find two more different people than Harry Dalton and Buzzie Bavasi would be an understatement. Generationally, they were night and day, which colored how they saw themselves and did their jobs. Dalton was generally seen as a tough but fair negotiator and a GM who, while not friends with the players he oversaw, put players at ease due to his approach that valued players as people. Bavasi was legendary for taking a tough stand against players financially and socially. These differences are primarily explained by the fact that each man came from a different generation of baseball executives. Bavasi had cut his teeth in the Dodgers organization under Larry MacPhail, Hall of Fame cheapskate Branch Rickey, and, as we have already seen, the equally thrifty Walter O'Malley.

With those mentors, Bavasi quickly learned to minimize costs and put the team ahead of the player. Stories of his negotiations with players are legendary. One of his favorite tactics was the use of fake contracts to get a player to sign for less than the player thought he was worth. In one prime example, Bavasi convinced a player (through a fake contract conveniently left on his desk in plain view) that Tommy Davis was making less than the player in his office who glimpsed the fake document. Faced with this faux reality, the second player, who knew he did not stand to make as much as Davis, signed for a much lower figure than he had initially requested.

This result was precisely what Bavasi wanted. In 1965 he took a hard-line stance with Don Drysdale and Sandy Koufax during their mutual holdout. Bavasi told these stories with pride and saw them as examples of doing the work expected of him.[34] This stance put him in a direct contrast to Harry Dalton, which made Bavasi's hiring in Anaheim akin to pouring gasoline into a burning house.

As soon as Bavasi came to Anaheim, he saw his mandate as getting the Angels out of debt, estimated at $3.5 million.[35] At the heart of that debt, as far as Bavasi saw it, were the policies of Harry Dalton. As Bavasi noted in 1987, when he came on board he curbed the number of tickets the Angels gave away (a policy Dalton first instituted to drum up interest in the club) and did not allow Dalton to expand the staff.[36] In the mind of Harry Dalton, Bavasi's policies and actions had one combined effect: he was out of a job, even if Autry did not fire him. This led him to send an impassioned letter to Autry, not only asking for clarification about his duties and the new reporting structure but also reminding Autry that he believed his own policies as GM were on the cusp of making the Angels a winner.

That letter may seem a like a man grasping for straws in an attempt to keep his job, but Dalton's experience contradicts that view. Dalton knew better than Autry that it took time to build a winner and that there were bumps in that road. It is also the opinion of the author that Autry, by using the Dodgers as his benchmark and routinely listening to former Dodgers staff, was blinding himself to the cold hard fact that even the Dodgers had not become winners overnight.

It took Bavasi and his bosses years to build a self-sustaining farm system. Because Autry thought he needed a winner to validate his position in the league and in his city, he did not have that kind of patience. The result was that Harry Dalton got caught in a position in which he had run out of time to produce a winner. Dalton ran out of patience as well.

Looking back at their time in California, Pat Dalton remembered that in 1977 "Harry became discouraged with front office and corporate politics and his inability to win one for the cowboy."[37] However, he could only leave the Angels if another team was willing to take a chance on him and if Autry would let him out of his contract. Luckily for Dalton, in the Midwest another owner was tired of losing and chasing a ghost in his city. This would set the stage for the last ride of the Dalton Gang. It would be a time filled with winning, mentoring the next generation of baseball executives, one last chance to set policy to make the game better, and, finally, an inglorious end to a long and fulfilling career, thanks in large part to the changing nature of baseball.

13

Working on His Terms

NOVEMBER 1977–
OCTOBER 1978

Wisconsin has a rich history of participating in competitive baseball at the grassroots and professional levels. At the heart of this history is the city of Milwaukee. The city had hosted high-level grassroots teams, Minor League pennant winners, and Major League champions.[1] Still, by 1977 the memories of the last champion in the city were thirty years old and had been overwhelmed by the nightmare of bad baseball. Harry Dalton would change all that and return the city to the ranks of baseball royalty, all while reestablishing his reputation and ensuring that he would dictate his future working conditions. As had been the case when Dalton dealt with his teams in Baltimore and California, making Milwaukee a winner again would take time, patience, and every skill he had acquired to that point in his career. Milwaukee baseball was in the midst of hard times. It had not always been like that.

Good times had visited the city's baseball fans in the past, in what became known as the "Milwaukee Miracle." In 1953, under a cloud of secrecy, the lowly Boston Braves left town for spring training and, as the season began, resurfaced as the Milwaukee Braves. Almost overnight, the Braves went from ugly duckling to the belle of the baseball world.

A young roster of exciting position players and a mix of veterans and young stars on the pitching staff spurred the transition. Position players included center fielder Billy Bruton, third baseman Eddie Matthews, first baseman Joe Adcock, shortstop Red Schoendienst, and prospect Henry Aaron, who would join the team in 1954. Milwaukee would also assemble a great group of bench players, including Bob "Hurricane" Hazel, Felix

"The Cat" Mantilla, and Frank Torre. Meanwhile, the pitching staff was the talk of baseball and included veteran tandem lefty Warren Spahn and righty Lew Burdette, along with young righty Bob Buhl. From 1953 to 1959, this conglomerate would win 651 games, two National League pennants (1957–58), and one World Series (1957) and would qualify for a playoff for a third pennant in 1959. They would also set attendance records that were the envy of baseball. The Braves would average 1,992,224 fans a year over seven seasons, from 1953 to 1959.[2]

This success, especially at the gate, would leave owners throughout the league scrambling to find cities willing to give them the "Milwaukee treatment" of a government-funded stadium and sweetheart financial breaks that saw the team keep most of the money earned during the first contract period. Still, even though the team kept winning as the 1950s turned into the 1960s, attendance would drop. Finally, after a two-year long process, including a court injunction and trial that threatened to change the landscape of baseball thanks to the effects of baseball's antitrust exemption, the Braves would leave Milwaukee after the 1965 season and land in Atlanta.[3]

The state of Wisconsin and Milwaukee itself were devastated by the loss. As such, a civic effort to replace the team was launched even before the Braves left. Known as Teams Inc., this group comprised various business and civic leaders, including shipping magnate Edmund Fitzgerald, future U.S. senator Herb Kohl, Oscar Mayer Jr. of Oscar Mayer and Company of Madison, and a junior member of the Milwaukee business community named Allan H. Selig. Selig, whose family was in the automotive leasing industry, set out to prove that Milwaukee was still "a major league city in every respect."[4] This mission required a public relations campaign that saw Teams Inc. attend every American and National League meeting for almost four years.

Selig, who went by "Bud," was a University of Wisconsin–Madison graduate and a huge baseball fan, and he was the one tasked with attending these meetings. His method was to show two things: that Milwaukee and the state could still support a Major League baseball team in terms of an adequate fan base and appropriate Major League facilities and that certain myths about the Braves' time in Milwaukee were not true. Selig's goal at all league meetings was to dispel these myths. Among the falsehoods circulating was that Milwaukee had "an unfriendly press, a small radio-TV market, [and a] loss of fans to the Minnesota Twins." In his presentations, Selig would do an admirable job of debunking these myths, such as the supposed loss of fans to the Twins. As to the size of the area's media footprint, he offered ideas for how Teams Inc. would mitigate the issue.[5] Nevertheless, a new team was not forthcoming. Although the city did not have a team, Major League Baseball returned to Milwaukee in spurts during the late 1960s.

In 1967 the Chicago White Sox played an exhibition before over fifty-one thousand fans at Milwaukee County Stadium. The Sox, who were testing the waters and thinking of moving out of Chicago, also played nine regular-season games in Milwaukee during the 1968 season.[6] This development gave Teams Inc., rebranded the Milwaukee Brewers Baseball Club Inc. during the late 1960s, some cachet with the American League. Still, the city would remain without a team thanks to a no vote by the NL when the league considered expansion for 1969 and a corresponding no vote by the American League for the same season. Milwaukee did not count on mismanagement by the American League when the league selected Seattle as an expansion city in 1967.

In a reflection of how some viewed Milwaukee's baseball future, in the late 1960s some saw Seattle as a Major League city. The only problem was that, unlike Milwaukee, Seattle's civic leaders were lukewarm toward baseball, which would not help in the effort to finance a new stadium. Moreover, Seattle did not have a well-heeled backer in the wings. Seattle was a town of "middle-class millionaires. . . . When in need, the city could not call on any exceedingly rich group."[7] The lack of a significant corporate backer meant that when the time came to find an ownership group for the team, Seattle was left with only Max and Dewey Soriano, who were grossly underfunded. When all of these factors were put together, the Seattle Pilots were doomed after one season. Seattle's failure opened the door for Milwaukee Brewers Baseball Club Inc. to get the franchise when the Sorianos defaulted into bankruptcy in the spring of 1970.[8]

The birth of the Milwaukee Brewers had much in common with the Braves' geographic shift in 1953. The team went to spring training as one team and left as another. The roster was a mix of young and old, thanks to the franchise relying on players acquired through the expansion draft prior to the 1968 season. The Brewers team, like the Braves, was also welcomed with open arms. The only difference was that the Brewers would not become a juggernaut on the field.

The Brewers could not reach the .500 mark for the first seven years. They would have six different managers during that time and four different GMs. Still, the people of Milwaukee embraced the club and the various individual stars who would spend time there during the club's early years. First baseman George "Boomer" Scott, reliever Ken "Bulldog" Sanders, third baseman Don Money, and Tommie Harper would all become fan favorites. Fans also welcomed Henry Aaron back to Milwaukee, where the home run king would play his last two seasons and hit his last home run before ending his Hall of Fame career.[9] Brewers fans were also introduced to three young stars who would become legends with the club during the Harry Dalton years.

In 1973 GM Jim Wilson had selected Robin Yount with the third overall pick of the June draft. The seventeen-year-old shortstop from Woodland Hills, California, would spend sixty-four games in Newark in the New York–Penn League in 1973. Then, in 1974, he would become the Brewers' everyday shortstop at eighteen. He would be in the team's lineup for the next twenty years. Later in the summer of 1974, Wilson drafted the player who would become Yount's double-play partner for almost ten years and his teammate for the next eighteen. Jim Gantner played his college baseball at the University of Wisconsin–Oshkosh and would become a fan favorite for his home state team during his long career because of his blue-collar approach to baseball. Finally, in 1977 the team picked Paul Molitor from the University of Minnesota in the June draft with the third overall pick. After taking some time to find his best position, Molitor would become one of the best pure hitters in baseball history during a twenty-one-year career.

The various GMs during the mid-1970s also brought in via trade several players who would leave an indelible mark on the Brewers franchise. First, in December 1976 GM Jim Baumer would trade George Scott and outfielder Bernie Carbo to Boston for first baseman Cecil Cooper, who would quickly become a weapon in the Brewers lineup thanks to a hitting approach that saw him use all fields with power and the consistency born of a quiet approach. Then, in June 1977, Baumer would trade for left-hander Mike Caldwell. Caldwell would spend the next eight years in Milwaukee and become a stalwart on the pitching staff.

Despite all these individual additions, the Brewers would still struggle on the field. As for what caused the continued problems despite an increase in talent, both Yount and Caldwell felt the Brewers lacked a professional attitude. Yount remembered that the early Brewers teams did not expect to win, and the city did not have great expectations for them.[10] The team and city were just happy to be in the Major League fold. That kind of attitude can only sustain a city so long, however, and the losses and the need to be a financial success weighed heavily on Bud Selig, now the team's principal owner. This forced Selig's hand one final time after the end of the 1977 season.

In what would become known as the "Saturday Night Massacre," Selig cleaned house on another staff. This time the victims included Jim Baumer and manager Alex Grammas, who had come to Milwaukee after working for Sparky Anderson in Cincinnati.[11] As for a replacement for Baumer, Selig has noted that there was only one option: Harry Dalton. "I had known Harry for a long time, and I really had faith in his ability," Selig wrote. "He was the only guy I wanted."[12]

Evidence suggests that Dalton knew that Bud Selig would come calling even before the Saturday Night Massacre. In an undated document titled "Lakeside," Dalton outlined his conditions for coming to work in Milwaukee.[13] At the top of that list was the stipulation that Dalton would have "*Full Authority*" (his emphasis) to run every aspect of the baseball operations, and this would see him report only to Bud Selig. Dalton was done having to justify the moves he felt were necessary for his club to be competitive; he felt he needed the "time-money-authority to do the job." That job constituted a total institutional overhaul of the Brewers, which included boosting the development budget by at least $400,000 and creating a new "organizational spirit from top to bottom."[14]

Beyond getting Selig to agree to an overhaul of team mentality and an increase in money for development, Dalton also felt that Selig needed to understand that profits would have to be a secondary concern for some time if Dalton was to lay the foundation for a winning program. At that point, Dalton asked Selig what his expectations for him were. It came down to one thing. In short, Selig wanted to increase civic pride in the team. Selig indicated that civic pride in the Brewers would be reflected in increased season ticket sales and a return to the halcyon days of the Milwaukee Miracle, when winning baseball was synonymous with the city.[15]

In order to meet those goals, Dalton felt that he would require a six-year deal worth $650,000 and a signing bonus of $50,000.[16] Selig agreed to give it to him and hand over the authority to remake the team that Dalton envisioned. All that was left to do was to break it to Kim, Cindy, and Debbie that it was time for another move. All three daughters remembered that they knew something was up as soon as their dad came home. "We had dinner at the dining room table," Kim Dalton recalled. "That never happened unless something big was happening or a holiday."[17] Dalton informed the girls that they were moving to Milwaukee.

Cindy recalled that she did not even know where Milwaukee was. That was when Harry pulled the pop culture card. "Dad looked at us and asked, 'Girls, do you watch *Laverne and Shirley*?'"[18] When they answered that they had indeed seen the show featuring characters working in a Milwaukee brewery, Dalton let them know that the city was their new home. Cindy felt better, but Kim, who was a sophomore at Tustin High School, could not be assuaged by the connection with a TV sitcom. "I was a teenager; I had friends. I was being told that I was moving from Southern California to a place where the temperature when we got there in January was −27. I was upset," she recalled.[19] As for Pat, she would recall that she felt the move out of California would be good for her family as they began the next part of their lives.[20]

As had been the case with the move to California, Harry Dalton would arrive in Milwaukee ahead of his family. Milwaukee scout Dee Fondy, one of the few men whom Dalton would retain, met Dalton at Mitchell Airport on November 21, 1977. At that time, Dalton played things close to the vest but suggested that writers could put "two and two together."[21] Dalton was in town, and there was a press conference scheduled for 1:00 p.m. that day. That press conference immediately showed Milwaukee and the state of Wisconsin that the days of the Brewers just being happy to be back in the Major League were over.

After some initial comments from Selig, Dalton made it clear that Selig had given him the authority to bring about a complete change in his new team. He also let it be known that his first step would be "getting rid of the dogs—the chronic losers. . . . Every team has some losers and some winners and those in the middle ground. . . . The first thing we've got to do is get rid of the losing attitude and a losing group of players if we have one."[22]

From there, Dalton made a few things clear to the assembled media. As had been the case in California, he was not in a hurry to hire a manager to replace Alex Grammas. "Unlike some of you, I don't think there is an urgency to name a manager," he announced. Instead, Dalton let it be known that he would spend his early days evaluating talent in the organization.[23]

At first glance, Dalton did not think the Brewers were in bad shape. The position player pool was "talented but shallow." Dalton liked Yount, outfielder Sixto Lezcano, Don Money, Sal Bando, Cooper, and a new free agent acquisition, Larry Hisle. Dalton also liked the pitching, though he felt they needed an ace. As for the rest of the organization, Dalton announced he was ordering a review of the Minor League system.[24]

In terms of what he thought of Milwaukee as a franchise, Dalton said that the team was "ready to explode." Dalton's barometer for that assessment was the team's attendance figures. Despite fans being subjected to lousy baseball, the Brewers had averaged 1.1 million fans since 1972. For Dalton, this meant that fans would come in droves if the team ever had a winning season. This spurred him to do the work needed to build Milwaukee into a winner, though he reminded the Milwaukee media and the fanbase that it might take a while to reach the top of the mountain. "When a .500 or winning season comes," he said, "I see a 2-million attendance potential in Milwaukee again. When that will happen is impossible to say. There are a few meteoric rises in this business, but for some franchises, it takes 20, 30, or 40 years." With Dalton in charge, it would take much less time for Milwaukee.[25]

After his introductory press conference, Dalton would identify three goals that he claimed would improve the Brewers and set them on the path to winning baseball. In a reflection of his experiences in Baltimore and California, his first goal was upgrading the Minor League system. Dalton hoped to do this by signing more players and possibly adding a team to the Minor League system, which would account for a large chunk of the money Selig agreed to spend on development. Second, Dalton wanted to bolster the Major League roster through another dip into the free agent market. Finally, he would look to swing a trade that would help transform the team. In these last two areas, Dalton would score big early and add two elements that would provide even more offensive punch while helping cement Milwaukee's identity under Dalton for years to come.

Dalton's first move occurred on December 9, 1978, when he sent veteran left-handed pitcher Rich Folkers and longtime Brewers starting pitcher Jim Slaton to Detroit for Ben Oglivie. It is a move that would be seen as a stroke of genius in later years. Born in Panama and raised in New York City, Oglivie was a strongman built into a rail-thin 6-foot-2-inch frame, and he would give the Brewers a power-hitting lefty who was also an above-average defender in left field. Finally, Dalton would add a power-hitting righty in February when Milwaukee claimed center fielder Gorman Thomas off waivers from the Texas Rangers after Jim Baumer sent Thomas to Texas in October as the "player to be named later" in an August trade.

Thomas was an interesting prospect on a team stacked with outfielders. Drafted out of South Carolina by the Seattle Pilots in 1969, Thomas broke into the Majors with Milwaukee in 1973. He would spend parts of the next four seasons in and out of the Brewers' lineup before being traded to the Rangers. Once he returned to Milwaukee, writers and team officials saw him as a dark horse coming off a big year at Triple-A Spokane before he was traded to Texas.

With the addition of Oglivie and Thomas, the Brewers seemed to be set in the outfield, with Hisle and Sixto Lezcano joining Oglivie and Thomas as options, along with Lenn Sakata. The same could be said about the pitching staff. As camp opened in Sun City, Arizona, the returnees Mike Caldwell, Wisconsin native Jerry Augustine, twenty-two-year-old Lary Sorensen, and twenty-five-year-old Bill Travers were in the rotation. Dalton also hoped to get innings from Bill Castro out of the bullpen along with youngsters Bob McClure and Eduardo Rodríguez. At catcher, Charlie Moore and Buck Martinez looked to get most of the time, while Dalton Gang favorites Andy Etchebarren and Larry Haney were also on the roster, albeit at advanced ages. If there were any battles in camp, they were in the infield, where a glut of players competed for very few spots.

Cecil Cooper was a lock at first base. By 1978 he was coming into his own as a hitter, and he would anchor the Brewers' infield for the next ten seasons. As for who would play third, the original plan was to have Sal Bando play primarily as the designated hitter. However, he would become the Brewers' best option at third and play 134 games there in 1978. When Bando did not play there, veteran infielder Don Money, who would divide his time between third, first, and second, would spell Bando. The two biggest questions were in the middle infield, and the main question was how to incorporate the two best young players in the organization.

Coming into spring training in 1978, Robin Yount seemed to be on the cusp of big things. On a team of veterans, Yount was an up-and-coming star. In 1977 he had flashed moments of power with 34 doubles and a .288 batting average while still only twenty-one years old. This upside made Yount critical to the Brewers' future. As a case in point, Yount's signability was a huge factor in whether Dalton would come to Milwaukee, and Dalton saw him as a large part of the team's success in 1978.

Another part of the Brewers' future was gearing up for his first Major League camp in the spring of 1978. Paul Molitor, after being the team's first pick in 1977, went to the Brewers' Class A affiliate in Burlington, Iowa, where he was the player and prospect of the year in the Midwest League. This was thanks to an offensive burst that saw Molitor hit .346

and drive in 50 runs during the second half of the season. Along the way, Burlington won the league title. This performance earned Molitor an invite to the Major League camp for 1978.

With both Yount and Molitor playing shortstop, it seemed that one of them would change positions to make room for the other. Whether this was actually Dalton's plan in 1978 became a moot point as spring camp opened for the Brewers. In 1978 Yount was set to play on an option year included in his original contract. The accepted wisdom was that he would negotiate a new deal with the Brewers in time for 1978. Yount threw a wrench into this understanding when he refused to sign a contract for 1978 upon reporting to camp at the end of February. The reasons for this move depended on whom you asked.

Yount himself was mum about his reasons, saying they were personal. "I'm going to wait and see. It depends on a lot of things," he said.[26] This explanation stoked the rumor mill and led some to articulate the view that Yount's biggest problem was the treatment given to Molitor by the club. Initially, Harry Dalton was not worried about whether Yount would ink a deal and would not consider trading Yount. In keeping with his people-first mentality, Dalton also quickly pointed out that he and the Brewers would not give Yount an ultimatum to sign a contract or risk being traded. Dalton was willing to work with Yount.[27] That does not mean there were not a few tense moments. Later in March, after a few challenging games, speculation mounted that Yount might quit baseball and try his hand at professional golf.[28] The Brewers would then place Yount on the disabled list with various injuries. Finally, Yount would ask for a leave of absence late in the spring.

Again, the reason he was leaving was worked over and over in the media. Officially he had a nagging shoulder and tendinitis in his ankles. Yount said his reasons for leaving the team were even more complicated. "He [Harry Dalton] was the reason I went AWOL," Yount stated. "I was afraid to tell him I hurt myself on a motorcycle." Yount remembered that in the end he told Selig what had happened, and "Bud talked with Harry."[29]

Whatever the reason, the Brewers would be without Yount for the first month of the season. As a team, they managed to keep their heads above water. They ended the month 9-11, but they did score more runs than they allowed and had won their first five games. Another upside was Molitor. The rookie hit .290 for the month and had an OPS of .732 in fourteen games. Finally, as a team trait for the season and most of Harry Dalton's time in Milwaukee, the Brewers would hit home runs at a prodigious rate. They cracked 31 in April, and Gorman Thomas (6 HRS, 17 RBIS), Larry Hisle (8 HRS, 19 RBIS), and Cecil Cooper (7 HRS, 18 RBIS) paced a Brewers offense that was quickly seen as one of the best in the American League.

The offensive burst of the first month would continue for the rest of the season. In May, with Yount back in the fold, Milwaukee went 14-11 and continued to hit homers with abandon. This time, they tallied 21 as a team. There was no doubt that, barring any significant injuries, the offense would keep them in games. The only question some fans had was whether the pitching staff would get anyone out. Into May, the youthful staff had pitched well enough, especially with the offense averaging 4.12 runs per game. Harry Dalton did not think his team needed another arm, especially if it would cost him one of his everyday players. "We would obviously pick up a pitcher if we can improve over what we have, but what's the price?" he asked rhetorically. "I'd hate to sacrifice a regular to get a pitcher. We can put a pretty good front-line club on the field right now if everyone is healthy."[30] In June fans in Milwaukee found out what Harry Dalton was talking about.

The Brewers finished 21-9 for the month, moving into contention in the American League East. At the heart of the Brewers' attack were two of the newcomers. Molitor had the best offensive month of the season as he hit .330 (.350 on balls in play), stole 11 bases, and created 19.43 runs for the month while batting at the top of the lineup.[31] Meanwhile, Molitor's teammates were still hitting the ball over the fence at a frenetic pace. In June the team hit 35 homers and drove in 159 runs in the process. This style of play earned the club a nickname that would last for over forty years: "Bambi's Bombers."[32] More importantly, thanks to the offensive burst, the Brewers stood at 44-31, which was good for second place in the American League East.

Despite his team's achievements, the biggest question Harry Dalton got in May and June was whether he was going to trade Robin Yount. There was even speculation that Dalton was ready to offload the California native to the Angels at the end of May. This finally led Dalton to give an emphatic answer: "I swear to you it's not true."[33] Re-signing Yount was a closer reality in mid-June. "There are still some things that have to be resolved. . . . But I don't see a problem with him playing and staying here," Dalton said.[34] Looking back, it is easy to see that Harry Dalton worked with inside information. On June 21 Yount would sign a five-year contract that would be the first of numerous extensions he would sign to stay in Milwaukee. As for Yount's importance to the Brewers, Harry Dalton summed it up perfectly: "He [Yount] is a very important part of our plan to bring a championship to Milwaukee."[35]

That championship would not come in 1978 despite winning ninety-three games. The team would post a winning record in the second half and continue to hit. They averaged over 5 runs a game for the season, and the middle of the lineup featured five players who hit for double-digit figures in home runs. This group was paced by Larry Hisle, who would bat 34 hits and drive in 115 RBIs on his way to finishing third in the AL MVP race. As for Yount and Molitor, they both had solid years that boded well for the future. Molitor hit .273, stole 30 bases, and finished second in the Rookie of the Year voting. Meanwhile, in 127 games, Yount hit .293 and drove in 71 runs.

As for the pitching, the results were mixed. On the one hand, Mike Caldwell seemed to be the ace Dalton felt the young staff needed. The crafty lefty finished 22-9 with a 2.36 ERA and led the league in complete games with twenty-three. Along the way, he would finish second in the Cy Young voting. The real problem was that the bullpen did not feature a go-to arm for when games were close. Going forward, this deficiency would plague the team and keep the Brewers from being a serious contender in a highly competitive American League East.

Regardless of any shortcomings of the Brewers, baseball in Milwaukee was back largely thanks to Harry Dalton. This return to prominence for Milwaukee had fringe benefits for Harry Dalton beyond baseball. He was remembered in his hometown. On August 10, 1978, "Flash"

Dalton got his day in West Springfield, Massachusetts. It was a day filled with remembrances of a man who never forgot where he came from. He never would. That's what his friends from back home appreciated. Long before he was a baseball executive, Dalton was a subpar sandlot player who valued his hometown and his friends. Because of this loyalty, Dalton was still a favorite son. This brought the whole town together to laud Dalton. A luncheon, awards, and trips to his childhood home filled his itinerary, along with a win by his Double-A team, which was in nearby Holyoke. It was the type of trip that would affirm Dalton's love of home, family, and baseball.

The year 1978 was also affirming if you were a fan of the Milwaukee Brewers. For the first time in the team's brief history, you could root for a winner. Milwaukee was a relevant baseball city again. Moreover, it was evident that Harry Dalton did not see winning baseball as the end of the road for Milwaukee; he wanted to win a title. He and his gang would spend the next two years paving the way for that. Along the way, they would lay the foundation that would not only propel the Brewers to a new level of competitiveness in the short term but guarantee that the Brewers would be a competitive organization for years to come, despite growing financial troubles.

14

Laying the Foundation for a Winner

1979–80

Heading into his twenty-sixth season in baseball, Harry Dalton knew one thing for certain: that winning begat winning and that losing was equally contagious. What mattered most was the groundwork a team did to ensure that winning happened more frequently than losing. Building on the foundation of 1978, at both the Major League level and in the Minor League system, was the goal of Harry Dalton and his charges over the next two seasons.

At the Major League level, the 1979 and 1980 seasons looked much like 1978. The Brewers would routinely win by using a mix of power hitting and timely pitching. In 1979, despite Larry Hisle suffering a career-ending rotator cuff injury twenty-six games into the season, the Brewers would hit 185 home runs, score over 5 runs a game, and win ninety-five games, although they would finish in second place, eight games behind the Baltimore Orioles.

Offensively, the outfield was perhaps the most productive in the big leagues. Gorman Thomas built on his 1978 season by blasting a Major League–leading 45 homers and driving in 123 RBIs. Left fielder Ben Oglivie broke out, hitting 29 home runs while driving in 81 RBIs. Finally, right fielder Sixto Lezcano delivered 28 homers and 101 RBIs while hitting .321 with an OPS of .972.

Not to be outdone, Cecil Cooper would hit .308, smash 24 homers, and drive in 106 runs to pace the infield. Meanwhile, Paul Molitor was again the catalyst at the top of the lineup. The second-year man would hit .322, have 188 hits, score 88 runs, and steal 33 bases while getting most of the starts at second base. Fans would quickly start to refer to the Minnesotan as "The Ignitor."[1]

All of this offense was backed by a better-than-average pitching staff. Mike Caldwell was a workhorse for the second straight year. This time the lefty finished 16-6 with a 3.29 ERA in 235 innings. Close behind Caldwell, twenty-nine-year-old Jim Slaton, who returned to Milwaukee as a free agent after spending 1978 in Detroit in the wake of being traded for Oglivie, finished 15-9 with a 3.63 ERA in 233.2 innings. The Brewers would also get effective innings from their third and fourth starters. Lefty Bill Travers had arguably his best season in nine years in the league in 1979. All told, he would go 14-8 with a 3.89 ERA. Finally, twenty-three-year-old Lary Sorensen would go 15-14 in 235 innings.

The bullpen was also improved from a statistical standpoint. If there was one drawback, it was that once again the team did not have a "fireman" who could help them win a close game. To that point, the bullpen was 5-5 in save situations and featured a revolving door in the "closer" role all season. For a contending team, that could be the death knell of an otherwise productive season. It was also evident that the Brewers needed a solid fifth starter.

Coming into 1979, Dalton had placed great hope in the return of another twenty-three-year-old, Moose Haas, who was sidelined with an injury in 1978. In 1979 he went 11-11 with an ERA of 6.16. This result had Dalton acknowledging that his team needed pitching help if it was to win a pennant. "Pitching is the area where we need help," he said.[2] When asked about how he hoped to remedy this deficiency, Dalton let it be known that the Brewers were keeping their options open. "If we sign a starter, we would move one of our starters out of the rotation into the bullpen," he said. "Our goal is to strengthen the bullpen."[3]

Pundits and fans alike wondered if Dalton might fix both problems by acquiring a free agent pitcher. This was even more intriguing when the list of free agents for the 1980 season included Nolan Ryan. After Dalton left the Angels, the "Ryan Express" continued to roll on in Southern California. Ryan and MVP Don Baylor would propel the Angels to their first AL West title in 1979 as the finally healthy team fulfilled Dalton's erstwhile timeline for producing a winner. Despite this success, Ryan was ready to explore leaving California. The primary reason was that Buzzie Bavasi was not Harry Dalton. As the 1979 season progressed, Bavasi let it be known that he was less enamored with Ryan than others. The GM's displeasure reached a pinnacle when, in response to Ryan's preference for a long-term deal worth $850,000 to $1 million per year, Bavasi let the press know that he could do better by signing two 8-7 pitchers for less money.[4]

When Dalton was asked about the chance he might leverage his relationship with Ryan to bring the fireballer to Milwaukee, the GM was quick to downplay any interest. One reason was that Dalton did not know if the Brewers needed another drawing card. "We've got enough stars to draw people to the park," he said.[5] The more critical issue for Dalton was the rising cost of improving or maintaining a winner. When a reporter suggested that adding Ryan would show Brewers fans that the team was serious about winning, Dalton replied that the writer was correct if he was okay with "tying up three quarters of a million a season for the next three or five years in one arm."[6] To Dalton, the investment was not worth it if the return was not better than what you could develop internally.

This would be an overriding principle in Milwaukee. As he had said numerous times in his career, Dalton would not leverage the future for the present unless the return was something extraordinary. Over the long run, this would make the Brewers one of the most stable organizations, in terms of record, in the Major Leagues and put them in possession of the most prolific Minor League system in MLB during the 1980s.

The overhaul of the Brewers' player development program (scouting and Minor League system) began concurrently with the 1979 season, and any work done was in response to the study commissioned by Dalton when he came on board in 1978. That study, done by Tony Siegel, showed that while the Brewers had signed a fair number of players between 1970 and 1977, the team could benefit from an increase in the number of scouts. As of 1976, the Brewers employed only five full-time scouts.[7] They also subscribed to the Major League Scouting Bureau, a clearinghouse run by the league. The first thing Dalton did was look to expand his own scouting staff and limit the amount of information the team got from the MLSB.

To oversee the scouting department, Dalton tabbed Ray Poitevint, who had returned to the Dalton fold after a stint with the Orioles and the MLSB. Poitevint is a complicated individual historically but deserves his fair share of credit for the Brewers developing a system that had become self-sustaining by the mid-1980s. His initial move was to expand the Brewers' scouting operation per Dalton's request. By 1982 Poitevint had increased the scouting department to thirty individuals.

The professional scouts (those who would evaluate players on opposing teams in case of possible trades) included Walter Shannon and Dee Fondy, whom Dalton retained from the Baumer regime, in the West and Walter Youse and Ray Scarborough in the East and the Carolinas.[8] On the amateur side, each of the pro scouts and Poitevint would work in their areas as cross-checkers. Under each cross-checker would be a scouting supervisor overseeing a group of scouts.

In the early 1980s these supervisors included Nelson Burbrink for the Midwest, Roland LeBlanc for the Southwest, and Walter Youse for the East Coast. In addition, the Brewers had a large international and overseas footprint; Dalton and Poitevint had scouts looking for players throughout Latin America and Asia and in Hawaii as well.[9]

In Central America, South America, and the state of Florida, the Brewers employed a Cuban expat named Julio Blanco-Herrera Jr. He had come to the United States in the fallout of the Cuban Revolution. At that time, capitalizing on his family's history as the operators of La Tropical, the oldest and most popular brewery in Cuba, Blanco-Herrera got a job at National Brewery in Baltimore.[10] From there, word filtered out that beyond brewing, baseball was a passion of the Blanco-Herrera family.[11] This led to Julio Jr. being asked to work for Harry Dalton as a Latin American scout. Working with Poitevint, he would make a name for himself in Baltimore, his claim to fame being the signing of pitcher Dennis Martínez out of Nicaragua in the early 1970s.

Blanco-Herrera would follow Poitevint to Milwaukee. There, he would become known as a loyal scout who knew every baseball contact in Latin America and who had a way of establishing a good rapport with the families of players. This would let him help the Brewers secure the rights to another Nicaraguan amateur star, David Green, in 1978. Green would become a quick riser in the Minors and was considered the best prospect in the Brewers system at eighteen years of age and in the big leagues at twenty.

In addition to Blanco-Herrera, the Brewers employed former Negro League star Félix Delgado in Puerto Rico. Delgado would be incredibly prolific in his career with Milwaukee prior to players from Puerto Rico being subject to the same MLB draft rules that governed players from the mainland United States. From 1970 to 1997, Delgado signed thirty-one Major League players, including Sixto Lezcano and Eddie Romero.[12]

Below the supervisory level, the Brewers had twenty-four area scouts in place by 1983. This diverse group worked in every corner of the United States. Sam Suplizio scouted in Colorado, Tom Gamboa and Billy Moffitt in California, Paul Tretiak in Missouri, former Major League player Johnny Neun in Baltimore, and so many more. Each had a unique story and a drive to make the Brewers the best team in baseball.[13]

Neun, for instance, had been in baseball since the 1920s. He had played for Ty Cobb and was a Minor League manager and scout for the Yankees during their postwar dynastic years in the 1950s, with a brief stop as a Major League manager in Cincinnati. After New York, he went to work for Lou Gorman and John Schuerholz in Kansas City. Finally, he would work for the Brewers as a scout and instructor.[14] Harry Dalton saw him as an invaluable member of the scouting department for the attitude he brought to the organization. "He was one of the finest men I have known," Dalton said. "He took exceptional care of himself, which is why he was coaching in our minor-league camp. He never drank or smoked and wouldn't allow himself to put on weight. He respected modern players and was never jealous of the salaries. Truly a joy to know, respect, and yes, even revere."[15]

The area scouts made it possible for the Brewers to begin to strike pay dirt with their drafts. In 1979 they picked catcher Bill Schroeder out of Clemson in the eighth round. Schroeder made it to the Majors in 1983 and played six years of an eight-year Major League career in Milwaukee. In 1980 the Brewers would draft high schooler Dion James with the twenty-fifth pick in the June draft, as well as infielder Randy Ready. Like Green and Schroeder, James and Ready were high-ceiling prospects who, it was hoped, would start to make the Brewers less reliant on outside talent in the coming years.

Associated scouts were the last level of scouting for the Brewers. They were loosely affiliated with the area scouts and were true baseball junkies. From the Dominican Republic to California, they scoured fields looking at players whom they would then pass up the chain; depending on the area scout, the number of associates could be huge.

For example, in the early 1980s Sam Suplizio had over 250 associates reporting to him. These men would not draw a salary from the Brewers and could not ask the club to reimburse them for the costs of their work. Instead, their pay was on a case-by-case basis. At that time, associates received $100 for each player signed by the club. They would then receive an extra $200 when the player got promoted for the first time (from rookie ball to Class A, for example). The associate would earn $700 if a player they found made the forty-man roster.[16]

To support the scouting structure, Milwaukee employed two full-time assistants. Dalton would give the people he hired in that role the same opportunity Jim McLaughlin once gave him. And as had been the case in Baltimore when he hired Gorman and Schuerholz, Dalton's eye for talent, even at the administrative level, would make Milwaukee a great team and provide a breeding ground for the next generation of baseball executives.

In 1979 Dalton hired Bruce Manno, who hailed from Cleveland, as an administrative assistant in the farm department. Working for Ray Poitevint, Manno thus began what would be a fifteen-year career with Milwaukee and forty-three years in baseball, with stops in Baltimore, Atlanta, and Cincinnati before his retirement in 2022.

Everywhere Manno went, he took the things he learned from Harry Dalton. "Harry was so good to work for. The first thing he taught me was that if I wanted to work in baseball for a long time to not compromise my word," he said.[17] This foundation was pure Dalton and would form the bedrock of Manno's career.

Dalton would impart many of these off-the-field life lessons to Manno and others. "One of the things that Harry taught me was to clear my desk at the end of the day," Manno recalled. "To put things away when I went home. That way the next day you had a clean slate."[18]

Dalton also taught Manno that he would never know everything about the game or the players playing it. But you wanted to be prepared and understand the human element of player evaluation. To that end, when it came to baseball, Dalton taught Manno early on that no matter what his job was supposed to be, Dalton wanted him to watch the game and learn to evaluate talent so that he could be a better decision-maker if that day ever came.

"It was my first spring training, and I was taking care of the paperwork," Manno recalled. "One day in the first week of games, Harry stopped me and asks how many games I had seen. I told him that I hadn't been to any games yet because I had been busy with the paperwork. He told me that he appreciated that I was working hard but that every day he wanted me to stop what I was doing at three or whenever and go to the game so that I would learn how to evaluate players. Harry would always ask me what I was seeing. He showed me the right way to do our job."[19]

In many cases, an executive would be lucky if he produced one former aide who would continue to shape an industry long after starting out. In 1980 Dalton would get to hire a second transformative talent. Dan Duquette was a western Massachusetts kid like Dalton. He was even from a town called Dalton and went to Dalton's alma mater, Amherst College. There he double-lettered, in football and baseball, each of his four years. After graduation, the career counselor from Amherst brought Duquette to the attention of PR man and Amherst alum Bob Brown, who then gave his name to Dalton.

Duquette remembered that when he first met Dalton, he was nervous and worried that he would blow his chance to work in baseball. According to Duquette, Dalton sensed this and quickly put the younger man at ease once he knew that Duquette had shown him enough to get the job: "Harry said, 'Listen, you are from Dalton, Massachusetts, you went to Amherst; if I don't hire you, I may not be able to go back home.'"[20]

Like Manno, Duquette learned both life and baseball lessons from

Dalton. One of the biggest ones for Duquette was that baseball had as much to do with people as any other variable. Dalton reinforced this in meetings when he would ask for the opinion of anyone seated around the table. Duquette recalled that Dalton fostered an "inclusiveness" among the older and younger staff members thanks to his way of running a meeting. "Harry wanted you to debate," Duquette recalled.[21] Dalton was also not above giving the younger members of the staff opportunities to show their abilities. Like Dalton did in his early years in Baltimore, Duquette spent much of his time tracking player movements on the organizational board or out on the road. In Duquette's case, he was on the road helping Manno, Poitevint, or one of the area scouts run tryout camps much like those that the Dalton Gang had utilized in California.

Duquette remembered that the tryout camp was Dalton's favorite promotional tool as much as it was a way to look at players. "We would go all over," he said. "We would be in Stevens Point [three hours from Milwaukee] and in La Crosse [two hours southwest of Stevens Point] or somewhere else the next day."[22] The camps would bring out high school stars and small college standouts. Scouts even saw the occasional Cuban refugee. This was the case in 1980, shortly after Duquette was hired, when seven Cuban expats housed temporarily at a nearby army post, Fort McCoy, attended a camp at La Crosse.[23]

No matter who the players were or where they were from, they typically set their sights on going to a bigger camp. For example, in a tryout situation in Wisconsin, a player would first go to his local tryout camp and then perhaps be asked to move up to an area tryout in Madison. Ultimately, the goal was to get invited to a workout at Milwaukee County Stadium in front of senior members of the Brewers' scouting staff and Dalton himself.[24] Speaking of the whole process, Duquette recalled that the results did not matter to Dalton: "We might find one or two players. Harry loved them [tryouts], though. He wanted people knowing that we were out there looking."[25]

As had been the case in California and Baltimore, it would take a few years for Milwaukee's farm system to bear fruit for the Major League team. With this in mind, Dalton did try and improve the Brewers for 1980 via free agency and various trade proposals.

The Brewers bid on ten players in the 1979 free agent draft. Among those were Nolan Ryan, as expected; veteran relievers Al Hrabosky and Don Stanhouse; righty starter Dave Goltz; outfielder Roy White; and left fielder/first baseman Bob Watson. They would miss all their targets. Ryan was not interested in Milwaukee because of an overriding desire to be home in Texas. Goltz and Stanhouse would sign with the Dodgers. Watson would move to the New York Yankees. White would retire. Even with the Brewers missing out, Dalton would go to the winter meetings happy with his roster.[26]

Still, when Dalton went to the winter meetings in Toronto, he came home with right-handed Minor League slugger Mark Brouhard following a pick in the Rule 5 draft. Dalton was familiar with the big outfielder thanks to the Angels spending a draft pick on Brouhard in 1976. Since that time, he had steadily moved up through the Angels system. In 1978 the twenty-four-year-old Brouhard almost won the Triple Crown in the Double-A Texas League. He led the league in homers with 28, as well as RBIs with 109, and he missed the batting title by one point when he marked .350. With numbers like that, Brouhard won MVP honors in the Texas League. On paper, Brouhard seemed redundant thanks to the Brewers' glut of outfielders, all of whom had the potential for putting up tremendous power numbers. However, since the young outfielder was still available, Dalton could not pass him up. "He's got real power, his bat was just too attractive not to take a chance," Dalton said. "We thought he had an outstanding bat when we were in California and we still do."[27]

With Brouhard in tow, the Brewers' roster was set for 1980, and the results were much the same as 1978–79, although the win total was nine short of 1979's figure. Like the first two years of the Dalton regime in Milwaukee, pitching was an issue.

Once again, the back end of the bullpen was shaky, and this deficiency again reared its ugly head in games where the Brewers could have saved a win. In save situations, the bullpen was 2-8 with thirteen blown saves.

Once again, the ninth inning was a revolving door. Lefty Bob McClure got the most opportunities. McClure joined the Brewers in 1977 and appeared in seventy-six games out of the bullpen between 1977 and 1979. To that point, he had saved twenty games using a combination of a fastball, a hard-breaking curve, and a changeup to get hitters out. In 1980 McClure would amass a 5-8 record with ten saves in fifteen chances. Behind McClure, Bill Castro would save eight games and blow four more chances. Swing man Reggie Cleveland would also save four games in six chances.

As for the main problem with the bullpen, there was a diverse set of theories. The media in Milwaukee blamed the bullpen's poor pitching, exacerbated by a lack of concentration before entering the game. Various articles pointed out that the bullpen was seen engaging in activities that did not include watching the game.

Pitching coach Cal McLish, who spent eighteen years as a pitcher in the Majors, felt that the writers and the fans were making poor outings worse by not supporting the bullpen. "Even before the season started, our bullpen was reading stories about how bad they were," McLish said. "Then, early in the season when they were doing a good job, they were still reading about it." As for the fans, McLish admitted that they had a right to express their opinion but felt they crossed a line when they started being antagonistic toward a player. Finally, in terms of preparation, McLish defended Larry Haney, the bullpen coach: "He's an excellent instructor. He knows the game and he and the pitchers watch the hitters." Still, McLish admitted late in 1980 that the Brewers would need to change the bullpen for 1981 if they were to take the next step toward winning a title.[28]

Results also pointed to a need to change up the rotation. In 1980 the top three pitchers in the rotation (Mike Caldwell, Moose Haas, and Lary Sorensen) were a combined 41-36. Individually, none of the three was better than two games above .500. Caldwell's performance was especially troubling. After a stellar year in 1979, the lefty was 13-11 in 1980 with a 4.03 ERA. All these things pointed to a trend of the Brewers having too little pitching for a contender.

If pitching was a problem for the Brewers in 1980, once again hitting was not. Bambi's Bombers continued to terrorize American League pitching. The Brewers would be third in Major League Baseball in runs scored per game at 5.03. They were fourth in the league in batting average (.277), first in slugging (.448), first in OPS (.777), second in doubles (298), and first in home runs, with a positively gaudy 203.

The power came from up and down the lineup. Cecil Cooper hit 25 homers and led the Majors in RBIs with 125. Meanwhile, Gorman Thomas finished third in the American League in homers with 38 and drove in 105. The breakout star was Ben Oglivie. The Panamanian tied for the American League lead in home runs with 41. He would also finish second in RBIs with 118. In addition, Yount had his first big year statistically. The now twenty-five-year-old shortstop would hit .293, lead the Majors in doubles with 49, hit 23 home runs, drive in 83, and score 121 runs.

If it seems like the Brewers should have won more games with that amount of offensive output, the math shows that they indeed should have. For the season, the club would have a +129 run differential (811–682). Using a hybrid of Bill James's Pythagorean winning percentage, which computes a theoretical winning percentage based on the number of runs scored versus the number of runs allowed, Baseball Reference had the 1980 Brewers going 94-68 instead of 86-76. Either of these totals would have seen them finish third in the AL East. Still, eight more wins is a significant number. That begs the question: other than the poor pitching, which the offense worked around all year, why were the Brewers, as Baseball Reference explains it, "unlucky" in 1980?

To begin with, injuries suffered by Paul Molitor would mean that the budding star would miss fifty-one games during what was, to that point, an All-Star campaign. It was a hole that an aging Don Money and the scrappy Jim Gantner worked hard to fill. Money hit 17 home runs and drove in 46 RBIs in eighty-six games. Gantner would play stellar defense in his first extended time in the lineup. What Molitor gave the Brewers, however, was continuity. By 1980 the combination of Molitor at the top of the lineup with Yount hitting behind him (and in front of the power trio of Cooper, Thomas, and Oglivie) had given the Brewers the most potent 1-5 in baseball. Molitor being in and out of the lineup robbed the Brewers of that comfortable setting.

Beyond Molitor's injuries, which would become a more significant issue in the years ahead, the 1980 Brewers suffered a more stunning loss when George Bamberger was forced to miss almost three months of the season due to a heart attack suffered in spring training. He would return on June 6, but many saw a man not up for the job. Bamberger would confirm this and step down as manager in September.

The loss of a popular player's manager left the Brewers a half step behind for most of the year. It was not that Bamberger's replacement, first base coach Bob "Buck" Rodgers, did not do an admirable job. He just wasn't Bamberger. This is especially true considering that the pitching staff struggled most of the summer. According to pitchers like Mike Caldwell and Lary Sorensen, having Bamberger in the dugout was like having another pitching coach.[29] In addition, players like Yount appreciated Bamberger's positive, easygoing nature. "George always kept everyone relaxed," Yount said. "Very few times in three years have there ever been any conflicts with the manager with anyone. Keeping your players happy is a big part of managing and George did a great job of it."[30] Finally, as the fans saw it, with Bamberger out of the dugout, there was none of the old spark of the previous three seasons. Whatever the catalyst was, it left the Brewers short of the division title and a shot at the American League pennant.

When asked what he planned to do to try and finally get the Brewers over the hump and win the East, Dalton acknowledged that the Brewers would be looking to add players at the winter meetings in Dallas. He also preferred that the Brewers add via trade rather than free agency. When asked why that was, Dalton was his usual straightforward self: "We frankly don't see a lot out there [in the free agent draft] that is better than what we have." This comment not only applied to the 1980 draft class but was also indicative of Dalton's thoughts on free agency as a whole. Speaking in 1979, Dalton likened the free agent sweepstakes in baseball to the goings-on of the local auction house: "You go to the auction and see an old moose head that you hadn't thought about [needing] until you got there. The auctioneer says, 'Available today only and never again. Here's your once in a lifetime chance.' So you get the auction fever. Then when you get the damn moose home it looks hideous . . . and you want to throw up."[31]

On the surface this seems like the comment of an underwhelmed GM. However, it points to Dalton's developing thoughts on free agency. As the free agency era continued, Milwaukee would have a more challenging time competing for players with teams that could take on more payroll. This led Dalton to the conclusion that if the Brewers were going to bring in new outside talent in 1980 and beyond, it would be through the trade market. Brewers fans would quickly find that this is where the work of Dalton and his gang set them apart from the competition. The Brewers would go to the winter meetings with holes to fill and come out with a pennant contender.

15

A Taste of Things to Come

1981

In Wisconsin the deal that "Made Milwaukee Famous" is also known simply as "The Trade." It marked when the Brewers stopped being a dark horse and started being seen as a serious Major League contender. In three short days, Harry Dalton would remake his team and create an indelible memory that cemented his legacy in Wisconsin and baseball. How he did it was a perfect example of how the Dalton Gang worked. However, much like when Dalton would trade for Nolan Ryan, issues within baseball jeopardized the work of the Dalton Gang. In the end, thanks in part to the work of Dalton, the 1981 season would end on the field, and the Brewers were one of the last teams standing.

Coming into the winter meetings in Dallas, it was obvious that the Brewers would be looking for a stopper for the back of their bullpen. Dalton even said that he wanted one of the best late-inning relievers in baseball, either Bruce Sutter or Rollie Fingers. Both pitchers would have fit the needs of the Brewers perfectly.[1]

Fingers was the longest-established fireman in the game.[2] He was the primary reliever for the Oakland World Series teams, etching 85 saves from 1972 to 1975 in the regular season and 9 more in the postseason. After Charlie Finley blew up his team in Oakland, Fingers, with his signature handlebar mustache, moved to San Diego, where he led the NL in saves in both 1977 and 1978. He saved 108 games for the sometimes listless Padres between 1977 and 1980.

While Fingers was the longest-tenured closer in the game, Bruce Sutter was arguably the best reliever, thanks to one devastating pitch. As a Minor Leaguer in the Chicago Cubs system, Sutter learned how to throw a split-finger fastball from the Cubs' Minor League pitching instructor. Known colloquially as a "splitter," the pitch is thrown by spreading the first two fingers of the throwing hand across the seams so that they form a V. The ball is then thrown with the arm action of a fastball. If the ball is thrown correctly, the hitter senses a fastball—just before the pitch tumbles downward, thanks to a reduced speed caused by the "choking" nature of the V grip and varying degrees of pressure placed on the index finger. The tumbling nature of the pitch means that the hitter, geared up for a fastball, swings over the splitter as it lands in the dirt.[3]

Although it took Sutter time to master the pitch, it helped him make the Cubs' Opening Day roster in 1976. As the Cubs' fireman with the splitter as his out pitch, Sutter would save 10 games in 1976 and go 6-3 in his rookie year. Over the next four seasons, Sutter would save 123 games and lead the National League in saves in 1979 and 1980.

The Milwaukee Brewers were in the mix for snagging their prime targets as the winter meetings got underway. According to Dalton, Milwaukee "had the inside track on getting Fingers from the San Diego Padres" until the Cardinals went and acquired him in a three-for-eight player deal that saw Fingers and his teammate Gene Tenace go to St. Louis on December 8.[4] Missing out on Fingers, Dalton then prepared to make his substantial move to land Sutter. As it turned out, Dalton was circling back to Sutter. He had had a deal in place with the Cubs on the first day of the meetings, one that would have seen Paul Molitor go to Chicago for Sutter. According to multiple sources, Dalton's advisors were deadlocked when he asked for a vote (4–4). Then, as he did throughout his career, Harry Dalton decided to "sleep on it" before making a decision.[5] Ultimately he would keep Molitor, and Sutter would go to the Cardinals on December 9.

Suddenly the St. Louis Cardinals were the best team in baseball, at least on paper, thanks to the trades they had made; the players they had at the Major League level, including veteran catcher Ted Simmons; and the free agent signing of Darrell Porter, the former Brewers and current Royals catcher. Some Major League managers felt that Whitey Herzog, who had worked for Dalton in California and was now the Cardinals' manager and GM, had too much of a good thing, and Harry Dalton was one who thought so. He quickly set out to reorganize his team so that he might make a deal with Herzog and the Cardinals.

Ultimately, Dalton and Brewers manager Buck Rodgers decided that the best way to free up room for new talent was to move Paul Molitor from second base to the outfield. In the mind of the Brewers' brain trust, this was possible because Molitor had the speed, agility, and arm strength to play in center. Moving Molitor to center opened second base for Jim Gantner. With that accomplished, Dalton could offer right fielder Sixto Lezcano to St. Louis for pitching and move slugger Gorman Thomas from center to right.

The trade talks with the Cardinals started small. At first the deal was Milwaukee sending pitcher Lary Sorensen for Fingers. Then, when Simmons balked about the possibility of moving to first base to accommodate Porter, Herzog threw him in the deal. Finally, Herzog also offered Dalton no-nonsense right-hander Pete Vuckovich. In return, Herzog wanted Lezcano, Sorensen, pitcher Dave LaPoint, and Minor League outfield prospect David Green. This was when conversations reached critical mass inside the Dalton Gang. The late Brewers public relations director Tom "Sky" Skibosh loved telling the story.

"It got so heated that Ray Poitevint and [special assignment scout] Ray Scarborough almost came to fisticuffs in a meeting," Skibosh recalled. "Poitevint was saying, 'David Green is the future of this organization,' and Scarborough was saying, 'Forget the future. We have a chance to get these guys; we want to win now.' They almost went at it. They had to separate them."[6]

Dalton's reaction was almost one of pride. According to Duquette and others, Dalton wanted the real opinions of those who worked for him. This went beyond the people who worked for him directly. Tim Trovato was one of a group of young employees who dotted the Brewers offices during Dalton's tenure. He remembered that one day he got a call from Dalton, even though he was a junior staff member, asking how a player's potential trade might affect the team at the gate. Trovato was astonished that Dalton wanted his opinion, rather than that of his boss. In the end, Trovato gave his opinion that they could make up the sales if the team could be helped. Dalton thanked him for being honest and went back to negotiations.[7] That was Harry Dalton. He did not care who you were; he wanted you to give your honest assessment.

In this case, while Dalton appreciated Poitevint's willingness to fight for his prospect, he also understood that the deal was "too attractive to pass up" and could launch the Brewers into the role of a contender.[8] There was only one problem. Thanks to Simmons's ten-year Major League career, during which he spent more than five years with the Cardinals, he could veto his role in the deal, which would jeopardize the whole trade. Luckily for Dalton and the Brewers, the team had three things going for it as far as Simmons was concerned.

First, the Brewers were an up-and-coming team, and they wanted Simmons to become their everyday catcher. Second, Milwaukee wanted Simmons to be their everyday catcher to solidify and lead their defense. Finally, Simmons was excited by the players Milwaukee was set to acquire.[9] He recalled, "I asked Whitey [Herzog], 'Who's going to Milwaukee?' He said, 'Fingers is going and you're going, Vuckovich is going.' I said, 'Let me get this straight: those two guys, Fingers and Vuckovich, are coming with me to Milwaukee?'" Once Herzog confirmed that was the deal he had made, Simmons was on board to try and work out a deal with the Brewers to get him to waive his right to veto the trade. Ultimately, it would take a $750,000 inducement, but Dalton had his catcher.[10]

"The Trade" would quickly become the talk of baseball, and, as Simmons would say in 2020, the deal transformed the careers of himself, Vuckovich, and Fingers and the perception of the Brewers as a franchise. Overnight Dalton became the toast of Milwaukee, and according to Dalton, his team became a legitimate contender for 1981. There was one dark cloud hanging over the Brewers, however. Mirroring 1972, baseball was heading toward a work stoppage.

The possibility of a stoppage became a concern in the spring and summer of 1980. At the heart of the argument were two interconnected issues. On the surface was the owners' belief that they needed direct compensation for the loss of free agents in order to keep a semblance of competitive balance in the game.[11] Compensation was only a smoke screen for a more significant issue, however. At the heart of the disagreement was the inability of the owners and the players to come to a mutual understanding of how they would "interpret the game's exploding salary structure."[12]

On the players' side, they saw the owners pushing for direct compensation to roll back free agency. Direct compensation would allow the owners to keep salaries low and forgo bidding in the free agent market if they wanted.[13] This was unacceptable to players, who finally felt they were being paid a fair wage for providing an irreplaceable skill. Owners saw this fair market value as the end of their financial profitability. Free agency had led to rising salaries stemming from free agent bidding wars and multiple-year extensions meant to protect teams from losing players to free agency. In the eyes of the owners, both things drove down profits.[14]

In addition to their concerns over profitability in this new era, the owners saw the 1980 collective bargaining agreement as an opportunity to help reassert their dominance in the game following the losses to the players union in 1972 and 1975–76. As Commissioner Bowie Kuhn explained during a luncheon with union head Marvin Miller in the fall of 1979, in the owners' mind, they "needed a win." This did not bode well for a quick negotiation.[15]

Talks between the two sides progressed at a slow pace. The players set a strike date for May 23 and expected the strike to be lengthy. At the eleventh hour, however, both sides were able to get a working deal in place on the morning of the deadline. This was nothing but a Band-Aid on an open wound. The new agreement did not address free agency compensation. Instead, what it bought both sides was more time. With this extension, both sides would utilize a four-person research committee tasked with developing their side's take on compensation for free agency. Those ideas would then be integrated into the negotiating platforms for each side.[16]

Representing the MLBPA would be veteran catcher Bob Boone of the Phillies and Brewer Sal Bando. On the owners' side, Player Relations Committee (PRC) head Lee MacPhail selected two of his trusted lieutenants: Harry Dalton and Frank Cashen. History shows that the work of this group meant very little. Owners wanted to induce a strike over free agency and used the fight over direct compensation to get one. That does not mean that the work of the group was useless. Especially when looking at it through the lens of time, the compensation study group is an example of how fans would hope labor negotiations would work in baseball. Nowhere is this more evident than in the work of Harry Dalton.

Dalton was the secretary for the PRC group, and his notes show that while both sides had their ideas over what made a reasonable attempt at direct compensation, the small group settings, when devoid of influence from either Ray Grebey (the head negotiator for the owners) and Marvin Miller or Donald Fehr for the players, there was a great deal of compromise. This was most evident when the two groups got together to draft a joint plan for direct compensation.

The joint study was never released, as both sides exercised the option to release their own report from the study group. However, Dalton developed an outline for the joint study, showing that both sides agreed on a great deal if left to their own devices:

1. A Compensation system is appropriate. It is found in all other major professional sports.
2. Re-entry draft seems to have worked well overall.
3. The parties (on the Joint Study Committee) [parentheses in original] seem to agree that there is need for equity for a quality player.
4. There may be some procedural problems in the re-entry draft.
5. There is a limited source of supply of professional players.
6. An Amateur draft choice is a risky compensation at best as a possible major league replacement for a lost free agent.[17]

Whatever goodwill was found in the study group quickly evaporated when both sides decided to issue their own reports in the aftermath of the meeting sessions. This led to increased distrust, and ultimately the issue of compensation remained unsolved. This led the owners, as was their right, to unilaterally institute a compensation plan in February 1981. The players union saw this as a nuclear option, and both sides girded for a strike.

Harry Dalton was asked in March whether there would be a strike, given all that had happened with the study committee. He was, in the minds of many reporters, the perfect source. Not only had Dalton featured heavily on the study committee, but he was also known to honestly assess any situation for reporters when he could.

Peter Gammons, who covered the strike for the *Boston Globe*, and Tim Kurkjian, who covered baseball for the *Washington Post* in the early 1980s, both paint Dalton as a man willing to work with reporters and give them as much as he could on and off the record. Kurkjian recalled that "Harry really understood our job as reporters. He would give you things if he felt he could, and he wouldn't hide things from you if he didn't have to, which is rare in our business."[18] Every journalist who worked with Dalton has chalked this up to the fact that Harry had spent time doing their job. However, as Kurkjian was quick to point out, Dalton often used his time on the sports beat as a self-deprecating way to make others feel important. The key to dealing with Dalton was establishing a two-way street of trust. If Dalton was going to give a reporter access and personal insights, he did not want those ideas he thought were private to become headline material. With those stipulations in play, he was willing to be the most candid, media-friendly GM in the game.

The need for those ground rules was reinforced to Dalton during his time with the joint study committee. Coming off the heels of two separate reports that were driven by the positions of Grebey and Miller and seemed to fix none of the issues surrounding direct compensation, Thomas Boswell, an up-and-coming reporter for the *Washington Post*, sought out Dalton for his opinion on the possibility of avoiding a baseball strike.

History shows that Dalton phoned Boswell, to whom he had given quotes for attribution numerous times leading up to 1981, and a discussion of the labor situation ensued. It is at this point where the stories of the two men diverge. Boswell has always claimed that what Dalton told him was on the record, and Dalton was sure he was commenting privately to Boswell. What was said would not only make Harry Dalton very clear about his rules with the media going forward but also make him an unintended martyr in baseball's labor struggles because of his willingness to speak the truth.

On March 6 Boswell quoted Dalton as saying, "I hope that management is really looking for a compromise and not a 'victory.' But I'm not certain that's the case. I hope that we are not about to witness another macho test of wills. From what I hear, the players association is genuinely looking for a compromise, if we'll just give them something that they can accept without losing too much face."[19]

Given his position on the joint study committee, what Dalton said was unequivocally the truth as he and many others saw it. It also broke ranks with the owners. Because of that, ownership made an example of Dalton by fining him $50,000 for comments detrimental to the ongoing negotiations during a kangaroo court proceeding in which Dalton was not allowed representation or a character witness. Dalton, the national media, and even the players union were stunned.

When informed of the fine, Marvin Miller quickly took the opportunity to call out management for punishing one of their own who had dared to tell the truth: "The fact of the matter is everybody has been talking about the negotiations . . . all of them. . . . The gag rule is if you don't parrot the party line."[20] Mark Belanger also came to the defense of his former boss: "It's bush. It's not fair to have someone like Dalton express an opinion and have it cost him money. That's really sad."[21]

Dalton quickly became the subject of editorials in some of the most prominent newspapers in the country. Even an aged Red Smith, the dean of sports columnists, weighed in. "Harry Dalton's crime was not speaking out in violation of the gag rule known as the 'Grebey discipline code,'" Smith wrote. "He sinned by suggesting that management was unwilling to compromise on the issue of compensation for players lost to free agency. . . . Nobody has suggested that Dalton didn't know what he was talking about when and if he made the comments that were published."[22]

Dalton himself was officially silent, as were Bud Selig and the Brewers. However, the team would initially pay the fine. Privately, Dalton was hurt. The hurt stemmed from the assertion that the disciplinary committee, composed of hard-line owners like Jerry Hoffberger, Walter O'Malley, and Gussie Busch, believed that Dalton would do anything "detrimental to baseball." Dalton was also quick to point out in a letter to Bowie Kuhn that he felt that the work he did for the study group was hypocritical, and he reminded Kuhn that he served on the study group against his better judgment because he and Frank Cashen wanted to be "good soldiers" for the game. In Dalton's mind, the work was hypocritical because the PRC had no intention of putting the best system in place in regard to compensation. Their actual goal was to "Beat Marvin." In the same letter, Dalton admitted to saying what Boswell had printed. He also took the time to point out that he understood that the reaction of the PRC was aimed at setting a precedent and that it was also political because Kuhn felt the necessity to curry favor with Gussie Busch.[23]

In the end, Kuhn tried to backtrack in a follow-up letter. In it, he lauded Dalton for his years of good work for baseball. In a response that was never sent, Dalton replied that "the letter did not make me feel any better." He then proceeded to outline why he thought that Kuhn was politically motivated to punish Milwaukee and thereby distance himself from a very public friendship with Bud Selig. Dalton also wrote in his draft letter that he resented the fact that as a result of Kuhn using Dalton as a scapegoat for his own gain, "my wife and daughters who—with a strong belief in right and wrong—must cope with the public perception that I have been grievously at fault."[24]

Dalton closed the matter with words reminiscent of his letter to Frank Cashen and Jerry Hoffberger in the lead-up to his leaving Baltimore.

"I will say nothing publicly in my own defense as long as I continue my employment within baseball, since I do not wish to do anything that will complicate problems in this industry," he wrote. "If however, the hypocrisy, direct lieing [*sic*] and press misinterpretation which have gone on to date continue to the point where I feel the record must be set straight, then I will speak out with as accurate a portrayal of what happened as possible. In order to do that however, I will first resign from baseball."[25]

It never came to that. Months later, Kuhn would quietly rescind the fine, and the rhetoric and hypocrisy Dalton warned against would lead to a strike that would last well into the summer.

With the PRC fiasco behind him, Dalton could finally return to what he loved: trying to get his team to a pennant. Under the threat of a looming strike, the Brewers had ended April with a 9-7 record. They then went 18-12 in May and looked like they were about to hit their stride. They were 31-25 when the strike came in June, after ten games had been played that month. Everything showed that the Brewers would be a force if the season continued.

Vuckovich had stabilized the starting pitching, going 6-2 in thirteen starts with a 3.67 ERA. Meanwhile, Fingers saved twelve games. As for the offense, it was as potent as Dalton and the fans could have hoped. Gorman Thomas would slam 15 homers in the first half, with 34 RBIs. Ted Simmons made everyone understand that he was a dual threat by helping control the game behind the plate and hitting 9 home runs and 30 RBIs. Then the season came to a halt.

Initially, players stayed in and around Milwaukee and worked out on their own in case of a quick resolution. That was not to be the case. The strike would drag on into the height of the summer. With extra time on his hands, Harry Dalton would return to his roots in the game and spend time with the scouts and the Brewers' Minor Leaguers. During that time, he realized that Ray Poitevint was not the best fit for the role of director of player development. It was a huge revelation that would immediately impact the Brewers' development efforts going forward.

Bruce Manno has recalled that although Poitevint was a great scout and the consummate salesman, he was not a great administrator and was prone to making deals that put the team in a bad position from a development standpoint. "Ray really protected our scouts and was promising players at least three spring trainings [before they would be cut] which was crazy!" Manno remembered. The result was that Dalton realized that the Brewers were overloaded with players who would never make the Majors. In addition, Poitevint created his own fiefdom in which the Minor League managers did not feel they had a voice. Finally, Poitevint would, according to Manno, "let his personal relationships get in the way and it clouded his judgement."[26]

Seeing this dynamic for himself, Dalton prepared to make sweeping changes in the development area. First, though, he would prepare to watch his Major League club on the field. The players and owners would battle their way to an agreement that included a form of free agent compensation that was finally signed on July 31. As for games, the end result of the forty-nine-day work stoppage was that the season would feature a format with winners for both halves and a round of divisional playoffs before the league championship series.

With the split-season parameters applied to the first half of the season, the Brewers officially finished that half in third place, three games behind the Yankees, who were enjoying the fruits of a huge first half thanks to free agent acquisition Dave Winfield. In the second half, the Brewers finished 31-22, which was good enough for the second-half AL East title. At the heart of the charge to the top was a 13-9 record when play resumed in August and an offensive burst from Oglivie and Cooper, who together hit 17 homers and 79 RBIs. For the pitching staff, both Vuckovich and Fingers achieved exactly what Dalton had hoped when he brought them to Milwaukee. Vuckovich went 6-2 in thirteen starts and pitched to a 3.67 ERA. Meanwhile, Fingers notched 16 saves, 5 wins, and an ERA of 0.72. The result was a game-and-a-half lead over Boston and Detroit when the dust cleared.

Milwaukee's sun-drenched County Stadium was the site of the clincher. In that game on October 3, 1981, the Brewers outlasted the Detroit Tigers on the next to last day of the season. Vuckovich started for Milwaukee and would surrender a single run over six and two-thirds innings. Any other day that would be a stellar start, but Tigers ace Jack Morris was better for the first seven innings by shutting out the potent Milwaukee offense. Then, in the eighth, Paul Molitor and Robin Yount, as they did throughout their Hall of Fame careers, kickstarted a rally that would change the Brewers' fortunes.

Molitor walked to start the inning. Yount then reached when the Detroit infield failed to get an out at either base on what was going to be a sacrifice bunt. Milwaukee loaded the bases when Cecil Cooper bunted for a base hit on a ball back to Morris that he fielded cleanly but could not turn into an out. At that point, with the bases loaded and no outs, Simmons, who went 2-4 that day, drove in the tying run on a groundball out that deflected off Morris before being gathered by Alan Trammell, who threw out Simmons at first.

With one out and first base open, Tigers manager Sparky Anderson instructed Morris to walk Oglivie and again load the bases. That led to a matchup between Morris and Gorman Thomas. Morris's first pitch was a fastball high and wide on the outside corner to the right-handed Thomas. Morris then threw another fastball. This one caught the plate, and Thomas was able to loft it into the right-center field gap, where it was corralled for an out by Rick Leach. It was deep enough, however, to score Yount from third. The Brewers now led 2–1.

It was 2–1 Milwaukee as the game headed to the ninth. From there, Rollie Fingers took over. For the first out, Fingers, who came in for Milwaukee with two out in the eighth, got Leach to fly out to Oglivie in left. He then struck out pinch hitter Champ Summers. That left Fingers facing the dangerous Lou Whitaker with two out and no one on. Fingers missed high with a breaking ball on the first pitch. He then evened the count with a fastball on the outside corner. On the 1-1, Fingers threw a breaking ball that Whitaker fouled toward first after just getting a piece of the ball, which otherwise would have been in the dirt. Fingers then returned to the fastball with the count at 1-2. This one was on the inside corner to Whitaker, and the lefty swung right through the offering.

The pandemonium that followed was reminiscent of what happens when the valve is released on a pressure cooker. After the game, Sal Bando and Fingers, both of whom had played on title-winning teams in Oakland, were ecstatic to be on a winner again.[27] Other players, such as Charlie Moore, quickly pointed out that Harry Dalton had turned Milwaukee into a winner. Forty-one years later, Robin Yount agreed. From the minute he took over, Dalton provided a steady influence. As he had in Baltimore, Dalton was quick to downplay his role in the snaring of the division title. Soaking wet from being thrown in the whirlpool, Dalton noted, "Personally this isn't as big a thrill for Harry Dalton as it is for the whole organization. It's a great, great day."[28]

Having secured the division title, the Brewers played their first playoff series in team history, going up against the New York Yankees. It was a hard-fought series for the team, and the turning point occurred in the first two games.

In game one at County Stadium, the Brewers took a 2–0 lead into the top of the fourth. The Yankees would score four times before the end of the inning. Moose Haas walked Reggie Jackson before giving up a home run to Oscar Gamble. The Yankees would get two more when catcher Rick Cerone plated two runs on a one-out double three hitters later. The next night, Dave Righetti, who would win the American League Rookie of the Year after the season, and Goose Gossage, the Yankees' fireman and a future Hall of Famer, shut down the Milwaukee offense in a 3–0 loss.

Down two games to none, the Brewers would win the next two games in New York. In game three, Milwaukee roughed up Tommy John, who had undergone a surgical procedure that now bears his name, with a 5–0 final tally. The next afternoon, Vuckovich defeated Rick Reuschel 2–1 behind RBIs from Oglivie and Cooper. In the fifth and final game, it looked as if the Brewers might come from behind to take the series.

Trailing 5–3 in the eighth, Goose Gossage retired Thomas and Oglivie quickly. He walked Sal Bando and pinch hitter Roy Howell ahead of Don Money. Money, who by this time was a part-time player, fell behind 1-2 and then seemed to catch lightning in a bottle. Gossage's fastball was right down the middle of the plate, and Money swung and drove the ball deep to left. At first it seemed that the ball would clear the fence and give the Brewers the lead. Money did not get fully extended on the swing, however. Because of this, the ball ran out of steam one step before the wall, allowing Dave Winfield to haul it in. The Brewers would then surrender two runs in the ninth and fall to the Yankees 7–3.

After the series, Harry Dalton was as upbeat as a GM whose team had lost could be. "I'm disappointed, naturally," he said. "But that disappointment is cushioned by how well we played in September (16-12) and by the fact that we pushed the Yankees to the wall after losing the first two games."[29] Dalton's optimism came from his understanding of the team's talent. "Pete Vuckovich . . . Rollie Fingers . . . Cecil Cooper . . . they all had great years," Dalton said.[30] He was pleased with the pitching as well. Fingers would go on to win both the American League Cy Young Award and the American League Most Valuable Player Award.

Meanwhile, while Vuckovich would not win any hardware in 1981, he gave the Brewers the ace they needed, and the season would be the start of a lifelong mutual admiration between the gritty pitcher and the entire Dalton family.

What Harry Dalton loved about Pete Vuckovich was that he was a gamer on the mound and unapologetic when telling people that he would do anything to help his team win. He also did both things with an edge that made him one of the most imposing people in baseball. He was just the type of player whom Dalton felt the Brewers needed. Dalton also loved that there was more to Vuckovich than met the eye.

While the national media and the fans loved Vuckovich for his pitching and his gruff exterior, Dalton's affinity for the righty extended to his intelligence, which was present both on the mound and off. For example, Dalton constantly pushed Vuckovich to take the entrance exam for Mensa International, the high IQ society of which Dalton was a member. In keeping with his what-you-see-is-what-you-get personality, Vuckovich always told Dalton that he would be a better candidate for "Densa." This flippant approach belied an individual who knew how to use his mind in conjunction with his ability to become one of the most potent pitchers in baseball during his years in Milwaukee. That made Vuckovich a perfect Harry Dalton player.

In turn, Vuckovich loved that Dalton wanted to win on the field, and he cared about him off it as well. The duality of their relationship bred a level of loyalty between Dalton and Vuckovich, and even Dalton's family, that still exists. As Vuckovich explained it, with a warmth and introspection that few people can convey, "I loved Harry Dalton, and he loved me."[31] This mutual feeling was the foundation of a lifelong friendship and a season that still lives in Brewers lore as the greatest in team history.

16

The Wallbangers

OCTOBER 1981–OCTOBER 1982

After the Brewers' showing against the Yankees, it did not seem that Harry Dalton would have too many holes to patch in the last weeks of the 1981 calendar year. This was indeed the case on the field. The winter of 1981 did not see Dalton make a move to strengthen his team beyond the release of much-maligned pitcher Reggie Cleveland.[1] Off the field, however, Dalton would make a series of moves that would have an impact on 1982 and beyond.

Before the season ended, Dalton completed the overhaul of the scouting and player development departments he had started during the strike. In the end, Dalton would reshuffle some existing staff and bring back an old face. In the reshuffle, Dalton named Bruce Manno as the director of Minor League operations (read: farm director), and Ray Poitevint became the head of player procurement (scouting). Dalton hoped these moves would allow the Brewers to perform better in both the scouting and development areas. Finally, George Bamberger would rejoin the team as the head of the Brewers' player development effort, though he would leave the team later in October to manage the New York Mets.[2]

With the front office taken care of, Dalton inked Buck Rodgers to a one-year deal as manager for 1982. At various points, it seemed that Rodgers might have been on his way out of Milwaukee in 1981—especially when Ted Simmons, Pete Vuckovich, Gorman Thomas, and Mike Caldwell were publicly vocal about how, in their opinion, Rodgers was over-managing the team.[3] Still, Dalton believed that Rodgers had "the team driving down the stretch."[4]

With Rodgers inked for another year, the rest of the winter moved quickly for Dalton. Once again, due to growing constraints of the costs associated with dipping into the free agent market, Dalton did not see the Brewers being significant players at the winter meetings unless it was through a trade. Even Dalton admitted that this was less likely heading into 1982 because the Brewers roster was "virtually set" for the season.[5]

The strength of their lineup did not stop the Dalton Gang from trying to swing a deal. At one point, Milwaukee offered Mike Caldwell to Philadelphia for a twenty-one-year-old second baseman named Ryne Sandberg. Sandberg would play thirteen games for the Phillies in 1981 and be traded to the Chicago Cubs the following off-season. There he would launch a Hall of Fame career that saw him smash 282 career homers, hit .285, and steal 344 bases.

After the winter meetings, time moved quickly for the Brewers and Harry Dalton. January saw Dalton make the rounds on the Brewers caravan and put out fires in Milwaukee. The most important task was to try and appease Charlie Moore. The 1982 season would be the catcher's ninth year in the Major Leagues with Milwaukee; the Brewers had drafted him out of high school in Alabama in 1971. Since then, the team had used Moore as a backup and a starter in a mission to find an offensive threat at the catching spot. Now, with Simmons, the Brewers had an everyday player. They also had two other backups besides Moore in the winter of 1982. This led the solidly built Moore to let Dalton know he wanted to be moved to somewhere he could play on a steady basis.[6]

Dalton let it be known that he understood Moore's stance on playing time and did not blame the player for wanting to be in the lineup more often. However, when asked about the situation in interviews, the cagey Dalton again pointed out that "things might happen that would change his [Moore's] mind."[7] This was one of those times when Harry Dalton knew what the public did not.

In December Dalton had been unceremoniously told by Bud Selig that the carousel that had moved Paul Molitor to the outfield in 1981 was about to stop for the final time; Molitor would move to third base and stay there. With this in mind, Dalton and Rodgers thought they could move Gorman Thomas back to center, where he wanted to be, and make Moore, who had one of the strongest arms in the league and good mobility for a catcher, to right field.[8] When Moore was clued in to this fact in March, he promptly dropped his trade request.[9]

The events surrounding Moore's chance in the outfield, brought about by Selig interceding with Dalton on behalf of Molitor, lends itself to a more extensive discussion of the dynamic between Selig and Dalton as it stood in 1982.

Generally, from the day that Dalton came to work in Milwaukee, he and Selig had enjoyed an amicable, productive relationship. They were close enough to allow each other open-door access to one another's office.[10] Still, there is no doubt that the two men handled people and stress differently. When asked about the difference between her father and Dalton, Wendy Selig, who worked for the club in various capacities during Dalton's tenure, recalled that, in her mind, "my father was a lunatic."[11] This included pacing around, chain-smoking cigarillos on his box's balcony, or confronting sportswriters in the press box who he felt had wronged his team in the newspapers.[12]

In contrast, Dalton was "stoic and calm" during games and spent the innings on the phone or with beer and peanuts and his ubiquitous scorebook close by. The most demonstrative thing he would do was occasionally rap his ring on the table during a critical moment that did not go as he would have liked.[13] Selig was also standoffish with fans and people who could be considered below his station.[14] Selig's demeanor was the opposite of Dalton's. Even when working during a game (he was constantly on the phone), Dalton took time to spend a few innings with friends of his daughters or friends whom Pat had invited to watch a game with her and Harry. At these times, he would give those interested an insight into how he and his scouts watched a game to evaluate talent.[15]

The difference in the demeanors of the two men went beyond their interactions with the public. At times, those who worked for Dalton felt their boss was undercut by Selig's insistence on quarterbacking things he felt could not be left to Dalton. In the early years of their partnership, most of these situations revolved around Selig taking a special interest in handling Paul Molitor and Robin Yount.

Selig promising Molitor that he would not move positions after 1982 was one of these situations. When asked about that instance, Dalton, much like he did when Mike Epstein swore Dalton had promised to trade him, flatly replied that the team "could never make such a promise" to Molitor.[16] At this, Selig countered that if Dalton did move Molitor, he "wouldn't be happy," thereby cutting Dalton's options on how he and the manager could use Molitor.[17]

As for Yount, Selig made a point of negotiating his contracts personally.[18] On the surface, this did not cause any outward problems between Yount and Dalton. Yount categorized their relationship as professional yet warm and was quick to laud Dalton for what he did to help the Milwaukee franchise.[19] However, Selig's insistence on negotiating with Yount did, in the minds of some, including Tom Skibosh, create a precedent in which stars of the team could go to Selig if they were unhappy with a decision made by Dalton.[20]

Dalton himself never showed any animosity toward Selig in these situations. An owner taking a special interest in a star was a regular occurrence, and in Dalton's mind the team owner had every right to weigh in or step in during a given situation.[21] One thing that Dalton did not let Selig do, however, was use the front office staff, especially those in the baseball operations department, as a verbal punching bag.

As Dan Duquette noted, "By 1982, Harry had been around. He had seen it all."[22] This professional experience gave Dalton a certain cachet with the tightly wound Selig when the owner was on the verge of taking his frustrations out on those who could not openly defend themselves.

Finally, Selig did not handle criticism well and always excelled at shaping the narrative surrounding events in which he was involved. Sometimes this meant painting himself as the victim of an unfair story. Dalton did a fantastic job ensuring that he could defuse Selig and still allow his boss to vent when needed. One case is legendary.

During 1980–82, Dan Okrent, then a freelance writer for various publications, was looking to give fans insight into the life of a Major League franchise using one game in the middle of one season as his lens. For various reasons, he chose Milwaukee. During his time with the team, he developed a good relationship with Harry and Pat Dalton. Selig did not take to Okrent, especially after Selig felt that the final product, the book *Nine Innings*, showed him in an unfair light. According to Okrent, this led to Selig voicing his displeasure in a tirade during a phone call in 1983 and frosty relations between the two men after that.[23]

Okrent found it odd that Dalton did not call about how he was presented in the book. The reason why he did not shines a light on how well Dalton understood Selig. Years later, Okrent received a call from the former GM. During it, Dalton complimented Okrent for his work and admitted that he liked the book. Okrent thanked Dalton and asked why he had waited seven years to tell him that. Dalton was forthright. He knew from conversations with Selig that the Brewers boss did not like the book, and Dalton felt the best way to minimize any strife with Selig was not to read the book. That way, Dalton could honestly tell Selig that he did not have an opinion on Okrent and his book when Selig came to discuss it.

With Molitor settled in at third base, the rest of the spring was devoid of controversy and significant injuries and fell into the rhythm of endless day games and nights building camaraderie at the tables of various restaurants around the Brewers' spring training home in Sun City, Arizona.[24] Calm prevailed until Rollie Fingers tried to break up the boredom that sets in at camp by participating in an impromptu tackling drill. During the incident, Fingers was "horsing around" with left-handed pitcher Randy Lerch. It is unclear whether he was the tackler or the target, but Fingers would injure his left shoulder. Dalton's response was blunt: "We aren't paying him [Fingers] to play linebacker."[25]

Luckily for Milwaukee, Fingers would not miss any time as the season began. Still, the team struggled. Milwaukee was 9-8 and two and a half games back at the end of April. May started much the same way. A five-game winning streak in early May was followed by a four-game losing streak. As for what was causing the erratic play, the players, much like in 1981, laid the blame at the feet of Buck Rodgers.

Asked about Rodgers, Robin Yount said the biggest problem was that he wanted the Brewers to play what was known as a "National League" style of baseball.[26] Rodgers wanted to hit and run, bunt, and play for one run.[27] That was not the team he had. The overmanagement led to resentment. As that resentment festered, the Brewers slipped further behind in the standings. The end of May saw Milwaukee go 2-6 in a home stand against the Angels, the Seattle Mariners, and the Oakland A's. At that point, the club left for a West Coast road trip against the same clubs. They were seven and a half games out of first place and in sixth place in the seven-team American League East.

Following a four-game split against the Angels in Anaheim, the team dropped the first game in Seattle. They were forty-six games into the season, and Harry Dalton had seen enough. After a win during the second game of a series with Seattle, Dalton decided to fire Rodgers. As for who would manage the club, Dalton felt the best fit was Harvey Kuenn, a Milwaukee hitting coach and longtime Major Leaguer.

Kuenn, who hailed from the Milwaukee area, was the AL Rookie of the Year in 1952, a ten-time All-Star, and the American League batting champ in 1959, when he hit .359. Kuenn had been with the Brewers as a hitting instructor and coach since the team's early days. Known as "Arch" thanks to an uncanny likeness to fictional everyman Archie Bunker, Kuenn built a rapport with every homegrown player on the team at one point. This familiarity gave Kuenn a familial relationship with most of his players, which was hugely influential in a team as close as the Brewers.[28]

It also did not hurt Kuenn's standing with his team that he went out of his way to show that he was not Buck Rodgers. The one moment that still stuck in players' minds forty years later was Kuenn's opinion of team meetings. Ted Simmons remembered that Kuenn called a meeting before a game against Seattle at the Kingdome. The veteran catcher considered it the best opening address to a team he ever saw: "Harvey comes in there and says, 'Boys, I hate meetings, and this meeting is over.'"[29]

When asked about his new skipper, Harry Dalton quickly pointed out that Kuenn was the interim manager, but that had more to do with Kuenn's physical condition.[30] As of 1982, the fifty-two-year-old had undergone bypass surgery and reconstructive stomach surgery and had had his right leg amputated below the knee due to a collapsed artery.

Despite all these challenges, Kuenn was an upbeat person. As might be expected following his take on clubhouse meetings, he carried that attitude over to how he ran a team: "I like the club to be loose, have a laugh. Go out and have fun."[31] The freewheeling Brewers took to this like a fish to water.

The team that became known as "Harvey's Wallbangers" quickly reeled off five wins in a row. They would finish June 20-7 and never look back, and they would suffer only one losing month the rest of the year. The offense was firing on all cylinders, including an MVP-like effort by Robin Yount. Meanwhile, Pete Vuckovich was giving the team a Cy Young–winning performance. Through the end of August, the Brewers held a four-and-a-half-game lead.

With all of this success, it would have been easy for Harry Dalton to stand pat. True to form, however, when he thought his team could win, Dalton looked to make a deal that could strengthen the odds. In addition, unbeknown to the outside world, despite his success, Pete Vuckovich had suffered an injury that threatened to weaken the Brewers' starting staff. That is how, at the August 31 trade deadline, Dalton traded outfielder Kevin Bass and pitchers Frank DiPino and Mike Madden to Houston for future Hall of Famer Don Sutton.[32]

The year 1982 was Sutton's sixteenth in the Majors, and he was the epitome of a top-of-rotation starter. Coming up with the Dodgers, Sutton was the heir apparent to Sandy Koufax and Don Drysdale, and he would win 233 games for Los Angeles. With that track record, Sutton was one of the most sought-after free agents in the 1981 reentry draft. At that time, Milwaukee was making a huge play for Sutton. In fact, Sutton said he gave Milwaukee the "right of first refusal" because of how impressed he was with the organization and Harry Dalton.[33] "Of all the people who dealt with me [in the winter of 1980]," Sutton remarked, "he was the only one who sent me a letter wishing me well."[34] After signing with Houston, Don Sutton, Nolan Ryan, and J. R. Richard formed one of the best rotations in baseball. Sutton was 11-9 in 1981 and 13-8 in 1982 when he was traded to Milwaukee.

It could not have come at a better time. As noted earlier, although Pete Vuckovich was having a great season, he was pitching at less than 100 percent. His throwing shoulder started hurting in early August whenever he threw a pitch. This was not the first time his shoulder had given him trouble. In 1980 Vuckovich had told St. Louis he was having pain in his shoulder, and after not initially believing him, they eventually administered a cortisone shot that allowed Vuckovich to finish the year. With the help of the shortened season in 1981, the pain did not return. However, in early August 1982 the pain came back. This time, an examination showed that Vuckovich had torn the rotator cuff in his right shoulder. Despite this result, Vuckovich once again proved that very little would get in his way of helping his team win. He would not miss a start due to the injury even though by the end of the year he was a shell of the pitcher he was at the beginning.[35]

The Brewers were not so lucky when injury struck their bullpen in early September. During an appearance in the first game of a doubleheader against the Cleveland Indians in Milwaukee, Rollie Fingers experienced tightness in his right forearm. At first, Fingers hoped he would be back on the mound in a few days.[36] However, as the month went on and a tear in the muscle was discovered, Fingers's return became doubtful.[37]

To replace Fingers, Harvey Kuenn slotted in a host of relievers, including rookie Pete Ladd, Moose Haas, Jim Slaton, and Dwight Bernard. As might be expected, the combination of Ladd and company was not as productive as a healthy Fingers. With this fluctuation, the Brewers stopped building a lead.[38] Still, after taking two of three from the Boston Red Sox at Fenway, Milwaukee went into Baltimore for the final series of the year with a three-game lead over the Orioles with four games to play.[39]

Needing to win only one game to clinch the pennant, it looked like a sure thing that Harry Dalton's Brewers would capture their first pennant in a city full of great memories for Dalton and his family.[40] However, manager Earl Weaver, in his final regular-season series and with his team still utilizing the tenets of the Oriole Way, had a team stacked with a combination of young talent in soon-to-be Rookie of the Year Cal Ripken, switch-hitting first baseman Eddie Murray, and a talented pitching staff anchored by Jim Palmer.

Weaver's crew would take the first three games in a cakewalk. In the first game of a doubleheader on Friday, they beat up Vuckovich behind Ray Poitevint find Dennis Martínez, with a final tally of 8–3. In the nightcap, rookie Storm Davis shut down Milwaukee 7–1. Finally, on Saturday right-hander Sammy Stewart would defeat Doc Medich behind an eleven-run offensive frenzy. The Brewers now needed to win on Sunday to capture a pennant that had seemed all but assured.

The mood in the Brewers' traveling party on the eve of the game was mixed.

Bud Selig could not sleep Saturday night.[41] The Brewers' young PR man, Mario Ziino, was equally nervous as he prepared to leave the team hotel in Cross Keys, Maryland. Ziino recalled that as he was waiting for the second bus to the ballpark, Harry Dalton was leaving the hotel and asked Ziino to tag along.[42]

"I got in the car," Ziino said, "and after Harry got us on the highway he looked over at me and asked what was wrong. He started telling me that we were going to win the game and he was so confident that I started to relax. By the time we got to the ballpark I believed we were going to win the game."[43]

Dalton carried his positivity into the clubhouse as well. As Ziino recalled, "I walked into the clubhouse with Harry. There were a few players in there having breakfast and as he walked in everyone waited to see how he was going to react. Especially having lost three games. Harry calls everyone round and he starts telling them how proud he was of them and how he thought we were going to win. You could see everyone relax."[44]

The looseness seen in the clubhouse carried onto the field. Legendary Brewers radio play-by-play personality Bob Uecker recalled that on the final day, the Wallbangers were less worried about the game and more worried about being the last man standing in a team-wide game of "flip." Flip was a form of the game pepper, in which players were eliminated if they let the ball hit the ground. The Wallbangers turned it into a game that often saw players bloodied or sporting broken fingers from getting maimed by a ball rocketed at them by a teammate. At one point during the year, Harry Dalton had even banned the game due to the physical nature of the contest. That last Sunday in Baltimore, the game was back. This told Uecker everything he needed to know about the team's psyche.

Once the game started, Milwaukee was ready to play. Facing Jim Palmer, who won fifteen games in 1982, the Brewers were able to build a lead early. Milwaukee got one run in each of the first three innings. Included in the tallies were two home runs by Robin Yount. With a three-run lead, Don Sutton stymied the Orioles with pinpoint control. "I'm not going to overpower anybody. I'm probably not going to be that over-impressive," he said. "But if I can keep 'em off stride, then that's the key for me to pitch."[45]

That did not mean that he sailed the whole day. Sutton gave up a home run to Glenn Gulliver in the third inning. In the fifth, he worked out of a bases-loaded jam unscathed. Then, in the eighth, Sutton struggled, and the O's looked set for a big inning. With one run in and two Orioles on base, Sutton got some help from his defense; left fielder Ben Oglivie made a sliding catch into the left-field sidewall with inches between him and the foul line. This killed the O's rally, and it was still 5–2 Brewers.

With the boost provided by Oglivie, the offense exploded in the top of the ninth. By the time the inning ended, the team had roughed up Dennis Martínez and former Cy Young Award winner Mike Flanagan for five runs to give the Brewers a 10–2 lead. From there, Bob McClure worked around two hits to preserve the Milwaukee win.[46]

The scene in the Milwaukee clubhouse was pure pandemonium. Bud Selig openly wept to celebrate a day he had longed for since he helped bring a team back to Milwaukee. As for Harry Dalton, celebrating another title in Baltimore, even if it was in the visiting clubhouse, had him reflecting on the fickle nature of baseball. "The last two days they [close plays] went for them," he said. "But all their close ones today were foul, and we came up with the plays when we needed them. The cliché is still correct. It's a game of inches and we got the inches today."[47]

With the lens of history applied, it seems that the 1982 playoffs were set up as a way for Harry Dalton to conquer any residual demons from his first two stops in his baseball career. The Brewers defeated Baltimore to make the playoffs, and they then took on California to bring the first pennant to Milwaukee since 1958.

There is no evidence that Harry Dalton saw the world that way. For all of his understanding of history and the dramatics of a good story, Dalton could stay focused on the present at all times. Still, the fact that

Dalton found himself back in Anaheim, trying to beat the team that had given up on him, with a chance to go to another World Series, showed that baseball was a small world.

The 1982 California Angels were of course different from the team that Dalton had left five years earlier. Buzzie Bavasi had turned the Angels into a virtual All-Star team using a series of trades and free agent signings. In addition to Bobby Grich and Don Baylor, who had become the players Dalton thought they were when he signed them, Bavasi had swung deals using players acquired by Dalton as trade bait. Among them were a deal for home run threat Brian Downing in 1977; perennial .300 hitter Rod Carew, acquired from Minnesota in 1979; and center fielder Fred Lynn, gained from Boston in 1981. This deal sent a group of players, including Joe Rudi and Frank Tanana, to Boston.

In addition, the Angels had added catcher Bob Boone in a smaller deal with Philadelphia in 1981 and had acquired third baseman Doug DeCinces, a former Dalton draft pick, from Baltimore. Finally, on the free agent front, Bavasi signed one of the most sought-after free agents in all of baseball when he lured to California a former World Series MVP, Reggie Jackson, who was coming off a series of tremendous performances for the Yankees.[48]

With all that firepower, California did not have a marquee pitcher at the top of its rotation. Still, in 1982 they got solid performances from 1980–81 free agent Geoff Zahn; veteran righty Steve Renko, who came over with Fred Lynn; and 1978 draft choice Mike Witt. The Angels also relied on former Pirate Bruce Kison, whom they got in free agency (after he won a second World Series with Pittsburgh) in time for 1979, and lefty Tommy John, who came over from the Yankees at the trade deadline in 1982.

After eliminating Baltimore, the Brewers opened the 1982 American League championship series at Anaheim Stadium, and they were flat.[49] In game one of the ALCS, Tommy John beat Mike Caldwell, 8–3, behind a double from Bobby Grich, a triple from Don Baylor, and a homer from Freddy Lynn in a four-run fourth inning. The next night Bruce Kison held the Brewers offense to two runs on an inside-the-park home run from Paul Molitor that skipped past Lynn in center field. Meanwhile, the Angels got a homer from Reggie Jackson and RBIs from the bottom of their lineup off Pete Vuckovich, thanks to one from second baseman Tim Foli and two from Bob Boone. The final was 4–2 California, and they led the series 2–0.[50]

As the Brewers headed back to Milwaukee, the odds of reaching a World Series were long. To that point, no team in the playoff era had overcome a 2–0 deficit to win a series. Three wins in a row from Milwaukee would be the biggest comeback in any type of elimination situation in baseball history.[51] Despite the odds, the Brewers remained confident and loose. That was how the team had been since Kuenn took charge, and it continued that trend even as they trailed California.

The Brewers' business-as-usual approach came from several sources. To begin, the 1982 Brewers were one of the last clubs that truly bonded around the game. Mario Ziino is fond of the story that would see a core group of players—Yount, Thomas, and Vuckovich among them—that after a game would spend hours in the clubhouse rehashing wins and losses over "a couple of pops" until equipment man Bob Sullivan gave them the keys and told them to turn out the lights and lock up.[52] There was none of the "twenty-five guys, twenty-five cabs" mentality that began to permeate big league clubhouses as the disparity in salary between the highest- and lowest-paid players created different socioeconomic groups within a team.[53]

That is not to say that the Brewers' clubhouse did not have personality problems. It was often said that players were put off by Paul Molitor's wife being allowed to travel with the team so often that Dan Okrent remembered that she was called the "twenty-sixth man."[54] Still, more often than not, the Wallbangers could be found together even off the field. They did not allow outsiders like writers or opposing fans, looking to say they had tangled with a Major League player in a bar or club on the road, to take a free shot at a teammate.[55]

This willingness to back each other off the field allowed the team to stick together when their backs were against the wall on the field. As Robin Yount would remember, "We were a whole team of gamers. Guys didn't take days off."[56] They also did not give up.

Their GM had the same mentality. One famous incident from the California series proves this in spades. Dan Duquette recalled that Thursday morning, after the flight home from California, Bud Selig called an all-hands meeting (including salespeople, PR staff, and administrative assistants) in the team's executive dining room. At that meeting, in a fit of panic over what getting swept meant to his team, including the ever-present and ever important (to Selig) financial implications, Selig began working up to one of his famous tirades as he questioned staff members, including his daughter Wendy, to see if they understood what losing the next game could mean.

Before he could become fully engulfed, however, Harry Dalton calmly held up a hand to get Selig's attention. He then thanked the owner for reminding everyone of the stakes and that he and the rest of the staff were "going to get back to work" preparing for the first home playoff game so they could do their part to win the series.[57] During times like these, the younger staff members found Dalton to be at his best.

Wendy Selig remembered that Dalton was "driven and inspiring" to her and others.[58] Those others included the young "clubhouse kids" who ran errands for Bob Sullivan on behalf of the players. Bill Zito, who went to the University (High) School of Milwaukee with the Dalton girls and would become the GM of the Florida Panthers of the NHL, was a "Clubbie" for that 1982 team. He recalled that Dalton was always making sure that Zito, an outstanding hockey player remembered by players like Pete Vuckovich as a "hardworking kid who knew how to act" in a Major League setting, was taking care of his responsibilities away from the park.[59]

"Mr. Dalton would come find me and ask if I had any homework. If I did, he would take me up to his office, and I would sit and do it before I got started with my clubhouse work," Zito recalled. He added that Dalton taking an interest in his life away from the park would influence how he dealt with his players when he became GM of the Florida Panthers in 2020.[60]

Taking an interest in his players and other staff as people did not mean that Dalton was unwilling to show his employees a sterner side. His drive could make life complicated for some staff members when

Dalton focused on putting what he felt were the ball club's best interests in front of his employees' best practices.

For instance, Dalton and Sky Skibosh often argued over the content of the game notes created by the public relations department. "The game notes are there for the media to use. To allow them to inform readers or listeners or the people watching on TV," Skibosh said. "Harry would edit the game notes. With red pen and everything. He would take out what he thought were 'negative' stats. I would say, 'Harry we can't do that. Let Mario [Ziino] and I do our jobs.'"[61]

Still, every person who worked for Harry Dalton came away with more good stories than bad because he was primarily always positive and knew that baseball was a game that favored people who could maintain an even keel. The rest of the ALCS would prove Dalton right.

Much like the last game of the season in Baltimore, the Brewers were able to play another day following a solid effort by Don Sutton and timely hitting. Sutton shut out the Angels for seven and two-thirds innings with eight ground ball outs and nine strikeouts. As for the hitting, the Brewers would manufacture a rally in the bottom of the fourth that would net them three runs.

Yount walked to lead off the frame, then Cooper doubled deep to right to score Yount. Ted Simmons then singled and moved Cooper to third. The next hitter, Gorman Thomas, drove a ball to the outfield, allowing Cooper to score on a sacrifice fly. Next, Ben Oglivie singled, and Ted Simmons, in one of the series' most memorable plays, went first to third on the play with a belly-flop, head-first slide. This paid off one batter later when designated hitter Don Money lofted a ball to left fielder Brian Downing on the first pitch of the at bat, allowing Simmons to score.

The Brewers would score again in the fifth. Money would lead off with a walk against Mike Witt (who replaced Geoff Zahn in the fourth after Money's sacrifice fly). Reserve outfielder Marshall Edwards then moved to second on a sacrifice bunt by Charlie Moore. Jim Gantner made the second out on a fly ball to center that was deep enough for the fleet-footed Edwards to move on to third. That brought up Paul

Molitor. Witt got Molitor to a 2-2 count. On the fifth pitch of Molitor's at bat, Witt tried to throw a slider away, and he hung the ball over the inside corner to the right-handed Molitor, who pulled the pitch into the left-field bleachers: 5–0 Milwaukee.

With that lead, Sutton continued to blank the Angels until he tired in the top of the eighth and gave up three runs on a home run to Bob Boone and doubles to Fred Lynn (whose base hit scored Rod Carew) and Don Baylor. This forced Harvey Kuenn to go to the bullpen. From there, Pete Ladd would pitch one and a third innings of scoreless baseball for the win.[62]

The Brewers would win the next day as well. This time the game was a pure slugfest, with rainy weather more befitting a Green Bay Packers football game at County Stadium. The Brewers scored three runs on one play thanks to a single by left fielder Mark Brouhard, who was playing for a gimpy Ben Oglivie; the Angels promptly misplayed it, making two errors. The Brewers got three more runs in the bottom of the fourth in a rally fueled by Angels mistakes. This time two walks and two wild pitches led to the Milwaukee runs. By the end of the inning, they had chased off the starter, Tommy John.

The game was still 6–0 Milwaukee when an error by Yount at short led to an unearned run, making it 6–1 Milwaukee heading to the bottom of the sixth. Milwaukee then got that run back when Mark Brouhard hit a ground rule, fan interference double and was driven in two batters later by Jim Gantner.

It was still 7–1 Brewers when, in the top of the eighth, the lack of Rollie Fingers would come back to bite the home team. During an inning that would have been a prime spot for the mustachioed closer, starter Moose Haas gave up a single to Brian Downing and a double to Rod Carew in the first two at bats. Haas then got Reggie Jackson looking at strike three before walking Fred Lynn on six pitches to load the bases. Next, Don Baylor showed America why Harry Dalton had brought him to California in the first place. On the first pitch from Haas, the man sometimes called "Groove" lined a fastball into the left-center-field stands to make it 7–5 going to the bottom of the eighth. That gave Baylor ten RBIs in the series, and it was a whole new ballgame.

That was when Mark Brouhard, who already had two hits and had scored three times, put the game on ice for Milwaukee. This time, with Marshall Edwards at second (Edwards pinch-ran for Don Money and then stole second), Brouhard would tuck a two-run homer inside the left-field foul pole to make it 9–5 Milwaukee. That was the final score after Jim Slaton, who got the last two Angels hitters in the eighth, retired Tim Foli on a groundout, Bob Boone on a pop-up to Gantner at second, and Brian Downing on a fly ball to Brouhard.

The Brewers were now one win away from the World Series. Mark Brouhard was the man of the hour, and no one was happier and more pragmatic than Harry Dalton. "Look at that smile, he's [Brouhard] just in seventh heaven," Dalton said. "In fairness to him, we knew that we hadn't given him the chance to play much[;] that's why we sent him down in August just to scrape the rust off so coming up in September he would be ready for the pennant drive if we needed him."[63]

Game five was played in front of another raucous sellout crowd at County Stadium. If it had been a random game in July, the Brewers faithful would most likely have seen a lineup devoid of a few of the team's stars. Pete Vuckovich took the mound with a torn rotator cuff, and Ben Oglivie was back in the lineup despite a lower-body injury that would hamper his movement. Finally, Gorman Thomas had a swollen knee thanks to a play at the plate in game four that saw him get caught between running over catcher Bob Boone and sliding around him to try and score.[64] In an elimination game, however, Harvey Kuenn had all his weapons available.

The action was fast and furious early. The Angels would score in the top of the first on a single by Fred Lynn. Milwaukee would tie the game in the bottom half when Molitor, who reached on a hustle double to short center to start the game, scored two hitters later on a Ted Simmons sacrifice fly.

The Angels retook the lead in the top of the third. This time Lynn would drive in catcher Bob Boone with a two-out single. Throughout the early innings, it seemed that the Angels had Vuckovich on the ropes, but each time he would channel a fighting spirit evocative of a modern-day mixed martial artist and minimize the damage. Then

Vuckovich would get picked up by his defense, and momentum would swing to the Brewers.

California would score again in the top of the fourth when a lead-off double and a Milwaukee error led to Boone scoring Doug DeCinces on a suicide squeeze bunt hit, giving the Angels runners on first and second with one out. However, as he did throughout his career, Vuckovich made a big pitch when he had to have one, this time getting Brian Downing to ground into a 5-4-3 inning-ending double play. Holding California to one run became magnified in the bottom half of the fourth when Ben Oglivie hit an 0-1 changeup from Bruce Kison into the right-field stands to make it 3–2 California.

The game remained 3–2 heading to the bottom of the fifth when it looked like California was ready to put the Brewers away. With one out, Vuckovich walked Reggie Jackson. The next batter, Fred Lynn, then looked to set up the Angels with a big inning when the former "Gold Dust Twin" hit a bouncing seeing-eye-single to right field that looked to certainly be enough to allow Jackson to go from first to third. No one told Charlie Moore that, however. The catcher-turned-outfielder came up with the ball like he was picking a wild pitch out of the dirt and gunned a perfect throw to Molitor, who blocked the sliding Jackson off the bag. From that moment forward, Milwaukee, whose players had committed four errors in the game, was a different team.

Two innings later, Milwaukee finally had a lead. First, Charlie Moore, proving that, in baseball, outstanding defense often leads to good offense, singled. Jim Gantner followed this with another single. At that point, relief pitcher Luis Sánchez, who came on for Bruce Kison in the bottom of the sixth, got Paul Molitor to pop up to Bob Boone for the second out. Sánchez then walked Yount to load the bases. Cecil Cooper was the next hitter.

If you ask any Brewers fan of a particular vintage who they wanted up in a big situation with the game on the line, they would simply say, "Coop."[65] Since his entry into the league with Boston, the rangy first baseman had had a knack for coming up with big hits in big moments. That was especially true in Milwaukee, where haunting, elongated chants of his shortened last name cascaded through County Stadium following big knocks for the home team. The seventh inning of game five was one of those moments.

On a 1-1 pitch, Cooper would take an outside fastball and line it to left. Once he did so, Moore and Gantner began a mad dash to home plate as Cooper willed the ball to get down, much like his then teammate Carlton Fisk had once willed a ball to stay fair in Game Six of the 1975 World Series. Moore would score the tying run easily, and seconds later, with Moore telling him to slide, Gantner scored the go-ahead tally.

With the Brewers in the lead, the onus fell on the bullpen to protect it. Kuenn turned to Bob McClure in the top of the seventh. McClure would get Lynn on a fly ball to left to lead off the bottom of the eighth. With the next hitter, the Brewers defense once again helped the pitching staff. This time reserve outfielder Marshall Edwards, who came in for Gorman Thomas to begin the inning, would make a play that would ring down through the years. On the seventh pitch of his at bat, Don Baylor seemed to drive a double to the gap in left-center, or that's what it looked like until Edwards, running to his left at a full sprint, leaped and corralled the ball with two hands as he slammed against the wall. Two hitters later, Edwards would make the final put-out of the inning when Grich flew to Edwards two steps short of the warning track in straightaway center field.

The Brewers would go quietly in the eighth's home half, and Bob McClure would take the mound in the top of the ninth to try and secure the win. To start the inning, longtime Angel Ron Jackson led off with a single before Rob Wilfong did pinch-running duty. This caused Harvey Kuenn to go to the Milwaukee bullpen for Pete Ladd. Ladd, a corrections officer in the off-season, would retire Bob Boone on a sacrifice bunt that moved Wilfong to second. Ladd then got Brian Downing on a hot-shot grounder to Molitor at third. That brought Rod Carew, arguably the best hitter in the American League, to the plate with the tying run on second.

The 1982 season was the fourteenth in a row that Carew hit .300 or above. During that time, he had won seven batting titles and an MVP. As Ned Yost would recall in 2007, just hearing longtime County Stadium PA announcer Bob Betts utter his name was enough to strike fear into Yost and others.[66] Rod Carew was a tough out, and he proved it that night.

Carew would foul off two pitches and take another to make it 1-2. On the fourth pitch Carew got a fastball out over the plate. The lefty swung and hit a one-hop bullet that looked on television like it would find a hole, but as the ABC camera panned to a wider angle, the viewer saw that the ball was ticketed right to Robin Yount at shortstop. Yount took half a beat to steady himself and gunned the ball across to Cooper, who leaped in the air, for the out. The Milwaukee Brewers had won the American League pennant.

The chaos that ensued on the field seems out of place today, but it was an excellent allegory for the love affair between the Brewers and their fans. Fans and players mixed in a mass of humanity on the field, where it was almost impossible to define the space between one and the other. They were one and the same.

As for Harry Dalton, he would spend the minutes immediately after the game kissing Pat in a warm embrace. Later Dalton looked out on a now-empty stadium from the mound with Bud Selig. Selig was very candid in the days ahead about how happy the World Series berth made him and how instrumental Harry Dalton had been in making it possible. "The coming of Harry Dalton turned it around," Selig said. "Before he came, I thought he was the greatest general manager in baseball. But I underestimated him."[67] Dalton quickly gave credit to Selig for laying a foundation on which Dalton could build.[68] Finally, later that night, Dalton and his family would celebrate at one of Milwaukee's famous German rathskeller taverns. The respite was deserved and short. The Brewers' first World Series would begin in St. Louis just two days later.

If the life of Harry Dalton were a film franchise, the 1982 season would be the movie that brings resolution for our hero. In the first movie, of course, the unknown twenty-something achieves beyond his wildest dreams and ends up with a great job and a great family. The sequel would see the tides turn as our protagonist reaches middle age and feels he is underappreciated and needs more. This would set him up for personal growth and a realization that his relationships and family are the keys to happiness as he fails for the first time. Finally, in the third installment, the now older man realizes that in the right place, he can have both personal happiness and professional success as he raises his family and vanquishes the antagonist he had had dealings with in the past.

The 1982 World Series would not be Harry Dalton's Hollywood ending. It was a dramatic series, to be sure. It also conformed to author Tyler Kepner's model for what makes or breaks a great World Series. It featured outstanding normative play from both teams and the proverbial October hero. It was also a series with individual and institutional outliers, and all these things would help sink Milwaukee's hopes for a championship.

In Game One, on the AstroTurf in St. Louis, they played to their norm. The team that led the American League in homers with 216 slugged their way to victory. They scored 10 runs on 17 hits. Paul Molitor had 5 hits, and Robin Yount chipped in with 4 hits. The team had 3 extra-base hits and RBIs from six different players. This was more than enough for Mike Caldwell as the lefty threw a complete-game shutout.[69] The Brewers did not make many mistakes. The biggest faux pas of the night occurred when Pat Dalton committed a fashion mistake that she never lived down.

Always impeccably dressed, especially for a national event like the World Series, Pat Dalton wore a very flattering suit to Game One. The problem arose when it was noted that the suit was Cardinals red. The story would make the Series news cycle, and Pat would smartly defend her fashion choices by stating that it was a "Cardinal Sin." She also said she would wear red again if it were good luck for Harry and the Brewers.[70]

The next night, the Cardinals won 5–4. Offensively, both teams would play to their strengths. Milwaukee got a second homer from Ted Simmons and three more extra-base hits from Charlie Moore, Robin Yount, and Cecil Cooper. Meanwhile, the Cardinals, who stole a league-leading two hundred bases during the regular season, swiped three bags off the pitching tandem of Sutton and Simmons. Game Two was also the first but not the last time an outlier was heard from in the Series.

In the 1982 Series, outliers would take the form of individuals and operating framework. This is the type that the Brewers dealt with throughout the Series and during Game Two especially. The injuries that had been building up over a long season finally took their toll. Pete Vuckovich won with more guile than substance, and Gorman Thomas and Ben

Oglivie were hobbled. Most important, despite trying to be ready to pitch, Rollie Fingers would miss the Series. This meant that when the Brewers went to their bullpen, they could not rely on Rollie Fingers to hold leads or help maintain tie games. This allowed St. Louis to climb back into a game and often take the lead late.

The Brewers had a 4–2 lead into the sixth inning in Game Two. The Cardinals then tied it in the bottom half of the inning on an opposite-field double by catcher Darrell Porter. Then Whitey Herzog would turn to Bruce Sutter to shut down the Brewers' attack. Meanwhile, Harvey Kuenn handed the ball to Bob McClure and Pete Ladd.

McClure pitched a clean seventh inning, striking out David Green and rookie center fielder Willie McGee. Then, after a single by Ozzie Smith and a walk to second baseman Tommy Herr, McClure retired pinch hitter Gene Tenace. McClure came out to pitch the eighth with the game still tied 4–4. Keith Hernandez led the inning off with a walk and would be erased on a force out at second. Darrell Porter would then come up with another hit when he singled to center, putting runners on first and second with one out.

Following the single, Kuenn went to the Milwaukee bullpen for Pete Ladd, who walked left fielder Lonnie Smith on a borderline 3-2 pitch to load the bases and then walk in the go-ahead run with a four-pitch walk to pinch hitter Steve Braun. Ladd would avoid any other damage, but the Cardinals had enough room to secure the win with Bruce Sutter working the ninth.

For Game Three, the series shifted to Milwaukee, and this time the Brewers were stung by the first appearance of the October hero. Game Three will always be remembered as the one where Willie McGee single-handedly took over and got the Cardinals a win. In the first, McGee robbed Paul Molitor, who continued to have an outstanding series, of an extra-base hit. Then, with two runners on in a scoreless game in the top of the fifth, McGee homered to put the Cardinals up 3–0 off Pete Vuckovich.

McGee's coming-out party continued in his next at bat in the seventh. This time, with the Cardinals leading 4–0, McGee hit a Vuckovich off-speed pitch to right for another homer, making it 5–0 Cardinals. Then, in the ninth, with the Brewers threatening while down 6–2, McGee robbed Gorman Thomas of what would have been a two-run homer off Bruce Sutter.

Despite the setback in Game Three, Milwaukee won the next two games (7–5 and 6–4) and was on the verge of a World Series title as the teams headed back to St. Louis. Once there, however, the Brewers fell victim to another outlier and one last dose of heroic play in the form of another Bruce Sutter appearance.

As for the outlier, this time an individual performance outside the norm hurt Milwaukee. In Game Six, played on a wet night that saw multiple rain delays, the Brewers' offense was shut down by rookie John Stuper, who gave up one run on four hits in a complete game that saved the Cardinals' bullpen. In contrast, the Cardinals hit starter Don Sutton for seven runs (five earned), and then, following a 2:13 rain delay in the sixth, they would score six runs (four earned) off long relief man George "Doc" Medich. The 1982 World Series would go to seven games. In Sutton's opinion, Stuper saved the series for St. Louis.[71]

In Game Seven, the Brewers not having Rollie Fingers and the Cardinals having a rested Bruce Sutter made the difference one final time. With the Brewers leading 3–1 with one out in the sixth and two runners on, Harvey Kuenn lifted Pete Vuckovich, who finally emptied the tank in a stellar 1982 season. Bob McClure would relieve Vuckovich and walk the bases loaded after a free pass to Gene Tenace. Keith Hernandez then singled home two runs to tie the game before George Hendrick got a go-ahead single in the very next at bat.

With a 4–3 lead, starter Joaquín Andújar worked a clean seventh before handing the ball to Bruce Sutter. Sutter got Molitor, Yount, and Cooper in the eighth. Then, after the Cardinals scored two more runs off Moose Haas, Sutter retired his former teammate Simmons and the next hitter, Ben Oglivie, on groundouts before striking out Gorman Thomas to end the game and the Series.

The atmosphere in the Brewers' camp was a direct contrast to the one it had been for most of October. The entire team was dejected, and this included Harry Dalton.

Pat Dalton remembered that in the days leading up to and during the Series, her husband was "the coolest man." That is to say that the pressure did not get to him. This coolness did not mean that Dalton was not dejected by the result. Pat Dalton would remember that "HID [Pat's nickname for Harry Dalton] did not lose well. I often commented that he was never as happy commensurate with the despair of losing."[72] His sense of disappointment did not blind Dalton to what he saw on the field, however. Even in the loss, Dalton could see areas where his team fell short of expectations. "It was surprising the way they outhit us. Even going into the ninth inning today (game seven), I kept thinking that we were going to break loose," Dalton said. Ultimately, Dalton gave credit to the Cardinals for executing: "If they execute the scouting report, they're going to stop you and they stopped us."[73]

As for what Dalton planned to do in the aftermath of the loss, it was time for the baseball operations staff to "go home and sit back and look at the whole picture." Even preliminarily, Dalton did not foresee a large amount of tinkering. "I don't think there will be a lot of changes on this ballclub," he said.[74] Dalton was not the only one who thought that.

In the aftermath of the Game Seven loss in St. Louis, Sky Skibosh and Mario Ziino sat in the press box at Busch Stadium and pictured a period in which the Brewers were going to be a force in baseball for years to come. "Mario [Ziino] and I just said, 'Well, we'll be back,'" Skibosh recalled. "There was no question that this was just the first chance."[75]

If this was the first World Series of many for the Brewers, the city of Milwaukee was ready to celebrate, even if it was to practice for when they would finally win. When the Brewers took a 3–2 lead in the Series, word began to leak out that a parade was in the offing, win or lose. In the aftermath of Game Seven, the city delivered. A throng lining Wisconsin Avenue was reminiscent of the halcyon days when the city turned out for the Braves in the era of Aaron, Adcock, Matthews, and Spahn.

Befitting a team that had just lost, the players were not enthused about being up early the next morning to celebrate a defeat that still stung. Neither was Harry Dalton. However, like the players and Bud Selig, when Harry and Pat saw all the people lining the parade route, the memory of the loss faded momentarily.

Dalton's joy even continued when his starting shortstop, on a dare from Pete Vuckovich and Ted Simmons, decided to rev up the crowd gathered at the terminus of the parade—County Stadium—by riding his dirt bike (which he illegally rode to the parade that morning) out of the tunnel and around the warning track. On that bright October day in Milwaukee, the city felt like a winner, and Harry Dalton was the catalyst that had made it all possible.[76]

Little did Dalton know that 1982 would be his last chance at a title. If he had known, chances are Dalton would have understood. He had been around long enough to understand that nothing in baseball was guaranteed. He often told his charges that you worked in baseball to be fired because you were being paid to win.

Still, although there would be no more pennants in his future, as baseball continued to evolve off the field, Harry Dalton would work tirelessly to put Milwaukee back on top, even if it meant shepherding his team through injuries, scandal, and an evolving economic structure.

17

Reversal of Fortune

WINTER 1982–OCTOBER 1985

The notion that the Milwaukee Brewers could repeat as American League champions in 1983 does not seem like a stretch when you look at the team that finished the 1982 season in the World Series. The Brewers had the executive of the year in Harry Dalton, Pete Vuckovich as the American League's Cy Young Award winner, and the AL MVPs for that year, and the previous one, in Robin Yount and Rollie Fingers. They also had had Don Sutton for an entire year; the veteran leadership of Ted Simmons; one of the best pure hitters in the league in Paul Molitor; a core group of power hitters in Cecil Cooper, Ben Oglivie, and Gorman Thomas; and a steady group of role players led by Jim Gantner.

Baseball seasons, however, are not played on paper. Injuries, scandal, and age would all derail the Brewers' momentum that began building the day Harry Dalton took over the baseball operations. On the injury front, Yount, Fingers, Vuckovich, and Molitor would all suffer debilitating issues that called their careers into question. Others, like Oglivie and Thomas, had injuries that, combined with their age, would hamper their offensive production.

Fingers continued to have issues with tendinitis. He would miss all of 1983, have a solid year for anyone but Fingers (23 saves) in a shortened year in 1984, and would struggle so much in 1985 (1-6 W-L, 5.04 ERA, 17 saves) that he would make his final appearance in mid-September and be released by the Brewers at the end of the year.

Much like Fingers, Vuckovich suffered an arm injury in 1982 that would curtail his career after that year. He would only make three starts in 1983 while recovering from a torn rotator cuff before being shelved in August with a bad hamstring. Vuckovich then missed all of 1984 with a bone spur in his right shoulder. In 1985 he had twenty-two starts and went 6-10 with a 5.51 ERA before "a shoulder strain landed him on the DL in May and June, and he underwent surgery for a large calcium deposit and another small bone spur in mid-September."[1] At the end of 1985, Vuckovich retired and started to scout for the Brewers. When the team designated Vuckovich for assignment in November 1985, Dalton would take that move harder than others. As was noted earlier, Dalton saw Vuckovich as a link to his past in the game because of the pitcher's mentality. Dalton appreciated the pitcher's loyalty. "It's really difficult to see it come to this," Dalton said. "I hope there's one more bounce back for him."[2]

With Molitor and Yount, their injuries were not career ending, but it was close.

Molitor would have a sore elbow that would limit his productivity in 1983. He then suffered a torn ligament of the same elbow in his throwing arm in 1984, limiting him to thirteen games. It also required that he undergo the relatively new "Tommy John" ligament replacement surgery, and there was no guarantee that he would be the player he was before the injury.[3]

As for Yount, he suffered a back injury in 1983 and a shoulder injury in 1984, and both would have repercussions for his career. Most importantly, the shoulder injury would mean a move to the outfield to prolong his career, even though Yount maintained that he would be back at shortstop. Recovery from these injuries meant that 1983–85 were wasted seasons for the former MVP.[4]

Finally, Ben Oglivie and Gorman Thomas had their future production sapped thanks to injuries suffered in 1982. Despite being an almost everyday player, Oglivie's power numbers dropped precipitously thanks to a series of lower-body issues. From 1983 through 1985, Oglivie hit thirty-five home runs, only one more than he hit in 1982 alone. Thomas suffered much the same fate.

In 1983 Thomas's knee was a question mark following the injury he suffered in October 1982. Still, he was in center field every day for the season's first two months. It was evident that he was not the prolific power hitter who terrorized the American League from 1978 to 1982. Through forty-six games and almost two hundred plate appearances,

Thomas had only hit five home runs, and his average, which was never robust, had plummeted to .187. This type of performance finally forced Harry Dalton's hand.

On June 6, the same day the team would draft a core group of players in an eventual rebuild, Dalton traded Thomas and pitchers Jamie Easterly and Ernie Camacho to Cleveland for center fielder Rick Manning and veteran left-handed pitcher Rick Waits. Dalton knew that what he did in trading Thomas was a potential powder keg. If there was one player whom Brewers fans identified with the most, it was Thomas. "Obviously there is going to be some fan fallout," Dalton admitted. "But if you can get better balance on the club and make a move that improves you, you have to try to do it."[5]

In terms of fan reaction, Dalton was clairvoyant. In the coming days, he would receive letters and calls from every corner of the state voicing displeasure with the move. In a far more serious incident, someone would go as far as to shoot a hole in Dalton's office window.[6]

The consensus of the notes received was that Dalton had dealt away the heart and soul of the team and that he did not care. Dalton did care. He cared enough to save the letters and write back to many of the correspondents.[7] What he would not do was bow to pressure. The year 1983 was Dalton's twenty-ninth in the game, and he understood that sometimes you had to make an unpopular decision to make a team better.

From 1983 to 1985 Dalton was faced with plenty of unpleasant choices, as age also played a role in forcing Dalton to turn over the Brewers roster. Most importantly, despite Ted Simmons's transitioning to designated hitter, years of catching finally caught up with him. He would struggle offensively from 1984 to 1985 after a solid season in 1983 and leave Milwaukee in the winter of 1985.

As would befit a team facing significant turnover among key players, play on the field suffered for the first time since Harry Dalton took over. A late-season slump in 1983 saw the Brewers finish fifth despite winning eighty-seven games. This disappointing end to the 1983 season led Dalton to remove Harvey Kuenn from his managerial role. It was speculated that the dismissal was what Dalton was aiming to do for most of the summer, and it is backed by the fact that he named a successor the same day Kuenn was fired. Rene Lachemann was the new manager. The thirty-eight-year-old, universally referred to as "Lach," had been fired midseason in 1983 by the Seattle Mariners. Still, Harry Dalton believed he had the right man to oversee any possible rebuild of the Brewers roster. "Lach is one of the fine young managing talents coming up in baseball," Dalton stated. "He worked his way up the ladder in the minor leagues and did a good job with a young team in Seattle."[8]

It turned out that Dalton had hired another manager before his time. Tom Trebelhorn was the new third base coach for the Brewers in 1984, and he believed that the roster had reached critical mass that year and that no amount of managing from Lachemann could have changed the outcome. "We were excited to have a contending team," Trebelhorn stated, "but did not realize that the less than contending play of the second half of 1983 was what his team was—an aging second division team, and '84 was a great disappointment."[9] The Brewers would finish in last place in the AL East at 67-95, and Harry Dalton opened himself up to scrutiny for the first time since he came to Milwaukee.

In an exposé in *Milwaukee Magazine* in the spring of 1984, author Michael Uruske put words to the thoughts of many Brewers fans: "Harry Dalton's team isn't winning games anymore, and some people (fans) are wondering whether it might not be his fault. Whether he's [Dalton] lost his touch."[10] Those who knew Dalton did not think so. Even with his club losing, he was one of the most respected GMs in the game. He was also self-aware enough to know that he knew it was time to change over his roster. Furthermore, Dalton knew that the Brewers would need to rely on the farm system to provide the replacement players.

When Harry Dalton took the GM job in Milwaukee, it was with the understanding that the purse strings would be open for Dalton to improve the club. This was possible for a small-market club in the early days of free agency as everyone in baseball tried to figure out how the system worked. As noted earlier, Milwaukee could not compete in a spending war with its rivals, and Dalton knew this. As the 1980s progressed, Dalton operated under a team policy that precluded it from attempting to sign free agents. In 1987 Dalton opined that the policy was in place because the Brewers could not simultaneously reward well-performing players, maintain a robust farm system, and compete in the free agent market.[11]

With the Brewers locked into a building program in the coming years, the question became what type of player to focus on in the scouting and development process. In keeping with his managerial style of building a consensus, Dalton opened the matter up for discussion. There were two schools of thought among those eligible to sit in a team conference. The Brewers could go with a "power team (1978–1982) plus adequate pitching and defense," or they could build a team based on "pitching, defense, and speed." In the end, Dalton and his gang tried to split the difference.[12]

In the run-up to the 1982 World Series, Dalton and the scouting and development department started to lay the foundation for the next generation of players. In 1981 the Brewers selected six players who would serve considerable time in the Majors with Milwaukee or would be flipped by Dalton for Major League talent that filled a need. The 1982 draft produced seven players who would join the team later in the 1980s. Seven was also a lucky number in 1983. In 1984 that number dropped to two but rebounded in 1985 to five, including the overall No. 1 pick, catcher B. J. Surhoff, out of North Carolina.[13]

In addition, the money Dalton invested in the international scouting department began to pay off. In 1983 the Brewers landed hard-throwing Puerto Rican left-hander Juan Nieves, who was not part of the baseball draft despite being in a prep school in Connecticut. The same year, on the recommendation of international scout Lee Sigman, the Brewers signed a diminutive lefty with a big arm: Teddy Higuera, from Mexico. After Higuera, the Brewers would scout extensively in Mexico for the rest of the 1980s.[14] Finally, with nothing to lose, the Brewers made their first foray into the Asian market for a player in the spring of 1985.

Yutaka Enatsu, as he was known in America, was one of the best pitchers in the Nipponese Professional Baseball League (NPBL) from the late 1960s until the early 1980s. As both a starter and a reliever, he was so good that the lefty would be compared to Sandy Koufax and Steve Carlton by Americans who saw the strikeout pitcher in his prime as a starter and would rank second in saves in the history of NPBL when he left Japanese baseball. His on-field performance was only half of the story, however.[15]

As noted by Robert K. Fitts, an expert on Japanese baseball, Enatsu was a lightning rod for controversy. He would be implicated in a league-wide gambling scandal in the early 1970s and wore out his welcome in Japan when he shoved his manager during the 1984 season.[16] At that point, Ray Poitevint, in keeping with his tendency to overinflate players' abilities, described Enatsu as "a Jim Palmer–type pitcher" and convinced Dalton to let Enatsu try and make the Brewers bullpen for 1985.[17]

Harry Dalton made it clear that the opportunity extended to the lefty contained two factors. First and foremost, he trusted Ray Poitevint. Second, the Brewers needed bullpen help. "While [Enatsu] hasn't made the team yet[,] we think he can pitch," Dalton said. "This is not glitz or box office. We're not into gimmicky things because our self-belief is that if our people are healthy, we're going to be a contender."[18] In the end, Enatsu did not make the team, but it wasn't for lack of ability. Much like the rest of the pitching staff, Enatsu was too old to take a chance on by 1985. Still, it speaks to the lengths to which Harry Dalton would go to rebuild the Brewers into a winner after 1982.

Rebuilding his roster was only part of Dalton's focus through the 1984–85 season. In May 1984, Dalton had to navigate issues surrounding Milwaukee's embroilment in a league-wide cocaine epidemic that produced several high-profile cases and federal convictions.[19] In the case of Milwaukee, Anthony "Tony" Peters was identified as the ringleader of a major drug operation in the city that sold to Major League players.

Among Peters's clients from 1979 to the time of his arrest in 1983 were six current and former Brewers, including Paul Molitor, Ben Oglivie, and Mike Caldwell, along with former outfielders Dick Davis and Sixto Lezcano and pitcher Lary Sorensen. Of the three active players, Molitor was the most visible.

Various people associated with the Peters case stated that Molitor began using cocaine in "April or May 1979" and purchased the drug from Peters "30–40 times between 1979 and 1982."[20] Molitor's drug usage was so pronounced that he almost overdosed on Christmas Eve 1980 after a "wild night of cocaine abuse."[21] Molitor was even with Peters the night the FBI arrested him, although Molitor was spirited away from the scene of the arrest and never charged.[22]

As Dan Okrent anecdotally remembered in 2022, the signs of drug use in the Milwaukee clubhouse were evident when he was there from 1981 to 1982. *Milwaukee Sentinel* beat reporter Vic Feuerherd backed Okrent's assertion. Buck Rodgers would back this up in 1985 when the *New York Times* ran a special report on drugs in baseball. At the time, Rodgers was the manager of the Montreal Expos, and he recalled that, while in Milwaukee, "one of my players came in late for a Sunday game in Minnesota. Being late was just part of it. He couldn't stop sniffing. He walked in and every player on the team watched him walk across and then everybody looked at me to see if I was watching. So everybody had some idea."[23]

As for Harry Dalton's knowledge of the drug problems in his clubhouse, there is no evidence to suggest that he actively covered up the story or that he turned a blind eye to the usage of narcotics when he did find out. Dick Davis recalled in 1985 that, in the 1980 season, Dalton told both him and Molitor that they were to "stay away from Peters" and where he did business.[24]

In addition, there is evidence to show that Dalton, who always believed in having high-character players on his rosters, tried to eliminate the problem from his clubhouse once he understood its scope. This is backed by the fact that by the winter of 1980, Dalton had traded Sorensen, Lezcano, and Davis and had attempted to trade Caldwell and Molitor. Finally, Dan Duquette remembered that in the fallout of the stories that ran in 1984–85, Dalton, Milwaukee-based counselor Gary Crites, and Bob Dupuy from the Milwaukee law firm of Foley and Lardner and, later, Major League Baseball helped to develop an employee assistance program (EAP) that quickly became the model for all of Major League Baseball.[25]

In addition to having to work through the repercussions of baseball's cocaine problem on his team, in the spring of 1985 Dalton was subpoenaed to testify in connection with an arbitration case between the MLBPA and

Major League Baseball stemming from the assertion of the players that the owners had colluded with each other in suppressing the acquisition of free agents in the winter of 1984. While being deposed, Dalton outlined why the Brewers were more likely to strengthen their team using players from the farm system than dabbling in the free agent market.

Dalton's eye-opening testimony asserted that his club was not colluding with the league's other teams. As noted earlier, Dalton pointed out that the Brewers would not enter the free agent market unless the standings and the team's finances made it prudent. In Dalton's mind, this was not as bad as it would seem to some simply because he would instead use the funds provided him to develop young talent and retain the already contracted players who had proven themselves.

When all the off-the-field issues combined with the poor performance on the field, it would have been easy for Harry Dalton to lose his ability to find the bright side of life. However, those who worked for him recall that even when under duress, Dalton could find a way to smile. This often meant participating in a practical joke that helped keep the office loose.

Jimmy Bank came on as the traveling secretary for the Brewers in 1983 after having spent time with Charlie Finley and the Oakland A's. Bank recalled that during his first spring training, Dalton managed to welcome Bank to the team while taking aim at his friend, trainer Freddie Frederico, who had come over to Milwaukee with Dalton from California:

> It was the end of spring training and we were getting ready to check out of the hotel. As I was packing my stuff up, I got a call from a guy claiming to be from the front desk. He said we had a problem with one of the rooms assigned to the team. This guy has a really thick Spanish accent and he tells me that the night before, they had received complaints that the person in the room had thrown a wild party and had destroyed the room. When I asked what room, he tells me that it was the room Freddie was in. After questioning the guy, because Freddie is the last person who would be throwing a party, I told him I would be down to sort it out.
>
> This whole time, I am wondering how I am going to tell Harry that his friend caused all this damage to his hotel room. When I get

to the lobby, I see Harry coming towards me. I told him that I would be back to talk to him in a minute but I had something to do first. He wouldn't let me go. Finally I said, "Harry, I have to go take care of something then I have to tell you what happened to Freddie's room." At this point, he looks at me and tells me that he was the one who called me![26]

Bank also remembered that Frederico was one of Dalton's favorite targets. Another year in spring training, Dalton charged a few days of his meals and other incidentals to Frederico's room, thus running up a large bill. When Frederico came down and was told of the charges, he was incredulous; Dalton was standing to the side laughing.

Dalton was also not above having fun with the younger members of the front office. Jon Greenberg, who would begin his tenure as a bat boy and then work in the PR department of the team until 2005, recalled the time Dalton participated in one of the oldest traditions in baseball. "We had this kid in the office and one day we decide to tell him to go get the key to the batters box and the left-handed curveballs. Stuff like that," Greenberg related. "Well, the joke is to send him all over the stadium looking for something that doesn't exist. So when we would do this to someone, the last stop was always in Harry's office. Harry looks at this guy who is so embarrassed that he can't find what we need and goes, 'Welcome to the big leagues kid, you've just been had.' He knew when to work and play."[27]

Dalton also took the time to relax away from work when he could. In the winter, Dalton could be found at school functions for Kim, Cindy, or Debbie at University School of Milwaukee. The few breaks he could take during the season gave Dalton the time to cut the grass on his riding lawnmower or go fishing on Lake Michigan or drive his family on a cross-country vacation that factored in plenty of stops to use a phone to call the office. He used all these opportunities to recharge his batteries for the long season, especially in years when the losses mounted up.[28]

Losses were the norm in 1985. With George Bamberger back at the helm for a second stint as manager, the Brewers went 71-90 and struggled at the plate and on the mound. Specifically, for the second year in a row, the Brewers went through a huge power drought while short of pitching. In 1985 the team would hit only 98 homers and have a scoring differential of −112. This added up to Harry Dalton announcing that changes to the roster would be the order of the day in 1986. "There will be some veterans that won't be with us," he warned.[29]

The turnover of the Brewers roster was possible because, as Dalton often noted both in private and in public, the Brewers had a group of players in the Minors who were knocking on the door of the big leagues. At the end of the 1985 season, this group included position players Billy Jo Robidoux of Ware, Massachusetts, for first base; corner outfielders Joey Meyer and Glenn Braggs, signed by Ray Poitevint out of the University of Hawaii; and center fielder Mike "Tiny" Felder. In addition, pitchers Chris Bosio, Dan Plesac, Bill Wegman, Tim Leary, and Juan Nieves all looked like they could contribute at the big league level.

At Double-A, Robidoux would have won the Triple Crown (with his .342 average and 132 RBIs) if Joey Meyer had not beaten him for the league lead in homers with 37. Meanwhile, their teammate Braggs, who possessed unbelievable strength on a rail-thin frame, hit .310 with 20 home runs and 103 RBIs. On the mound, Bosio, Plesac, and Nieves would form a formidable rotation for the El Paso Double-A club.[30]

In Triple-A, club manager Tom Trebelhorn had a team that featured Wegman, Leary, and a promoted Nieves. In addition, Chuck Crim, one of the University of Hawaii signees by Ray Poitevint, and Bryan Clutterbuck, signed from Eastern Michigan University, would also pitch well in 1985. Meanwhile, at the plate, Tiny Felder would hit .314 and steal 61 bases, and Jim Adduci would hit 20 homers and drive in 77 runs.

Each one of those teams would win a pennant in 1985, and the Vancouver Triple-A club, which Trebelhorn called a "very good group who worked hard and had fun playing," would win the Pacific Coast League title.[31] It was one of many the Brewers would capture at the Minor League level in the 1980s. As an organization, the Brewers' clubs would win the most games at the Minor League level during the 1980s, and by 1990 a league-high 48 percent of Brewers players at the Major League level were homegrown. This effort would not go unnoticed. The Brewers would win Baseball America Organization of the Year honors from 1985 to 1987.[32]

With all that success, it seemed as if Harry Dalton had a chance to get the Brewers to the top again. It was not to be. Still, from 1986 to 1988 the Brewers under Harry Dalton would continue to make strides to return the Brewers to respectability while providing their fans with some of the most memorable moments in the franchise's history.

18

Streaking

WINTER 1986–FALL 1988

Four years after the Harry Dalton–built Brewers secured a division title, an American League pennant, and a World Series berth, he was on the verge of turning over almost his entire team. This process would be accomplished quicker than anticipated, and by 1988 the Milwaukee Brewers were looking like they would be ready to contend again, despite severe financial difficulties. Along the way, the influx of new talent, mixed with the veteran presence of Robin Yount, a now healthy Paul Molitor, and fan favorite Jim Gantner, would provide Dalton and his team with a new level of respect among their fans as the excitement returned to County Stadium.

Spring training of 1986 was the most critical camp that Harry Dalton had during his time as general manager of the Brewers. A poor season in 1986 could call Dalton's abilities further into question despite the goodwill he built from 1978 to 1982. Conversely, a good season could cement Dalton into the Brewers GM role as he approached his fourth decade in the game. In the winter of 1985, Dalton set out to find the talent that he could combine with a young core of players that spring to make a top-flight season possible.

Heading to the winter meetings in San Diego, the first without an interleague trade deadline, Dalton looked to help fill the problem areas on his team. Specifically, he was looking for a bullpen arm and a "run-producing" outfielder.[1] He also took time to once again speak on behalf of the owners in their ongoing war of words with the union regarding collusion.

This time Dalton appeared on NBC's *Today Show* with Bryant Gumble as part of a panel discussion. In it, the veteran GM clearly stated why he felt the market was slower than expected: fear of paying for underperformance. "The problem simply is this," Dalton said, "that after 10 years of free agency I think that baseball's management suddenly—not suddenly—but now has an overwhelming history of evidence of financial mistakes, serious financial mistakes."[2] As for collusion, much as he did with his testimony in the arbitration hearing the previous year, Dalton made it known that while he understood some agents would see a slow signing period as collusion, "if there is any indication of a directive or an order that we are not supposed to do things in the way of free agents it hasn't gotten back to me and I know that's not true."[3]

As for his team, Dalton was true to his word on trying to make his team better. On December 4 Dalton reacquired David Green as an option in the outfield. By this time, the once highly touted prospect was playing for the San Francisco Giants after underachieving in St. Louis, thanks in part to a prolonged struggle with alcohol, but Dalton felt that his age (Green was listed as twenty-four in the spring of 1986) was enough of an upside for the Brewers to try him that spring. One week later, Dalton acquired veteran bullpen arm Mark Clear. Finally, on December 19 Dalton swung another deal with the Giants. This time Dalton sent two Minor Leaguers to San Francisco for "free swinging outfielder" Rob Deer.[4]

As expected, the Brewers were quiet on the free agent front. As noted before, much of the inactivity could be explained by an organizational belief that free agency was not worth the cost. However, what few people realized at the time, when Milwaukee carried the fourth-highest average player salary in the big leagues through 1985, was that the Brewers were having major financial issues.

The financial difficulties hamstrung Dalton to an extreme degree. He would spend most of the mid-1980s trimming payroll at the behest of Selig and Dick Hoffman, the chief financial officer. As an indication of how serious it got, in the winter of 1985–86, the Brewers announced they would likely go with a twenty-four-man roster instead of the allowed twenty-five for most of 1986.[5]

This level of austerity would prevent Dalton from making any significant, costly trades for the rest of his career. Most importantly, in 1986, despite offering "several different proposals," the Brewers had to pass on a trade for Andre Dawson of the Montreal Expos primarily because they could not have taken on Dawson's $1.2 million salary.[6]

As he prepared for spring training, for which the Brewers would be moving into a new complex in Chandler, Arizona, Dalton did manage to re-sign free agent Danny Darwin to a two-year deal before a scheduled arbitration hearing. Beating the deadline for a hearing was nothing new for Dalton. Since he had come to Milwaukee, he had avoided having a hearing with any eligible player. Dalton was quick to downplay this achievement in the press, saying, "It's not necessarily a point of pride. I just believe in negotiating hard and firm with the player and his representative."[7]

A "hard and firm" negotiating style did not mean that Dalton was against a player trying to argue what he was worth with Dalton. However, what Dalton felt was unnecessary was the combative nature of an arbitration hearing. He truly believed in maintaining a cordial relationship with a player if possible. Moreover, as he articulated in 1986, "I have a belief the club and the player are in the best position to know what the player's performance contributed to the club. They should be able to work it out—not a third party who may not know quite as much about baseball."[8]

Once most of the contractual work was done for the spring, Dalton turned his eye to preparing for the season. However, one event drastically threw the Brewers' plans for 1986 askew and reminded Dalton and others in his organization that life was fragile and the matters of baseball, as serious as they were, palled in comparison to the happenings of real tragedy.

On February 27 Dalton was in the manager's office at the new training facility with George Bamberger when work being done to "bleed" air from the gas lines in the coach's locker room next door caused an explosion. The explosion produced a flash fire that sent a "bolt of fire" through the door into Bamberger's office and threw bullpen coach Larry Haney, on fire, into the office from the adjoining clubhouse. Bamberger and Dalton were knocked to the floor, and when they got back up, they quickly moved to assist the group of coaches. Bamberger moved toward Haney to smother the flames. Meanwhile, Dalton, who would suffer "singed hair" and a burned scalp, moved to help plumber Jeff Sutton, who was engulfed in flames. Dalton also helped third base coach Tony Muser, who suffered second- and third-degree burns on almost half of his body.[9]

In total, nine people suffered injuries in the event, including rookie hopeful pitcher Bill Wegman and catcher Bill Schroeder, who were standing in an adjacent hallway. In the immediate aftermath, the focus was not on baseball. Dalton, speaking the next day, guaranteed that the Brewers, despite their desire to occupy the building, did not move into the facility too soon: "Accidents happen. We don't feel that we rushed in here. . . . Some people got hurt. That's the worst part. The building can be fixed."[10]

In the aftermath of the explosion, camp got underway, and it quickly became apparent that the Brewers seemed to have a wealth of young pitching talent to go with a mix of position players, both prospects and veterans. Anchoring that mix was Juan Nieves, who went a combined 16-5 in Double-A and Triple-A in 1985, and Teddy Higuera, who won a Brewers rookie record fifteen games in 1985. Dalton hoped they would carry the standard for the team's starters in 1986 and beyond. It turned out that he had the first part correct.

Higuera, the flame-throwing lefty who drew comparisons to Fernando Valenzuela of the Dodgers because of his arm and his "bad body," would become the third twenty-game winner in Brewers history in 1986. He would finish 20-11 and come in second behind Roger Clemens of the Boston Red Sox in the American League Cy Young vote. Higuera would follow that up with 18 wins and 240 strikeouts in 1987 and 16 wins in 1988. During those three years, the 57-30 record he compiled was the third-best tally in the American League behind only Frank Viola of the Twins and Roger Clemens.

As for Nieves, his overall record in 1986 was 11-12, but he would show flashes of brilliance in his rookie year. May was his best month, as he went 5-1, including a 6–3 complete-game victory over Minnesota in which he struck out six batters. It was in 1987 when the lefty would make his mark. For the season, he would go 14-8, and in April he would make

Brewers history on a cold, windswept night in Baltimore when he threw the Brewers' only solo no-hitter ever, notching a 7–0 Brewers win.

The Brewers also seemed to find an early leader in the clubhouse to replace Rollie Fingers as the team's late-inning reliever. Lefty Dan Plesac from North Carolina State was a starter for the Brewers all through the Minors after being drafted twenty-sixth overall in 1983. The 6-foot-5-inch Plesac, who featured a mid-90s fastball and a wipeout slider, would move to the bullpen in 1986 and become the Brewers' "closer" as bullpens became more specialized than they were in the time of the firemen. From 1986 to 1988 Plesac had 67 saves, which was fourth best in the American League. The 1988 season saw him earn 30 saves in 35 chances.

With the abundance of pitching talent, the Brewers featured an evolving offense that became more diversified as the decade progressed. Thanks to Rob Deer, the Brewers had a long ball threat in the middle of their lineup. The all-or-nothing slugger would average 28 homers from 1986 to 1988 and lead the league in strikeouts twice, averaging 173 punchouts during those seasons. Still, Harry Dalton's roster construction began to rely more on putting the ball in play, taking the extra base, and stealing bases.

Robin Yount, who had become a full-time outfielder thanks to the shoulder injury suffered in 1983, continued to be a driving force in the Brewers' lineup even as his power numbers declined. He carried a .310 average from 1986 to 1988, collected 551 hits, and averaged 91 runs scored. Yount would also begin to rack up milestone achievements. In 1986 he reached 2,000 career hits on a bloop single against the Cleveland Indians. In May 1988 he would become the Brewers' all-time RBI leader, hit for the cycle on a sun-soaked afternoon in Chicago in June against the White Sox, and drive in his 1,000th RBI in August at home versus Detroit.

In addition to Yount's production, for the first time in his career the Brewers were reaping the benefits of a mostly healthy Paul Molitor. He had a solid year when he hit .281 and stole 20 bases in 105 games in 1986. In 1988 he hit .312, stole 41 bases, and had 190 hits, including 34 doubles. In between those two years, he was even better.

For Paul Molitor, 1987 was a season for the ages. He hit .353; led the league in runs scored, with 114 and 41 doubles; stole 45 bases; and had an OPS over 1,000 for the only time in his Hall of Fame career. All of this paled in comparison to what he achieved between July 16 and August 26. In the sweltering summer of 1987, Molitor went on a thirty-nine-game hitting streak, mesmerizing the country. Looking back at the hit streak in 2020, J. R. Radcliffe of the *Milwaukee Journal Sentinel* summed up Molitor's excellence perfectly: "During the streak, Molitor went 68 for 168 (.405 batting average) with seven homers, three triples, 17 doubles, 25 walks, and 23 strikeouts. He posted a 1.151 OPS and .485 on-base percentage. The Brewers went 24-15, and Molitor's status each night became the talk of Milwaukee."[11] Molitor's streak was the fifth longest in Major League Baseball history behind Ty Cobb (40), George Sisler (41), Pete Rose (44), and Joe DiMaggio (56).

With the steady play of Yount and Molitor, the Brewers could slowly integrate some of their young talent into their everyday lineup between 1986 and 1988. Outfielders Mike "Tiny" Felder and Glenn Braggs would contribute alongside shortstop Dale Sveum and catcher Bill Schroeder. It seemed that Harry Dalton had accomplished what he set out to do. He had rebuilt the Brewers into a formidable team in the American League East. The new look Brew Crew would have their coming-out party in 1987.

The Brewers opened the '87 season at home and swept the Boston Red Sox. They then swept the Texas Rangers in Arlington before heading to Baltimore on the second leg of the road trip. The Brewers would run their record to 8-0 after a 7–4 victory against the Orioles. The next night, Juan Nieves would no-hit the Orioles thanks to outstanding defensive plays by left fielder Jim Paciorek and Paul Molitor and a diving catch by Robin Yount to secure the final out.

After Nieves's no-hitter, Harry Dalton had optimistic praise for his young lefty and the team overall: "Young players have a tendency to be inconsistent for a while [Nieves was 1-0 but walked five and gave up six runs in five and a third innings in his first start]. But you see the raw ability. You know, the physical ability is there—the ability to throw the fastball, the breaking ball, the command on the mound. And it's a matter of pitching enough experience in this league to be consistent."[12]

As for his take on the team, the 9-0 start shocked Dalton despite his belief in the team: "We know there's talent there. We knew we'd come home and have a chance to play well, but we couldn't tell you what was going to happen to this extent. . . . There's a lot of confidence for the youngsters and we just want to capitalize on it."[13]

The Brewers continued their hot play on the next home stand. In the first game of a series against the Rangers, the Brewers won their tenth game in a row 10–2, thanks to a seven-run seventh inning and a complete game with twelve strikeouts from Teddy Higuera. On Saturday, another of the Brewers' young arms, right-hander Bill Wegman, gave Milwaukee seven and two-thirds innings in a 4–3 Brewers win that featured four stolen bases and a home run from Rob Deer.

The party continued in Milwaukee the next day. Easter Sunday was an unseasonably warm day in Milwaukee and featured one of the biggest moments in franchise history. This time the Brewers trailed 4–1 heading into the ninth inning. In keeping with the month's magic, Glenn Braggs was walked by Rangers closer Mitch Williams. The next hitter, first baseman Greg Brock, for whom Dalton had traded in the winter of 1986 in a deal with the Dodgers for pitchers Tim Leary and Tim Crews, singled. With two on, that is when the inning got wild.

After Williams retired Cecil Cooper on a fly ball for the first out, Rangers manager Bobby Valentine made a pitching change for veteran righty Greg Harris. On the first pitch, Harris made Deer look bad on a slider breaking down and away on the big righty. On the next pitch, Harris tried the same approach. This pitch hung over the plate, and Deer deposited the ball three-quarters of the way up in the jam-packed bleachers. Tie game. The next hitter, rookie catcher B. J. Surhoff, struck out for the second out, then Jim Gantner walked on five pitches.

Now, with the winning run on base, up stepped second-year shortstop Dale Sveum. Over twenty-nine thousand Brewers fans were at full throat. On the first three pitches, Harris worked Sveum away with a fastball and missed with each one. On 3-0, Harris threw his first strike, making it 3-1. Harris then got back in the count when the lefty Sveum fouled away an outside fastball with Gantner on the move. Harris then tried to climb the ladder on Sveum with a fastball. With his closed, pigeon-toed stance, Sveum was able to get on top of the ball away from him and hooked it into the right-field stands. The Brewers had won 6–4 on a walk-off homer.

The twelfth win in a row set off a joyous celebration the likes of which Brewers fans had not seen since the parade after the 1982 World Series. This time, the excitement centered on free hamburgers. Like many businesses in the Milwaukee area looking to play into "Brewer Fever," George Webb Restaurant, a Milwaukee diner with a long history of supporting Milwaukee baseball since its founding in 1948, offered free hamburgers for twelve wins in a row. In the end, Webb's served 168,194 in three days and drew fans from all over the state.[14]

The next night the Brewers defeated the rival White Sox 5–4 in a game at Comiskey Park that featured three innings of relief from rookie Chuck Crim (another player Ray Poitevint got from the University of Hawaii) and Dan Plesac's fifth save of the season. The thirteen wins in a row tied the Major League record for most wins to start a season. The rebuilt Milwaukee Brewers were the darlings of the sports media.

On April 27, with their record at 16-1 following a loss on April 21 against the White Sox and four more victories in a row, including another sweep of Baltimore, the new-look Brewers made the cover of *Sports Illustrated*. When asked if they could keep up their winning ways, Juan Nieves was pointed in his response: "People probably think this is a joke, but it is not. It's a taste of what's to come the rest of the way. We're back. No mercy." As for the catalyst for the unlikely first-place team, Rick Manning felt a large part of the Brewers' success sprang from who was in the dugout.[15]

Tom Trebelhorn, a piano-playing former teacher and a career Minor Leaguer, took over the Brewers on an interim basis at the end of 1986. In late September Harry Dalton decided not to bring George Bamberger back for 1987. When he heard of the impending change, Bamberger, citing his iffy health, decided to go home without finishing the season. Initially, Dalton was instructed to offer the job to Sal Bando, who had been serving as a special assistant to Dalton since his retirement. Bando turned the Brewers down, and Trebelhorn, the third base coach, stepped into the breach.

According to Dalton, "Treb" became his interim manager for myriad reasons: "First he has managed six or seven players currently on the ballclub. Secondly, he has managed most recently among all our coaches (that included no one with big league experience)."[16] Even on an interim basis, it was a meteoric rise for the man who is credited with teaching Rickey Henderson how to harness his blinding speed to steal bases. In 1984 Trebelhorn was the first base coach on Rene Lachemann's coaching staff. After Lachemann's dismissal, the Brewers were impressed enough with Trebelhorn that Dalton and Bruce Manno offered him a job as the manager at Triple-A Vancouver in 1985. There, he was exposed to the Brewers system and, as mentioned earlier, led his team to a title.

Despite his success, Trebelhorn would decline a chance to return to Vancouver because of the strain a full season schedule placed on his family dynamic. However, he did accept a spot as a roving instructor and a chance to manage a Brewers short-season team that would start after the draft in June. It was at that point that fate intervened.

When Tony Muser was injured in the Chandler clubhouse explosion, Dalton asked Trebelhorn to become the Brewers' third base coach. Much like when he was given the managerial job a year later, Trebelhorn was supposed to fill in for Muser just until he could return. That would see him back in either Class A Short Season or rookie ball. However, when Muser did not return in 1986, that made Trebelhorn the best option, in Dalton's mind, to manage the team.[17]

Those nine games cemented Trebelhorn as the Brewers' manager for 1987. However, as he remembered it, he felt his team did not do him any favors off the field:

> We went 6 and 3 and knocked Toronto out of the pennant race with a double header sweep on the final Sunday of the season. This followed a Saturday night team party that got a little rowdy as somehow we lost a bed out of one of the rooms that the Sheraton people never found. I had a team meeting and told the team that they really ruined my one and only chance to be a real major league manager and that if they had so much fun last night you better have more fun this afternoon

> as I am going to play you until you drop[,] so get ready. They did and under miserable final day conditions we played two terrific games.[18]

Trebelhorn was correct. It was the performance down the stretch that mattered. Specifically, Dalton loved how prepared the cerebral Trebelhorn was and how he seemed to get the players to respond. "He's done extremely well," Dalton said, "not just with his nine-inning performance but his preparation and contact with players."[19] In short, he was the type of manager that Harry Dalton loved.

Less than a year later it seemed that Dalton, with his team at 18-3, had struck gold with his new manager. His players loved playing for Trebelhorn, who was youthful and vibrant on the field and off. Moreover, he had a managerial style that fit his team.[20] "I'll tell you what I like," Trebelhorn said. He then named "a Paul Molitor bunting for a base hit. A steal of second. A Jimmy Gantner take-it-with you [a drag bunt for a base hit] to the right side getting Molitor over to third. A Robin Yount hard groundball to the backhand side of the second baseman whose only play is to first, Paulie scores. That's what I love."[21]

Trebelhorn also loved to run. Under his watch, the Brewers had the most diverse offense at any time in the Dalton era. In 1987 they would steal 176 bases and lead the league. They would again lead the league in 1988 (with 159). Still, even with this new approach, the Brewers could not come close to a pennant in Trebelhorn's first two years. One of the reasons was an unbelievable number of debilitating injuries that would sideline key players.

In truth, injuries would help define the rest of Harry Dalton's career and make the job he did building a competitive team even more impressive. Upon Dalton's retirement in 1994, Dalton's friend and colleague Roland Hemond, who in 1994 was the GM of the Orioles, took a stand in defense of Dalton's abilities and the impact that injuries had on the final product Dalton put on the field: "I told him once, 'Harry you're just not lucky.' It was like a hex over them. He didn't like making excuses, so I'll make them for him. I can't think of a club that's had that much tough luck."[22]

In 1987 injuries to several key players, including Paul Molitor (elbow and hamstring); Rob Deer (knee); Dan Plesac, rookie starting pitcher Mike Birkbeck, and Jim Gantner (hamstring), would force all to miss significant amounts of time that would weaken the Brewers after their hot start. Combined with a stretch of bad play, the same team that went 18-3 in April finished May at 6-18 and lost twelve in a row from May 3 to May 19. The rest of the season was a microcosm of the first two months. A stretch of good play followed a stretch of bad and vice versa.

According to Tom Trebelhorn, the one person who did not lose his cool in the face of these swings in fortune was Harry Dalton. "Harry was very patient during the roller coaster of 1987," Trebelhorn wrote, "and with the return of Molitor and his 39-game hitting streak we did OK. I stopped in to see Harry every day on my way to the clubhouse and if he had time we talked about the team and what we might be able to do to be a little more consistent. He would come down to the clubhouse every once in a while to encourage players and staff. He was terrific to work for and with."[23]

Aside from support of the emotional and intellectual variety Dalton provided Trebelhorn, the GM also tried to shore up the Brewers' pitching staff, whose performance mirrored that of the team. Dalton even asked Pete Vuckovich if he would attempt a comeback. There was a precedent for such a request; Dalton had done the same thing in 1986. As Vuckovich later recalled, in 1986, while the former pitcher was working as a scout for the Brewers, Dalton had asked if the competitive Vuckovich would want to try and get back to the big leagues. Vuckovich would go to Vancouver and earn a call-up to Milwaukee after six appearances in Triple-A. He would go 2-4 with a 3.06 ERA before his arm troubles resurfaced.

In 1987 Dalton was hoping that, with rest, the righty was willing to try again. This time, Vuckovich knew better and was not about to get Dalton's hopes up with another trip to Triple-A. "Harry called me again and asked if I wanted to pitch," Vuckovich recalled. "Now, even then, I knew I could go to Double-A [where Dalton wanted him to rehab] and get hitters out with what I had left. What I couldn't do was get big league hitters out. I told Harry that I didn't want to embarrass myself, my teammates, or the organization."[24]

In the end, rookie righty Chris Bosio, who had made a brief appearance with Milwaukee in 1986, made nineteen starts in 1987 after being in the bullpen for the first part of the year. He would go 8-7 as a starter and have some effective moments as the team's fifth starter. Bosio was not the only rookie contributing to the pitching staff that season. Rookie Mark Ciardi would make his only appearances in the Majors that summer; three were starts. Finally, relievers Chuck Crim and Mark Knudson would also make starts for the beleaguered staff.

Even with injuries and streaky play, Milwaukee would end 1987 with ninety-one wins, which was good for third in the AL East behind the Detroit Tigers. Still, there was enough potential in Milwaukee for pundits to proclaim them the American League favorite for 1988. Harry Dalton took a guarded approach when he was told.

"I'm sure there will be people picking us first or second in the winter publications," he said. "Treb and I have talked a lot about it and were going to stress to our players that you can't take anything for granted."[25] This was a prophetic approach as the 1988 Brewers were once again a streaky team.

In truth, for most of the 1988 season, the Brewers were a .500 team that caught fire at the end of the year and made a memorable late push for first place. Otherwise, play on the field was a mix of pedestrian and stellar. Once again, the starting pitching was anchored by Teddy Higuera, who went 16-9. The Brewers also got an unexpected boost from rookie hurler Don August, who went 13-7 with a 3.09 ERA in twenty-two starts. Finally, coming back from his injury-plagued 1987 and fighting through an early-season demotion to Triple-A, Mike Birkbeck would go 10-8.

In addition to the pitching, the offense was also solid thanks to a healthy Paul Molitor (.312 average, 13 home runs, 60 RBIs, 41 stolen bases), another solid year from Robin Yount (.306, 13 home runs, 91 RBIs), Jim Gantner (.276, 47 RBIs, 20 stolen bases), and a typical power showing from Rob Deer (23 home runs, 85 RBIs). Despite success in both areas, the Brewers' 1988 roster also had some glaring concerns.

Offensively, the team was beholden to the production of Yount, Molitor, Gantner, and Deer. Greg Brock would grossly underachieve in 1988 after a solid 1987. Also, Jeffrey Leonard, whom Dalton acquired in June from San Francisco, would struggle mightily during his time in Milwaukee and leave at the end of the season.

As for the pitching, outside of Higuera and the emergence of Don August, the team struggled to find a third starter. Chris Bosio went 7-15, and Bill Wegman would finish the year at 13-13. Both had moments, but neither impressed to a great degree. Then there was Juan Nieves. One year removed from what many thought would be stardom, the lefty had an injury-plagued 1988, thanks partly to overuse after pitching in winter ball, and would make only 15 starts.

Finally, despite the hype associated with the upcoming youth movement in Milwaukee, many of the players whom the Brewers were counting on to make an impact began to show chinks in their armor. In 1988 the Brewers would finally be forced to move on from Billy Jo Robidoux after a series of injuries and merely lackluster performance even when healthy. By 1988 the Brewers had also given up on a one-time prospect, shortstop Ernie Riles, who ended up being a part of the Jeffrey Leonard deal. Lastly, rookie slugger Joey Meyer and 1987 hero Dale Sveum suffered injuries that sapped their production going forward.

Still, when he looked ahead to 1989, Harry Dalton saw a team that could compete. He did not know that the new faces in his clubhouse would need a different sort of motivation than any group of players he had previously encountered. This would put Dalton at odds with some in the clubhouse, and it led the veteran GM to suffer ever-increasing frustration as his team struggled to reach their potential on the field and as he tried to keep them unified off it. In the end, this battle played out in full view of the media and fans. Combined with a perception that he had lost his magic as a talent evaluator, that battle would be the death knell of Harry Dalton's storied career as a team builder.

19

The Last Ride of the Dalton Gang

WINTER 1988–FALL 1991

From 1989 to 1991, the off-the-field news surrounding Harry Dalton and the Brewers, as well as the growing perception in the media that the game had passed Dalton by, swallowed up any positives that occurred on the field. That news would lead to an inglorious end for Dalton and his supporting cast of scouts and advisors. Still, he conducted himself with great dignity even as others looked to tarnish his reputation, call his legacy into question, and insinuate that he did not understand the modern game. However, the beginning of the end emerged when Dalton's hopes for another pennant were dashed by another set of roster-changing injuries.

The most significant blow for the Brewers regarding how injuries would affect 1989 occurred before the season started. In December Teddy Higuera underwent surgery to repair a herniated disc resulting from a back injury. Happening just six weeks before spring training, his injury guaranteed that he would miss all of camp and the season's first month. In addition, once camp did start, it became evident that Juan Nieves had lost the zip on his fastball from a combination of nagging shoulder issues and a bulked-up physique born of an off-season weight-training regimen. Tom Trebelhorn would sum up the situation in March: "He can't get loose and he can't throw the ball hard. It looks again like he's the victim of the vanishing fastball. He can't pitch that way."[1]

Nieves would not play at the Major League level in 1989; he had surgery in May for a torn rotator cuff following three starts at Triple-A Denver. He would also miss all of 1990 after multiple surgeries, and Milwaukee finally released him in 1991.

The dual loss of Higuera and Nieves had devastating consequences for the Brewers' starting staff. First, as Trebelhorn would remember in 2017, the loss of his two power lefties resulted in a one-dimensional pitching staff in terms of approach. "When we lost Higuera and Nieves," Trebelhorn said, "every pitcher we ran out was right-handed and they all pitched the same. It became real easy to scout us at that point."[2] The other issue for Trebelhorn when the two lefties went down was finding capable big league starters to fill the top two spots in the rotation. Injuries to Bill Wegman and righty Tom Filer compounded this issue. The Brewers were forced to use twelve different starting pitchers in 1989, and they would use the same number in 1990 and thirteen in 1991. The lack of continuity would hurt the team during each of those years.

In addition to the issues with the starting pitching, the middle of the Brewers' infield was decimated by injuries thanks to two horrific collisions. Dale Sveum was slated to return in time for the 1989 season after he broke his shin upon making contact with rookie left fielder Darryl Hamilton. However, Sveum's leg did not heal right, and doctors had to re-break his shin and do more surgery. He would miss all of 1989, and when he returned for brief stretches in 1990 and 1991 he was not the player the Brewers saw in 1987.

As Sveum recalled in 1998, "People talk about losing a step, I lost two steps. I just didn't have strength in that leg to go to my right."[3] It also affected his hitting. Before the injury, Sveum was rounding into one of the best hitters on the Brewers. As Tom Trebelhorn would recall, Sveum was as clutch as any hitter on the Brewers. "He was a very rare commodity: a middle infielder who could produce runs," Trebelhorn said. "He was as good as anybody I had in terms of being a player who could produce in those situations. As good as Robin Yount, Paul Molitor, anybody."[4]

For much of the time Sveum was missing from the lineup, the Brewers would also be without Jim Gantner. Gantner sustained his injury in August 1989, when a rolling slide by Yankees rookie Marcus Lawton took him out. It was the second time he tore his ACL in his career. This time, he was sidelined until June 1990.

In an attempt to fill in the injury-induced gaps in the middle infield, the Brewers called up two promising rookies from their farm system: shortstops Gary Sheffield and Bill Spiers. Dalton believed that both players had a future with the team if he could move one or the other to a new position. This method of playing the best athletes in the best spots was something that Dalton had done often enough, with both Boog Powell and Bobby Valentine, for example. This time, however, Dalton's instincts on where to play his best players to help his team win would become the issue that would split his clubhouse apart and detract from any good that might happen on the field.

Looking back on the careers of Gary Sheffield and Bill Spiers, there is no question in the minds of even a casual fan that the two are not comparable from a statistical standpoint. Sheffield would play twenty-two years in the Majors, with 2,600 hits, 509 homers, and a lifetime batting average of .292. It is said that the only thing keeping the slugger out of the Hall of Fame in Cooperstown was his becoming embroiled in baseball's steroid scandal during the early 2000s.

Bill Spiers also had a long Major League career. He would play parts of thirteen seasons before retiring. That is where the comparison with Sheffield ends for most fans, if they even remember Spiers at all. Three back surgeries drastically changed the course of his career, and he was a utility player for much of the time thereafter. Nevertheless, in the mid-1980s Sheffield and Spiers were seen as two of the best prospects in baseball in a loaded Milwaukee system.

The Brewers drafted Sheffield, a shortstop, sixth overall in 1986. He was just out of high school in Tampa, Florida, where he grew up in the shadow of drugs and gang violence and where his uncle, All-Star pitcher Dwight "Doc" Gooden, would be a role model for the kid everyone called "Sheff." Dalton and company took Spiers, also a shortstop, thirteenth overall the following year. Spiers came out of Clemson University, where he was a standout for the Tigers baseball team and a punter for the football squad. With the proximity of their draft dates and the outstanding Minor League seasons both players would produce for winning teams, Harry Dalton and his gang saw them as inseparable and envisioned a day when Spiers and Sheffield would help form the core of the team, much like Molitor and Yount had for so many years.

When asked in the spring of 1989, Dalton was quick not to compare the two players directly or speculate on when both might make the Major

League roster. "Where they play and what date they both become regulars, we're not sure," Dalton said. "But it's nice to look forward to that, having Sheffield and Spiers in the same lineup."[5] Because of the injury to Sveum and concerns about Molitor's ability to play defense, thanks to his arm issues and a broken finger suffered at the end of March, the future came early in Milwaukee.

Because of Sveum's injury, Sheffield would make it to the Major League roster at the end of the 1988 season and would show flashes of the talent Dalton and others thought would make the skinny nineteen-year-old a star. In all, he would make twenty-four starts at short, and while he only hit .238, he would slug .400 and have an OPS of .695, and it seemed that he would have the inside track on the starting shortstop job in 1989.

At the same time, Spiers would have a solid year between Class A Stockton and Double-A El Paso. His play was good enough that he would open 1989 at Triple-A Denver. Plans changed when Paul Molitor broke a finger near the end of training camp. The injury allowed Spiers to play almost every day, and he took that opportunity to make the twenty-four-man Major League roster.

The hype surrounding the two rookie players, their demeanors, and the expectations of each man were wholly different and colored their early days with the team. It may seem cliché, but Spiers remembered that he was "wide-eyed" and just wanted to take everything in. To him, that meant watching how veterans like Robin Yount, Paul Molitor, and Jim Gantner went about their work. "Watching those guys, Robin, Paul, and Jim, was a great experience," Spiers said. "Robin really taught me how to be ready to play. . . . Those guys were gamers, and I tried to work the same way."[6]

Sheffield was seen as the heir apparent to men like Yount and Molitor and, as the starting shortstop, was touted as the top candidate for American League Rookie of the Year honors. However, he would increasingly feel that the veterans on the team did nothing to help him, and he quickly made it known that he was not going to soak in the atmosphere of a big league clubhouse. He felt it was the clubhouse's job to adjust to him and his expectations. In his mind, he was a star and should be treated like one.

Nowhere was this attitude more apparent than in how Spiers and Sheffield viewed their playing time. Although he was hoping to one day be the starting shortstop, Spiers was, as the saying goes, "just hoping to help the ball club." To that end, he would play wherever and whenever Harry Dalton and Tom Trebelhorn thought he would benefit the team. For Sheffield, the starting shortstop job was his. He wanted to play there every day, and there was to be no adjustment to those parameters.

The numerical evidence shows this was the case. Sheffield would start forty-eight of the first fifty games, playing forty of those as the starting shortstop. Meanwhile, Spiers would start twenty-four of the first fifty games. Nine of those were at short, and seven of those games occurred in April. He would also start nine games at third, one each at first and second, and another four games as the designated hitter. This breakdown shows that the Brewers believed that Sheffield was the starting shortstop. Sheffield was not so sure. He quickly made it known that he was not happy.

After a Brewers loss in late May to Seattle, Sheffield made his frustrations with the team public and scapegoated Spiers as the reason for his displeasure. Specifically, Sheffield took umbrage at what he perceived as special treatment of Spiers. In Sheffield's mind, the organization was "setting the table" for Spiers while disrespecting Sheffield, giving Spiers starts at short.[7]

Sheffield then broadened his attack, taking aim at his manager and his other teammates. He would accuse the club of overcoaching him (in the form of making him take extra infield) as a whole. In his mind, Tom Trebelhorn had a "chip on his shoulder" because of the "type of person" Sheffield was. Sheffield also believed that his teammates did not care about him. This was especially true, he said, of the pitchers who were slow to defend him when he was knocked down.[8] As for why he decided to react the way he did, Sheffield quickly pointed out that the advice he got from Gooden was not to "kiss anyone's butt" if he had issues.[9]

As expected, Sheffield's comments did not sit well with most of his teammates, and they blindsided others. Spiers had been under the impression that they had a good relationship, so he did not understand where Sheffield's animosity was coming from.[10]

Two days later, the situation looked much better from where Harry Dalton sat. "I think the net fallout effect of this is going to be positive,"

Dalton said. Sheffield "had some things eating away inside of him. It's better to have the problems on the table so that you can attack them."[11] As for what Sheffield said, Dalton was sympathetic when he told reporters that Sheffield was right to speak to the problems as he saw them with the team, even if not everything he said was correct. Where Dalton felt Sheffield erred was in taking his issues to the media instead of coming to Trebelhorn or Dalton right away.[12] It was a misstep that Sheffield would repeat numerous times in the coming years, and it would help to erode the relationship between Dalton, Selig, Trebelhorn, and Sheffield.

Beyond putting a strain on relationships in the clubhouse, Sheffield's response helped foster an environment where it was acceptable to question management on almost every decision. This was a new phenomenon for Dalton, who, despite having adjusted to players having more power in the era of free agency and being more combative with the GM, had maintained good relationships with players. That all changed in 1989.

Contrary to how Sheffield saw events, Dalton did not create the rifts that began to appear in the Milwaukee clubhouse. Neither did Sheffield, and what the situation did was bring to light changes occurring naturally.

The average age of the Brewers was 28.6 in 1989. This was just above the league-average age. However, it was deceiving in their case because of a handful of older players among the position player group who appeared in fewer than fifty games that season. When the fifty-game threshold is considered, the average age falls to 27 among position players. This would make the Brewers the second-youngest group of position players in the American League in 1989. According to Robin Yount, the youth began to change the dynamic in the clubhouse.[13] The most significant difference to Dalton was a lack of patience and a change in motivation. He would articulate this to his team in June 1989.

In 1989, a month after Sheffield voiced his opinion, Dalton took the opportunity in a closed-door meeting that was tape-recorded to give his opinion of the team after seventy-six games. What he found in front of him was perplexing. Dalton admitted to being "pissed" and saddened by his team. The duality of his emotions was because he felt that the younger players were "trapped by money . . . by the financial system in the game today and by agents" who constantly reminded players of the financial rewards to be made as a Major League player.[14] This, according to Dalton, led players to forget why they played the game. It also led to what frustrated Dalton.

According to Dalton, the instant gratification experienced in other facets of their lives tricked the new generation of players into believing that baseball would be as easy as the other things they did. In Dalton's mind, this led to the belief that the natural ability that got players to the Major Leagues would be enough to allow them to stay. The veteran GM reminded his team that baseball did not work that way, that players would have to "bust their ass" to stay in the big leagues.

Dalton understood that his thoughts made him seem like an "old bastard," but he was trying to bring his thoughts to the forefront to make the players understand that part of their work was to hold themselves accountable. "Some of you have never experienced failure so you pout and sulk," he said. "When you are twenty-three, or twenty-five or twenty-six you are too old to pout and sulk." Dalton reminded his team that contrary to popular belief the players were expected to "work baseball," not play it. Dalton did not feel that most of the players on the roster understood that it was their job to give "a maximum mental and physical performance" to hold up their contract. Dalton then pointed out that the lack of effort and the "attitude problems" displayed by his club started changing the team's perception among their peers.

"I've got a friend on the Yankees, and we talk about things that are going on, and a lot of the Yankee players laugh at this ball club. Your nickname is 'Candy Ass Kids.'" This moniker stemmed from the belief that the Brewers were too quick to show their emotions when things did not go right instead of playing through the frequent failures the game provided. In Dalton's mind, this behavior "gave the other team an advantage."

Dalton then concluded his discussion by reminding the team of what they had going for them, including pitchers who threw 94 mph and a potential MVP for 1989 in Robin Yount. In his mind, if every player turned their thoughts to what they had and what they could do to help the team, they could right the ship and make a push for the playoffs. He still believed in his team and needed the players to believe along with him.

He needed them to play as a team, however. As he concluded, Dalton wanted the players to give him "four months in which you forget your selfishness . . . and grind it out, day by day, play by play, pitch by pitch." Dalton had no qualms about putting his team forward for a playoff or World Series berth if they did that.

After Dalton's talk, the team would play better down the stretch. When righty Tom Filer beat Boston 5–2 on an August Friday night in Milwaukee, the Brewers were a half a game out of first place. Unfortunately, that was the high-water mark for the team. Even with Dalton's impassioned pleas, the team would sink to .500 on the season, which was good for fourth in the AL East. When the bulk of the season is considered, it was precisely the result the team deserved. Once again, however, there were enough injuries to make fans wonder what a healthy team could have accomplished. The media was not as forgiving, however.

Much like during the downturn of the 1984–86 seasons, the media began questioning Harry Dalton's decisions. In early October Peter Jackel of the *Journal Times* in Racine announced that when looking for why the Brewers underachieved, Dalton needed to "look in the mirror." That journalist's view included the indictment that Dalton had "failed to develop a legitimate Major-League hitter since he joined the Brewers in November of 1977."[15] To prove his point, Jackel would point to the offensive woes of Glenn Braggs, who had a solid season in 1989 but was not the player Dalton and company had envisioned.

Andy Baggot of the *Wisconsin State Journal* of Madison also hit on possible player evaluation issues with the Dalton Gang in a tongue-in-cheek imagining of the Brewers' future and present if they had drafted first baseman Will Clark with the first overall pick in 1985 instead of underachieving catcher B. J. Surhoff. In Baggot's mind, Clark, who finished second in the NL MVP race and was a silver slugger in 1989, would have put the Brewers in line for a World Series berth.[16]

These types of anti-Dalton commentaries became more commonplace in 1990–91. Harry Dalton also began to get pushback from his clubhouse. Mike Felder felt betrayed by Tom Trebelhorn thanks to a reduction in playing time; he blamed Dalton for clouding Trebelhorn's perception of

Felder.[17] Dan Plesac was often a vocal opponent of Dalton, though his comments were veiled.[18] Perhaps in the most significant salvo uttered by someone not named Gary Sheffield, Robin Yount announced at the end of 1989 that unless significant changes were made with the Brewers for 1990 and beyond, he would seriously consider leaving the team in free agency coming off his MVP year.[19]

Yount was not specific about what changes he thought needed to be made but was clear about the catalyst for his request. In an interview with Andy Baggot, it became clear to the sportswriter that "the reason for his [Yount's] change in attitude appears to center around the current mix of individuals on the club and the direction it is heading."[20]

Dalton agreed with his detractors, but he did not know how those changes would take place or at whose behest. As the calendar turned to the 1990s, the Brewers' farm system was as thin as it had been when Dalton got to Milwaukee. The farm system would produce several Major Leaguers after 1991, but they were all years away.

Joey Meyer and Glenn Braggs are often the position players whom fans of that generation point to as "busts." LaVel Freeman is another. Freeman was a standout in the loaded Brewers system. He would hit .395 with 24 homers and 96 RBIs in 1987 while playing for Double-A El Paso. He followed that up with a .318 average for Triple-A Denver the next year. However, after three at bats with Milwaukee in 1989, Freeman was never heard from again at the Major League level.

In hindsight, however, the Brewers' farm system produced more talent than Baggot and others gave it credit for. Yes, Joey Meyer would not pan out. Braggs was a solid Major League outfielder who would win a World Series with the Reds. Talent-wise, Chris Bosio would become the type of pitcher Dalton envisioned. He would go 14-10 for another angst-ridden Brewers club in 1991 and follow that up with a 16-6 record for a ninety-two-win Brewers team in 1992. That 1992 club is the proof that, as Tom Haudricourt, now retired from the *Milwaukee Journal Sentinel*, would say in 2017, "Harry [Dalton] didn't get dumb" in the early 1990s.[21]

On a team eliminated from playoff contention in the season's final weekend, nine of the top twelve wins above replacement were from homegrown players drafted by the Dalton Gang. This included Bosio, as mentioned earlier; seventeen-game winner Jaime Navarro; Bill Wegman; and outfielder Darryl Hamilton, who would have arguably his best year of a thirteen-year career by hitting .298 and stealing 41 bases. In addition to the veterans mentioned above, two standout rookies drafted by Dalton would make their presence felt in 1992.

Pat Listach, drafted in 1988 out of Arizona State, would hit .290, steal 54 bases, and make only 24 errors over 711 chances in 148 games. When the dust settled on the season, this was good enough to win Rookie of the Year honors in the American League. While Listach helped transform the offense, rookie right-hander Cal Eldred would provide the Brewers with their best fourth starter in the Dalton era.

The Brewers drafted Eldred in 1989 out of the University of Iowa in the first round. He would make his Major League debut in 1991 and win two of his three starts following a September call-up. He would go back to Triple-A Denver for the start of the 1992 season and then explode on the Major League scene by going 11-2 with a 1.79 ERA in fourteen starts, including winning ten in a row from August 8 to September 29.

There is no question that the 1992 Brewers were one of the top three teams that Harry Dalton built while in Milwaukee. The team had speed (a Major League–leading 256 stolen bases) and defense (their 89 errors were the fewest in MLB), and they put the ball in play (.268 team batting average, good for second in MLB). They were missing only two things: a transformative power bat in the middle of the lineup and Harry Dalton. How those things came to be interconnected resulted in long-term damage to the Brewers.

The 1990 season was a repeat of 1989, just in reverse order. Milwaukee suffered from debilitating injuries early, clubhouse turmoil late, and poor baseball in the middle. Consequently, pressure continued to mount on Harry Dalton as his team finished 74-88 and in sixth place.

Much like in 1989, the injuries centered on the pitching staff. In total, twelve different starters appeared for Milwaukee, and Juan Nieves would not make an appearance in 1990. Bill Wegman had his season curtailed by injuries and only made eight starts, and Chris Bosio made twenty starts before landing on the disabled list. In addition, Bill Spiers suffered a shoulder injury that would keep him out for most of the season. Then there was the case of Gary Sheffield.

Despite his issues with Trebelhorn early in the previous season and his souring on the Brewers as a whole thanks to a misdiagnosed broken bone in his foot in 1989 that caused him to play poorly enough to be demoted before it was discovered, Sheffield was having a fantastic year in 1990. Much of the credit for this turnaround came from two off-season moves that seemed to satiate the young star in the making and solidify in Robin Yount's mind that Milwaukee would work to be competitive in the coming years.

First, late in the season in 1989, Harry Dalton hired the retired Don Baylor as a special assistant to the GM. He would become the hitting coach for the Brewers in 1990. On the surface, it was a way for Baylor to evaluate the Brewers for Dalton.

This was a move Dalton often employed with his coaches. For instance, every coach for the 1982 Brewers had a connection with Dalton. He felt this was a way to get an unvarnished look into the goings-on with his team. Some felt it amounted to having a built-in spy. Andy Etchebarren was notorious for telling Dalton things as a way to stay in his former boss's good graces. The only problem for "Etch" was that everyone knew he was the information pipeline to Dalton.

Most famously, as 1988 got underway, the Brewers celebrated the season opener together the day before the first game. It happened to be Easter Sunday, so trainer John Adam organized a traditional Easter egg hunt in the clubhouse in Baltimore. As Jimmy Bank remembered, "We come in from the workout, and everyone starts looking for their egg. Harry walks over and goes, 'Found mine!' At that point, Treb yells, 'Andy, did you pipeline that to Harry!' The whole room, including Harry, broke up laughing."[22]

Don Baylor was not a spy for Dalton, but he played an important role. Baylor was one of two men the GM hoped would mentor some of the young players on his team. Most important among these was Gary Sheffield. That was also the role of the second addition, whom Dalton signed in December 1989 as his first free agent since 1980. This new hire was former MVP and perennial All-Star Dave Parker. With his coming to Milwaukee, he could help keep Yount in Milwaukee, and he seemed to help with Gary Sheffield as well.

Looking back on the event, Parker was on the fence about coming to Milwaukee. However, because Milwaukee needed to impress Yount, they were willing to offer Parker more money than the other teams in the bidding for the veteran outfielder. Ultimately, this brought Parker a two-year contract worth over $3 million.[23] Even at the steep price, it seemed like a good deal for the Brewers for two reasons.

To begin, even at age thirty-nine, Dave Parker, whose nickname was "The Cobra," was still highly productive at the plate. Even though he thought he underachieved in 1989, Parker had contributed 22 homers and 97 RBIs to an Oakland team that won the World Series in four games over the San Francisco Giants. Second, as Parker would outline, Bud Selig told him through Dalton that Parker would be the perfect mentor for Gary Sheffield.

"Dalton had heard about my work with young players like Eric Davis, Barry Larkin and Kal Daniels and was hoping I could be a positive influence on Sheffield," Parker wrote. "Milwaukee offered me a raise, a nice signing bonus, two years guaranteed and an option for a third with a buyout."[24]

Parker indicated that his role was reinforced when he met with Bud Selig, who "made continued reference to the young, Black players on the club—Glenn Braggs, Greg Vaughn, and especially the prize possession of the organization. Gary Sheffield."[25]

For most of the year, the mentorship of Baylor and Parker helped Sheffield begin to achieve the greatness Dalton and company saw when they drafted him. He would hit .294 heading into September after carrying an average of over .300 for most of the season's early months. This success even seemed to let Sheffield be okay with being at third base and not his preferred position of shortstop. Along the way, Parker was an All-Star, and even though injuries would derail the pitching staff, it seemed as if the Brewers had turned a corner with the interpersonal issues that had prevailed during the previous season. Then September happened, and all the work Dalton and men like Baylor and Parker had done was over in one brief moment.

The unraveling began when Sheffield was admitted to a hospital in Arlington, Texas, for an illness that tests could not identify. He would stay in the hospital for almost a week, and when he returned to Milwaukee, Sheffield announced that he would not play any further in 1990.[26] A few weeks later, he said he wanted a chance to win the shortstop job in 1991. Parker wrote that Tom Trebelhorn's inability to understand Sheffield was the biggest hurdle to establishing healthy relations with the player, and so when Trebelhorn responded to Sheffield's request with "tough shit," Sheffield left the stadium.[27]

Parker recalled that the subsequent phone call from Bud Selig was frantic and seemed to blame Parker for Sheffield's abrupt departure.[28] Ultimately it was the straw that broke the camel's back with Sheffield, the Brewers, and Parker.

Parker said that during his talks with Selig that night, the owner tacitly promised to pick up the slugger's option at the end of the 1991 season in thanks for helping with Sheffield. According to Parker, Selig would pull that offer off the table following Parker having off-season knee surgery. Selig then traded him to the Angels for outfielder Dante Bichette, and Parker saw it as retribution.

"The Brewers shipped my ass out West, to the Angels, trading me for a young player they didn't know what to do with named Dante Bichette, the kind of kid I would've mentored if they chose someone else to send in the deal," Parker stated. "The trade really made no sense on either side. The Angels didn't really need more home-run power from the left side and Milwaukee didn't need another outfielder. This was all about Selig reneging on the spiritual deal we had for mentoring Gary."[29]

As for what Dalton did in the aftermath of these events, he spent many of the last days of the season assuring writers and fans that Tom Trebelhorn's job was safe, his team still had the talent to compete, and that issues with Sheffield were not as bad as the newspapers made them out to be. Dalton also spent time defending his work over the last few seasons.

The way that the 1990 season ended—with another Brewers team finishing short of its promise—put Dalton in further trouble with his clubhouse and fanbase. Once again his ability to pull the trigger on a trade was questioned. He would also become associated with two of the biggest financial blunders in Brewers history, both occurring within days of each other.

As for the trades, in the minds of fans and his team, Dalton acquiring the likes of Jeffrey Leonard, Jerry Reuss, and pitcher Don Robinson, whom Dalton got for Glenn Braggs and utility player Billy Bates in June 1990, did not have the same appeal as acquiring players like Vuckovich, Fingers, and Simmons.

Dalton could not make a blockbuster trade that would have transformed his team. That type of trade was probably impossible by then, given how Harry Dalton liked to work a deal. Former Cubs GM Dallas Green characterized dealing with Dalton this way: "He does drive a hard bargain. He thinks his players are special and he puts that kind of thought into deals to the point where he wants to get a little bit extra."[30] Dalton could not accomplish that when he did not have a marquee prospect or a healthy set of stars to move. Even Sheffield was underperforming.

Moreover, Dalton, like many others, felt that his prospects could still work through their immaturity and become professional players in every sense. If that was possible, he did not want to trade talent away. No matter what the issues with his team, Dalton took the blame for the Brewers' underperformance. "I'm responsible for the people on the roster," he said. "If you're going to look at the club and say the club is not good enough, the buck stops here."[31]

Dalton is right, of course, but it must also be said that the clubhouse in Milwaukee during the 1990–91 season was a different situation than anything Dalton had ever faced. It was not a matter of him trading away one malcontent or adding a stabilizing force. In August Don Baylor would openly call some of the players who had stopped working "losers." In September 1990 Baylor gave an even bigger glimpse into the priorities in the clubhouse: "You can put a college [football] or an NFL game on television [in the clubhouse] and the enthusiasm is unbelievable. They know who's hurt and who can't play. But you ask them who is pitching against them [the next day] and they don't know. Get your priorities in line and then maybe you can win a championship."[32]

Given that environment, it would have been easy for Dalton to try and parent his wayward players. No evidence points to that, however. Dalton did not see himself as a father figure for the team. At this point in his career, he did not try to be overly friendly with anyone simply because of the difference in age between him and his clubhouse.[33]

This did not mean that people did not accuse him of overstepping in his role as their boss. In an article published in the *Los Angeles Times* in June 1992, Sheffield claimed that Dalton had his daughters spy on him if they saw him out in Milwaukee at night.[34]

Even after extensive interviewing of Sheffield's teammates, there is no anecdotal evidence to corroborate his assertion. Many of Sheffield's teammates and Brewers front office personnel from that time have said that Sheffield fabricated other events to suit his narrative of how bad Milwaukee got for him.

Reliever Mark Knudson would become a Sheffield target in 2004. In a story by Tom Verducci for *Sports Illustrated*, Sheffield said he fought Knudson sometime in 1990–91.[35] Knudson said the fight never happened.[36] Verducci would go back and ask Sheffield about it, and by then his story had changed.[37]

In another well-worn story, Sheffield claimed to have made errors on purpose during his time in Milwaukee, hoping that he would get traded.[38] Extensive independent research by Tom Verducci, as well as by Jay Jaffe of *FanGraphs*, has shown the story to be untrue.[39] Even Sheffield would walk his comments back after his revelations almost led to an investigation by then-commissioner Fay Vincent.[40] According to Bruce Manno, the only aspect of that story with an element of truth was that Sheffield made an error on purpose in the Minors and was benched for "2–3 games until he apologized to the manager and his teammates" with the Stockton Ports.[41]

Finally, in direct reference to Dalton, Sheffield claimed he was blamed for giving Dalton a heart attack, and the author has confirmed that Dalton never suffered a heart attack. Moreover, given the importance of Harry Dalton in the Milwaukee media market, such an event and Sheffield being blamed for causing it would have been a story too big not to report. However, there are no stories about Dalton being hospitalized for any reason between 1989 and 1991.

Beyond the above examples of Sheffield shaping the narrative around his time in Milwaukee, one last attribute lends credence to the fact that Dalton's daughters never spied on Sheffield. Harry Dalton would never have asked his daughters to engage in such behavior because, at home, he was invested as a parent and looking to shield his girls from any goings-on with the team.

By the winter of 1991, Dalton did not need further information on Sheffield. He knew Sheffield was unhappy.

With all the conflicts in his clubhouse, it would have been easy for Harry Dalton to quit caring about winning. Those who spent time in that front office quickly pointed out that that never happened. Wendy Selig would remember that Dalton was always the first in the office and would announce his presence with big band music.[42] This was augmented by a box or two of sticky buns from a local bakery. Dalton's administrative assistant, Sandy Ronback, said that when she got to the office, Dalton's Dictaphone was full of things for her to transcribe.[43]

Dalton was also often the last to leave, and Ronback said a nap in the afternoon often helped Dalton offset the fact that even in his sixties, Harry Dalton drove himself as hard as he did in his twenties to try and make his team a winner.

The factors keeping Dalton from winning were mounting by 1991. Internal memos show that Dalton was continuously under pressure to cut payroll or keep it manageable.[44] He also began to face more and more input from Bud Selig, which put Dalton in awkward positions vis-à-vis player decisions. In the winter of 1991, the pressure led to one of the worst financial decisions in team history. In addition, Dalton compounded the difficulties when he made a wrong move in free agency, which would be equally debilitating to his team.

Because of another round of arbitration over collusion between the MLBPA and MLB and a stalemate between Major League Baseball and the National Association of Professional Baseball Leagues (the parent organization for Minor League clubs) over a new development contract, the winter meetings scheduled for the fall of 1990 in Los Angeles were canceled, while MLB held its winter gathering in Rosemont, Illinois, in early December.

Before those meetings, Dalton indicated that the Brewers would be looking for pitching help in the hope of offsetting the injuries the staff had suffered since 1988. The team would also be seeking a left-handed power-hitting outfielder to replace the disgruntled Rob Deer, who had departed in the winter of 1990 for Detroit.[45]

Once again, Dalton was true to his word. He would leave the meetings having achieved both of his overall targets. Unfortunately, Dalton would also err on both signings. One was certainly not his fault, while the other was, and it would be held over the head of Dalton as evidence that he had lost his ability to evaluate properly the available talent in the era of big-money free agency.

Dalton's first mistake of the 1990 winter meetings occurred on December 5. In the lead-up to the meetings, Dalton, Dr. Paul Jacobs, who was the Brewers' orthopedic surgeon, and the rest of the Dalton Gang met to discuss whether, given Teddy Higuera's injury problems, the Brewers should even attempt to re-sign him. At that meeting, according to Sky Skibosh, Jacobs made it clear that the Brewers should pass on the lefty because his shoulder was an injury waiting to happen and thus would not be worth the three-year investment the pitcher and his agent sought.[46]

Armed with that information, Dalton was ready to let Higuera go. Bud Selig would overrule Dalton by citing the Brewers' need to keep a star player.[47] The Brewers would offer Higuera a fourth year to get him to stay. The deal would be worth $13 million over four years and was the most lucrative contract in club history.

According to Tom Haudricourt, in the immediate aftermath of the deal he saw Harry Dalton walking across the hotel lobby heading for the press conference to announce the move. Haudricourt mentioned to Dalton that he must be thrilled. At that point, Dalton looked at him and announced that he did not know whether to "laugh or cry."[48]

It turned out that crying was the appropriate response. Higuera would suffer multiple injuries in 1991 and make only seven starts. Left shoulder inflammation led to a tear in his rotator cuff. Higuera would then miss all of 1992 and be ineffective in twenty total starts in 1993–94 (eight in '93 and twelve in '94). Dalton would be made the scapegoat for the signing in the aftermath and beyond without the public ever knowing he had not wanted to commit to the deal.

As for the second decision of the 1990 winter meetings that went south on Dalton and the Brewers, critics of the move called it a gross overestimation of the player the Brewers were getting. In this case, Milwaukee inked outfielder/first baseman Franklin Stubbs of the Houston Astros to a three-year deal worth $6 million. This came on the heels of Stubbs's best offensive year in the big leagues when he hit 23 home runs and batted .271.

In the end, Stubbs would hit 20 homers and drive in 80 in the first two years of his contract combined. He also gained a reputation for not working hard. It is Dalton's worst signing of his career by far when everything is considered. It also highlighted Dalton's most significant challenge when building a team in Milwaukee.

Michael Hamacher of Milwaukee was one of a young group of employees who dotted the baseball office in the last few years of Harry Dalton's tenure in Milwaukee. Others included Judd Schemmel and Scott Martens. Hamacher served as Dalton's "Guy Friday" during most of his time with the team and worked on special projects. He has said that Dalton looked at him one day at lunch and said there were not enough "six-digit successes to make up for a seven-digit mistake."[49]

In the end, Dalton was right. The financial structure of the game changed in the early 1990s and finally caught up with Dalton and the Brewers. In September 1990 Bud Selig acknowledged that Dalton was working from a distinct disadvantage. "Harry Dalton's margin for error because of the market size is unquestionably a factor. . . . We can't throw money around like a drunken sailor," Selig stated.[50] As Dalton would say, the vagaries of working in Milwaukee made it especially important that he not "shoot at false targets."[51]

Unfortunately for Dalton, that is exactly what he did in the case of Stubbs. Like every signing he made, Dalton was not the sole decision-maker, but he would acknowledge that it was his choice. However, to say this came about because he was getting older or did not care is to misunderstand the pitfalls of team building. All GMs have an example of the time they made the wrong choice. In the end, Stubbs was the wrong choice for the Brewers, both statistically and from a makeup standpoint. No matter how Stubbs ended up in Milwaukee, it did not matter. It was another crack in the dam where Harry Dalton had to put his finger. Bud Selig and Jim Gantner would deliver the final blow.

As noted earlier, since the beginning of arbitration in baseball as a means to settle contract disputes, Harry Dalton had not experienced a single hearing. To him, it did not make good sense and was utterly counterproductive to argue with the players. In his view, if you were telling players they were essential, they should be expected to perform as such. That streak of no hearings, guided by Dalton's principle, was still intact in the winter of 1990–91.

That all changed with Jim Gantner. Gantner, the thirteen-year veteran, was on an expiring contract of $700,000 in the winter of 1990 and was eligible for free agency if he and the Brewers could not come to an agreement. What Dalton intended to do with Gantner is unrecorded. However, before the winter of 1990–91, Dalton saw Gantner as the heart and soul of the team because of his tireless work ethic.[52] This belief in Gantner allowed Dalton to maintain a good relationship with the player known as "Gumby" by fans and employees of the Brewers.

That all changed thanks to an edict from Bud Selig. According to Sky Skibosh, in the fall of 1990, as Dalton and his team prepared for the off-season, Selig announced that Dalton would take a player to an arbitration hearing. Hamacher recalled that Dalton knew it was a bad idea and not something Dalton wanted to do. Still, Dalton would never buck an edict of that magnitude from Selig.

In the end, the veteran Gantner was chosen as the test case when he and his agent, Ron Simon, submitted a figure of $2 million for the 1991 season while the Brewers came in at $1 million. Armed with ammunition compiled by Hamacher and PR staffer Jon Greenberg, Dalton and the Brewers confronted Gantner with their case. The result was disastrous for Dalton's morale and that of the Brewers.

Hamacher remembered that Gantner saw his worth to the Brewers in more of an intrinsic way, that is to say, he believed he was a part of the team's core with Robin Yount and Paul Molitor.[53] That is not how the arbitration process works in professional sports. It is a hearing driven by the side with the best statistical basis for its claim. In this case, the Brewers outlined how Gantner had nowhere near the statistical output of those second basemen who would earn a $2 million contract.

More importantly, team research showed that Gantner's performance aligned with the $1 million figure the Brewers proposed. Specifically, Dalton noted that the Brewers had signed veteran second baseman Willie Randolph, who had comparable stats to those compiled by Gantner, to an $875,000 deal as a nonroster invitee for 1991. This caused Gantner to boil over in the hearing, and a rift that Dalton did not have to contend with previously blew wide open. Harry Dalton told Hamacher in the car ride home to Milwaukee from Chicago that the situation distressed Dalton so much he would never sit in another arbitration hearing.

The pressure Selig placed Dalton under from 1989 to 1991 was indicative of a new approach by the owner. Selig put Dalton and those who worked for him in increasingly compromising situations aimed at undercutting the GM. As for what brought about the change, those associated with the team felt that Selig was being swayed behind the scenes. Most importantly, Sky Skibosh and Pete Vuckovich claimed that Sal Bando increasingly influenced Selig. Bando had worked as a special assistant to Dalton since his retirement. During that time, he was seen as a valuable set of eyes for the organization and got along with Dalton and his team of advisors.

However, in the 1990–91 season, Bando began letting Selig know that he could manage the current issues with the team better than Dalton. This included the personal conflicts in the clubhouse and the financial situations that were starting to become more of an aspect of the GM job.

In addition to lending credence to Bando's thoughts on Dalton, Selig began to believe that Dalton should have been replacing some of the Dalton Gang as they aged. Whether Dalton held on too long to members of the gang is hard to say. What is not debatable is that the group was older than their peers in Major League Baseball. Walter Shannon was eighty-four in 1991 and still working, and Walter Youse was seventy-seven and had only just cut back his workload in the winter of 1990. Of course, Dalton continued bringing in younger people to his front office, but the only one with enough experience in Dalton's view was Bruce Manno.

All of these issues made life harder for Harry Dalton. Then the volcano that was Gary Sheffield erupted and buried Dalton in turmoil. Contrary to popular belief, Harry Dalton was not why Gary Sheffield finally forced his way out of Milwaukee. What Dalton did was his job. He wanted to build his roster how he saw fit, as did Tom Trebelhorn. Sheffield, who felt that he had the same star leverage as Dwight Gooden or other high-profile veterans, seemed to think that he carried enough weight to have input into decisions Dalton made. When Dalton pushed back against that notion, Sheffield took every chance he could to undermine Dalton and disparage him in public. The most famous instance of public comments occurred right before the end of spring training in 1991.

The catalyst for this development was Dalton trading Dave Parker at the behest of the owners. Sheffield saw Parker as an ally in a tenuous environment where most of his teammates did not like him. Thus, when Parker was sent to California in a cost-saving measure triggered by the financial measures put in place by Selig, Sheffield saw it as Dalton "breaking his heart."[54] This caused him to tell reporters that Dalton was ruining the team.[55] After Sheffield left Milwaukee, he would even say, "I hated [Dalton] so much that I wanted to hurt the man."[56]

As he did with Sheffield's earlier tirades, Dalton took the high road and refused to comment on any aspect of the situation. Once again, Dalton did not want to put his team in a bad light. This was also the case when Selig went around Dalton and tried to mend fences later that spring by inviting Sheffield's parents to Milwaukee for a conference. The summit was another move Selig made unilaterally and showed Dalton and those who worked for him that Selig did not trust Dalton. Through all this, Dalton would remain quiet.

As for how it affected him, anecdotes from players, the media, and Dalton's staff provide the best insight. Mark Knudson, now a media personality in Colorado, said Dalton seemed like a wounded man because all he had ever tried to do was make Sheffield as comfortable as possible.

"We [the players] didn't understand what Gary was complaining about," Knudson said. "When we looked at it, it seemed like the organization was giving Gary everything."[57] According to Knudson, this had the effect of demoralizing Dalton.

While Dalton was fending off attacks from Sheffield and others in his clubhouse, his team would steadily get worse on the field. They would start 10-9 in April and go 12-15 in May and June. The stretch at the end of June would have Dalton saying that not everyone on the roster gave 100 percent.[58] As frustrated as he was becoming, Dalton still appreciated outstanding effort even as his team struggled. This is best encapsulated by his interaction with Don August.

August, a 6-foot-1-inch righty, came to Milwaukee with Mark Knudson for pitcher Danny Darwin. He would make the big league roster in 1988 and go 13-7 with a 3.09 ERA. From there, he would go 12-12 in 1989. August then had a reversal of fortune in 1990 when he spent most of the year at Triple-A. However, he was back in Milwaukee in 1991. It was during this stint that August would endear himself to Harry Dalton.

On May 1, August would enter a game against the White Sox at County Stadium in the fifteenth inning. As August related it, he was the last true pitcher Milwaukee had, and Gary Sheffield was the next man out of the bullpen if the game went any longer. With that in mind, August threw five innings in relief and won the game in the nineteenth inning when Willie Randolph knocked in Jim Gantner.

After the game, the man affectionately known as "Auggie" said Harry Dalton did something he never forgot.

"Harry comes over to my locker and thanks me for pitching like I did," August said. "He says he wants me to take my wife out the next time we are back in Milwaukee (the Brewers were getting ready to leave on a road trip) and he wants me to bring him the bill. He says the club will reimburse me. I thank him and then we go on the road. A few weeks go by and I don't really think Harry is serious. One day he comes to me and asks where the receipt is for the dinner. I tell him we hadn't gone and not to worry about it. He tells me to go. So we go out and we have a great meal and order wine and everything and it was expensive. The next day I go and I leave the receipt with his secretary. After the game that night he comes down to the clubhouse and writes me a check out of his personal checkbook. I never forgot what he did."[59]

Despite efforts like August's, it was this stretch in June that Trebelhorn felt decided the fate of himself and Dalton. "Sal Bando and Mr. Selig along with some others started planning a shakeup that would include Harry and myself," Trebelhorn said. "We had some interesting players at AAA (Listach/Eldred/Henry) that appeared to be ready to help us out[,] but they were not quite ready although we did get Doug Henry, who helped out significantly down the stretch. We were kind of on our own."[60]

The subpar June was followed by a 9-18 July. By August 6 the Brewers had fallen to fifteen and a half games out of first at 45-61. From that moment on, the Brewers gelled, and they played their best baseball of the season. They would finish the season on a tear and end the year at 83-79. Despite the strong finish, the writing was on the wall for Dalton.

Trebelhorn remembered that Bando and Selig were not around the club while the late-season push was underway. Trebelhorn believed this made it easier when the ax was readied for Dalton when the season ended. There is evidence that Dalton knew this to be the case. Michael Hamacher remembered that Dalton began preparing his younger staff for the day they would be fired.[61] Before that happened, however, the Dalton Gang had one last laugh.

In a twist of fate, the Brewers ended the 1991 season in Boston. It would be a fitting send-off for one of their biggest fans. Dalton would see his team go 3-0 with wins by Cal Eldred (in his Major League debut), Mike Ignasiak, and Julio Machado. He would even have some unexpected company.

Knowing this was likely to be his last series as GM, Cindy, Kim, and Debbie made their way to Boston to see their parents. They planned to surprise him, and all was going well until they asked for Dalton's room number. Respecting the privacy of their guests, the front desk refused to give the girls their parents' room number. It finally took a call to Jimmy Bank to clear the situation up.

Once the Brewers returned to Milwaukee, the day Dalton anticipated finally arrived. He was let go from his GM duties on October 8, 1991. At the press conference, Dalton would tell the assembled reporters that he was disappointed but not bitter about the end of his time as the GM.

As for why Selig decided that Dalton needed to go, he was evasive in his reasoning. Even in retirement, Dalton said that Selig never gave him a reason. The decisive factors behind Dalton's dismissal are still unknown to Dalton's family and his bevy of supporters. Even now, all Selig will say is that he felt it was time to make a change.

Whatever Selig's reasoning, Dalton was pragmatic about the situation. As he would tell Pat, his daughters, or anyone who wanted to know, Selig "was the owner, he paid me well, and he could do what he wanted."[62] Even with that classic Dalton logic, others did not understand the move or how their friend and colleague stayed so even-keeled about the matter. In countless letters, people like PR professional Jerry Sachs, office staffer Bill Zito, and football executive Ernie Accorsi told Dalton they could not understand why he was suddenly out.[63] What made the situation much worse was that, on paper, it looked as if Dalton had received a promotion.

Sky Skibosh recalled that the day Dalton was to be told he was being let go, Selig, Dalton, CFO Dick Hackett, and Skibosh met to have a final discussion. At that time, Selig gave Dalton the option to either retire with a club-issued buyout of the three remaining years on his contract or continue to work for the club. No one expected Dalton to keep working. However, when some debate arose over the buyout amount, Dalton shocked everyone in the room by staying on. As such, although Dalton would no longer be the GM, he would be listed on the books as a senior vice president.

The truth was Dalton had no more responsibilities. The press conference was the first in a long line of days that would anger people who knew Dalton and understood what Selig was doing to him. He would become a man in exile until the day he retired. Through it all, Dalton would maintain an upbeat attitude and even manage to make the game better one last time. From there, he would become a retired statesman of the sport who lived a quiet life away from baseball in a land he cared about with people who loved him. All too quickly, though, life would become a living nightmare for Dalton and ultimately rob baseball and the world of a great man.

20

Exile, Carefree Days, and Living Nightmares

1992–2005

From the minute Harry Dalton stopped being the GM of the Milwaukee Brewers, his relationship with the man who considered Dalton the main reason his team became a winner changed forever. From 1992 until Dalton retired in 1994, Bud Selig was cold, distant, and, some would say, mean to Harry Dalton. It was an inglorious end to a great career, and countless people who know the full extent of the situation believe that what Selig did to a man to whom he owed so much was wrong.[1]

Still, Dalton would make the most of his time and pass on his memories of baseball to others. He would then retire as quietly as he began his career and rejuvenate himself in the American West, which he came to love, with his family and friends around him. That was until he was struck down by a horrendous disease that would rob him of his mobility but not his mind, dignity, or love for others.

Much like when he fired his GM, Bud Selig would never say why he treated Harry Dalton so poorly during the last three years of his career. Chances are, Harry Dalton would have said the reasons did not matter and that the owner could do what he wanted. This is exactly what Selig did, and the memory still hurts those who learned to love working for Dalton.

Dalton would work the rest of his days in a cramped space (described as a closet) in a section of County Stadium once dedicated to the Milwaukee Braves' clubhouse. He shared the space with junior PR professional Mario Ziino. Most days, Ziino said, Dalton had no real work of his own. Still, he came to work every day. As Tom Haudricourt reported in 1994, Selig hardly acknowledged Dalton's presence when they saw each other.[2]

That treatment lasted for three years. At that time, the Brewers would have one last winning team of players drafted by the Dalton Gang. The organization would then begin a slow decline, during which Selig would transfer ownership of the team to his daughter Wendy as he transitioned into his new role as commissioner of baseball. Throughout the ensuing period, the farm system and the roster that Dalton and his colleagues had constructed from virtually nothing disintegrated.

While what he built fell down around him and his work relationship with a man he considered close degraded almost as fast, Dalton continued to be loyal to baseball. He would speak to college coaches; he looked to see how best to support the next generation of scouts; he helped the Brewers sell tickets by setting up meetings for Tim Trovato with the head of corporations like Briggs & Stratton. Most important, he helped expand the footprint of Major League Baseball.

From 1992 to 1994 Dalton would make periodic trips, at the behest of Selig, in search of two new cities for the league. The reports Dalton filed from Orlando, Phoenix, Tampa/St. Petersburg, and Charlotte are colored by his inquisitive nature, his understanding of baseball, and his ability to convey information in a clear and concise format. His city scouting work surveyed every central question, from weather, existing facilities, and size of the market to major employers, media footprint, and thirst for baseball. In addition, Dalton helped Selig and the expansion group consider things as mundane as how traffic patterns would affect the ability of a team to draw fans.

In the end, Dalton was very impressed with Charlotte and Phoenix and would help the latter transition to a big league city by serving on the board of advisors to the Triple-A Phoenix Firebirds, run by Robin Yount's brother (and agent), Larry Yount. Dalton undertook this role with the understanding that he and others would help the city prepare itself for Major League Baseball if the league decided to expand.[3] It is not a stretch to say that baseball expanded in the late 1990s because of his efforts.

When Dalton was not on the road, he was telling stories. Mario Ziino recalled that in the days and years after losing the GM position, Dalton became talkative about his days in the game and life in general. When he was away from the stadium, Dalton would duck hunt and fish, and he and Pat would design their dream home in Arizona, where they planned to retire surrounded by their growing extended family.

Never once did Dalton let it be known that he had regrets about his career. One exception, as Dan Duquette said, was that Dalton let slip that he, like so many other children of New England, wished he could have run the Red Sox. Still, Dalton would bask in the light of the fact that Duquette and Lou Gorman, two men he trained, got that very opportunity.[4]

As he sat on the cusp of retirement, he was even asked to run one more team. In 1994, shortly before he left the game for good, the Chicago Cubs asked Dalton to take over as their president and CEO in an effort to end an almost fifty-year drought between World Series appearances. Dalton politely declined, and the Cubs would give Lee MacPhail's son Andy the job.[5] Dalton did not want the spotlight. He also thought the game of baseball was changing too much for his tastes. To him, the best thing he could do was follow his own advice and leave the game while he still enjoyed it. It got to the heart of his belief that one should leave while the party's good. He did it his whole career, and when he retired it was no different. He left Baltimore on top and California when his team was getting better but his voice was on the verge of being marginalized. With Milwaukee, Dalton, despite his being phased out as GM, was still widely regarded in the game, and he was okay with leaving.

Mario Ziino would occasionally see Dalton during spring training once Dalton became a full-time Arizona resident. "Harry would never make a fuss," Ziino said. Dalton would sit and watch the game, maybe say hello to a few people, and then slip away unnoticed.[6] Dalton never truly became impressed with being "Harry Dalton, Baseball Executive," and he was comfortable in his own skin.

Dalton would take that demeanor with him everywhere in retirement. There were trips with Pat, nights with neighbors on their balcony off the "Carefree Highway" (of Gordon Lightfoot fame) in Arizona, gaining weight on Ding Dongs, walks to the Dairy Queen, and homemade brownies prepared by a granddaughter whose given name was Dalton. Harry Dalton would genuinely enjoy being a grandfather and even take time to instruct his grandson Tripp in the finer points of T-ball.[7]

He also understood the pull of his celebrity, though he did not bask in it or call attention to himself. In this way, Dalton could lend his fund-raising talents to the Desert Foothills Land Trust. Today you can walk the Harry I. Dalton Trail as part of the Jewel of the Creek Nature Preserve in Cave Creek.

Amid all this work, his old occupation would occasionally come calling. The Baltimore Orioles inducted Dalton into their Hall of Fame in 1995. He would be on hand as the club showed off their new "old" stadium in the Camden Yards area of the Inner Harbor. Dalton would also attend Earl Weaver's induction in Cooperstown. The Brewers would induct Dalton into their Walk of Fame in 2003.

Many people did not know that as he adjusted to retired life, Dalton's body would begin to betray him. Andy Etchebarren recalled seeing Dalton in Florida and noticing his former boss walking with a slight shuffle.[8] The same altered stride can be seen in the video of Dalton's Orioles Hall of Fame induction speech in Baltimore. What that shuffle betrayed was that Dalton was in the early stages of Lewy body dementia (LBD).

This condition is a common yet underdiagnosed form of dementia in which proteins build up in the brain and cause both physical and cognitive impairment.[9] Physically, Dalton developed the rigidity of movement most associated with Parkinson's disease, which would lead to a common misdiagnosis of Parkinson's. In addition, he would begin to suffer from violent living nightmares, among other symptoms. Soon, the progression of the disease meant that he would require constant care from social companions and medical staff.[10]

Even during this time, however, Dalton continued to impact the lives of those around him by providing lasting final memories. His sister-in-law Winki remembered the last time she saw him. It was a struggle for Dalton to move at that point, but he would make one of his final trips to his elevated deck at the house in Carefree, Arizona. As she recalled, "He stood up and looked at me as I was walking up the driveway and just said, 'I love you, Winkipoo.'"[11] It is one of her favorite and saddest memories of a man she loved dearly.

Dalton's grace in illness also influenced those who had had no contact with him previously. He would make friends with an unlikely caregiver named Kerry Wood (unrelated to the big league pitcher), who shared countless adventures with Dalton until he passed away. Included in this was meeting Wood's son Brandon, a highly rated Major League prospect at the time. Wood remembered that Dalton balked at meeting his son initially: "Harry told me he didn't want to meet another ballplayer. I looked at him and said, 'Harry, I'm not bringing him to meet you. I want you to meet him.'" Dalton laughed and set up a visit.[12]

No matter how many good days he had, LBD would eventually catch up with Harry Dalton. Still, he would make the best of the situation when he could, like the day Bobby Grich, Don Baylor, and Joe Rudi visited him at his daughter Kim's house. Kim recalled that it was one of her father's last good days. He would smile to the degree he could, and the four men would laugh over stories from days gone by.[13]

It should be no surprise that baseball played a role in Dalton's life even as he approached his death. He had given his life to the game and was still a fan even though the game had become something that was not fun for him anymore. What was fun was seeing the favorite team from his boyhood finally win a World Series after eighty-six years of frustration. Debbie remembered that the last Series her dad ever watched before he became too ill to follow the game anymore was in 2004, when the Boston Red Sox finally took home a title.

Harry Dalton would pass away the following October. As could be imagined, it was a time of great sadness for the people in his life. Still, even in death, Dalton would comfort the people in his life, as his memories provided a way for people to laugh and smile and see the positives in their life through their relationship with him. This included his longtime boss Bud Selig. Dalton's celebration of life event even gave his friends and family one last opportunity to hear "Take Me Out to the Ballgame" as they exited the service. One last time, Harry Dalton made sure that everyone who knew and cared about him got to "leave while the party's good."

Epilogue

LEGACY

When I sat down to research this book, I wanted to tell the story of a man's life and how he fit into the larger world around him on a personal and professional level. I then wanted to project what kind of legacy he left in those worlds. The preceding pages have, I hope, achieved the first two goals. It is now time to end with a consideration of the third and final piece of my work.

In terms of a personal legacy, there should be no question that Harry Dalton was a man of integrity, wisdom, intelligence, and humility. This does not mean he was infallible. He was often the first person to acknowledge the mistakes he made. Still, he strove to minimize his faults as they pertained to his interactions with others and was always the first to admit when he failed. Even with his wife and children, he never claimed to be perfect. By being this way, he truly allowed those around him to be themselves, whether they worked for him, knew him socially, or were his family.

Of course, his professional life was informed by his personal traits. In addition, as a baseball executive, he was intelligent, shrewd, stern, charitable, charismatic, and funny. All of these things led him to be a once-in-a-lifetime talent.

How good was that talent? Well, statistically, Dalton won. A lot. Most important to some was that he won on the biggest stages. His teams took home five American League pennants and two World Series titles. He would also finish with a winning record overall for his career.

Harry Dalton was much more than his statistics, however. Despite him being out of the game for almost thirty years, there are still people working in the game who learned their baseball from Harry Dalton. His lessons live on every day in the minds of Dan Duquette, Bruce Manno, and John Schuerholz. In turn, the things that Dalton taught them live on in the minds of those they taught and so on down the line. In this way, Harry Dalton's impact on the game and business of baseball will carry on for another half century, if not more.

Finally, Dalton's legacy lives on in the deeds of the great players he put together and the ideas he used to move the game forward. Whenever a highlight reel of Brooks Robinson and Frank Robinson, Nolan Ryan, Don Baylor, Robin Yount, or even Gary Sheffield is shown, it's good to remember that those highlights were made possible partly by Harry Dalton and the men he empowered. As for ideas, baseball would not be where it is today without the contributions of Harry Dalton. He took on every major issue of his day and improved the game. Every step he took got the game to where it is now.

In the minds of many Dalton knew, all these contributions lead to one thing: Harry Dalton must be enshrined in the Baseball Hall of Fame and Museum. To be sure, this is not an honor he would have considered for himself. He would likely also have seen others petitioning on his behalf as pursuing the errand of fools. Neither of those things detracts from the validity of the statement.

The Baseball Hall of Fame is where the most excellent, well-rounded players and executives are supposed to reside. That does not mean they are perfect in every way, and some parts of their game shine brighter than other parts. Nevertheless, they are Hall of Famers because they were excellent for long periods, excelled in multiple areas, and excited those around them with their passion for the game. By that definition, Harry Dalton deserves to be in Cooperstown.

The call for Dalton's inclusion is more than the hyperbole of an oversaturated author. It is the opinion of men like Bud Selig, Peter Gammons, Ted Simmons, Dan Duquette, and countless others. Harry Dalton proved that the best decisions are made by a group of informed advisors. With that in mind, it is time to listen to them and invite Harry Dalton to the best party in baseball.

Notes

1. AN ALL-AMERICAN SON

1. Bruno Ramirez, "Canada in the United States: Perspectives on Migration and Continental History," *Journal of American Ethnic History* 20, no. 3 (2001): 59.
2. Ramirez, "Canada in the United States," 59.
3. Information on James Dalton and family can be found in "1881 Canadian Census," Ancestry.com Operations, accessed May 26, 2018, https://search.ancestry.com/cgi-bin/sse.dll?indiv=try&db=1881Canada&h=1854894.
4. For information on the Harry H. Dalton family, see "1901 Canadian Census," Ancestry.com Operations, accessed 2018, https://search.ancestry.com/cgi-bin/sse.dll?db=1901canada&h=10099519&indiv=try&o_vc=Record:OtherRecord&rhSource=1577.
5. For information on Thomas and Hattie O'Malley prior to the birth of their children, see Government of Canada, "1881 Canadian Census" and "Marriages for the Year 1892," Ancestry.com Operations, accessed May 26, 2018.
6. The early details of Hattie and Thomas O'Malley's family can be pieced together using "1900 Federal Census," Ancestry.com Operations, accessed 2018, https://search.ancestry.com/cgi-bin/sse.dll?indiv=try&db=1900usfedcen&h=2847634.
7. The death records of Roy and Catherine O'Malley can be found in "Massachusetts Death Records for 1899," Ancestry.com Operations, accessed May 26, 2018.
8. Edna O'Malley's birth information is available from "Birth Records for 1902," Ancestry.com Operations, accessed May 26, 2018.
9. Details of Jack and Edna's lives prior to their immigration to the United States came from their obituaries that appeared in the *Baltimore Sun* following their deaths (Jack passed away in November 1964 in Towson, Maryland, and Edna passed away in August 1979 in California). Speculation on when Jack and Edna met comes from my email correspondence with Pat Dalton.
10. The Daltons' early life in the United States was pieced together using myriad sources, including "Records of Aliens Pre-Examined in Canada," Ancestry.com Operations, 1925, accessed May 26, 2018, https://search.ancestry.com

/cgi-bin/sse.dll?indiv=1&dbid=2055&h=949024&tid=&pid=&usePUB=true&_phsrc=WrA209&_phstart=successSource; "Declaration of Intention for Arthur J. Dalton," Ancestry.com Operations, 1942, accessed May 26, 2018, https://search.ancestry.com/cgi-bin/sse.dll?db=MANaturalizations&h=1033942&indiv=try&o_vc=Record:OtherRecord&rhSource=61084; and "Orlando City Directory for 1926," Ancestry.com Operations, accessed May 26, 2018.

11. The marriage records for the Dalton brothers and their wives can be found at "Florida County Marriage Records for 1926," Ancestry.com Operations, accessed May 26, 2018.
12. "Orlando City Directory for 1928," Ancestry.com Operations, accessed May 26, 2018.
13. Information on West Springfield can be found in Massachusetts Historical Commission, *MHC Reconnaissance Survey Town Report: West Springfield* (Boston: Commonwealth of Massachusetts, 1982).
14. This population figure was originally conveyed in the 1930 federal census and was found in "West Springfield Massachusetts," Wikipedia, accessed May 26, 2018, https://en.wikipedia.org/wiki/West_Springfield,_Massachusetts.
15. "1930 United States Federal Census," Ancestry.com Operations, accessed May 26, 2018.
16. "106 at Junior High Attain Honors List," *Springfield (MA) Daily Republican*, June 25, 1941, 4.
17. Dalton's junior and senior years in high school were recapped using the West Springfield High School yearbook, *The Terrier*, for 1945 and 1946.
18. West Springfield High School yearbook, *The Terrier* (1946).
19. "Excursion" as printed in West Springfield High School yearbook, *The Terrier* (1946).
20. West Springfield High School yearbook, *The Terrier* (1946).
21. West Springfield High School yearbook, *The Terrier* (1946).
22. Pat Dalton, interview by author about Harry Dalton's teenage years, 2018.
23. Academics have extensively covered the "New Curriculum" at Amherst College. The best overall view of the nature of this change can be found at Amherst College, "The New Curriculum: Toward an Oral History," YouTube.com, June 3, 2016, https://www.youtube.com/watch?v=adLewmNH9J0.
24. "Amherst College Timeline," accessed September 23, 2023, https://www.amherst.edu/about/history/bicentennial/amherst-college-timeline.
25. "Amherst College Timeline."
26. Amherst maintains a War Materials Collection in its archive. See also Sarah Walden McGowan, "The Introduction of World War II to Amherst College,"

March 7, 2019, https://digitalcollections.wordpress.amherst.edu/2019/03/07/the-introduction-of-world-war-ii-to-amherst-college.

27. Of the two, Frost is the most well known in a popular sense. In and around his career at Amherst he became poet laureate of the United States, and his crowning achievement was reading "The Road Less Traveled" at the presidential inauguration of John F. Kennedy in January 1961. On the other hand, Baird is renowned among scholars of the teaching of English. The innovations that he brought to Amherst are chronicled in Robin Varnum, *Fencing with Words: A History of Writing Instruction at Amherst College during the Era of Theodore Baird, 1938–1966* (Urbana IL: National Council of Teachers of English, 1996).
28. Course requirements for the Amherst class of 1950 can be found in Amherst College, *Amherst College Bulletin 1946/1947* (1946).
29. Harry Dalton's extracurriculars were pieced together using the Amherst College yearbook, *Olio* (1950).
30. Dayle Jones, interview by author about Harry Dalton in college, 2018.
31. The friendship between Nesbitt, Galbreath, and Dalton was described to the author in the Jones interview. Background on the Galbreath family can be found at "John Galbreath, 90, a Sportsman and Real Estate Developer, Dies," *New York Times*, July 21, 1988, https://www.nytimes.com/1988/07/21/obituaries/john-galbreath-90-a-sportsman-and-real-estate-developer-dies.html.
32. "To Confer Seven Honorary Degrees at Amherst Sunday," *Holyoke (MA) Transcript-Telegram*, June 9, 1950, 15, https://www.newspapers.com/image/837972394/?terms=%22Amherst%20College%22%20and%20%22confer%22&match=1.
33. Harry Dalton, "Third Round of City Golf Tournament Today," *Springfield (MA) Sunday Republican*, July 9, 1950, 27.
34. Harry Dalton, "Cornell Grid Coach Foresees Four-Way Battle for Ivy League Honors," *Springfield (MA) Sunday Republican*, July 16, 1950, 8B.
35. Harry Dalton, "Amherst Gridders Open Practice September 4," *Springfield (MA) Sunday Republican*, August 20, 1950, 4B.
36. Harry Dalton, "Colorful Midget Derby at Forest Park Today," *Springfield (MA) Sunday Republican*, September 10, 1950, 3B.
37. For a comprehensive study of the fighting in Korea and the situation leading to the war, see Clay Blair, *The Forgotten War: America in Korea, 1950–1953* (Annapolis: Naval Institute Press, 2003).
38. For a discussion on the rise of the U.S. Air Force in the public mind, see Jeffrey G. Barlow, *The Revolt of the Admirals: The Fight for Naval Aviation: 1945–1950* (Washington DC: Naval Historical Center, 1994). The historiography of the air force in the Korean War is expansive, and every other branch

of the service has also left a historical record. A good starting point for a new reader is Richard P. Hallion, ed., *Silver Wings, Golden Valor: The USAF Remembers Korea* (Washington DC: Air Force History and Museums Program, 2006).

39. "SDF History," Louisville Muhammad Ali International Airport, accessed September 6, 2023, https://www.flylouisville.com/corporate/sdf-history/.
40. The details of Dalton's air force career prior to going to Korea are pieced together from "Dalton to Join Eastern AF," *Springfield (MA) Daily Republican*, July 27, 1952, 15.
41. "Dalton Is Top Honor Graduate," *Springfield (MA) Union*, February 24, 1951, 28.
42. "Dayle Fort to Wed Lt. Nesbitt," *Springfield (MA) Union*, May 30, 1952, 7.
43. For a further discussion of the GOC, see Bruce D. Callander, "Ground Observer Corps," *Air Force Magazine*, February 2006, http://www.airforcemag.com/MagazineArchive/Pages/2006/February%202006/0206goc.aspx.
44. "Dalton to Join Eastern AF," 15.
45. Dalton's decorations were confirmed with his family and the U.S. Air Force in the spring of 2018. The Bronze Star is routinely referenced in various articles that appeared throughout Dalton's career in baseball as well as his obituary and personal correspondence from that time.

2. PRESENT AT THE CREATION

1. The advertisement announcing Jack Dalton's arrival and credentials can be found in a Bacharach's advertisement, *Baltimore Sun*, November 12, 1950, 37.
2. John Eisenberg, *From 33rd Street to Camden Yards: An Oral History of the Baltimore Orioles* (New York: McGraw-Hill, 2001), 10.
3. Bill DeWitt's comments can be found in James Edward Miller, *The Baseball Business: Pursuing Pennants and Profits in Baltimore* (Chapel Hill: University of North Carolina Press, 1991), 23.
4. The reasons for not allowing the Browns to move to LA are best articulated in J. E. Miller, *Baseball Business*.
5. Because of his penchant for showmanship, there are many takes on the life and times of Bill Veeck. Most of them are supplied by Veeck himself. The most well-rounded account, however, is Paul Dickson, *Bill Veeck: Baseball's Greatest Maverick* (New York: Walker & Company, 2012).
6. Historiography of the Milwaukee Braves is expanding. The most complete book on the rise and fall of the Milwaukee Braves is Bob Buege, *The Milwaukee Braves: A Baseball Eulogy* (N.p.: Douglas American Sports Publications, 1988). The best source on the move from Boston is the documentary

film directed by William Povletich, *A Braves New World* (Milwaukee Public Television, 2009). More recently, Patrick Steele has outlined why the Braves left Milwaukee in his book *Home of the Braves: The Battle for Baseball in Milwaukee* (Madison: University of Wisconsin Press, 2018).

7. J. E. Miller, *Baseball Business*, 26–27.
8. The best recap of the work done to get the Browns to Baltimore is in Eisenberg, *From 33rd Street to Camden Yards*, 5–7.
9. For information on the early days of the Baltimore Orioles, see an interview with Harry Dalton in Eisenberg, *From 33rd Street to Camden Yards*, 10.
10. Eisenberg, *From 33rd Street to Camden Yards*, 10.
11. Eisenberg, *From 33rd Street to Camden Yards*, 11.
12. McLaughlin would eventually develop a chart of both the tools that could be seen and those that could not; he called this concept "The Whole Ballplayer." It is replicated in Kevin Kerrane, *Dollar Sign on the Muscle: The World of Baseball Scouting* (N.p.: CreateSpace, 2013).
13. Characteristics of life in Thomasville can be found in Eisenberg, *From 33rd Street to Camden Yards*, 71–76, with Jim Palmer's recollections at 72, 74.
14. Eisenberg, *From 33rd Street to Camden Yards*, 72.
15. For a recap of the technological innovations Enos tried, see "Orioles Try Push Button Baseball," *Thomasville (GA) Times Enterprise*, March 19, 1954.
16. "Orioles Try Push Button Baseball."
17. Dalton's remembrances of the Bird's Nest can be found in Eisenberg, *From 33rd Street to Camden Yards*, 74–75.
18. Period evidence of Dalton's Thomasville dating life can be found in his personal papers along with a very tongue-in-cheek "press release" about his successful attempts to date Claire Varnedoe, found in folder 1, box 2, Harry Dalton Papers, Giamatti Research Center, National Baseball Hall of Fame and Museum, Cooperstown NY (hereafter Dalton Papers). The author also conducted various phone interviews in the spring of 2019 with Claire Varnedoe-Thomas, who still lives in Thomasville. Her recollections are that Dalton dated a friend of hers and was also a very good friend of her own.
19. Dalton's comments on an average trip on the road can be found in a letter to his parents dated September 16, 1954, in folder 1, box 2, Dalton Papers.
20. "Waxahachians Pay Tribute to Paul," *Daily Light* (Waxahachie TX), September 16, 1954.
21. The best description of that first meeting can be found in Kerrane, *Dollar Sign on the Muscle*.

3. COMPETING PHILOSOPHIES

1. The four players were Matt Batts, Don Ferrarese, Don Johnson, and Fred Marsh. All were journeymen. Only Don Ferrarese spent more than one

season with the team, and Matt Batts did not play a single game with the Orioles.

2. John Eisenberg, "'Reckless' Richards Cracks Open O's Coffers," *Baltimore Sun*, October 29, 2003, C1.
3. Dalton's comments come from Eisenberg, *From 33rd Street to Camden Yards*, 47. Claude "Dutch" Dietrich was a longtime scout and had known Richards since he scouted him as a youngster in the 1930s. Information on Dietrich came from Warren Corbett in a discussion with the author.
4. Bob Maisel, "Orioles Sign Two Rookies," *Baltimore Sun*, February 3, 1955, 21.
5. Recap of the 1955 season was put together using the season timeline provided at "1955 Baltimore Orioles," Baseball Reference, accessed August 24, 2019, https://www.baseball-reference.com/teams/BAL/1955.shtml.
6. Bob Maisel, "Confidence Vote Given Richards," *Baltimore Sun*, September 27, 1955, 21.
7. J. E. Miller, *Baseball Business*, 48.
8. J. E. Miller, *Baseball Business*.
9. There is a small discrepancy with the number of teams in the Orioles' farm system during 1954. James Edward Miller indicates in *Baseball Business* that the Orioles had a thirteen-team system. However, the 1954 media guide lists twelve teams. Because the media guide is an official team document, twelve is the number used here. (The Orioles' media guides were digitized in 2014 for the team's fiftieth anniversary; see Major League Baseball, https://www.mlb.com/orioles/history/media-guides.)
10. McLaughlin's comments were made at a press conference held in connection with the off-season meetings of the Orioles' Minor League clubs in Baltimore in November 1954. Those comments appear in James Ellis, "Orioles to Trim Farm System to Seven Clubs," *Evening Sun* (Baltimore), November 29, 1954, 29.
11. Hoffman's trip is described in Hugh Trader, "Orioles European Bird Dog Flushes Couple of GI Chicks," *The Sporting News* (St. Louis), November 3, 1954, 20.
12. For Rex Greaves's work in Germany, see "Sandlot on the Rhine" in the "Events and Discoveries" column, *Sports Illustrated*, February 20, 1956.
13. O'Connor's November 1957 note to Dalton can be found in folder 1, box 2, Dalton Papers.
14. Hamper quoted in Eisenberg, *From 33rd Street to Camden Yards*, 69.
15. Tasby would make his Major League debut at the end of 1958. Dalton's comment about him is from Bob Maisel, "Willie Tasby Called Best," *Baltimore Sun*, August 21, 1958, 18.
16. Maisel, "Willie Tasby Called Best," 18.

17. Pat Booker's life at Goucher was pieced together using the Goucher College yearbook, *Donnybrook Fair* (1958).
18. Pat Dalton relayed highlights of her courtship with Harry Dalton in a letter to the author, March 2023.
19. The best recap of the Orioles' overtures to Lee MacPhail, his thoughts on staying in New York, and his ultimate decision to move to Baltimore can be found in Lee MacPhail, *My 9 Innings: An Autobiography of 50 Years in Baseball* (Westport CT: Meckler Books, 1989), 59–60.
20. Eisenberg, *From 33rd Street to Camden Yards*, 67.
21. The best synopsis of Bob Brown's early life is found in John Steadman, "Brown: Peerless among PR Men, Pride of O's," *Baltimore Sun*, April 30, 2000, 4E.
22. Larry Desautels, "Nicholson Unloads Big Bat after Being Sent to Class C," *The Sporting News*, May 20, 1959.
23. Dalton's temporary promotion and his fall schedule were pieced together using two separate articles that appeared in the "Bird Seed" section about the Orioles in *The Sporting News*, July 15, 1959, and October 14, 1959.
24. Wedding details from Pat Dalton, email to author, November 19, 2019.
25. Eisenberg, *From 33rd Street to Camden Yards*, 70.
26. Lou Hatter, "Jim McLaughlin Quits as Orioles' Farm Director: Assistant Dalton Is Successor," *Baltimore Sun*, January 12, 1961, 17.
27. The public understanding of the situation with the Orioles' front office is best summed up in Hatter, "Jim McLaughlin Quits as Orioles' Farm Director," 17.
28. "Dave McNally Strikes Out 27," *Billings (MT) Gazette*, July 3, 1960, 11.
29. The best source on McNally's life, including his American Legion experience, is Mark Armour, "Dave McNally," in *Pitching, Defense, and Three-Run Homers: The 1970 Baltimore Orioles*, ed. Mark Armour and Malcolm Allen (Lincoln: University of Nebraska Press, 2012). For McNally's recollections of the Orioles' pursuit of him, see Eisenberg, *From 33rd Street to Camden Yards*, 133–34.
30. Dalton's comments on McLaughlin's firing are in Eisenberg, *From 33rd Street to Camden Yards*, 70.
31. For a recap of Dalton's pedigree at the time of his hiring, see Hatter, "Jim McLaughlin Quits as Orioles' Farm Director," 17.

4. THE WORLD OF HARRY DALTON

1. Dalton's comments on Orioles farm policy come from Hatter, "Jim McLaughlin Quits as Orioles' Farm Director," 17.
2. Dalton's views on the importance of the scouting department can be found in an internal budget memo for 1961 in folder 7-1, box 7, Dalton Papers.

3. Bob Maisel, "The Morning After," *Baltimore Sun*, March 5, 1961, 2D.
4. The scouting department of the Orioles is outlined in the Baltimore Orioles' media guide for 1961.
5. Dalton's appraisal of his scouting staff can be found in Maisel, "Morning After," March 5, 1961, 2D.
6. Dalton's comments on the core members of his scouting department are from Eisenberg, *From 33rd Street to Camden Yards*, 133.
7. Bill Tanton, "Dalton Listens to People and That's Why He Is Where He Is Today," *Evening Sun* (Baltimore), January 13, 1989, 2B.
8. Tanton, "Dalton Listens to People," 2B.
9. Bob Maisel, "The Morning After," *Baltimore Sun*, June 26, 1961, 15.
10. Jerry Sachs, interview by author about working with Harry Dalton, December 28, 2017.
11. Eisenberg, *From 33rd Street to Camden Yards*, 133.
12. Russo's negative views about Harry Dalton are laid out in Jimmy Russo and Bob Hammel, *Super Scout: Thirty-Five Years of Major League Scouting* (Chicago: Bonus Books, 1992), 89.
13. Eisenberg, *From 33rd Street to Camden Yards*, 133.
14. The best recap of the scouting reshuffle following Richards's departure can be found in John Steadman, "Top Sleuths Stock Orioles Farms with Talented Kids," *The Sporting News*, November 1, 1961, 17.
15. Lou Hatter, "Ed Robinson Leaves Birds," *Baltimore Sun*, September 8, 1961, 25.
16. Steadman, "Top Sleuths Stock Orioles," 17.
17 Steadman, "Top Sleuths Stock Orioles," 17.
18. The birth of the "Oriole Way" is detailed in Eisenberg, *From 33rd Street to Camden Yards*, 76.
19. Tim Sommer, *Beating about the Bushes* (West Conshohocken PA: Infinity, 2008), 34–35.
20. The Paredes event is described in Sommer, *Beating about the Bushes*, 39. There is no follow-up as to whether Paredes returned to Thomasville proper.
21. Fay Vincent, *It's What's Inside the Lines That Counts: Baseball Stars of the 1970s and 1980s Talk about the Game They Loved* (New York: Simon and Schuster, 2010), 162.
22. Vincent, *It's What's Inside the Lines That Counts*, 88.
23. Weaver taking on the opposing team is recounted in Eisenberg, *From 33rd Street to Camden Yards*, 192–93.
24. Minor League pennant wins and records were compiled from data at Baseball Reference, https://www.baseball-reference.com. These totals encompass games recorded by that website.

25. Tim Sommer, interview by author about playing in the Orioles' Minor League system, July 20, 2019.
26. Weaver's exploits and Dalton's reaction are recorded in Eisenberg, *From 33rd Street to Camden Yards*, 193–94.
27. These stories are related in Doug Brown, "Orioles Draw Blank on Pheasant Hunt," *The Sporting News*, June 20, 1964.
28. Doug Brown, "Orioles Stunned, Proud at Losing 18 in Draft," *The Sporting News*, December 8, 1962.

5. CHANGES

1. For basic biographical information, see "Ford Frick," National Baseball Hall of Fame, accessed February 14, 2020, https://baseballhall.org/hall-of-famers/frick-ford. On Frick's plan for the restructuring of the Office of the Commissioner, see Brian McKenna, "William Eckert," Society for American Baseball Research, accessed February 14, 2020, https://sabr.org/bioproj/person/4691515d. The best full-length treatment of Frick's time in office can be found in John P. Carvalho, *Frick*: Baseball's Third Commissioner* (Jefferson NC: McFarland, 2016).
2. Eckert's background pulled from McKenna, "William Eckert."
3. Neal Eskridge, "Lee MacPhail Sees Post as a 'Mandate,'" *The Sporting News*, December 4, 1965, 33.
4. The best recap of the Yankees sale to CBS can be found in Marty Appel, *Pinstripe Empire: The New York Yankees from Before the Babe to After the Boss* (New York: Bloomsbury, 2012), 346–47, 353–54.
5. Eisenberg, *From 33rd Street to Camden Yards*, 152–53.
6. Eisenberg, *From 33rd Street to Camden Yards*, 147.
7. Eskridge, "Lee MacPhail Sees Post as a 'Mandate,'" 4.
8. Eskridge, "Lee MacPhail Sees Post as a 'Mandate,'" 4.
9. Hamper's comments can be found in Eisenberg, *From 33rd Street to Camden Yards*, 154.
10. Pat Dalton, email to author, August 11, 2018.
11. Hamper's comments on Hoffberger are in Eisenberg, *From 33rd Street to Camden Yards*, 153–54.
12. J. Frank Cashen, *Winning in Both Leagues: Reflections from Baseball's Front Office* (Lincoln: University of Nebraska Press, 2014), ebook.
13. Cashen, *Winning in Both Leagues*.
14. Cashen, *Winning in Both Leagues*.
15. Lou Hatter, "Club Drops GM Title in Alignment," *Baltimore Sun*, December 8, 1965, 33.
16. Pat Dalton, email to author regarding the relationship between Harry Dalton and Frank Cashen, December 1, 2017.

17. J. E. Miller, *Baseball Business.*
18. Eisenberg, *From 33rd Street to Camden Yards,* 147.
19. Doug Brown, "MacPhail Scouring Swap Marts, Seeks Flyhawk for Birds," *The Sporting News,* December 4, 1965, 33.
20. MacPhail, *My 9 Innings,* 79.
21. Brown, "MacPhail Scouring Swap Marts, Seeks Flyhawk for Birds," 33.
22. Brown, "MacPhail Scouring Swap Marts, Seeks Flyhawk for Birds," 33.
23. Doug Brown, "Knowles Proving Orioles Scouts Know Talent," *The Sporting News,* January 23, 1965, 15.
24. Lou Smith, "Statistics Show Why DeWitt Seeks Pitchers," *Cincinnati Enquirer,* December 5, 1965, 90.
25. For a recap of Robinson's early career, see Maxwell Kates, "Frank Robinson," in *Pitching, Defense, and Three-Run Homers,* ed. Armour and Allen.
26. These insights come from Fay Vincent, *Frank Robinson Oral History,* SABR Oral History Collection (Society of American Baseball Research, 2004), digital audio recording.
27. Mark J. Schmetzer, *Before the Machine: The Story of the 1961 Pennant-Winning Reds* (Cincinnati: Clerisy Press, 2011), 32–37.
28. Eisenberg, *From 33rd Street to Camden Yards,* 148.
29. All quotes dealing with Dalton's trade negations and Lee MacPhail's input come from an interview with Harry Dalton appearing in Eisenberg, *From 33rd Street to Camden Yards,* 148.
30. Eisenberg, *From 33rd Street to Camden Yards,* 149.
31. Eisenberg, *From 33rd Street to Camden Yards,* 149.
32. Eisenberg, *From 33rd Street to Camden Yards,* 149.
33. Eisenberg, *From 33rd Street to Camden Yards,* 150.
34. Doug Brown, "Ticket, Ad Buyers Come Alive with Robinson in Birds' Nest," *The Sporting News,* December 25, 1965, 11.
35. Jim Elliot, "Orioles Get Frank Robinson from Cincinnati Reds for Milt Pappas, Dick Simpson, Jack Baldschun," *Baltimore Sun,* December 10, 1965, 27.
36. Elliot, "Orioles Get Frank Robinson from Cincinnati Reds for Milt Pappas, Dick Simpson, Jack Baldschun," 27.
37. Elliot, "Orioles Get Frank Robinson from Cincinnati Reds for Milt Pappas, Dick Simpson, Jack Baldschun," 27.
38. Elliot, "Orioles Get Frank Robinson from Cincinnati Reds for Milt Pappas, Dick Simpson, Jack Baldschun," 27.

6. CAN YOU BELIEVE IT?

1. Lou Gorman, *High and Inside: My Life in the Front Offices of Baseball* (Jefferson NC: McFarland, 2007), 41.
2. Gorman, *High and Inside,* 50.

3. Gorman, *High and Inside*, 66.
4. "Brooks Robinson Advanced Fielding Stats," Baseball Reference, accessed March 3, 2020, https://www.baseball-reference.com/players/r/robinbr01-field.shtml#all_advanced_fielding_3b.
5. Eisenberg, *From 33rd Street to Camden Yards*.
6. Bob Maisel, "The Morning After," *Baltimore Sun*, March 10, 1966.
7. Andy Etchebarren, interview by author, October 19, 2017.
8. Ron Kasper and Boog Powell, *Baltimore Baseball and Barbecue with Boog Powell: Stories from the Orioles' Smokey Slugger* (Charleston SC: History Press, 2014), 63.
9. The history of housing segregation and desegregation in Baltimore is covered in thorough detail in Antero Pietila, *Not in My Neighborhood: How Bigotry Shaped a Great American City* (Chicago: Ivan R. Dee, 2010).
10. Mike Klingaman, "Fifty Years Ago, Frank Robinson's Search for Housing in Baltimore Helped in 'Opening the Door for Others,'" *Baltimore Sun*, January 22, 2016, https://www.baltimoresun.com/sports/orioles/bs-sp-frank-robinson-housing-0124-20160122-story.html.
11. Basic statistics on the Orioles' 1966 season were garnered from "1966 Baltimore Orioles Game Log," Baseball Reference, accessed April 14, 2020, https://www.baseball-reference.com/teams/BAL/1966-schedule-scores.shtml.
12. Harry Dalton's opinion of the Kangaroo Court and his participation is detailed in the author's correspondence with Pat Dalton from June 18, 2020.
13. Alan H. Selig, interview by author about working with Harry Dalton and Dalton's legacy in baseball, August 26, 2019.
14. There is no explanation as to why this proposal called for an odd number of games.
15. Bill Kaegel, "Execs Cool to Dalton Proposal for Cutting 18 Games off Sked," *The Sporting News*, August 13, 1966.
16. Russell Schneider, "Brooks Should Study Rule Book on Schedules, Declares Gabe," *The Sporting News*, August 13, 1966, 8.
17. Kaegel, "Execs Cool to Dalton Proposal for Cutting 18 Games Off Sked," 8.
18. "Weary Mays Fires Blast at Day-Night Twin-Bills," *The Sporting News*, August 13, 1966, 8; Schneider, "Brooks Should Study Rule Book on Schedules, Declares Gabe," 8.
19. "Orioles Exec Dalton Praises Columns on the College Issue," *The Sporting News*, July 30, 1966, 22.
20. "A Big Boost from Andy," *The Sporting News*, July 30, 1966, 22.
21. Dalton quote from Eisenberg, *From 33rd Street to Camden Yards*, 166.
22. Lacy's comments on Dalton can be found in Sam Lacy, "Baltimore Orioles and Harry Dalton; and Harry Who . . . ," *The Afro-American* (Baltimore), July 26, 1966, 13.

23. Powell quoted in Eisenberg, *From 33rd Street to Camden Yards*, 168.
24. The pool party is described in Eisenberg, *From 33rd Street to Camden Yards*, 168.
25. A recap of the day's events, on and off the field, can be found in Lou Hatter and Gordon Beard, "Wild Scene Follows Birds Flag-Clinching," *Baltimore Sun*, September 23, 1966, A1.
26. Al Kubski and Jim Russo provided these insights into the Dodgers in their "1966 World Series Scouting Report," which they compiled for the Orioles late in the season in 1966. Harry Dalton not only kept the Baltimore scouting reports on their possible World Series opponents but was also in possession of the Dodgers' scouting report on Baltimore. Al Campanis, the Dodgers' scouting director, mailed a copy of this report to Frank Lane in the summer of 1967. These reports are available in folder 2, box 2, Dalton Papers.
27. Kubski and Russo, "1966 World Series Scouting Report."
28. The stories of Koufax's preparations before and after starts are legendary. Of particular note are the anecdotes he shared about covering his arm in "Atomic Balm," a highly potent capsaicin-based ointment, prior to games to loosen his arthritic arm and then dunking it in ice water (to keep inflammation down) for so long that he risked frostbite. He also recounted that in 1969 he was routinely given cortisone shots as a well as a mix of painkillers that caused him to pitch games "half high." Charles Maher, "Koufax Quits Because of Ailing Arm," *Los Angeles Times*, November 19, 1966.
29. Bob Maisel, "The Morning After," *Baltimore Sun*, October 6, 1966, C3.
30. Maisel, "Morning After," October 6, 1966, C3.
31. Travel arrangements prior to the third game in Los Angeles are covered in the Orioles' season review for 1966. A copy of this review, which was compiled by Bob Brown, can be found in box 2a, Dalton Papers.
32. Bob Maisel, "The Morning After," *Baltimore Sun*, October 9, 1966, A10.
33. Dalton's quotes appear in Bob Maisel, "The Morning After," *Baltimore Sun*, March 10, 1966, 26.
34. Etchebarren interview.

7. A DIFFERENT REALITY

1. The scout who was most vocal over the years about things that Harry Dalton did not do was Jim Russo. In his autobiography, Russo would openly challenge Dalton and Frank Cashen on not trading for Williams, saying that "Frank and Harry should have understood that I knew more than them about Billy Williams' ability to help the Baltimore Orioles because I had seen a hell of a lot more of him." Jimmy Russo and Bob Hammel, *Super Scout: Thirty-Five Years of Major League Scouting* (Chicago: Bonus Books, 1992), 91.

2. "Orioles Cling to Phenoms, Pass Up Deal for Williams," *The Sporting News*, March 4, 1967, 24.
3. Doug Brown, "Egghead Epstein: The Slugging Scholar," *The Sporting News*, April 3, 1965, 5.
4. "Statistical Register for Mike Epstein," Baseball Reference, accessed June 19, 2020, https:/www.baseball-reference.com/register/player.fcgi?id=epstei001mic.
5. A recap of Belanger's rise in the Orioles system can be found in Clif Keane, "Orioles Put Untouchable Tag on SS Belanger of Lanesboro," *Boston Globe*, February 5, 1967, 51.
6. Perceived issues with the Orioles for 1967 appear in Doug Brown, "Bunker and Barber Sore-Arm Question Marks on Oriole Hill," *The Sporting News*, February 25, 1967, 9.
7. Dick Kranz, "Dalton Spots Three Clubs as Rivals for A.L. Flag," *The Sporting News*, February 25, 1967.
8. Jim Palmer's recollections of his shoulder trouble in 1966–67 appear in Jim Palmer and Alan Maimon, *Jim Palmer: Nine Innings to Success; A Hall of Famer's Approach to Achieving Excellence* (Chicago: Triumph Books, 2016), ebook.
9. Doug Brown, "Epstein Insists He's Earned Wings—and Not Red Ones," *The Sporting News*, May 27, 1967.
10. Brown, "Epstein Insists He's Earned Wings—and Not Red Ones."
11. Jim Elliot, "'Confused' Frank Plays Full Nine," *Baltimore Sun*, March 31, 1967, C1.
12. Palmer's day in Boston is recalled in Palmer and Maimon, *Jim Palmer*.
13. The recap of Dalton's efforts can be found in J. E. Miller, *Baseball Business*, 128.
14. An example of fans questioning Dalton can be found in Doug Brown, "Bird Dealer Dalton Makes Clean Breast to Restless Natives," *The Sporting News*, August 19, 1967, 10.
15. Kim Dalton, initial interview by author about her father, October 10, 2017.
16. Doug Brown, "The Man Who Makes the Oriole Player Deals," *Baltimore Sun Magazine*, July 16, 1967, 18.
17. Recollections of the impact and heyday of the McAllister Hotel can be found in Buddy Nevins, "The End of an Era," *The Sun-Sentinel* (Fort Lauderdale), January 6, 1988.
18. The best chronicle of Operation Pedro Pan can be found in Monsignor Bryan O. Walsh, "Cuban Refugee Children," *Journal of Interamerican Studies and World Affairs* 13, no. 3–4 (1971): 378–415.
19. Recollections of the relationship between the Daltons and the Diaz family come from Miriam Diaz, telephone conversation with the author, October 13, 2017.

20. The Weis incident and Robinson's medical condition are detailed in John C. Skipper, *Frank Robinson: A Baseball Biography* (Jefferson NC: McFarland, 2014), 99.
21. Skipper, *Frank Robinson*, 99; J. E. Miller, *Baseball Business*, 129.
22. Lou Hatter, "Orioles Rehire Jim McLaughlin," *Baltimore Sun*, September 19, 1967, C1.
23. Hatter, "Orioles Rehire Jim McLaughlin," C1.
24. Lou Hatter, "3 Coaches Dropped in Bird Shift," *Baltimore Sun*, September 29, 1967, C1.
25. Hank Bauer's Marine Corps career is chronicled at "Hank Bauer," Gary Bedingfield's Baseball in Wartime, last updated 2008, http://www.baseballinwartime.com/player_biographies/bauer_hank.htm. Bauer's comments on being tougher in 1968 come from Doug Brown, "'I'm Going to Be Tougher,' Bauer Vows," *The Sporting News*, October 21, 1967, 17.
26. Buford's collegiate career is covered in Mark Armour, "Don Buford," in *Pitching, Defense, and Three-Run Homers*, ed. Armour and Allen.
27. For the media's thoughts on Buford being a throw-in, see Bob Maisel, "The Morning After," *Baltimore Sun*, November 30, 1967, C1. Harry Dalton's comments on the trade are found in W. Lawrence Null, "Orioles Trade Aparicio, Snyder to White Sox," *Baltimore Sun*, November 30, 1967, C1.
28. Thomas E. Van Hyning, *The Santurce Crabbers: Sixty Seasons of Puerto Rican Winter League Baseball* (Jefferson NC: McFarland, 2008), 103.
29. The career of Elrod "Ellie" Hendricks was pieced together using a series of sources, including Rory Costello, "Elrod Hendricks," Society for American Baseball Research, accessed September 25, 2020, https://sabr.org/bioproj/person/elrod-hendricks/; "Statistical Register for Elrod Hendricks," Baseball Reference, accessed September 25, 2020, https://www.baseball-reference.com/players/h/hendrel01.shtml; Phil Jackman, "Big Leagues Are Great—Just Ask Elrod of Orioles," *The Sporting News*, August 8, 1970, 8; and Van Hyning, *Santurce Crabbers*, 109.
30. Dalton's comments on the need for an exploratory committee on the 1968 expansion draft can be found in Jim Elliot, "A.L. Sets Liberal Expansion Plans," *Baltimore Sun*, January 30, 1968, C1.
31. Elliot, "A.L. Sets Liberal Expansion Plans," C3.
32. The new plan for the 1968 expansion draft and the reasoning behind it are given by Dalton in Elliot, "A.L. Sets Liberal Expansion Plans," C3.
33. The crash diet in the spring of 1965 was actually instituted by Hank Bauer. According to Powell, Bauer threatened Powell that he would charge him "ten dollars for every pound" over the mandated limit. This is what led to the larger confrontation with Dalton. Powell shares his recollections in Kasper and Powell, *Baltimore Baseball and Barbecue with Boog Powell*, 61.

34. The early meeting between Powell and Dalton is detailed in Lou Hatter, "Trim Powell Here for Pact Talks," *Baltimore Sun*, February 9, 1968, C1.
35. Boog Powell's contract details are found in Jim Elliot, "1968 Pact Agreeable to Powell," *Baltimore Sun*, February 29, 1968, C1.
36. This assessment was confirmed by players from every era of Dalton's career, including Bobby Grich, who played for Dalton in both Baltimore and California; Mike Caldwell, Pete Vuckovich, and Don August, who pitched for Dalton in Milwaukee; and Nolan Ryan, who pitched for Dalton in California.
37. Brooks Robinson, email to author, September 12, 2018.
38. Johnson's and Blefary's contract demands are discussed in Lou Hatter, "Powell Hit of Camp at 237 Pounds," *Baltimore Sun*, March 1, 1968, C1.
39. The signing of Johnson and Blefary is covered in Lou Hatter, "F. Robinson Lone Bird Holdout," *Baltimore Sun*, March 5, 1968, C1.
40. The Orioles' first offer to Robinson is chronicled in Lou Hatter, "Frank Robinson Says No to Pact," *Baltimore Sun*, January 24, 1968, C1.
41. Phil Jackman, "F Robby's Holdout Like a Chess Meet," *The Sporting News*, March 16, 1968, 10.
42. A recap of the Frank Robinson negotiations in March appears in Jim Elliot, "F. Robinson, Orioles in Salary Stalemate," *Baltimore Sun*, March 7, 1968, C1.
43. The Robinson signing is covered in Lou Hatter, "Robinson 'Satisfied' after Signing Contract for Estimated $115,000," *Baltimore Sun*, March 8, 1968, C1.
44. Maisel's recap of the relationship between Bauer and Weaver appears in Bob Maisel, "The Morning After," *Baltimore Sun*, March 30, 1968, B1.
45. Lou Hatter, "Dalton Likes Bird Chances," *Baltimore Sun*, April 3, 1968, C2.
46. The Orioles' itinerary was pieced together from the Orioles' media guide for 1968.
47. The details of King's trip to Memphis and the events of the day he was killed were taken from a number of sources. His reasoning for being in Memphis comes from a portion of the special series "1968: How We Got Here," broadcast on National Public Radio's *All Things Considered*. The report by Debbie Elliott is archived at "When MLK Was Killed, He Was in Memphis Fighting for Economic Justice," National Public Radio, March 28, 2018, https://www.npr.org/2018/03/28/597308044/the-memphis-sanitation-workers-strike-kings-last-cause-for-economic-justice#:~:text=Live%20Sessions-,When%20MLK%20Was%20Killed%2C%20He%20Was%20In%20Memphis%20Fighting%20For,went%20to%20Memphis%20to%20help. The timeline of King's final hour comes from PBS's *American Experience* website and was produced in conjunction with that show's documentary titled "Roads to Memphis." The timeline is archived at "King's Assassination: A Timeline," Public Broadcasting System, accessed August 8, 2020, https://www.pbs.org/wgbh/americanexperience/features/memphis-hunt/.

48. Charlie Roberts, ".400 Club Meets Braves, Orioles Don't," *Atlanta Constitution*, April 6, 1968, 12.
49. Paul Hensler, *The New Boys of Summer: Baseball's Radical Transformation in the Late Sixties* (Lanham MD: Rowman & Littlefield, 2017), 64.
50. Hensler, *New Boys of Summer*.
51. The best overall study of the riots in Baltimore in the wake of the King assassination is Jessica Elfenbein, Thomas Hollowak, and Elizabeth Nix, *Baltimore '68: Riots and Rebirth in an American City* (Philadelphia: Temple University Press, 2011).
52. Racial tensions in every walk of life continue to color the history of Baltimore. For a historical treatment, see Pietila, *Not in My Neighborhood*. For a more recent example framed within the context of Orioles baseball, see Kevin Cowherd, *When the Crowd Didn't Roar: How Baseball's Strangest Game Ever Gave a Broken City Hope* (Lincoln: University of Nebraska Press, 2019).
53. Don Buford, telephone interview by author, August 19, 2019.
54. Pat Dalton recalled the Atlanta trip in an email to the author, received on April 4, 2018, the fiftieth anniversary of King's death.
55. "1900 U.S. Troops Patroling [*sic*] City; Officials Plan Curfew Again Today; 4 Dead, 300 Hurt, 1,350 Arrested," *Baltimore Sun*, April 8, 1968, 1.
56. "1,900 More GI's Join Riot Forces as Snipers Peril Police, Firemen; Arrests in 3 Days Rise to 3,450," *Baltimore Sun*, April 9, 1968, 1.
57. The impacts of the war in Vietnam on Major League Baseball are discussed in Hensler, *New Boys of Summer*, 117–20.
58. In an interesting side note, when the Orioles ordered World Series rings for the players and front office staff in 1966, Dalton did not order one for Schuerholz because he was on active duty for most of the season and did not directly contribute to the success of the team. Schuerholz would go on to finish his military obligation with a unit in Kansas City after following Lou Gorman there to run the Royals. This story was related in John Schuerholz, interview by author, June 12, 2018.
59. The call-up of Belanger and Richert is discussed in Jim Elliot, "Makeshift Lineup Set for Orioles," *Baltimore Sun*, April 9, 1968, B1.
60. Dalton's comments on the realities of players facing military service is found in Lou Hatter, "Birds Gain Okay for Game Today," *Baltimore Sun*, April 10, 1968, C1.
61. Dalton's conversation with Richman and Dalton's unnamed friend is recounted in Richman's syndicated column "Today's Sports Parade," June 7, 1968. The article itself can be found in folder 1, box 2, Dalton Papers. Quotations in subsequent paragraphs come from this source until noted otherwise.

62. Lou Hatter, "Orioles Faced with Dilemma," *Baltimore Sun*, June 12, 1968, C1, C4.
63. The Orioles' options and Dalton's preference for promoting Rettenmund are found in Hatter, "Orioles Faced with Dilemma," C1, C4.
64. Bob Maisel, "The Morning After," *Baltimore Sun*, June 16, 1968, A1.
65. Quoted in Eisenberg, *From 33rd Street to Camden Yards*, 185.
66. Bauer's recollections can be found in Eisenberg, *From 33rd Street to Camden Yards*, 185.
67. Eisenberg, *From 33rd Street to Camden Yards*, 185.
68. Weaver recollections from Vincent, *It's What's Inside the Lines That Counts*, 101.
69. Vincent, *It's What's Inside the Lines That Counts*, 101.
70. Vincent, *It's What's Inside the Lines That Counts*, 102.
71. Dalton's reasoning for firing Hank Bauer can be found in the transcript of the press conference introducing Earl Weaver as manager, located in folder 6, box 1, Dalton Papers.
72. Comments found in Weaver Transcript, folder 6, box 1, Dalton Papers.
73. Dalton's comments in Weaver Transcript, folder 6, box 1, Dalton Papers.
74. Quoted in Terry Pluto and Earl Weaver, *Weaver on Strategy* (Washington DC: Brassey's, 2002).
75. Lou Hatter, "Blefary Shuns Versatile Role," *Baltimore Sun*, September 17, 1968, C1, C3.
76. The growing rift between Blefary and Weaver is covered best in Doug Brown, "Blefary Has Curt Reply: 'I'm No Peck's Bad Boy,'" *The Sporting News*, December 21, 1968, 34.
77. At the time, it seemed as if Dalton had simply dumped Blefary without picking up much in return. This was due in large part to the fact that Cuellar posted an 8-11 record in 1968 despite an ERA of 2.74. Three years later, the deal looked much different. Cuellar would go 67-28 for Baltimore from 1969 to 1971 and would win a Cy Young Award in 1969. Conversely, Blefary continued to decline, and he would spend the next three seasons paying part-time for three different teams. He would play his last game in the Majors in 1972.
78. The commissioner was set up as the lone arbitrator of player/owner disputes in the collective bargaining agreement (CBA) of 1968. Eckert's role as arbitrator is covered in Mark Armour, "Collective Barging Agreement (1968)," *In Pursuit of Pennants* (blog), February 15, 2018, https://pursuitofpennants.wordpress.com/2018/02/15/collective-bargaining-agreement-1968/.
79. The "speck of bias" comment comes from the syndicated column by Milt Richman, "Dalton's the Man," *Daily Times-Advocate* (Escondido CA), December 19, 1968, A-14.

80. Pat Dalton's comments came from her review of the manuscript for this work before she passed away in the summer of 2023.

8. THE BEST TEAM IN BASEBALL

1. "Statistical Register for Frank Robinson," Baseball Reference, accessed November 3, 2022, https://www.baseball-reference.com/players/r/robinfr02.shtml.
2. "Statistical Register for Brooks Robinson," Baseball Reference, accessed November 5, 2022, https://www.baseball-reference.com/players/r/robinbr01.shtml.
3. "MLB Team Position by Fielding Runs, 1969–1971," Baseball Reference, accessed November 3, 2022, https://www.baseball-reference.com/leagues/team_compare.cgi?request=1&year=1969&lg=MLB&stat=runs_fielding.
4. "Pitching Splits for the Baltimore Orioles Starting Pitchers, 1969–1971," Stathead, accessed November 3, 2022, https://stathead.com/baseball/split_finder.cgi?request=1&match=seasons&order_by_asc=0&order_by=year_game&year_min=1969&year_max=1971&split_1=total%3Atotal&split_total_comp=gt&class=team&type=p&sr_pitching_splits_output=view_pitching&team_id=BAL.
5. Bill Stetka, "4 x 20: Orioles 1971 Season Is One for the Books, Title or Not," *Birdland Insider*, Baltimore Orioles, December 14, 2021, https://www.mlb.com/orioles/news/featured/4-x-20-orioles-1971-season-is-one-for-the-books-title-or-not#:~:text=The%20%2771%20Orioles%20became%20the,the%201920%20Chicago%20White%20Sox.
6. "Statistical Register for Eddie Watt," Baseball Reference, accessed November 8, 2022, https://www.baseball-reference.com/players/w/watted01.shtml.
7. Quoted in Rob Neyer and Eddie Epstein, *Baseball Dynasties: The Greatest Teams of All Time* (New York: Norton, 2000), 251.
8. References to the manual will be italicized, while references to the concept of the Oriole Way will not.
9. Don Pries, *The Oriole Way of Baseball* (Baltimore: Baltimore Orioles, 1969).
10. Pries, *Oriole Way*, i (emphasis added).
11. Pries, *Oriole Way*, i (original emphasis).
12. Pries, *Oriole Way*, 1.
13. Pries, *Oriole Way*, 1–3.
14. Pries, *Oriole Way*, 3–4.
15. Pries, *Oriole Way*, 9.
16. Ernie Accorsi, interview by author on the impact of Harry Dalton on his career, August 12, 2018.
17. Jeff Hewett's comments come from an email provided to the author by Kim Dalton on December 18, 2017.

18. Mike Klingaman, "Harry Dalton 1928–2005," *Baltimore Sun*, October 24, 2005, D1, D6.
19. Pete Richert, interview by author about Harry Dalton, 2020.
20. Tim Sommer outlines the social goings on of Orioles farmhands in *Beating about the Bushes*.
21. Earl Weaver had ten ejections between 1969 and 1971. Off the field, his drinking was well known, though people who knew Weaver never considered him an alcoholic. Weaver was a fixture in the hotel bar after games on the road, and the stories of his consumption and the aftermath are legendary. Sources for this information include Cashen, *Winning in Both Leagues*, 39–40; as well as a telephone conversation with Weaver's stepdaughter Kim Benson in November 2022.
22. Grich's comments on Dalton appear in Eisenberg, *From 33rd Street to Camden Yards*, 240.
23. John Steadman, "Weaver Always Had the Fire, but Dalton Always Had Faith," *Baltimore Sun*, March 9, 1996, https://www.baltimoresun.com/news/bs-xpm-1996-03-10-1996070106-story.html.
24. Steadman, "Weaver Always Had the Fire, but Dalton Always Had Faith."
25. Weaver's comments come from an email that he sent to Debbie Dalton upon her father's death in 2005 and that was shared at Dalton's celebration of life.
26. Weaver's thoughts on managing shared by Dan Duquette in an email to author, July 22, 2020.
27. Pete Richert comments from undated telephone interview by author.
28. Pries, *Oriole Way*.
29. George Bamberger's preseason pitching philosophy appears in Pries, *Oriole Way*.
30. Bamberger's belief in changing speeds and throwing strikes is garnered from Dave Anderson, "George Bamberger, the Brewers [*sic*] Ph.D. in Pitching," *New York Times*, March 8, 1979, D-20.
31. Tyler Kepner, *The Grandest Stage: A History of the World Series* (New York: Doubleday, 2022), 3.
32. Kepner, *Grandest Stage*, 78.
33. "1969 World Series," Baseball Reference, accessed November 10 2022, https://www.baseball-reference.com/postseason/1969_WS.shtml.
34. Agee's Game Three is recapped in "BB Moments: '69 World Series Game 3, Agee Gets It Done," Major League Baseball, 2009, https://www.mlb.com/video/bb-moments-agee-gets-it-done-c3412634?q=ContentTags%20%3D%20%5B%22gamepk-67610%22%5D%20Order%20by%20Timestamp%20DESC&cp=CMS_FIRST&p=0. Ron Swoboda's catch in Game Four is available at "Swoboda Makes 'The Catch,'" Major League Baseball, 2010, https://www.mlb.com/video/swoboda-makes-the-catch-c13062803.

35. Robinson's performance in 1970 is recapped at "Robinson Leads O's to '70 Title," Major League Baseball, 2012, https://www.mlb.com/rays/video/robinson-leads-o-s-to-70-title-c25331825.
36. Clemente's performance is recapped at "Roberto Clemente STELLAR 1971 World Series! Clemente Crushes Orioles to Win MVP," YouTube.com, 2020, https://www.youtube.com/watch?v=7r5FuvQNCa8.
37. The performances of Blass, Briles, and Kison were garnered from the statistics available at "1971 World Series," Baseball Reference, accessed November 10, 2022, https://www.baseball-reference.com/postseason/1971_WS.shtml.

9. THE DALTONS GO WEST

1. Dalton's account of the call from Autry appears in Harry Dalton to Jerry Hoffberger, September 20, 1971, folder 1a, box 2, Dalton Papers.
2. Dalton to Hoffberger, September 20, 1971.
3. Dalton to Hoffberger, September 20, 1971.
4. Dalton to Hoffberger, September 20, 1971.
5. Dalton to Hoffberger, September 20, 1971.
6. For an understanding of the legal precedent for baseball's antitrust exemption and the interplay between that and the reserve clause, see Stuart Banner, *The Baseball Trust: A History of Baseball's Antitrust Exemption* (New York: Oxford University Press, 2013).
7. Curt Flood, letter to Commissioner of Baseball Bowie K. Kuhn, December 24, 1969, Exhibits of the Sheridan Libraries and Museums, Johns Hopkins University, accessed January 13, 2023, https://exhibits.library.jhu.edu/items/show/1226.
8. Harry Dalton to Jerry Hoffberger, undated but likely mid-September 1971, folder 1a, box 2, Dalton Papers. Quotations in subsequent paragraphs are from this source until noted otherwise.
9. Anonymous interview by author regarding Frank Cashen's relationship with Harry Dalton, June 20, 2020.
10. Pat Dalton, interview by author regarding the end of Harry Dalton's career in Baltimore, 2021.
11. Dalton to Hoffberger undated letter of mid-September 1971.
12. Dalton to Hoffberger undated letter of mid-September 1971.
13. Gene Autry and Mickey Herskowitz, *Back in the Saddle Again* (New York: Doubleday, 1978), 151.
14. Autry and Herskowitz, *Back in the Saddle Again.*
15. A general history of baseball in California is provided in Kevin Nelson, *The Golden Game: The Story of California Baseball* (Lincoln: University of Nebraska Press, 2015).

16. Andy McCue, *Mover and Shaker: Walter O'Malley, the Dodgers, and Baseball's Westward Expansion* (Lincoln: University of Nebraska Press, 2014), xv.
17. Lincoln Abraham Mitchell, *Baseball Goes West: The Dodgers, the Giants, and the Shaping of the Major Leagues* (Kent OH: Kent State University Press, 2018), 11.
18. The Dodgers would also finish second three times, winning over ninety games twice. Writing about the Brooklyn Dodgers has become a cottage industry among historians. The two best treatments of the rise of the Dodgers in the postwar New York era are Roger Kahn, *The Boys of Summer* (New York: HarperCollins, 2011); and Peter Golenbock and Paul Dickson, *Bums: An Oral History of the Brooklyn Dodgers* (Mineola NY: Dover, 2010).
19. This era of Dodgers baseball is best covered in a trio of works by Brian M. Endsley: *Bums No More: The 1959 Los Angeles Dodgers, World Champions of Baseball* (Jefferson NC: McFarland, 2009); *Finding the Left Arm of God: Sandy Koufax and the Los Angeles Dodgers, 1960–1963* (Jefferson NC: McFarland, 2015); and *Koufax Throws a Curve: The Los Angeles Dodgers at the End of an Era, 1964–1966* (Jefferson NC: McFarland 2018). Moreover, the transitional period of the late 1960s and the intersection of the Dodgers with a changing America is covered wonderfully in Michael Leahy, *The Last Innocents: The Collision of the Turbulent Sixties and the Los Angeles Dodgers* (New York: Harper, 2016).
20. Quoted in Rob Goldman, *Once They Were Angels* (Champaign IL: Sports Publishing, 2006), 81.
21. Quoted in Goldman, *Once They Were Angels*, 81.
22. OPS+ is a player's on-base percentage plus slugging statistic adjusted to factor in the parks in which he played.
23. Fregosi's comments can be found in Ron Rapoport, "Hatred 'Eats' at Alex—Conigliaro," *Los Angeles Times*, June 28, 1971, 34.
24. Alex Johnson's career is best summed up in Christopher Foster, "Alex Johnson Dies at 72; Angels' Troubled Batting Champ," *Los Angeles Times*, March 3, 2015, https://www.latimes.com/local/obituaries/la-me-alex-johnson-20150304-story.html.

10. GETTING HIS HANDS IN THE DIRT

1. Quoted in Milt Richman, "He Came to Deal," United Press International, November 29, 1971.
2. Rice's career is best summed up in Norm King, "Del Rice," Society for American Baseball Research, accessed December 15, 2021, https://sabr.org/bioproj/person/del-rice/.
3. Claude Anderson, "Rice Won't Predict Pennant Winner, Yet," *San Bernardino County (CA) Sun*, December 8, 1971, 41.

4. Dick Miller, "'We'll Have Fun,' Says New Angel Pilot Rice," *The Sporting News*, December 25, 1971, 29.
5. D. Miller, "'We'll Have Fun,' Says New Angel Pilot Rice."
6. Ross Newhan, "Dodger-Angel Report: Nothing to Announce," *Los Angeles Times*, December 2, 1971, 71.
7. Fregosi's propensity for the nightlife was outlined in Tom Sommers, interview by author, June 2, 2022.
8. Dalton's comments on the possibility of trading Fregosi and also the notion of Dalton even considering to trade Fregosi come from Bud Tucker, "Dalton Has Ridden into Town," *Independent* (Long Beach CA), December 9, 1971, 57.
9. Quotes from the Mets appear in Joseph Durso, "Mets Trade Ryan. No Kidding!" *New York Times*, December 10, 1971, https://archive.nytimes.com/www.nytimes.com/packages/html/sports/year_in_sports/12.10.html.
10. Ross Newhan, "Trade 'Thrills' Veteran Angel Fregosi," *Los Angeles Times*, December 11, 1971, 11.
11. Ross Newhan, "Trade 'Thrills' Veteran Angel Fregosi."
12. Nolan Ryan, interview by author about his time with the Angels and his dealings with Harry Dalton, March 18, 2018.
13. Ross Newhan, *The California Angels: The Complete History*, ed. Gene Schoor (New York: Simon and Schuster, 1982), 126.
14. [Angels fan], letter to the editor on Harry Dalton, *Progress-Bulletin* (Pomona CA), December 15, 1971, 46.
15. Ross Newhan, "Angels Make a Pitch off the Baseball Field," *Los Angeles Times*, February 17, 1972, 61.
16. Kim Dalton, interview by author about special events for the Dalton family, February 16, 2022.
17. Newhan, "Angels Make a Pitch off the Baseball Field," 61.
18. Newhan, "Angels Make a Pitch off the Baseball Field," 61.
19. Newhan, "Angels Make a Pitch off the Baseball Field," 61.
20. These day-to-day observations are found in Rob Goldman, *Nolan Ryan: The Making of a Pitcher* (Chicago: Triumph Books, 2014), 62–66.
21. The grazing fields of Holtville are best seen in a photograph from March 1972 taken by Art Rogers of the *Los Angeles Times*. It can be found online at "Los Angeles Angels Spring Training," *Los Angeles Times*, 2014, https://www.latimes.com/visuals/photography/la-me-fw-archives-lso-angeles-angels-spring-training-20190305-htmlstory.html.
22. Today the comparison of a POW camp and a baseball training facility seems cringeworthy at best. The original comparison was made by Bud Tucker of the *San Gabriel Valley Tribune* and was conveyed in Gene Lube, "Holtville-Stalag 17: Angels Still Love Palm Springs," *Desert Sun* (Palm Springs CA), February 9, 1967, 9. The actual Stalag Luft 17B was located in Austria and

was one of a series of camps run by the German military to house Allied airmen who were shot down in occupied territory. The prisoners' experiences there were the basis for a movie made in 1953, and the camp was lightheartedly portrayed in the television sitcom *Hogan's Heroes* during the late 1960s. Information on the camp is at "Krems, Austria—Stalag 17B," 392nd Bomb Group Association, accessed March 24, 2022, https://b24.net/powStalag17.htm.

23. Goldman, *Nolan Ryan*, 63.
24. Don Merry, "Dalton Optimistic," *Independent* (Long Beach CA), March 1, 1972, 39.
25. Merry, "Dalton Optimistic," 39.
26. Ryan interview about his time with the Angels.
27. Jimmy Hutto, interview by author about Harry Dalton, April 13, 2019.
28. The founding of the Brotherhood of Professional Base Ball Players is best covered in Lee Lowenfish, *The Imperfect Diamond: A History of Baseball's Labor Wars* (Lincoln: University of Nebraska Press, 2010), 27–37. The 1886 membership numbers of the Brotherhood appear in Robert B. Ross, *The Great Baseball Revolt: The Rise and Fall of the 1890 Players League* (Lincoln: University of Nebraska Press, 2016), 53.
29. The best work on the season of 1890 and the war between the PL and the NL is Ross, *Great Baseball Revolt.*
30. The period of the Players' Fraternity is covered best in Scott Longert, "The Players Fraternity," *Baseball Research Journal* 30, no. 1 (2001): 40–52.
31. The American Baseball Guild is covered in full in Lowenfish, *Imperfect Diamond*, 139–53.
32. On the "house union" years of the MLBPA, see Charles P. Korr, *The End of Baseball as We Knew It: The Players Union, 1960–81* (Urbana: University of Illinois Press, 2002), 16–34.
33. The hunt for a new union chief is best described in Larry Burke, Peter Thomas Fornatale, and Jim Baker, *Change Up: An Oral History of Eight Key Events That Shaped Baseball* (New York: Rodale Books, 2008), 90–95.
34. While there are numerous long-form treatments of Marvin Miller and his career, the information here is from Vincent, *It's What's Inside the Lines That Counts*, 298–300.
35. Vincent, *It's What's Inside the Lines That Counts*, 308.
36. Dalton quoted in J. E. Miller, *Baseball Business*, 136.
37. The best overview of the history of the pension fund is Charles W. Bevis, "A Home Run by Any Measure: The Baseball Players' Pension Plan," *Baseball Research Journal* 21 (1992): 64–70.
38. Robert V. Bellamy Jr., interview by author regarding the player pension fund, May 3, 2022.

39. Bellamy interview regarding the player pension fund.
40. Negotiations prior to 1972 are covered in Bevis, "Home Run by Any Measure," 68–69.
41. Angell's comments first appeared in 1972 and were later republished in Roger Angell, *Five Seasons: A Baseball Companion* (Hudson NY: Open Road Media, 2013).
42. Owners' responses to the possibility of a strike are from Jack Lang, "Owners Stand Their Ground, Nix Players Pension Raise," *The Sporting News*, April 8, 1972, 24.
43. Dalton's comments on the difference between the styles of the players union and management are from Harry Dalton, "Discussion of the Evolution of the Relationship between Ownership and the Players in Baseball, 1970–1982," 1991, in Charles P. Korr, "Charles Korr's Major League Baseball Interview Audio Tapes," #6355, Kheel Center for Labor-Management Documentation and Archives, Cornell University Library, Ithaca NY.
44. Dalton's comments and his plan for avoiding a work stoppage are found in Jeff Prugh, "Strike's End Brings Yeas, Yawns," *Los Angeles Times*, April 14, 1972, sec. 3, 6.
45. Dalton's comment from the BBWAA dinner can be found in John Hall, "The Last Hurrah," *Los Angeles Times*, April 3, 1972, 37.
46. Associated Press, "'Play Ball!' Strike Ends; Season Starts Saturday," *Los Angeles Times*, April 14, 1972, 14.
47. Associated Press, "'Play Ball!' Strike Ends; Season Starts Saturday," 14.
48. Ross Newhan, "Angels Lose Third Straight; Texas Scores 5–0 Blank," *Los Angeles Times*, April 23, 1972, 43.
49. Even in their Opening Day win, the Angels did not drive in a run. Their lone tally came on a wild pitch. The game recap can be found in Ross Newhan, "Messersmith Hurls Two-Hitter, 1–0," *Los Angeles Times*, April 16, 1972, 39.
50. Ross Newhan, "Rangers Smash Hit in Texas Premiere, Subdue Angels, 7–6," *Los Angeles Times*, April 22, 1972, 10.
51. Ryan's statistics for his starts in April 1972 were compiled from the game log at "Nolan Ryan Game Log for 1972," Baseball Reference, accessed March 24, 2022, https://www.baseball-reference.com/players/gl.fcgi?id=ryanno01&t=p&year=1972.
52. Stats for the Angels' bullpen in April 1972 compiled with tools found at https://stathead.com. Stathead is a subsidiary of Baseball Reference.
53. The Angels' injury woes are outlined in Ross Newhan, "Angels' Arms at Half Mast; BoSox Roll 8–1," *Los Angeles Times*, May 12, 1972, 18.
54. "1972 California Angels Game Log and Splits," Baseball Reference, accessed March 24, 2022, https://www.baseball-reference.com/teams/CAL/1972-schedule-scores.shtml; "Standings at the End of May 31," Retrosheet,

accessed March 24, 2022, https://www.retrosheet.org/boxesetc/1972/05311972.htm.

55. Ross Newhan, "Angels Are Still Trying to Jell [*sic*]," *Los Angeles Times*, May 31, 1972, 44. Quotations in subsequent paragraphs are from this article until noted otherwise.
56. Torborg describes his work with Ryan in George Castle, *When the Game Changed: An Oral History of Baseball's True Golden Age: 1969–1979* (Guilford CT: Lyons Press, 2012), location 1054–67 of ebook, https://books.google.com/books?id=9iuPBAAAQBAJ.
57. Ross Newhan, "Where Now, Angels?" *Los Angeles Times*, October 10, 1972, 33.

11. LOOKING FOR THE RIGHT COMBINATION

1. The agenda, participants, and notes from the fall organizational meeting of 1972 are found in folder 1, box 5, Dalton Papers.
2. Rating scales are from "Fall Meeting Agenda 1972," folder 1, box 5, Dalton Papers.
3. Scouting totals for 1972 and coverage areas come from Tom Sommers, Farm Director, memo to Harry Dalton, from the fall of 1971. The memo appears in series II of the Dalton Papers.
4. Biographical information on Nick Kamzic and Dick Weincek comes from P. J. Dragseth, *Major League Baseball Scouts: A Biographical Dictionary* (Jefferson NC: McFarland, 2011).
5. Sommers memo to Dalton, fall 1971.
6. Quote from Dalton appears in "Fall Meeting Agenda 1972."
7. Dalton quote from "Fall Meeting Agenda 1972."
8. Tom Sommers, interview by author, June 2, 2022.
9. Bruce Manno, interview by author about loyalty in baseball, February 3, 2022.
10. Sommers interview.
11. Information on tryout camp comes from C. Thomas Nelson, "Box Score of Tryout Camp: Few Hits, All Run, Most Err," *Los Angeles Times*, August 19, 1973, 7. The Angels were a member of the Major League Scouting Bureau, but unlike other clubs, they also maintained their own scouting department.
12. The presence of more college-age Angels draft picks comes from analyzing their draft log on Baseball Reference, accessed March 24, 2022, https://www.baseball-reference.com/draft/.
13. These percentages reflect players drafted and signed by the Angels. They are computed using information from Baseball Reference.
14. Ron Fimrite, "The Angels' Prospects Are Heavenly: With the Top Farm Clubs, California Could Soon Become a Devil to Beat," *Sports Illustrated*, August 2, 1976.
15. Fimrite, "Angels' Prospects Are Heavenly."

16. Dalton's efforts to improve the Angels' roster are recapped in part in Dick Miller, "New Faces Crowding Angels' Roster," *The Sporting News*, November 30, 1974, 50.
17. Peter Gammons, interview by author about the career of Harry Dalton, May 19, 2022.
18. Del Rice spoke about Harry Dalton's reasons for letting him go in John Hall, "The Old Pastime," *Los Angeles Times*, October 13, 1972, 51.
19. Ross Newhan, "Winkles Named Angels Manager," *Los Angeles Times*, October 12, 1972, 59.
20. Winkles's early life and career are recapped in Norm King, "Bobby Winkles," Society for American Baseball Research, accessed June 16, 2022, https://sabr.org/bioproj/person/bobby-winkles/.
21. Dick Miller, "'We'll Have Fun,' Says New Angel Pilot Rice," *The Sporting News*, December 25, 1971.
22. Newhan, "Winkles Named Angels Manager."
23. The Robinson trade to the Dodgers is recapped in Ron Rapoport, "Dodgers Trade Robinson to Angels," *Los Angeles Times*, November 29, 1972, 41.
24. Frank Robinson's starts and stats come from his registry page on Baseball Reference, https://baseball-reference.com/players/r/robinfr02.shtml.
25. Bobby Valentine and Peter Golenbock, *Valentine's Way: My Adventurous Life and Times* (New York: Permuted Platinum, 2021), 89.
26. Valentine covers the incident in detail in Valentine and Golenbock, *Valentine's Way*, 89–90.
27. Details on the 1973 season, including season record breakdowns, can be found on the team's Baseball Reference page for 1973, https://baseball-reference.com/search/search.fcgi?hint=&search=Angels&pid=&idx=.
28. Dalton's recap of the 1973 season is found in Don Merry, "Angels Finish on Optimistic Note for 1974," *Independent* (Long Beach CA), October 1, 1973, 23.
29. Merry, "Angels Finish on Optimistic Note for 1974," 23.
30. Ryan's spectacular 1973 season is recapped in Paul Hensler, "Revisiting Nolan Ryan in 1973: The Quest for 400 Strikeouts," *Baseball Research Journal* 42, no. 1 (Spring 2013): 71–82.
31. Ryan would throw seven no-hitters in his long career. Details of these games can be found in Steve Wulf, "Heaven for Seven: The Men behind Nolan Ryan's No-Hitters," *Sports Illustrated*, May 1, 2015, https://www.si.com/mlb/2015/05/01/si-vault-nolan-ryan-seven-no-hitters.
32. This event turned out to be a huge promotional boon for the Angels. It is best covered in Jonathan Hock, dir., *Fastball* (Legendary Entertainment and Major League Baseball Productions, 2016).

33. The Dalton family was kind enough to answer a multitude of important (and not so important) questions during the writing of this book. Pat Dalton et al., interview by author about the Daltons' favorite players, 2017.
34. Merry, "Angels Finish on Optimistic Note for 1974," 23.
35. Bud Tucker, "Angels Should Stage Harry Dalton Night," *Independent* (Long Beach CA), August 21, 1973, 24.
36. The Winkles way of baseball is described in Valentine and Golenbock, *Valentine's Way* (ebook).
37. The feud between Winkles and Robinson is recapped in Valentine and Golenbock, *Valentine's Way* (ebook).
38. Associated Press, "Winkles: 'I Couldn't Handle Robinson'; Raps Dalton," *Los Angeles Times*, June 28, 1974, 45.
39. Associated Press, "Winkles: 'I Couldn't Handle Robinson'; Raps Dalton."
40. The nontrade of Robinson to the Yankees is covered best by former Yankee Fritz Peterson on his blog; see Fritz Peterson, "The Four Times Frank Robinson Almost Became a Yankee," FritzPeterson.org, July 19, 2015, https://fritzpetersondotorg.wordpress.com/2015/07/19/the-four-times-frank-robinson-almost-became-a-yankee/.
41. Associated Press, "Winkles: 'I Couldn't Handle Robinson'; Raps Dalton."
42. Sommers interview.
43. Associated Press, "Winkles: 'I Couldn't Handle Robinson'; Raps Dalton."
44. For Winkles's comment and thoughts on how he saw the role of managers in team building, see Associated Press, "Winkles: 'I Couldn't Handle Robinson'; Raps Dalton."
45. Pat Dalton, interview by author regarding the hiring and firing of Bobby Winkles by Harry Dalton, November 6, 2018.
46. Dave Duncan's description of the demeanor of Dick Williams is found in Jason Turbow, *Dynastic, Bombastic, Fantastic: Reggie, Rollie, Catfish, and Charlie Finley's Swingin' A's* (Boston: Houghton Mifflin Harcourt, 2017), 8–9.
47. Autry and Herskowitz, *Back in the Saddle Again*, 162.
48. Jeff Prugh, "Angels Send Out SOS; Dick Williams Answers," *Los Angeles Times*, June 28, 1974, 11.
49. Prugh, "Angels Send Out SOS; Dick Williams Answers."
50. Prugh, "Angels Send Out SOS; Dick Williams Answers."
51. All quotes in the paragraph come from the anonymous letter to Gene Autry, dated June 22, 1974, in folder 1a, box 2, Dalton Papers.
52. The Angels' plans for Arthur "Red" Patterson are outlined in Ross Newhan, "Red Patterson Speaking: Anywhere and/or Anytime," *Los Angeles Times*, March 4, 1975.

53. Dalton's issues with Red Patterson are outlined in a recap of a meeting he had with Gene Autry in October 1975. It is found in the Dalton Papers.
54. Dick Williams and Bill Plaschke, *No More Mr. Nice Guy: A Life of Hardball* (San Diego: Harcourt Brace Jovanovich, 1990), 179.
55. Autry and Herskowitz, *Back in the Saddle Again*, 165.
56. Williams and Plaschke, *No More Mr. Nice Guy*, 188.
57. Statistics for 1975 are garnered from the Angels' register for 1975 at Baseball Reference, https://www.baseball-reference.com/teams/ANA/index.shtml.
58. Dalton's comments regarding college baseball and pro baseball are from a letter to Lou Pavlovich of *College Baseball Newspaper* found in the Dalton Papers.
59. Bill Bruns, "The Runs, Hits, and Errors of a Big-League General Manager," *Money*, June 1976.
60. Winki Winburn, interview by author, January 15, 2018.
61. For an overview of Pat Dalton's life in California, see Mary Lou Hopkins, "She Knows the Score, but Can't Keep It," *Los Angeles Times*, April 11, 1974.
62. Williams shares his thoughts on the Bobby Bonds trade in Williams and Plaschke, *No More Mr. Nice Guy*, 195–96.
63. "Statistical Register for Bobby Bonds," Baseball Reference, accessed 2022, https://www.baseball-reference.com/players/b/bondsbo01.shtml.
64. "1975 California Angels Game Log," Baseball Reference, accessed 2022, https://www.baseball-reference.com/teams/CAL/1975-schedule-scores.shtml.
65. Williams and Plaschke, *No More Mr. Nice Guy*, 196.
66. Williams and Plaschke, *No More Mr. Nice Guy*, 198.
67. Williams and Plaschke, *No More Mr. Nice Guy*, 199.
68. For Norm Sherry's career prior to becoming manager in Anaheim, see David E. Skelton, "Norm Sherry," Society for American Baseball Research, accessed 2022, https://sabr.org/bioproj/person/norm-sherry/.
69. The press release covering Dalton's extension and the signing of Red Patterson to a formal contract is in folder 3, box 5, Dalton Papers.
70. For the Angels' moves after Dalton's contract extension, see Dave Distel, "Angels Order Another Round of Sherry," *Los Angeles Times*, October 5, 1976.
71. Distel, "Angels Order Another Round of Sherry."
72. Distel, "Angels Order Another Round of Sherry."

12. NEW WORLD, NEW DALTON, SAME RESULTS

1. For more information on the Messersmith-McNally decision, see Ed Edmonds and Frank G. Houdek, *Baseball Meets the Law: A Chronology of Decisions, Statutes and Other Legal Events* (Jefferson NC: McFarland, 2017), 126.
2. Distel, "Angels Order Another Round of Sherry."

3. The mechanics of the first free agency, as well as of the player pool, are found in Ralph Ray, "Bidders Will Set Sights on 26 Free Agents," *The Sporting News*, October 16, 1976, 12, 32.
4. United Press International, "Don Baylor Can't Refuse Angels," *Valley News* (Van Nuys CA), November 17, 1976, 31.
5. United Press International, "Don Baylor Can't Refuse Angels," 31.
6. Ross Newhan, "Angels Sign Another Finley Alum: Rudi," *Los Angeles Times*, November 18, 1976, 68.
7. Rudi's career evaluated using "Statistical Register for Joe Rudi," Baseball Reference, accessed July 30, 2022, https://www.baseball-reference.com/players/r/rudijo01.shtml#all_batting_postseason.
8. Newhan, "Angels Sign Another Finley Alum: Rudi."
9. Eisenberg, *From 33rd Street to Camden Yards*, 240.
10. Bobby Grich, interview by author, October 22, 2017.
11. In the end, Steinbrenner's argument against Dalton was mostly crying over spilled milk. This included his saying that Dalton had gone back on his word that the Angels were only in the market for one marquee player. The episode is best described in Steve Jacobson, "Search Doesn't End with Gullett," *Newsday* (New York), November 19, 1976.
12. Dalton's comments come from Associated Press, "Angels Get Their Man—Grich," *Progress-Bulletin* (Pomona CA), November 25, 1976, 51.
13. Newhan, "Angels Sign Another Finley Alum: Rudi."
14. Dalton's quotes from the introductory press conference were available to the author in the format of a DVD of the original conference that is in the Dalton family's possession.
15. Dick Miller, "Bonanza or Bust Will Decide Angel Gamble," *The Sporting News*, March 5, 1977, 3.
16. D. Miller, "Bonanza or Bust."
17. Dalton diary, spring 1977, folder 1, box 5, Dalton Papers.
18. Dalton diary, spring 1977.
19. Dalton diary, spring 1977.
20. Insight into division rivals comes from the Dalton diary, spring 1977.
21. Dalton diary, spring 1977.
22. Dalton diary, spring 1977.
23. Dalton diary, spring 1977.
24. The opinions of Angels fans are found in "Faultin Dalton," *Los Angeles Times*, May 14, 1977.
25. Ron Rapoport, interview by author regarding covering Harry Dalton in California, June 30, 2022.
26. Tracy Ringolsby, interview by author regarding covering Harry Dalton in California, September 4, 2019.

27. Ross Newhan, "Dalton Rearms Angels and Price Was Right," *Los Angeles Times*, June 17, 1977, 40.
28. Newhan, "Dalton Rearms Angels."
29. Newhan, "Dalton Rearms Angels."
30. Comments from Dalton regarding Dave Garcia come from an interview that Harry Dalton gave on the Angels Hotline, July 11, 1977. This recording is in the Dalton family's private collection.
31. "1977 California Angels Game Log," Baseball Reference, accessed August 10, 2022, https://www.baseball-reference.com/teams/CAL/1977-schedule-scores.shtml.
32. United Press International, "Will Autry Rope Buzzie?" *Valley News*, October 14, 1977, 32.
33. Don Merry, "Angels Reshuffle; Autry in Charge, Bavasi No. 2," *Los Angeles Times*, October 21, 1977, 59.
34. Bavasi tells stories from his career in Bob Wolf, "Baseball by Bavasi," *Los Angeles Times*, September 21, 1991, 35.
35. Buzzie Bavasi and John Strege, *Off the Record* (Chicago: Contemporary Books, 1987), 167.
36. Bavasi and Strege, *Off the Record*, 167.
37. Pat Dalton, email to author, July 5, 2022.

13. WORKING ON HIS TERMS

1. Various authors have tackled the history of Milwaukee baseball up to the time the Brewers arrived. Dennis Pajot, *The Rise of Milwaukee Baseball: The Cream City from Midwestern Outpost to the Major Leagues, 1859–1901* (Jefferson NC: McFarland, 2009), covers the early days of the city's involvement in baseball, primarily at the grassroots level. Brian A. Podoll, *The Minor League Milwaukee Brewers, 1859–1952* (Jefferson NC: McFarland, 2003), takes a look at the Triple-A days of Milwaukee prior to the arrival of the Braves in 1953.
2. The best historical survey of the early days of the Milwaukee Miracle is Bob Buege, *The Milwaukee Braves: A Baseball Eulogy* (Milwaukee: Douglas American Sports Publications, 1988).
3. Two books cover the Braves' transition from Milwaukee to Atlanta. Patrick Steele, *Home of the Braves: The Battle for Baseball in Milwaukee* (Madison: University of Wisconsin Press, 2018), covers the reasons why the Braves considered leaving Milwaukee and the court case from the Milwaukee side. Clayton Trutor, *Loserville: How Professional Sports Remade Atlanta—and How Atlanta Remade Professional Sports* (Lincoln: University of Nebraska Press, 2022), looks at Atlanta's push to land the Braves and how that move would help to transform the city.
4. Teams Inc., *Milwaukee . . . Major League City* (Milwaukee: Teams Inc., 1965).

5. Teams Inc., *Milwaukee . . . Major League City.*
6. Chris Foran, "When the Chicago White Sox Called Milwaukee's County Stadium Home," *Milwaukee Journal Sentinel*, May 8, 2018, https://www.jsonline.com/story/life/green-sheet/2018/05/08/when-chicago-white-sox-called-milwaukees-county-stadium-home/576362002/.
7. Bill Mullins, *Becoming Big League: Seattle, the Pilots, and Stadium Politics* (Seattle: University of Washington Press, 2013), 13–15.
8. Mullins, *Becoming Big League.*
9. Chuck Carlson, *True Brew: A Quarter Century with the Milwaukee Brewers* (Dallas: Taylor, 1993), 88–103.
10. Mike Caldwell, interview by author, June 23, 2020; Robin Yount, interview by author, September 10, 2020.
11. Chris Zantow, *Building the Brewers: Bud Selig and the Return of Major League Baseball to Milwaukee* (Jefferson NC: McFarland, 2019), 166–67.
12. Bud Selig, *For the Good of the Game: The Inside Story of the Surprising and Dramatic Transformation of Major League Baseball* (New York: HarperCollins, 2019), 76.
13. "Lakeside" memo, undated, folder 2a, box 5, Dalton Papers.
14. "Lakeside" memo.
15. "Lakeside" memo.
16. "Lakeside" memo.
17. Kim Dalton, interview by author about growing up with Harry Dalton as a father, October 10, 2017.
18. Cindy Dalton, initial interview by author, October 10, 2017.
19. Kim Dalton, interview by author about moving to Milwaukee, August 26, 2022.
20. Pat Dalton, initial interview by author, October 10, 2017.
21. Associated Press, "Dalton New GM in Sweeping Brewer Purge," *Stevens Point (WI) Journal*, November 21, 1977, 16.
22. Lou Chapman, "Brewers Give Dalton Full Authority," *The Sporting News*, November 10, 1977, 52.
23. Chapman, "Brewers Give Dalton Full Authority," 52.
24. Chapman, "Brewers Give Dalton Full Authority," 52.
25. Chapman, "Brewers Give Dalton Full Authority," 52.
26. Yount interview, September 10, 2020.
27. Associated Press, "Dalton Denies Yount Trade Rumors," *Wisconsin State Journal* (Madison), March 16, 1978, 25.
28. "This Robin Is a Rare Bird," *Sports Illustrated*, September 27, 1982, https://vault.si.com/vault/1982/09/27/this-robin-is-a-rare-bird.
29. Robin Yount, interview by author regarding playing golf in 1978, September 25, 2020.

30. Mike Conring, "Brewer Offense Potent, but Pitching Sags," *The Sporting News*, May 20, 1978, 17.
31. "Paul Molitor 1978 Batting Splits," Baseball Reference, accessed October 17, 2022, https://www.baseball-reference.com/players/split.fcgi?id=molitpa01&year=1978&t=b.
32. The term "Bambi's Bombers" was coined in June 1978. It appeared on everything from T-shirts to book titles, such as Don Olson, *Bambi's Bombers: The First Time Around* (Milwaukee: NOSLO, 1985).
33. Associated Press, "Brewers Deny Yount to Angels," *Leader-Telegram* (Eau Claire WI), May 25, 1978, 21.
34. Don Langenkamp, "GM Dalton Plays It Cool," *Green Bay Press-Gazette*, June 14, 1978, 23.
35. Associated Press, "Yount Agrees to New Contract with Brewers," *Stevens Point (WI) Journal*, June 21, 1978, 11.

14. LAYING THE FOUNDATION FOR A WINNER

1. Funnily enough, Molitor is on record saying he did not really like his nickname.
2. Jim Kornkven, "Nolan Ryan, a Problem," *Kenosha (WI) News*, December 10, 1979, 17.
3. Kornkven, "Nolan Ryan, a Problem," 17.
4. J. Daniel, "The Courtship of Nolan Ryan," *1980s Baseball*, https://80sbaseball.com/the-courtship-of-nolan-ryan/.
5. Kornkven, "Nolan Ryan, a Problem," 17.
6. Kornkven, "Nolan Ryan, a Problem," 17.
7. Daniel Okrent, *Nine Innings: The Anatomy of a Baseball Game*, 2nd ed. (Boston: Houghton Mifflin, 2000), 220.
8. The makeup of the scouting department in Milwaukee is covered in Okrent, *Nine Innings*, 220–21.
9. Tom Skibosh, ed., *Milwaukee Brewers Official 1983 Yearbook* (Milwaukee: Milwaukee Brewers Baseball Club, 1983), 52.
10. The history of the Blanco-Herrera family in the brewing industry in Cuba is summarized best in Okrent, *Nine Innings*, 220.
11. La Tropical, with the Blanco-Herrera family as its owners, had a long association with baseball in Cuba. This included building the stadium that housed the Cuban League beginning in 1930. The stadium, known officially as Gran Stadium Cervecería Tropical, housed Cuban League and various exhibition games through the end of World War II. Although the baseball field is gone, the stadium itself is the home of the Cuban national soccer team. Information on the building and use of the stadium for baseball is found in Roberto González Echevarría, *The Pride of Havana: A History of Cuban Baseball* (New York: Oxford University Press, 1999), 186, 217.

12. Delgado played in the Negro Leagues from 1933 to 1942, spending those years with three teams: the Puerto Rican Stars, the Cuban Stars, and the New York Cubans. Information on his playing career is found at "Felix Delgado," Negro League Baseball Players Association, updated 2022, http://www.nlbpa.com/the-athletes/delgado-felix. Information on players he signed for Milwaukee comes from a report by Ray Poitevint for Harry Dalton on the Brewers' international scouting efforts. That report, dated January 5, 1989, is found in folder 5, box 6, Dalton Papers.
13. A list of the area scouts is found in Skibosh, *Milwaukee Brewers Official 1983 Yearbook*, 52.
14. Bob Maisel, "Johnny Neun: Baseball Man All the Way," *Baltimore Sun*, April 1, 1990, 28.
15. Dalton spoke of Neun upon his death in 1990. Maisel, "Johnny Neun," 28.
16. The associate scout pay structure comes from a contract found in folder 3, box 7, Dalton Papers.
17. Bruce Manno, initial interview with author, October 25, 2017.
18. Manno interview.
19. Manno interview.
20. Dan Duquette, initial interview by author, October 27, 2017.
21. Duquette interview.
22. Duquette interview.
23. Jacqueline Kaiser, "Seven Cubans among Brewer Tryout Hopefuls," *La Crosse (WI) Tribune*, July 20, 1980, 26.
24. Bruce Manno described the tryout camp process to the author via text message in 2022.
25. Duquette interview.
26. Bill Brophy, "Brewers' Dalton 'Won't Make a Deal Just to Make a Deal,'" *Wisconsin State Journal*, December 2, 1979, 31.
27. Tom Flaherty, "Brewers Surprised, Elated, to Get Brouhard's Big Bat," *The Sporting News*, December 22, 1979, 53.
28. The issues with the bullpen and McLish's comments are from Dan Vanderpas, "Changes Needed, McLish Admits," *Post-Crescent* (Appleton WI), August 31, 1980, 44.
29. Mike Caldwell, interview by author, June 23, 2020; Lary Sorensen, interview by author, April 16, 2020.
30. Mike O'Brien, "Bamberger Retires, Rodgers Will Take Brewer Reins," *Post-Crescent*, September 6, 1980, 9.
31. Quoted in Krister Swanson, *Baseball's Power Shift: How the Players Union, the Fans, and the Media Changed American Sports Culture* (Lincoln: University of Nebraska Press, 2016), 239.

15. A TASTE OF THINGS TO COME

1. Bill Brophy, “Pitchers, Naturally, Top Brewers Priority List,” *Wisconsin State Journal*, November 7, 1980, 22.
2. When discussing Fingers and the other first-generation, late-inning relievers, the author will use the period term “fireman.” This was the preferred term in the media because first-generation relievers were expected to come into tough situations and put out fires. This might see them tasked to work multiple innings in order to preserve a win. The best overview of the evolution of late-inning relief pitching is found in Fran Zimniuch, *Fireman: The Evolution of the Closer in Baseball* (Chicago: Triumph Books, 2010).
3. Sutter’s origin story with the splitter is covered in both Tyler Kepner, *K: A History of Baseball in Ten Pitches* (New York: Knopf Doubleday, 2019); and Zimniuch, *Fireman.*
4. Shawn Krest, *Baseball Meat Market: The Stories behind the Best and Worst Trades in History* (Salem MA: Page Street, 2017), 178.
5. Krest, *Baseball Meat Market*, 178.
6. “David Green,” Society for American Baseball Research, accessed November 20, 2022, https://sabr.org/bioproj/person/david-green/.
7. Tim Trovato, phone conversation with author, September 23, 2022.
8. Dalton’s comments on the deal are in Susan Shemanske, “Brewers Roll Dice in Search of Relief,” *Journal Times* (Racine WI), December 14, 1980, 17.
9. Ted Simmons, initial interview by author, September 11, 2020.
10. Simmons told this story in reference to an interviewer’s question on the day he was introduced as a Hall of Fame inductee. The video clip from the Baseball Hall of Fame and Museum, “Introductory Press Conference for Ted Simmons,” December 9, 2020, can be found on the Facebook page “Leave While the Party’s Good: The Life, Times, and Legacy of Harry Dalton,” https://www.facebook.com/KluckDalton2021/videos/229988028475903. Various sources report different figures paid to Simmons to waive his no-trade clause. The author uses a figure found in Krest, *Baseball Meat Market*, 178.
11. Ownership’s need for direct compensation for competitive balance is best articulated in Jeff Katz, *Split Season: 1981; Fernandomania, the Bronx Zoo, and the Strike That Saved Baseball* (New York: St. Martin’s Publishing Group, 2015), 5.
12. Katz, *Split Season*, 4.
13. Marvin Miller, *A Whole Different Ball Game: The Sport and Business of Baseball* (New York: Carol Publishing Group, 1991), 287.
14. The beliefs of the players regarding direct compensation are best summed up in Swanson, *Baseball’s Power Shift*, 236–37.
15. Katz, *Split Season*, 4.

16. Information on the use of a research committee is articulated in a Player Relations Committee press release found in folder 1, box 9, Dalton Papers.
17. Harry Dalton, "Notes from the Meeting of 1-15-81," folder 3, box 9, Dalton Papers.
18. Tim Kurkjian, interview by author, September 7, 2022.
19. Boswell's initial article is summed up by Mark Asher and Bart Barnes, "Team Pays $50,000 Fine Imposed on GM Dalton," *Washington Post*, May 7, 1981.
20. Asher and Barnes, "Team Pays $50,000 Fine."
21. Asher and Barnes, "Team Pays $50,000 Fine."
22. Red Smith, "Baseball's Star Chamber," *New York Times*, May 8, 1981.
23. Harry Dalton to Bowie Kuhn, April 20, 1981. That letter and all correspondence regarding Dalton's fine can be found in folder 6, box 7, Dalton Papers.
24. The draft of Dalton's unsent letter to Bowie Kuhn is stored in folder 6, box 7, Dalton Papers.
25. Dalton draft of unsent letter to Kuhn.
26. Bruce Manno assessed Poitevint's work in a text to the author in 2022.
27. Bando and Fingers shared their thoughts during NBC television's postgame coverage. The video of the game is available on Classic MLB1, "NBC Game of The Week: Detroit Tigers vs Milwaukee Brewers," YouTube.com, accessed September 25, 2023, https://www.youtube.com/watch?v=AJ8uM40gWgc.
28. Bill Brophy, "Brewers on Their Way," *Wisconsin State Journal*, October 4, 1981.
29. United Press International, "Dalton Pleased with Brewers," *Oshkosh (WI) Northwestern*, October 13, 1981, 20.
30. United Press International, "Dalton Pleased with Brewers," 20.
31. Pete Vuckovich, interview by author regarding Harry Dalton, November 22, 2017.

16. THE WALLBANGERS

1. Reggie Cleveland would go 14-17 with a 4.66 ERA for the Brewers in three seasons as the team's swingman.
2. Associated Press, "Bamberger: New Job," *Manitowoc (WI) Herald-Times*, September 18, 1981, 13.
3. The rift between Rodgers and players, including those mentioned, is covered in Okrent, *Nine Innings*, 11.
4. Associated Press, "Rodgers Awarded New Pact," *Wisconsin State Journal*, October 1, 1981, 17.
5. United Press International, "Brewers Not Close to Pitching Deals," *Kenosha (WI) News*, December 9, 1981, 29.
6. Associated Press, "Charlie Moore Wants a Trade," *Marshfield (WI) News Herald*, January 9, 1982, 10.

7. Associated Press, "Charlie Moore Wants a Trade," 10.
8. Discussions on moving Molitor to third, Selig's ultimatum to Dalton on behalf of Molitor, Dalton's response, and the comments of Molitor's teammates are covered in Okrent, *Nine Innings*, 52–54.
9. Associated Press, "Moore Drops Trade Demand," *The Reporter* (Fond du Lac WI), March 1, 1982, 16.
10. The positive nature of the relationship between Selig and Dalton in the early years was related to the author by everyone who worked for the club during that time. This includes Selig's biggest detractors and Selig himself. Bud Selig, interview by author about working with Harry Dalton and Dalton's legacy in baseball, August 26, 2019.
11. Wendy Selig-Prieb, interview by author about Harry Dalton, November 29, 2017.
12. Selig's demeanor is best captured in Okrent, *Nine Innings*, 138, 106.
13. Selig-Prieb interview.
14. Okrent, *Nine Innings*, 138, 232.
15. Like his relationship with Selig, Dalton's demeanor with friends who came to games is universally affirmed. It is best remembered by Arvid Tillmar and Mary Pat Tillmar, interview by author about Harry and Pat Dalton, August 23, 2020.
16. Okrent, *Nine Innings*, 52.
17. Selig's comments appear in Okrent, *Nine Innings*, 52.
18. Yount stated that Selig handled his contract negotiations personally in Yount interview, September 10, 2020. It is confirmed in print in Associated Press, "Yount Stays a Brewer," *Portage (WI) Daily Register*, December 20, 1989, 10.
19. Yount interview, September 10, 2020.
20. Tom Skibosh, interview by author, September 10, 2017.
21. Pat Dalton interview, October 10, 2017.
22. Recalled in a discussion about Dalton and Selig during a telephone conversation with the author in the summer of 2020.
23. *Nine Innings* is considered one of the top baseball books of all time, and Okrent still remembers his time following Milwaukee fondly. This includes Pat Dalton frantically informing him that his wife was in labor before telling him to forget about his work as she threw him in a cab to the airport in Dallas so that he could be home for the birth of his first child. As for his relationship with Selig, the writer admitted that Selig never got over Okrent's perceived slight of him. Daniel Okrent, interview by author about covering the 1982 Brewers for *Nine Innings*, November 11, 2017. As for his interactions with Selig, Okrent retold the story of Selig being upset and then holding a grudge in Justin McGuire, "*Nine Innings*," *Baseball by the Book* (audio

podcast), 49:42, December 4, 2017, https://baseballbythebook.libsyn.com/episode-97-nine-innings.

24. Although Dalton was not a big drinker, he was also not a teetotaler. As Dan Okrent recalls, one night in particular during spring training got the best of Dalton, and in the aftermath, he gave up beer for a period during the 1982 season. The story can be found in Okrent, *Nine Innings*, 21.
25. Bob Sudyk, "Just Horsing Around, Fingers Scares Everyone," *Kenosha (WI) News*, March 17, 1982, 23.
26. Yount interview, September 10, 2020.
27. Yount interview, September 10, 2020.
28. Players spoke about Kuenn being a father figure for some of them during interviews for the documentary film *Harvey's Wallbangers: The 1982 Milwaukee Brewers* (Hart Sharp Video, 2007).
29. Simmons interview.
30. Associated Press, "Several Factors Led to Rodgers' Dismissal," *The Reporter* (Fond du Lac WI), June 3, 1982, 20.
31. For a recap of the hiring of Harvey Kuenn, see Tom Flaherty, "Crises Nothing New for Kuenn," *The Sporting News*, June 21, 1982, 14.
32. All three players sent to Houston would make the Major League roster. Of those, Kevin Bass would have the most impactful career. Bass played for Houston for the rest of the 1980s, with his best season coming in 1986 during Houston's run to the NL West title.
33. Mike O'Brien, "Sutton: 'I Just Hope to Earn My Way,'" *The Reporter* (Fond du Lac WI), September 1, 1982, 13.
34. O'Brien, "Sutton: 'I Just Hope to Earn My Way.'"
35. Vuckovich would outline his shoulder problems to the author in a telephone conversation on November 13, 2022.
36. Vince Sweeney, "HR in 9th Beats Sutton; Brewers Split with Tribe," *Milwaukee Sentinel*, September 3, 1982, 17.
37. Vic Feuerherd, "Fingers' Arm Still Too Sore," *Milwaukee Sentinel*, September 27, 1982.
38. The bullpen usage for the Brewers in September comes from the "1982 Milwaukee Brewers Game Log," Baseball Reference, 2022, https://www.baseball-reference.com/teams/MIL/1982-schedule-scores.shtml. Each of the pitchers mentioned closed games for the Brewers in September.
39. The series in Boston at the end of September is best remembered in Brewers lore for a three-run home run by backup catcher and future Brewers manager Ned Yost in the bottom of the ninth of the second game.
40. The sentiment in the Brewers' clubhouse before the team headed out to play Baltimore is best articulated by Gorman Thomas in the documentary film *Harvey's Wallbangers*.

41. *Harvey's Wallbangers* documentary.
42. Mario J. Ziino, interview by author, November 28, 2022.
43. Ziino interview.
44. Ziino interview.
45. "Sutton Will Talk Forever," *Milwaukee Journal*, October 4, 1982, 22.
46. Lee Kluck, "October 3, 1982: Brewers Hold Off Orioles' Charge in Season Finale," Society for American Baseball Research, https://sabr.org/gamesproj/game/october-3-1982-brewers-hold-off-orioles-charge-in-season-finale.
47. Vic Feuerherd, "Kuenn Had 'No Doubt,'" *Milwaukee Sentinel*, October 4, 1982, sec. 2, 5.
48. The author tracked moves by the Angels in the post-Dalton era by consulting the transaction logs for the Angels from 1978 to 1982 on Baseball Reference, https://www.baseball-reference.com/teams/ANA/index.shtml.
49. Robin Yount would use the word "flat" to describe the Brewers in California in the *Harvey's Wallbangers* documentary.
50. Game recaps built by the author using information from the homepage for the 1982 American League Championship Series, Baseball Reference, accessed December 9, 2022, https://www.baseball-reference.com/postseason/1982_ALCS.shtml.
51. The 2004 Boston Red Sox broke this record when they won four straight games against the New York Yankees in the 2004 ALCS after falling behind 3–0.
52. The "pops" to which Ziino referred were, in the time-honored tradition of the baseball clubhouse, made with water, malted barley, and fermented hops. Ziino interview.
53. Perhaps the most famous examples of the twenty-five men, twenty-five cabs mentality from the same era include the 1978 Yankees and the Boston Red Sox of the 1980s.
54. Okrent interview in McGuire, "*Nine Innings*" podcast.
55. In terms of dealing with reporters, the '82 Brewers could be a tight-lipped group when they felt that a beat writer was particularly hard on a member of the club. For instance, Ted Simmons went most of the season not talking to the writers of the two daily Milwaukee newspapers. As for dust-ups with fans, the Wallbangers were not a hit-first-and-ask-questions-later kind of outfit. However, players have said there were times when a confrontation was unavoidable.
56. Yount interview, September 10, 2020.
57. Dan Duquette told this story to the author via a phone call in 2020.
58. Selig-Prieb interview.
59. Pete Vuckovich's comments on Bill Zito come from text message correspondence with the author in December 2022.

60. Bill Zito, interview by author about working as clubhouse attendant for the 1982 Brewers, October 29, 2021.
61. Skibosh interview.
62. Game recaps for the ALCS were constructed from the homepage for the 1982 American League Championship Series at Baseball Reference. The author also watched the ALCS from videos available on YouTube.com.
63. John Hughes, "Brouhard Merely Followed the Script," *Wisconsin State Journal*, October 10, 1982, 23.
64. Thomas described his injury in a pregame interview with Keith Jackson of ABC Sports. The game can be found at Classic MLB1, "Angels vs Brewers (1982 ALCS Game 5)," YouTube.com, accessed 2018, https://www.youtube.com/watch?v=9aQsVqw7cGY.
65. Fans gave their opinion of Cooper in the *Harvey's Wallbangers* documentary.
66. Yost described his thoughts on Rod Carew being introduced during game five in the *Harvey's Wallbangers* documentary.
67. Selig's comments on Dalton appear in Joe Karius, "Selig's Longest Day Ends in Victory Celebration," *Milwaukee Sentinel*, October 11, 1982, 16.
68. Karius, "Selig's Longest Day Ends in Victory Celebration," 16.
69. As he did for the 1982 ALCS, the author reconstructed the 1982 World Series using information found at YouTube.com and the homepage for the 1982 World Series, Baseball Reference, 2022, https://www.baseball-reference.com/postseason/1982_WS.shtml.
70. Lifestyle staff, "A Cardinal Sin in the Name of Fashion," *Milwaukee Sentinel*, October 15, 1982.
71. Kepner, *Grandest Stage*, 77–78.
72. Pat Dalton described her husband in the days leading up to, during, and after the World Series in an email to the author on December 17, 2017.
73. Jim Armstrong, "Power Failure," *Journal Times*, October 21, 1982, 17.
74. "What They're Saying about the World Series," *Journal Times*, October 21, 1982, 17.
75. Skibosh interview.
76. All involved with the Brewers in 1982 remember the parade fondly forty years later. Bud Selig remembered the parade for the documentary *Harvey's Wallbangers*.

17. REVERSAL OF FORTUNE

1. "Statistical Register for Pete Vuckovich," Baseball Reference, accessed December 12, 2022, https://www.baseball-reference.com/players/v/vuckope01.shtml. The quote appears in Rory Costello, "Pete Vuckovich,"

Society for American Baseball Research, accessed December 12, 2022, https://sabr.org/bioproj/person/Pete-Vuckovich/.

2. Associated Press, "Brewers Begin Youth Movement Plan," *Sheboygan (WI) Press*, November 15, 1985, 18.
3. Molitor's injury woes are recapped in Doug Skipper and Dan Levitt, "Paul Molitor," Society for American Baseball Research, accessed December 12, 2022, https://sabr.org/bioproj/person/paul-molitor/. Today, recovery from Tommy John surgery is taken as a given. In the early days of the procedure, this was not the case.
4. Yount's injury woes are recapped in Gregory H. Wolf, "Robin Yount," Society for American Baseball Research, accessed December 24, 2022, https://sabr.org/bioproj/person/robin-yount/.
5. Joe Karius, "Slump Settled Gorman's Fate," *Milwaukee Journal*, June 7, 1983, 11.
6. The gunshot fired at Dalton's window was kept out of the newspapers, but the story was relayed to the author by his daughters.
7. Correspondence surrounding the Gorman Thomas trade is found in folder 3, box 8, Dalton Papers.
8. "Welcome Aboard Lach!" *What's Brewing* (magazine of the Milwaukee Brewers), November 1983, 7.
9. Tom Trebelhorn, letter to the author received in 2017.
10. Michael J. Uruske, "Hard Times for Harry Dalton," *Milwaukee Magazine*, September 1984, 58–60.
11. This quote comes from Dalton's deposition in *Selig v. United States*, found in folder 7, box 7, Dalton Papers.
12. The types of teams considered by the Brewers are found in memos from various scouts to Harry Dalton in folder 4, box 6, Dalton Papers.
13. The number of prospects who made the Brewers' roster after being drafted by the club was computed using the MLB Draft Database, Baseball America, https://www.baseballamerica.com/draft-history.
14. The Brewers' efforts in Latin America and Mexico are recapped in Tom Tolan, "The Mexican Connection," *Milwaukee Magazine*, August 1990.
15. Robert Fitts, email about Enatsu to author, March 17, 2018.
16. Fitts email.
17. The running joke with people in the Milwaukee office was that every pitcher Poitevint saw was a "Jim Palmer type." This was very rarely the case.
18. Mike O'Brien, "Enatsu Makes Impressive Pitch for Roster Spot," *Milwaukee Sentinel*, March 28, 1985, 14.
19. The cases in question were in Kansas City and Pittsburgh in 1983–84. See Paul Hensler, "The Pervasion of Drugs," chapter 4 in his book *Gathering*

Crowds: Catching Baseball Fever in the New Era of Free Agency (Lanham MD: Rowman & Littlefield, 2021).

20. Testimony about Molitor and others is quoted in James Romensko, "Off Their Pedestals: The Baseball Drug Papers," *Milwaukee Magazine*, October 1985.
21. Molitor's drug use was recounted in his agent's book; see Ron Simon, *The Game behind the Game: Negotiating in the Big Leagues* (Stillwater MN: Voyageur, 1993). The author quotes Simon from Selig, *For the Good of the Game*, 104.
22. Molitor's involvement with the Peters case from a legal standpoint is complicated. In addition to him not being charged, any testimony Molitor provided to the U.S. attorney was not given in open court. Also, testimony that leaked in 1985 showed that the FBI agents went out of their way to keep Molitor's involvement secret so as to not harm his reputation. As it turned out, this included calling Bud Selig and having him intercept Molitor after the FBI arrested Peters. Selig, *For the Good of the Game*, 104.
23. Dan Okrent provided his observations to the author in a telephone call in the fall of 2022. Vic Feuerherd recounted his observations to the author via social media in 2022. Buck Rodgers's comments come from Murray Chass, "Cocaine Disrupts Baseball from Field to Front Office," *New York Times*, August 20, 1985, 1.
24. Davis is quoted in Murray Chass, "Cocaine and Baseball: A Deepening Problem," *New York Times*, August 19, 1985, 1.
25. Dan Duquette explained the development of the Brewers' EAP program in a telephone call to the author in the fall of 2022.
26. Jimmy Bank, interview by author about working for the Brewers and Harry Dalton, October 26, 2017.
27. Jon Greenberg, interview by author about working for the Brewers and Harry Dalton, June 1, 2022.
28. The Dalton family has shared memories of their husband/father off the field throughout the course of this project.
29. Associated Press, "Brewers Begin Youth Movement Plan," *Sheboygan (WI) Press*, November 15, 1985, 18.
30. The exploits of Joey Meyer and company are shared by their manager in Tom Gamboa and David Russell, *Tom Gamboa: My Life in Baseball* (Jefferson NC: McFarland, 2017).
31. Thoughts on the 1985 Vancouver team come from Trebelhorn letter to author.
32. Stats on the Brewers organization come from David Lamb, *Stolen Season: A Journey through America and Baseball's Minor Leagues* (New York: Random House, 1991). In addition, J. J. Cooper of Baseball America provided information from the organization's archives.

18. STREAKING

1. Bill Brophy, "Big Deal? Dalton Appears Ready to Make One," *Wisconsin State Journal*, December 8, 1985, 33.
2. A transcript of Dalton's appearance on the *Today Show* with Bryant Gumble can be found in the Dalton Papers.
3. *Today Show* transcript.
4. Associated Press, "Brewers Get Giants' Deer," *Wisconsin State Journal*, December 19, 1985, 21.
5. Associated Press, "Brewers May Go with 24 Players on '86 Roster," *Post-Crescent*, January 12, 1986, 47.
6. Susan Shemanske, "Dalton's Pocketbook Coughs and Wheezes at Dawson's Price Tag," *Journal Times*, January 12, 1986, 15.
7. Tom Haudricourt, "Darwin Agrees to Two-Year Pact," *Milwaukee Sentinel*, February 5, 1986, 19.
8. Haudricourt, "Darwin Agrees to Two-Year Pact," 19.
9. The author reconstructed the events around the explosion by using three articles that all appeared in the *Milwaukee Sentinel*, February 28, 1986, 13: Tom Haudricourt, "Clubhouse Had Been Given OK for Occupancy"; Tom Haudricourt, "Bamberger: 'It Was Like a War'"; and Joe Manning, "Fireball Engulfed One Coach."
10. Haudricourt, "Clubhouse Had Been Given OK for Occupancy," 13.
11. J. R. Radcliffe, "50 in 50: Paul Molitor's Hitting Streak Comes to a Dramatic Conclusion," *Milwaukee Journal Sentinel*, April 13, 2020, https://www.jsonline.com/story/sports/mlb/brewers/2020/04/13/50-greatest-wisconsin-sports-moments-no-40-paul-molitors-streak/2919121001/.
12. Rick Braun, "Nieves Shares Thrill with Fans," *Milwaukee Sentinel*, April 17, 1987, 15.
13. Braun, "Nieves Shares Thrill with Fans," 15.
14. George Webb Restaurant offered the same promotion during the days of the Minor League Brewers and the Braves. The information on the 1987 giveaway is found at "The Legend Is Real," George Webb Restaurants, accessed January 17, 2023, https://georgewebb.com/about/history#.
15. Nieves and Manning are quoted in Bruce Newman, "A Heady Start," *Sports Illustrated*, April 27, 1987.
16. Associated Press, "Trebelhorn Takes Charge," *Wausau (WI) Daily Herald*, September 27, 1986, 1.
17. Trebelhorn recounted coaching Rickey Henderson in George F. Will, *Men at Work: The Craft of Baseball* (New York: Macmillan, 1990), 54–56. He recounted his plans for 1986 in Trebelhorn letter to author.
18. Trebelhorn letter to author.

19. Tom Haudricourt, "Trebelhorn Earned the Job," *Milwaukee Sentinel*, October 2, 1986.
20. Insights into Trebelhorn's management style come from Mark Knudson, interview by author, September 16, 2022. Knudson was a Brewers relief pitcher.
21. Trebelhorn quoted in Will, *Men at Work*, 55.
22. Tom Haudricourt, "Silent Departure," *Milwaukee Sentinel*, October 31, 1994, 22.
23. Trebelhorn letter to author.
24. Pete Vuckovich, interview by author regarding Harry Dalton, November 22, 2017.
25. New York Times News Service, "Brewers Early Favorite for '88 Series," *Sheboygan (WI) Press*, October 27, 1987, 17.

19. THE LAST RIDE OF THE DALTON GANG

1. Associated Press, "Nieves Fighting Stiff Arm Again," *La Crosse (WI) Tribune*, March 8, 1989, 30.
2. Tom Trebelhorn shared these thoughts with the author via telephone in 2017.
3. Buster Olney, "Role Has Changed but Sveum Accepts It," *New York Times*, March 11, 1998, sec. C, 2.
4. Olney, "Role Has Changed but Sveum Accepts It," sec. C, 2.
5. Cliff Cristl, "Spiers Makes Jump," *The Sporting News*, April 17, 1989.
6. Bill Spiers shared his reminiscences with the author in a telephone call on January 17, 2023.
7. Tom Haudricourt, "Sheffield Blasts Trebelhorn, Mates," *Milwaukee Sentinel*, May 27, 1989, 9.
8. Haudricourt, "Sheffield Blasts Trebelhorn, Mates," 9.
9. Haudricourt, "Sheffield Blasts Trebelhorn, Mates," 9.
10. Haudricourt, "Sheffield Blasts Trebelhorn, Mates," 9.
11. Tom Haudricourt, "Sheffield, Dalton Clear the Air," *Milwaukee Sentinel*, May 29, 1989, sec. 2, 5.
12. Haudricourt, "Sheffield, Dalton Clear the Air," sec. 2, 5.
13. Yount interview, September 10, 2020.
14. There is no indication of who taped the clubhouse meeting in question. The author was given the master copy of the talk by the Dalton family, in a box of materials used for research. Quoted passages are from this September 1989 clubhouse tape recording until noted otherwise.
15. Peter Jackel, "Take a Look in the Mirror, Mr. Dalton," *Journal Times*, October 5, 1989, 13.
16. Andy Baggot, "What If Will Were a Brewer?" *Wisconsin State Journal*, October 12, 1989, 17.

17. Felder shared his thoughts on Dalton with the author during a public speaking engagement in the fall of 2022.
18. Plesac would make various comments between 1989 and 1991. For a sampling of these, see Associated Press, "Brewers Yank Hartenstein," *Capital Times* (Madison WI), October 2, 1989, 12; Pete Dougherty, "Dalton, Players Support Trebelhorn," *Green Bay Press-Gazette*, August 19, 1990, 25; "Finding Relief: Plesac Feels Better after Talk with Dalton," *Journal Times*, June 15, 1991, 11.
19. Associated Press, "Brewers Fire Batting Coach," *La Crosse (WI) Tribune*, September 28, 1989, 25.
20. Andy Baggot, "Yount Weights All His Options," *Wisconsin State Journal*, September 27, 1989, 13.
21. Tom Haudricourt, interview by author, October 6, 2017.
22. Etchebarren's propensity to report back to his boss was related in Jimmy Bank, interview by author about working for the Brewers and Harry Dalton, 2018.
23. Parker's take on his time in Milwaukee comes from Dave Parker and Dave Jordan, "Brother's Gonna Work It Out," courtesy MLBbro.com, "Exclusive Missing Chapters from Baseball Legend Dave Parker's Memoir," 2023, https://mlbbro.com/2022/03/01/exclusive-missing-chapters-from-baseball-legend-dave-parkers-memoir-cobra-a-life-of-baseball-and-brotherhood-part-3/.
24. Parker and Jordan, "Brother's Gonna Work It Out."
25. Parker and Jordan, "Brother's Gonna Work It Out."
26. "Sheffield's Season Comes to an End," *Milwaukee Sentinel*, September 25, 1990, 14.
27. Tom Haudricourt, "Trebelhorn Says Sheffield's Wish Won't Be Granted," *Milwaukee Sentinel*, September 27, 1990, 15.
28. Parker and Jordan, "Brother's Gonna Work It Out."
29. Parker and Jordan, "Brother's Gonna Work It Out."
30. Associated Press, "Dalton Accepts Blame," *Post-Crescent*, August 5, 1990, 37.
31. Associated Press, "Dalton Accepts Blame," 37.
32. Baylor's comments come from Associated Press, "Quoteworthy," *Green Bay Press-Gazette*, September 23, 1990, 26.
33. The changing nature of Dalton's relationship with players was shared in the author's telephone conversation with Cindy Dalton on December 22, 2022.
34. Bob Nightengale, "A Dugout from Hell," *Los Angeles Times*, June 9, 1992, https://www.latimes.com/archives/la-xpm-1992-06-09-sp-102-story.html.
35. Tom Verducci, "Swinging Away," *Sports Illustrated*, October 11, 2004.
36. Knudson interview.
37. Verducci's conversation with Sheffield was recounted in the Knudson interview.

38. Nightengale, "Dugout from Hell."
39. Jay Jaffe, "JAWS and the 2022 Hall of Fame Ballot: Gary Sheffield," *FanGraphs*, December 8, 2021, https://blogs.fangraphs.com/jaws-and-the-2022-hall-of-fame-ballot-gary-sheffield/.
40. Bob Nightengale, "Sheffield Now Caught between Articles on His Days as a Brewer," *Los Angeles Times*, September 1, 1992, https://www.latimes.com/archives/la-xpm-1992-09-01-sp-6844-story.html.
41. Bruce Manno shared the error story in a text message to the author in February 2021.
42. Selig-Prieb interview.
43. Sandy Ronback, interview by author, September 26, 2017.
44. The budget memos in question are found in folder 5, box 7, Dalton Papers.
45. Associated Press, "Dalton Targets Pitching," *Oshkosh (WI) Northwestern*, November 24, 1990, 15.
46. Skibosh interview.
47. Associated Press, "Brewers Hope to Get Their Money's Worth," *Post-Crescent*, December 7, 1990, 19.
48. Tom Haudricourt, interview by author, October 6, 2017.
49. Michael Hamacher, interview by author, October 17, 2017.
50. Associated Press, "Dalton Accepts Blame."
51. Associated Press, "Dalton Accepts Blame."
52. Dalton's thoughts on Gantner come from the September 1989 clubhouse tape recording.
53. Hamacher interview.
54. Gary Sheffield and David Ritz, *Inside Power* (New York: Crown, 2007), 93.
55. Andy Baggot, "Sheffield Says Dalton Ruining Team," *Wisconsin State Journal*, April 5, 1991, 20–21.
56. Nightengale, "Dugout from Hell."
57. Knudson interview.
58. Andy Baggot, "Dalton Targets Malcontents," *Wisconsin State Journal*, June 24, 1991, 7.
59. August recounted this story both to the author and in a tweet on X/Twitter.
60. Trebelhorn letter to author.
61. Hamacher interview.
62. Quoted in Pat Dalton, initial interview.
63. Letters to Dalton on his replacement are in folder 6, box 8, Dalton Papers.

20. EXILE, CAREFREE DAYS, AND NIGHTMARES

1. Tom Haudricourt outlines some of Selig's treatment of Dalton in Tom Haudricourt, "Silent Departure," *Milwaukee Sentinel*, October 31, 1994. Beyond the written record, others who have worked with Dalton shared details of

the nature of the rift between the two men and the consequences of that rift for Dalton. Sources include the Skibosh interview. A third group of people shared details with the author but asked to remain anonymous so as not to complicate their relationship with Selig.

2. Ziino interview. Haudricourt's reporting is covered in Haudricourt, "Silent Departure."
3. Dalton's feasibility studies and expansion correspondence reside in folder 8, box 8, Dalton Papers.
4. Duquette initial interview, October 27, 2017.
5. Pat Dalton initial interview, October 10, 2017.
6. Ziino interview.
7. Pat, Kim, Cindy, and Debbie Dalton shared memories of their dad in retirement at his home in Carefree, Arizona, with the author at various points during this project. Dalton's granddaughter Dalton Fusco recounted Harry Dalton's prodigious sweet tooth and interactions with her and her brother Trip in Dalton Fusco, interview by author, 2017.
8. Etchebarren interview.
9. Lewy body dementia information is from the Lewy Body Dementia Association (LBDA). They maintain information at "What Is Lewy Body Dementia," accessed January 20, 2023, https://www.lbda.org/what-is-lbd/.
10. Kim, Cindy, and Debbie Dalton have discussed their father's symptoms with the author at various times during this project via text, phone, and email.
11. Winki Booker Winbur, interview by author, January 15, 2018.
12. Kerry Wood, interview by author about serving as a companion for Harry Dalton, November 20, 2017.
13. Kim Dalton initial interview about her father.

Index